Economic Diversification Policies in Natural Resource Rich Economies

T0291161

Economic diversification remains at the top of the agenda for hundreds of regions around the world, from the single-commodity economies of African countries and the Caribbean to the many single-industry regions of Europe and North America, as well as the oil- and gas-rich but volatile hydrocarbon economies. Economic diversification policies have been around for almost a century with varying degrees of success and failure.

Economic Diversification Policies in Natural Resource Rich Economies takes a special interest in the policy experiences of a set of different countries for which extractive industries represent significant drivers of their economies and consequently are significant contributors to government revenues. The book explores eleven cases including upper-middle to high income economies such as Canada, Australia, Iceland and Norway, emerging economies such as Latin America, the GCC (Saudi and UAE), Kazakhstan, Malaysia and Russia, and the developing economy of Uganda. Each chapter provides a review of economic diversification experiences including policy environment, diversification strategies, desired outcomes, the role of government and a critical evaluation of achievements.

This book is suitable for those who study environmental economics, development economics, public policy and resource management.

Sami Mahroum is the Director of the INSEAD Innovation and Policy Initiative. Prior to that, he was a Senior Analyst with the OECD in Paris and a Visiting Reader at Birkbeck, University of London.

Yasser Al-Saleh is a Faculty Member at the Mohammed Bin Rashid School of Government. Prior to that, he was a Senior Research Fellow at the INSEAD Innovation and Policy Initiative.

Routledge Explorations in Environmental Economics
Edited by Nick Hanley
University of Stirling, UK

For a full list of titles in this series, please visit www.routledge.com/series/REEE

Economic Diversification Policies in Natural Resource Rich Economies

**Edited by Sami Mahroum
and Yasser Al-Saleh**

LONDON AND NEW YORK

First published 2017 by Routledge

2 Park Square, Milton Park, Abingdon, Oxfordshire OX14 4RN
711 Third Avenue, New York, NY 10017

Routledge is an imprint of the Taylor & Francis Group, an informa business

First issued in paperback 2018

British Library Cataloguing in Publication Data
A catalogue record for this book is available from the British Library

Library of Congress Cataloging in Publication Data
Names: Mahroum, Sami, editor. | Al-Saleh, Yasser M., editor.
Title: Economic diversification policies in natural resource rich economies / edited by Sami Mahroum and Yasser Al-Saleh.Description: 1 Edition. | New York : Routledge, 2016.
Identifiers: LCCN 2016009962| ISBN 9781138958883 (hardback) | ISBN 9781315660981 (ebook)
Subjects: LCSH: Diversification in industry--Case studies. | Agricultural diversification--Case studies. | Natural resources--Case studies.
Classification: LCC HD2756 E255 2016 | DDC 338.6--dc23
LC record available at https://lccn.loc.gov/2016009962

ISBN: 978-1-138-95888-3 (hbk)
ISBN: 978-1-138-32518-0 (pbk)

Typeset in Times New Roman
by Saxon Graphics Ltd, Derby

Contents

Figures

Tables

Contributors

Hamed Al-Hashemi, Cranfield School of Management, Cranfield University, UK

Yasser Al-Saleh, Mohammed Bin Rashid School of Government, Dubai

Thorvaldur Gylfason, University of Iceland

Richard Hawkins, Science Technology and Society Program, University of Calgary, Canada

Igor Hernandez, IESA, Venezuela

Peter Howie, Nazarbayev University, Kazakhstan

Kenneth Leong, Bankwest Curtin Economics Centre, Curtin University, Perth

Sami Mahroum, INSEAD Innovation and Policy Initiative, Abu Dhabi

Osmel Manzano, Georgetown University, US and IESA, Venezuela

Jean-Pascal Nguessa Nganou, World Bank, Washington DC

Abdillah Noh, Tun Abdul Razak School of Government, Malaysia

John Phillimore, Bankwest Curtin Economics Centre and John Curtin Institute of Public Policy, Curtin University, Perth

Hatem Samman, Saudi Arabian General Investment Authority, Riyadh

Sheikh Shahnawaz, California State University, Chico, US

Li-Chen Sim, Zayed University, Abu Dhabi

Olav Wicken, University of Oslo, Norway

Per Magnus Wijkman, University of Gothenburg, Sweden

Acknowledgements

The editors wish to thank Abu Dhabi Education Council for financially supporting
this international research project.

1 Economic diversification
New thinking

Sami Mahroum

1.1 Introduction

For decades the topic of economic diversification has been high on the agenda of governments in all natural resource-rich economies. In the past two decades, governments of these economies have been making substantial investments in what one might call diversification clusters of new economic activities. These have included high-tech sectors, energy renewables and creative industries. The investments reflect and support governments' thinking on how to achieve broader economic diversification, which rests on the assumption that government's role lies primarily in economic factors on the supply side, such as necessary investments in infrastructure and training.

A bonanza created by natural resources sometimes means that there is little in terms of market incentive to diversify away from this sector, and governments have even thought that a market failure case was there to encourage the diversification effort. We see this thinking in all the eleven cases discussed in this book, with varying degrees of intervention. In this regard, innovation policy has become a main framework for many government interventions, with the expectation that economic diversification will be delivered by high-tech sectors such as aerospace, semi-conductors and renewable energy. The role of government thus lies on the supply side of the intervention spectrum through support of the development of science, technology and innovation systems. This is somewhat different from earlier decades where import-substitution policies and policies pertaining to local content were used as demand-based policy instruments for economic diversification (Edquist et al., 2000; Geroski, 1990).

What we now have is a policy paradigm that sees an active role for government in the creation of high-tech or knowledge-intensive zones, known as clusters, incubators, valleys or any other fancy name that gives out the signal that something new is taking place here. For the majority of these initiatives, an underlying, albeit not always announced goal has been the creation of home-grown Silicon Valley-style unicorn firms such as Apple and Google. In fact, economic diversification policies in natural resource-rich countries are the same as economic development policies in developing countries and regional regeneration policies in advanced economies. What we have is a blend of terms for what is in reality a convergence of policy tools, and therefore sometimes we find cluster policies adopted as a policy tool for all three economic development purposes.

For example, this is evident in the case of diversification policies pursued in the Emirate of Abu Dhabi in the United Arab Emirates. Acting at the subnational level, the Abu Dhabi Government has adopted its own economic diversification strategy known as the Economic Vision 2030, which is entirely geared towards diversification into high-tech and knowledge-intensive sectors through the creation of clusters. However, what is often missing in these broad diversification policies is a clear business model. Future plans for production and employment pertaining to future-oriented industries have no clear portfolio of products and services linked to the investments, and neither do they have a clear client base or market to satisfy. It is not obvious that the massive investments made in future-oriented industries will result in any success whatsoever or produce a positive return on investment. In other words, the link between technology supply and market demand in many such economic development and diversification policies is often sketchy, speculative and based on wishful thinking.

In this chapter, I introduce and discuss an alternative model of economic diversification that has been advanced by Mahroum and Al-Saleh (2013), namely 'demand-led related diversification' (DLRD). The DLRD model stipulates that successful economic diversification and industrial renewal strategies have higher chances of success if: (i) they are based on existing or anticipated market demand, either domestically or globally; (ii) they can be – at least partially – supplied by existing domestic capabilities; and (iii) they aim to develop complementary capabilities that are – at least partially – compatible with an existing domestic ones.

1.2 Demand-led diversification

Market demand is essential for any economic growth, as both economic and innovation activities take place specifically to meet and satisfy the demand for goods and services. It is in the competition to meet various types of demand that opportunities for innovation and economic diversification emerge. Thus, many governments in the developing world (and in other parts of the world to various extents) have chosen to use demand power as an important driver of local economic development, for example by pursuing so-called 'import-substitution' policies. The latter necessitates that local demand is eventually met by local supply, achieved by using various incentives for local supply as well as levying tariffs on imports (Amsden, 1989; Wade, 1990). However, following the perceived failure of many import substitution policies that were put in place in the 1960s, governments began to discard domestic demand-oriented policies to adopt a global demand-led strategy fostered by market liberalisation policies. The latter saw the removal of most barriers to imports and the adoption of a strategy that fundamentally replaced local demand with global demand as a main driver of economic development and growth. Accordingly, local industries were expected to engage in a worldwide race to meet the greater and wider global demand for goods and services, subsequently resulting in a greater diversification of the domestic economy. To ensure that such a dynamic would ensue, local markets and industries had to be opened up to global competition too (Wade, 1990).

Just how demand (domestic or global) can be used to spur economic development has been an important subject of research among economic development scholars (e.g. see Amsden, 1989; Rodrik, 2007; Wade, 1990). It is often argued, for example, that small economies may be more dependent on global demand and hence on international trade and exports, whereas large economies are often fuelled by domestic demand (Chenery, 1982).

However, the debate about the role of 'demand' in economic development takes on a different dimension when it is perceived from the angle of innovation and the creation of new markets. In this context, demand may be classified into three types: (i) existing and satisfied demand; (ii) existing but unsatisfied demand; and finally (iii) dormant non-satisfied demand (Edler, 2007; OECD, 2011). When considering these three types of market demand, it is useful to also think of Hausmann and Rodrik's notion of countries' 'self-discovery'. According to Hausmann and Rodrik (2003), entrepreneurs across different economies are constantly looking for new opportunities to create new value. This is a costly process as it always involves making investments. The first type of demand is where most international trade and competition occurs, as goods and services tend to have their own established consumers and suppliers (i.e. markets). It is here that governments are often expected to play no role, or a very small one. Nonetheless, as Hausmann and Rodrik (2003) argue, even in mature markets where technology production techniques are well established, there will be a cost of learning for any new entrant. However, governments should not promote entrepreneurial activities that involve technology adoption and adaptation through imitation, because the return on investment in such learning activities will be low.

The second type of demand is where entrepreneurial activities are concentrated on the pursuit of radical innovations in the hope of making a market breakthrough. This is often the case when the demand (potential market) for certain goods and services exists, but it is not satisfied due to 'technology failure' or 'market failure' in general. It is in the context of this type of expected demand that Hausmann and Rodrik (2003), and indeed many governments, suggest that governments should support ex ante investments needed to create domestic capabilities to meet the market that is waiting to be tapped. Governments do so in a variety of forms, including the provision of a supportive physical infrastructure for firms and resources along a certain supply chain to mobilise and agglomerate.

The third type is 'greenfield' and 'blue ocean' areas, where supply triggers demand. These are goods and services where, once people become aware of their existence, they begin to demand them. For example, at one point there was no demand, and indeed no anticipation of a demand, for personal computers, mobile phones or wifi services. It was only after the introduction of these innovations that consumers for them emerged. Table 1.1 provides a schematic overview of these different categories of market conditions with their corresponding opportunity platforms.

Table 1.1 Type of demand and corresponding platform of related variety

Status of demand, market	Related variety platform
Existing, satisfied market	Opportunities lie in supply-chain variety
Existing, non-satisfied market	Opportunities lie in technological variety
Non-existing, non-satisfied market	Opportunities lie in knowledge variety

The first type, with a satisfied market and existing demand as per Hausmann and Rodrik (2003), arguably does not require a strong government role beyond the provision of broad basic services that are required in a modern economy, such as infrastructure, regulation for ease of business, education and training, and law and order. The third type, with a non-existing non-satisfied market – the blue ocean type of market conditions – is a typical case where government support is required in the provision of support for R&D activities, advanced infrastructure and human resources for science and technology. It is in the second type of market conditions where government actions and policies tend to be multifaceted.

1.3 Demand and supply varieties

These categorisations of demand and related variety platforms bring new dimensions to the debate about the role of demand in economic development and indeed competitiveness, but also the potential role of government. Economies not only compete in the same (but differentiated) product classes (Krugman, 1979), or in different segments of product classes according to their comparative advantage (Ricardo, 1817), but also in prospective markets for unmet existing and non-existing demand. This form of competition for prospective and anticipated markets is analogous to the notion of blue ocean strategy at the firm level (Kim and Mauborgne, 2005). The role of government here goes beyond the old debate about import-substitution, levels of trade liberalisation and industrial subsidies. This is not to say that these are irrelevant policy issues, but rather to indicate that a new dimension of policy becomes very relevant, and that the type of demand and the type of supply are most relevant for the development and growth of a particular economy.

For example, in the case of existing but not satisfied demand (second row in Table 1.1), a government is able to influence the technical standards and platforms for new products coming into the market. It can do this in a way that steers the development of certain innovations along trajectories that favour its potential local suppliers. These can be in the form of environmental standards, energy efficiency or health guidelines, as well as design features (OECD, 2011). These could have the power to alter market structure or affect the funds available for investment (Georghiou, 2007) in a way that helps to evolve what we call 'related demand'. In addition, governments may use public procurement to increase demand for certain products, or they can act as an articulator of a specific need, where they know their industrial base has related capabilities to generate the supply needed. In fact, in past years, as documented by Edquist et al. (2000), public procurement has been used to accomplish a wide range of objectives such as increasing demand for specific technologies, stimulating economic activities, creating employment, protecting domestic firms from foreign competition and remedying regional disparities. In this regard, one particular government intervention instrument that has been experimented with recently is 'lead markets'. The concept of a lead market builds on the notion of a lead user (Von Hippel, 2005), which has recently been popularised by several scholars (Beise, 2001; Georghiou, 2007; Jacob et al., 2005). In a lead market, a government decides to combine supply and demand measures to make its market a lead (pioneer) market for the introduction of a new innovation (e.g. electric buses). The support may include the provision of adequate R&D, seed capital and supporting infrastructure as well standard setting, regulations and public procurement to foster the development and take-off of a new class of products. The lead market country is then in an advantageous position to set the parameters for the shape of demand in a blue ocean market. That is what Zerka (2009), among others, called a 'smart' use of innovation policies that would entail applying several demand and supply-related mechanisms at the same time, while enabling the occurrence of synergies between these instruments.

1.4 The three roads of diversification

Economic diversification is an undertaking that is both costly and risky, especially when it is geared towards a distant future. Therefore, economic diversification experiences can be thought of in three broad groups. First, there are the countries that have successfully diversified their economies by becoming homes for manufacturing and outsourced services for existing demand. These are countries like China, Indonesia, Mexico and Vietnam, among others, that have aligned their development policies with current and existing market needs where costs and benefits can be calculated with a great level of accuracy. The second group includes countries that have managed to diversify by upgrading their existing industries and introducing new products and services into existing markets. Examples in this group include Brazil, Chile, Malaysia and Norway, who have innovated around their existing industrial legacies such as farming, fishing and forestry to create new industries related to corn, salmon, fisheries and palm oil. The final group adopted a less risky approach to diversification by considering the relatedness of existing infrastructure and natural advantages to new economic activities. These are countries that have adopted a longer-term, futuristic, costlier and riskier approach to economic diversification by pursuing a strategy aimed at the development of products and services that are new to the country and new to world. This group includes countries like Australia, Abu Dhabi, Saudi Arabia and other subnational regions in Europe and elsewhere. This is not to suggest that rich countries like Australia and Abu Dhabi are wrong in choosing to take greater risks in return for higher returns on investment. This strategy may well pay off, but would require a muddling-through approach that continues to guide new economic development activities in relation to emerging market demand.

Little attention has been paid by policymakers to the potential role of linking diversification policies with related domestic demand and supply. However, research elsewhere that was not undertaken with the aim of examining diversification issues has resulted in some findings that are helpful in understanding economic development dynamics and which are relevant to diversification issues too. For example, research conducted in the USA and the UK by Klepper (2002) and Boschma and Wenting (2007) respectively found some evidence that new (automobile) firms had a higher survival rate during the early stages of the life cycle of a new industry when the entrepreneur had a background in a related sector. Similar findings have been reported in a study of the economic evolution of seventy Swedish regions during the period from 1969 to 2002. Regions were most likely to create new industries when they focussed on industries that required competencies related to pre-existing ones (Neffke et al., 2011). These findings are important to bear in mind when considering the selection and development of new industries in a region. The relatedness of a new venture to existing ones could help make older industries into springboards for industrial renewal activities. To that end, the idea of a DLRD (i.e. Demand-led Related Diversification) model is an appealing one. A combination of policy mix (Flanagan et al., 2011) with demand-side policy instruments and supply-side instruments is more likely to yield higher levels of successful diversification in natural resource economies than one that seeks to establish new industries from scratch.

Using existing industries as a starting point can narrow the trial and error range and reduce the cost of failure by using existing infrastructure and available resources. Such an approach has helped make Brazil, for example, into one of the world's largest producers of ethanol, which was based on their already existing sugar industry. As the Brazilian government found, it is often more effective to choose new industries for which a country has natural advantages like environment or location. Another successful case of economic diversification within existing industrial structures is the Chilean salmon industry. Chile is currently the second largest producer of salmon in the world, despite the fact that salmon is not a local fish. This stems from its existing legacy as a fishing nation thanks to the country's long coastline. However, the traditional Chilean fish industry was aimed merely at local consumption. The industry had small space for mass production, let alone export, but the government eventually sought to diversify the economy by leveraging Chile's geography. It identified the advantage of the country's cold water and long coast by introducing salmon. The species was already produced for export in many countries such as Norway and Finland, but Chile soon became one of the largest salmon producers in the world.

A similar story of diversification based on existing industrial structures can be found on the other side of the world, in Malaysia. This country's climate and abundance of water resources enabled it to become a major producer of rubber. However, a fall in rubber prices pushed the country to diversify its agricultural production. An agricultural diversification programme was introduced by the Malaysian government in the 1960s to reduce the country's economic overreliance on rubber and tin. This resulted in the introduction of oil palm, which was based on the country's pre-existing experience from its long history of growing rubber trees. In a short time palm oil became a major product in the Malaysian economy; Malaysia is now a world leader in the use of palm oil in a wide range of industries, including biofuel and pharmaceutical glycerine.

These three examples show that diversifying an economy can happen within existing industrial structures, taking a shorter horizon yet higher added value route. New industries are born with the immediate advantage of being able to tap into existing pool of resources, supply chains and infrastructure. Arguably these conditions might not be available to all countries or regions, and a complete shift from existing and traditional legacies might be the only way forward. Nevertheless, an approach of muddling through would be still recommended to wed emerging capabilities with emerging market demand.

The rest of this book provides rich and deep insights about the different experiences of several natural resource-rich countries at various levels of economic development and diversification. These experiences come from all four populated continents of the world and cover a period of several decades of policy experimentation with varying degrees of success.

Note

This chapter is based on the paper 'Demand-led related diversification: an innovation policy approach to economic diversification and development' by Sami Mahroum and Yasser Al-Saleh, published in *Science and Public Policy* (2013, vol. 40, no. 3, pp. 406–418).

References

Amsden, A. (1989) *Asia's next giant: South Korea and late industrialization*, Oxford: Oxford University Press.

Beise, M. (2001) *Lead markets: Country specific success factors of the global diffusion of innovations*, Heidelberg: Physica-Verlag.

Boschma, R.A. and Wenting, R. (2007) 'The spatial evolution of the British automobile industry: Does location matter?' *Industrial and Corporate Change*, vol. 16, no. 2, pp. 213–238.

Chenery, H.B. (1982) *Industrialization and growth: The experience of large countries*, World Bank Staff Working Paper, no. 539.

Edquist, C., Hommen, L. and Tsipouri, L. (eds.) (2000) *Public technology procurement and innovation*, Norwell: Kluwer Academic Publishers.

Edler, J. (2007) 'Demand oriented innovation policy', in Smits, R., Kuhlmann, S. and Shapira, P. (eds.) *The co-evolution of innovation policy: Innovation policy dynamics, systems and governance*, Cheltenham: Edward Elgar.

Flanagan, K., Uyarra, E. and Laranja, M. (2011) 'Reconceptualising the "policy mix" for innovation', *Research Policy*, vol. 40, no. 5, pp. 702–713.

Georghiou, L. (2007) *Demanding innovation: Lead markets, public procurement and innovation*, London: NESTA.

Geroski, P.A. (1990) 'Procurement policy as a tool of industrial policy', *International Review of Applied Economics*, vol. 4, no. 2, pp. 182–198.

Hausmann, R. and Rodrik, D. (2003) 'Economic development as self-discovery', *Journal of Economic Development*, vol. 72, no. 2, pp. 603–633.

Jacob, K. et al. (2005) *Lead markets for environmental innovations*, Heidelberg: Physica-Verlag.

Kim, W.C. and Mauborgne, R. (2005) *Blue ocean strategy: How to create uncontested market space and make the competition irrelevant*, Cambridge: Harvard Business School Press.

Klepper, S. (2002) 'The capabilities of new firms and the evolution of the US automobile industry', *Industrial and Corporate Change*, vol. 11, no. 4, pp. 645–666.

Krugman, P.R. (1979) 'Increasing returns, monopolistic competition, and international trade', *Journal of International Economics*, vol. 9, no. 4, pp. 469–479.

Mahroum, S. and Al-Saleh, Y.M. (2013) 'Demand-led related diversification: an innovation policy approach to economic diversification and development', *Science and Public Policy*, vol. 40, no. 3, pp. 406–418.

Neffke, F., Henning, M. and Boschma, R. (2011) 'How do regions diversify over time? Industry relatedness and the development of new growth paths in regions', *Economic Geography*, Vol. 87, no. 3, pp. 237–265.

OECD (2011) *Demand-side innovation policies*, Paris: OECD.

Ricardo, D. (1817) *On the principles of political economy and taxation*, 3rd edition, London: John Murray.

Rodrik, D. (2007) *One economics, many recipes: Globalization, institutions and economic growth*, Princeton: Princeton University Press.

Von Hippel, E. (2005) *Democratizing innovation*, Cambridge: MIT Press.

Wade, R. (1990) *Governing the market*, Princeton: Princeton University Press.

Zerka, P. (2009) *Making innovation work: Towards a smart demand-orientated innovation policy in Europe*, Warsaw: Demos Europa: Centre for European Strategy.

2 Industrial diversification and the evolving position of natural resources in the Canadian economy

Richard Hawkins

2.1 Introduction

Canada possesses one of the largest and most diverse endowments of natural resources in the world. The popular national narrative has long been that Canada cannot escape being a 'hewer of wood and a drawer of water'. However, Canada stands with a tiny group of other OECD countries – most notably the US and Australia – that could claim to be virtually self-sufficient in human, intellectual, industrial, financial and natural resources. Accordingly, it would be incorrect to characterise Canada as a resource-based economy, structured around natural resources and dependent mainly upon the income from the export of undifferentiated resource commodities.

The relationship of natural resources to the Canadian economy is one of complexity, not dependency. Canada is simultaneously a resource economy and a knowledge economy. It is already an exemplar of the paradigm that most less-diversified resource-rich countries seek to embrace. The challenges Canada now faces concern how this relationship will be organised and managed in order to preserve and enhance an already diversified economy.

What has changed is that the export of just one type of natural resource – oil and gas – has acquired a very large share of Canadian exports, whereas the contributions of manufacturing sectors have stagnated or declined. This is a new trend, which is worrying for several reasons. First, most of the oil and gas industry is foreign-owned. Second, the resource is land-locked, making the United States virtually the sole export market. Third, most of the Canadian reserves yield heavier grades of oil with special extraction, transport and refining requirements. Fourth, Canada has very little domestic upgrading capacity. Thus, as an oil producer, Canada is a price taker, which typically means taking a 10–15% discount on the global price per barrel, apart from any external price shocks. Thus, Canada is becoming ever more reliant on just one export whose market structure and geo-politics are entirely beyond its control.

The volatility of this situation has led to many concerns about the future of Canada's economic diversity. Moreover, with recent rapid declines in the world oil price, these concerns have expanded from the medium and long term to encompass even relatively short-term economic prospects, especially in the oil-producing regions. The question motivating this chapter is whether current policies for science, technology and industry (STI) can continue to induce and support diversification as Canada acquires an increasingly specialised profile as an energy exporter.

The discussion begins with a look at how the Canadian economy developed historically through interaction between its resource base and the emergence of value-added industries. Evolution in the position of energy in this context is then discussed, focussing specifically on the role of the public sector in developing oil sands. This will be followed by a look at diversity in the current Canadian economy in terms mainly of changes in the value-added composition of exports. The evolution of Canadian STI policy will then be explored with reference to the declining efficiency of policy as it has shifted steadily away from creating industries towards subsidising firms. The chapter concludes with an assessment of what needs to be done to ensure that Canada does not move irrevocably in the direction of becoming a 'hewer of wood and a drawer of water' for the first time in its history.

2.2 Neither a hewer of wood nor a drawer of water – dispelling the great Canadian myth

The intellectual foundations of Canadian economic development are most often drawn from the economic historian Harold Innis (1894–1952) who saw Canada's economic development as being propelled forward as export markets for one staple commodity declined and markets for others opened up (Innis, 1923, 1940). This was a form of diversification in that each successive staple never entirely supplanted the others. In strictly Schumpeterian terms, it also represented innovation, specifically with regard to opening up new markets and new sources of supply for existing commodities (Schumpeter, 1912/1959).

However, as Zeller (1996) points out, the need to identify and exploit new resources was also the wellspring of organised scientific activity in Canada, and also of the rise of specialised technological and industrial capabilities. As most of Canada is a frozen desert most of the time, the full nature and extent of Canada's resource endowments were largely invisible to the early European colonisers. Early geophysical surveys were sceptical that agriculture was viable except in very small concentrations, or, ironically, that energy and mineral resources were adequate to support industrial development on a significant scale.

Canadian industries typically followed unique developmental paths that were indicated in the first instance by geographical, geophysical and demographic idiosyncrasies. Accordingly, Canada developed an aircraft industry that was highly specialised in serving remote and peripheral regions. Similar dynamics spurred activity in the communication industries, and the eventual migration of this expertise to a broad range of digital industries, from geo-observational satellites to cultural industries. Likewise a biotechnology industry evolved from the need to develop climate-specialised crop varieties. Such transformations have always been characteristic of Canadian technological and industrial development.

Gavin Wright and Paul David have argued that the actual pathway to industrialisation and economic diversification in the US, and also to scientific and technological advancement, lay in developing ever more efficient ways to exploit declining domestic reserves of raw materials (Wright, 1990; David and Wright, 1997). Canada's path was broadly similar. Resource exploitation supported the rise of manufacturing, logistics and high-value services sectors, including financial services (Pomfret, 1993). The pattern of economic development in Canada has always been for resource and non-resource sectors to develop concomitantly and symbiotically, a pattern not dissimilar to the US or to many of the major European economies (cf. Mitchell, 1984).

In policy terms, however, it would be fair to say that the natural resource industries have been regarded as standing somewhat apart from efforts to stimulate industrial diversification. These have always tended to focus on building up the manufacturing base, or more recently the service industries. Moreover, beginning the early 1980s, and mirroring similar developments in other OECD countries, Canadian policy for innovation and diversification became much more explicit and embodied in specifically tasked institutions and agencies. Essentially it was reoriented from a *vertical* approach, focussed on the support and/or creation of specific industrial capabilities and clusters, to a basically *horizontal* approach, patterned broadly after a *National System of Innovation* (NSI) model. This shift was well under way before the extent and significance of fossil fuel exports were fully evident. However, since at least the mid-1990s it has been impossible to detach any evaluation of the effects of this shift from shifts in broader economic strategies structured around the exploitation of fossil fuels.

2.3 Energy in the Canadian industrial mix

Canada has vast endowments of coal, shale, conventional oil and gas, and, of course, oil sands. Most of the known recoverable oil reserves, reckoned to be the third largest in the world, are contained in the Athabasca, Peace River and Cold Lake oil sands deposits, with close to 98% of these located in central and northern Alberta. Natural gas fields have been exploited in southern Alberta since the 1920s, with reserves of conventional crude in the central part of the Province coming on stream in the 1940s. British Columbia, Saskatchewan, Manitoba and Newfoundland are also producers of conventional oil and gas, although these reserves are much smaller (e.g. Newfoundland reserves stand at about two billion barrels). Attempts to exploit the oil sands as a source of compounds, such as bitumen for paving roads, date back nearly a century, as do early attempts to extract fuel stocks from them. The extraction and export of oil sands-based fuel stocks on a commercial scale became significant only within the last twenty-five years (Chastko, 2012).

Although the oil sands are usually associated in the media with huge open pit mines, only about 20% of the resource is close enough to the surface to be mined. The other 80% can be tapped only by drilling coupled with in situ extraction methods. Canada's total known reserves of recoverable oil now stand at about 176 billion barrels, of which 170 billion barrels are non-conventional crude (CERI, 2014). At present, however, the much smaller reserve of conventional crude (six billion barrels) is still commercially significant. As shown in Table 2.1, non-conventional oil contributes roughly 50% of total Canadian output, and is not expected to surpass the output of conventional oil for at least another twenty years. With the advent of new directional drilling, well profiling, controlled fracturing and other technologies, many of which were developed in Canada, along with the possible discovery of additional off-shore reserves in the Arctic Ocean, Canada's actual recoverable reserves of conventional oil may be much larger than current estimates (Alberta Chamber of Resources, 2011).

However, unlike the situation with many oil-producing regions, the prosperity generated by the oil sands has not been driven primarily by royalties, but by the huge range of goods and services associated with exploiting the oil sands, most of which are procured locally. Yearly investment in the construction and operation of oil sands plants now amounts to about CDN 55 billion per year. Total investment by 2013 was reckoned to be just over CDN 500 billion (CERI, 2014). This dwarfs virtually all other industrial investment in Canada in this period, and it explains why, since 2006, most of the real increase in Canadian GDP and employment has been generated in the western Provinces, mainly in Alberta. However, this also means that when oil prices fall, most of the impacts affect new rather than existing projects. If investment in new projects dries up, for example owing to global oversupply, much of the growth in employment could dry up also.

More relevant in the present context is the fact that as each new project typically involves technological advances, it is new development that is most likely to be associated with new R&D investments. In terms of diversification goals, any significant hollowing out of R&D activities in the oil and gas sector could have direct effects also in terms of capabilities to generate spin-offs, or markets for technology that is developed in related sectors, for example in environmental mitigation.

Energy and the national political economy

Ironically, Canada is not energy self-sufficient. Although Alberta gas flows to eastern Canada, along with a small amount of oil, the largest domestic oil markets of Quebec and Ontario are still almost entirely reliant on imports, mostly from

Table 2.1 Current and projected oil sands production by source, in barrels/day (CAPP, 2013)

Year	1980	2012	2025 E	2030 E
Crude oil (including oil sands)	1.5 million	3.2 million	5.6 million	6.2 million
Oil sands	0.1 million	1.8 million	4.2 million	5.0 million

Latin America. These have generally proven to be cheaper, partly because most of the pipeline infrastructure for Alberta oil is oriented north/south. This means that consumers in the industrial heartland can be held hostage to the vicissitudes of world prices, while oil-producing provinces sit on huge unexploited reserves. However, it also means that there is no infrastructure for exporting oil to countries other than the US, except via rail.

This situation is indicative of a long and troubled history of internal political strife with respect to how energy resources should be exploited and managed in the context of a continental Canadian economy (Chastko, 2012; Getman, 1980). It continues to be a critical factor in the difficulties encountered at both provincial and federal levels in leveraging diversification with oil wealth.

Under the Constitution, individual provinces have ownership of mineral resources in their jurisdictions, along with sole rights to set the terms under which they are exploited. This includes most areas of environmental regulation, although some elements, such as transport and conformance with international emissions targets, also intersect federal jurisdiction. Crucially, all of the royalty revenues flow only to the producing provinces. As a result, pipelines have never reflected national priorities, but rather those of mostly foreign-owned companies to move product into the US.

The economic significance of Canada's vast reserves dwindles when seen from this perspective. As shown in Figure 2.1, Canadian oil exports to the US have grown considerably since 2000, as that of other producers has declined. As Figure 2.2 shows, Canada now exports about three million barrels per day, but this amounts to only about 15% of the total US requirement. In effect, this is also the total size of the current export market for Canadian oil. Whereas countries like the Gulf States can make up lost US market share by exporting to other countries, Canada has few such options.

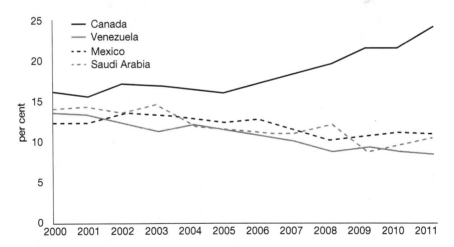

Figure 2.1 Canadian share of US oil imports.
(CAPP, 2013 – based on EIA data 2012).

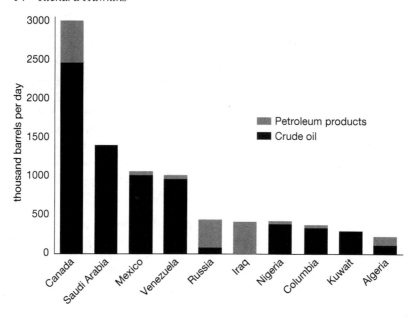

Figure 2.2 Sources of US oil imports.
(CAPP, 2013 – based on EIA data 2013).

Provincial control of the fossil fuel resource creates two additional problems. First, the producing provinces have relatively small populations. This means that the social costs of resource development must be borne by a relatively small tax base. Alberta has doubled in population in only twenty years, requiring massive new investment in public services, health, education and a host of other essentials. The other problem is rapid influxes of wealth as regions transform from minor to major exporters of energy. Alberta set up a sovereign wealth fund – the Alberta Heritage Trust – in the 1970s, but because it is owned by a province and not a country, the political and economic problems that would be caused by any provincially-based super-sized fund are considerable.

In the Alberta case, these problems never materialised for the simple reason that beginning in the 1990s the Provincial Government discontinued mandatory contributions to the fund, most of the royalty income being used instead to finance the provincial public sector. However, until relatively recently, most of the royalty income came from levies on the much smaller reserve of conventional oil and gas. Oil sands producers paid significantly lower royalties according to complex investment-to-profitability formulae. Basically, Alberta uses royalty revenues from conventional oil and gas both directly to subsidise a very low provincial tax rate, and indirectly to subsidise many of the development costs of non-conventional reserves.

Thus, in the current year the Heritage Trust stands at only about CDN 15 billion, which is equal to approximately 30% of an average Alberta provincial budget. This is miniscule, for example in comparison to Norway which has now accumulated close to USD 1 trillion in a sovereign fund from a resource that amounts to only 4% of the Canadian reserve. Accordingly, in Alberta oil price shocks can often translate directly into cuts in public services, like health and education, and to the postponement of essential public investments (Mansell and Schlenker, 2006).

The unique characteristics of Canada as an oil producer

Just how the intricacies of Canada's position as an oil producer play into the diversification issue must first be understood from the perspective that oil from the oil sands is *synthetic*; it must first be separated from the bitumen. Thus, it is a *manufactured* product with a supply and production chain that is closer to that of a manufacturing enterprise than a purely extractive one.

In effect, although measured officially as a resource export, synthetic crude is actually Canada's largest manufactured export. Projects require huge up-front capital investments to achieve commercially viable production levels in the first instance. Once operational, production costs decline steadily, but maintaining competitiveness depends upon increasing production efficiencies relative to lower cost alternatives. Achieving them also must take into account the life-cycle costs of mitigating a complex array of environmental externalities, ranging from water management and land reclamation to CO_2 reduction and sequestration (Rainville et al., 2014). These special life cycle requirements also involve significant and costly R&D investments, along with continuous applications of new technology (Bergerson and Keith, 2006). Thus, although its final product may be a relatively undifferentiated commodity, the oil sands industry is the product of one of the largest single science and technology investments in Canadian history, most of the critical early and mid-stage R&D being undertaken by publicly funded agencies (Chastko, 2006; Hester and Lawrence, 2010). For well over a decade, Alberta has consistently hosted the highest concentration of accredited science and technology professionals in Canada, and one of the highest concentrations in the world (Alberta Chamber of Resources, 2011).

For reasons explained in more detail below, resource industries present special problems for R&D measurement, but it is significant to note that even according to the standard indicators, Canada's resource industries rank among the very few that consistently perform R&D above the OECD average (see Figure 2.5). In a recent Statistics Canada Survey of R&D 'intentions' in Canadian industries (undertaken before the recent price drop), the oil and gas sector was one of very few to anticipate a significant increase in R&D spend (Statistics Canada, 2014).

The oil sands as an example of effective interventionist industrial policy

The popular narrative is that the synthetic crude industry is mainly the product of private sector entrepreneurship. The truth is very different. The enterprise became commercially viable only through a long-standing partnership between government, the research community and private investment both domestic and foreign. This effort amounted to a major industrial strategy, embodied in a succession of policies and measures undertaken intermittently by both national and provincial governments over a span of nearly a century. Moreover, although creation of the industry was to a large extent a provincially-centred initiative, it has many analogues with other Canadian industries which have employed particularly effective vertical approaches to industrial policy and diversification.

Paul Chastko (2004, 2012), the only authoritative critical historian of the oil sands, points out that this development was actually the last of several successive waves of economic diversification in the Alberta economy. This evolved from an economy based originally on hunting, trapping and forestry, to one based on ranching, then on farming, then on conventional hydrocarbons (oil, gas and coal), and ultimately on non-conventional oil. However, most of these industries still contribute to the provincial and national economies, and have spawned auxiliary processing, manufacturing, logistics and service industries, both regionally and nationally.

Chastko is also very clear that in the non-conventional sector, apart from the obvious special technical and logistical obstacles, the main historical reason for a lack of development in the oil sands was the lack of sustained commercial interest by multi-national oil companies. The original rationale for charging very low royalties was to encourage early investors to continue with the enterprise in the face of uncompetitive costs, a practice which remains embedded in the royalty regime. All of this changed radically in the early 1970s with the rise of OPEC and the oil embargoes, which raised the price of crude to the level where non-conventional oil began to be competitive.

However, although by 1970 US interests had declared the oil sands to be a strategic energy resource, and the Canadian Federal Government had reciprocated by becoming a more active participant in oil sands development, it was primarily a political initiative by the Alberta Provincial Government that triggered production on a commercial scale. Five key features of the provincial initiative were particularly significant in terms of creating a viable oil sands industry (Chastko, 2004, 2012; Hester and Lawrence, 2010):

1   The Alberta Government acted quickly to exploit a window of opportunity provided by the 1970s oil crisis to attract foreign commitment and investment around the then still radical idea of replacing a significant amount of fossil fuel requirements with non-conventional crude.
2   The initiative was predicated on an explicit understanding that merely exploiting a natural resource would not be enough to sustain prosperity in the longer term. Thus, exploitation plans, including regulation, investment staging and the management of social costs, were linked from the beginning with strategies to enhance and develop relevant locally-based capabilities and skills in science, technology and project management.
3   The Alberta Government commitment was long-term and insulated from other political exigencies through an arms-length institutional structure that was oriented to meeting the early and mid-stage costs of developing a whole industry over the long term, not simply to ensuring the survival of any individual company.

4   Policy recognised that the key to both initiating and controlling the wealth flows from the resource over the long term lay in acquiring a dominant stake in the key technologies required to exploit it. Thus, the Alberta Oil Sands Technology and Research Authority (AOSTRA) was created, which developed most of the cornerstone technologies and processes that made synthetic crude production possible at a relatively competitive cost. This was largely focussed on two basic in situ methods, namely Steam Assisted Gravity Drainage (SAGD) and Cyclic Steam Stimulation (CSS). Between 1974 and 2000 this constituted one of the largest R&D projects in Canadian history. The province retained ownership of these technologies, which are licensed to the oil companies (AOSTRA, 1990).

5   Government established funded institutions with the specific objective of transforming wealth from the oil sands into a broader range of industrial developments, mainly through knowledge investments in science and technology. In the early period this resulted in various public-private initiatives like Novatel, a mobile communications venture, and Nova Chemical, both of which remain in operation.

From about 1990 onwards the basic structure of this policy remained, although the self-financing strategy of the early years, whereby oil sands development would proceed at a pace equivalent to the provincial ability to pay the social and infrastructure costs, was abandoned. Instead, subsequent Alberta administrations encouraged a wide open development policy, which continues to this day.

Also, the general approach to diversification policy evolved into *Alberta Innovates*, a quasi-arms-length complex of technology development corporations funded partly through the Alberta Heritage Trust and other provincial agencies, partly by industry, and partly by revenues from the Provincial Carbon Tax. Although still significantly involved with energy and environmental research fields, this structure is now mainly oriented to the creation and growth of technology start-ups in a variety of related and unrelated sectors.

Energy, innovation and diversification

Development of the Alberta oil sands became indisputably the most significant innovation in recent Canadian history. Aside from producing wealth directly, it has induced massive demographic and wealth shifts from east to west. It has re-balanced the political structure along the same lines. It has re-oriented foreign and trade policy. It has affected (positively or negatively) virtually every other segment of the economy. It has dominated capital markets and captured the currency. No innovation ever generates bigger impacts than these. However, there remain questions concerning its ultimate significance in terms of maintaining or enhancing the diversity of the Canadian economy.

Any innovation of this nature and magnitude also creates major threats – not least the problem that the thrust of innovation in the energy sector globally has been shifting towards alternatives and renewables. Thus, if not managed carefully, arguably the biggest innovation in Canadian history may stop at the level of having created basically a high-cost producer in a global energy market that is showing signs of loosening its dependency on fossil fuels on the one hand, and of devising ever newer ways of producing more fossil fuels at lower cost on the other.

Arguments have emerged to the effect that a downturn in energy prices could be a boost for innovation and diversification in other industries. Some claim that lower energy prices hurt only energy producers; otherwise they free up capital for other purposes, encouraging more domestic consumption and lowering the prices of manufactures in export markets (Stanford, 2012). Thus, it is often proposed that declines in the energy sector will encourage diversification by boosting Canadian manufacturing.

Problematically, such reasoning ignores the fact that offshore competitors also benefit from lower energy prices, and that in high labour-cost countries, competitive advantages for manufacturing and services are not based upon prices alone, but also on the degrees of specialisation that are embodied in their exports (Plümper and Graff, 2001). Except maybe in the very short term, low energy costs do not compensate for lack of investment in product development, which statistics consistently indicate has become chronic and endemic in most Canadian sectors (CCA, 2009, 2013, 2014; Statistics Canada, 2011).

Most seriously, all such arguments ignore the fact that in an already diversified economy, the supply and production chains of capital intensive industries intersect virtually every other sector of the economy through procurement of a very broad range of specialised and non-specialised goods and services. Thus, although the oil and gas industry typically contributes only about 8% of Canadian GDP directly, its knock-on effects on a wide array of supplier sectors are very significant.

At this stage, however, virtually all arguments must contend with ignorance as to the actual relationship between the special dynamics of the Canadian oil and gas industry and the rest of the economy. In Canada, as in most other producing countries, the role of resource industries in the diversification mix is poorly characterised in the official statistics on innovation and diversification (cf. Schaan and Anderson, 2002; Arundel et al., 2008; Acha and Cusmano, 2005), although historically this relationship in Canada has generally been shown to be positive, especially if observed in terms of growth in national income (Baldwin and MacDonald, 2012). There is also some evidence from input-output analysis that there have been spillovers into other industries in other regions of the country, mainly in the form of domestic sourcing of equipment for oil and gas exploration, extraction and transport (CERI, 2005). If or how this sector contributes more systemically to innovation and diversification remains largely a matter of anecdote and speculation.

2.4 Coping with an inversion in Canadian exports

The importance of acquiring a better understanding of how the energy industry figures in the innovation and diversification picture in Canada can be seen easily by looking at evolution in the export profile. Currently, about 35% of Canadian

GDP is exported (compared with around 14% of US GDP and around 50% of German GDP). However, Figure 2.3 shows that nearly 80% of all Canadian exports go to the US, and that nearly 70% of Canadian imports come from the US. Indeed, in many key sectors the economies of these two countries are now practically inseparable.

As with all OECD countries, Canada has experienced a shift from manufacturing to services. Table 2.2 shows that about 70% of GDP is now produced in the services sectors. However, the 'goods' segment is split roughly evenly between manufactured and resource commodities.

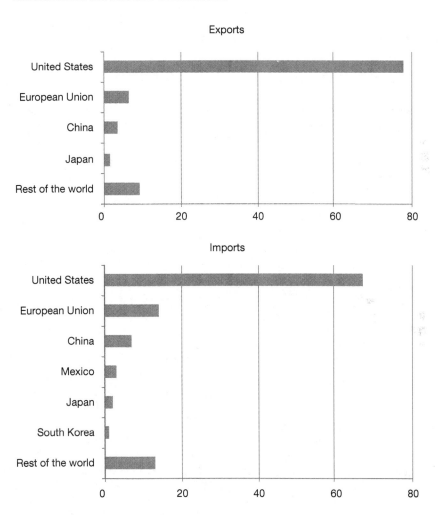

Figure 2.3 Canadian exports and imports.
(Statistics Canada, CANSIM, 2014).

Table 2.2 Sectoral contributions to Canadian GDP (Statistics Canada, CANSIM, 2014)

Industry	GDP contribution[1]	%[2]
All industries	1,643,825	100%
Real estate and rental and leasing	214,671	13.0%
Manufacturing	172,322	10.4%
Mining, quarrying, and oil and gas extraction	130,226	8.0%
Construction	120,447	7.3%
Finance and insurance	115,082	7.0%
Health care and social assistance	111,757	7.0%
Public administration	106,657	7.0%
Wholesale trade	93,580	5.7%
Retail trade	89,298	5.4%
Professional, scientific and technical services	88,423	5.4%
Educational services	85,782	5.3%
Transportation and warehousing	70,839	4.3%
Information and cultural industries	50,247	3.0%
Administrative & support, waste management and remediation services	42,587	2.6%
Utilities	37,053	2.3%
Accommodation and food services	33,893	2.0%
Other services (except public administration)	32,707	2.0%
Agriculture, forestry, fishing and hunting	25,416	1.5%
Arts, entertainment and recreation	12,294	0.7%
Management of companies and enterprises	12,260	0.7%

1 Millions of chained dollars at seasonally adjusted rates.
2 Nearest per cent to one decimal place.

These statistics are important for interpreting the relationship between what is exported and where the value is added. Figure 2.4 shows that unrefined resources constitute Canada's single largest export, with oil and gas exports accounting for just under 25% of all exports.

More interesting from a diversification standpoint is the value-added intensity of goods exports. Although R&D expenditures and innovation outcomes are not necessarily related, R&D spend is a reasonable proxy for firm capabilities in terms of product development and improvement, and the potential to diversify (Freeman and Soete, 2009; Gault, 2010).

Figure 2.5 shows the R&D intensity of key Canadian manufacturing sectors, including refined oil products. Comparing Figure 2.5 with Table 2.2, a strong tendency can be seen for the export and R&D intensity of many of Canada's leading industries to vary inversely. Industries like machinery, electronics and aerospace, which have the highest domestic R&D intensities, hold relatively small shares of total goods exports.

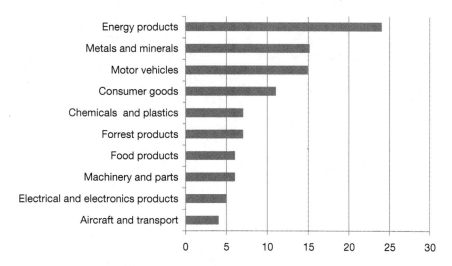

Figure 2.4 Principal Canadian exports 2013.
(Statistics Canada, CANSIM 2014).

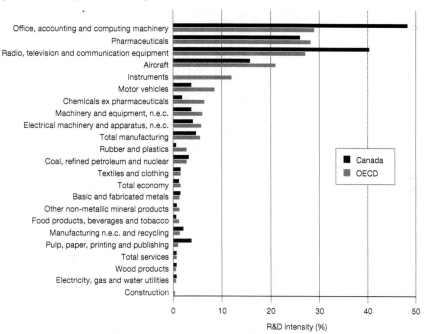

Figure 2.5 R&D intensity of Canadian industrial sectors.
(CCA, 2014 – based on Statistics Canada Data).

However, the situation is likely much more complicated with respect to the overall profile of the energy sector as an R&D performer. In the first place, the resource sector is comprised mostly of capital intensive industries that base their business models on the acquisition, configuration and deployment of technology, not on its development and production. Accordingly, they do not show up well in R&D statistics or in innovation surveys, which tend to be oriented to conventional manufacturing outputs with a strong bias towards technology producer goods (Gault, 2010; Hawkins, 2012). Thurston and Stewart (2005) note that upstream extractive industries do not even conceptualise their technological evolution in terms of R&D as conventionally defined. For example, 'research' costs are generally reckoned in terms of 'exploration' costs, not engineering costs.

2.5 Natural resources and current Canadian policy for science, technology and industry

Over the past ten years, several independent reports have warned about Canadian weaknesses on the STI front (CCA, 2009, 2013, 2014; Canada, 2011; Munn-Venn, 2006). Although they have different interpretations of the problem, all point broadly to the same three dominant issues: Canada has chronically low and declining business investment in R&D; the record of translating new ideas into products in the market is poor; and labour productivity is low. They also all note that STI policy since the 1980s has had little if any positive effect on this situation. All made recommendations advocating a more direct, coherent and coordinated approach by the Federal Government to leveraging knowledge resources into wealth. To date, no recommendation has been acted upon to any significant extent.

The current situation is somewhat fluid. Both the Canadian federal government and the Alberta provincial governments changed in 2015. In both cases, the parties that assumed power – the Liberals at the federal level and the New Democrats in Alberta – have indicated that they favour a more interventionist approach to economic strategy, and generally that they will pursue diversification measures and engage proactively with environmental concerns. However, both governments are very new and must deal with many challenging policy legacies that have accumulated under previous governments.

The economic strategy of the outgoing Conservative government (2006–2015) gelled mostly around the slogan 'Canada as an energy superpower', which in effect represented a significant reversal of Canadian STI policy. Since the 1930s federal policy had focussed mainly on those sectors that produce very high value-added products and services. Resource sectors were seen mainly as economic anchors whose direct benefits accrued largely in the producing regions in the form of wages (Pomfret, 1993; Atkinson and Coleman, 1989). In complete contrast, the present strategy would appear to be simply to enable the export of as much energy as possible, in the expectation that this will stimulate the rest of the economy to diversify.

Thus, diversification initiatives under the Conservatives focussed more on increasing the number of markets for existing Canadian exports than on diversifying the composition of these exports as such. Since 2007 the number of free trade initiatives has nearly doubled, with around fifty of them now concluded or in process, the most significant having associated status with the EU. However, Canadian exports to the vast majority of 'free trade' regimes currently extant or under negotiation are virtually negligible. The key question of what Canada will trade in these new regimes, and how this may need to diversify through innovation and product development, was never explicitly defined in the Conservative policies. These focussed instead on the removal of trade barriers and on fiscal measures to lower debt and taxation levels, in the expectation that such incentives would stimulate Canadian producers to innovate and export into new markets.

To date, however, there are no signs that this approach has been effective. On the industry front, as all of the reports noted above have shown, all of the key comparative indicators associated with diversification – R&D investment, innovation, advanced technology use and so forth – have continued to stagnate or turn negative. Recent OECD figures tend to confirm this analysis (OECD, 2013). On the energy front, little if any progress has been made towards building pipeline capacity east and west so as to exploit European and Asian markets, and on the environmental front, which has been one of the key obstacles to growing both new and existing markets for oil sands product, a recent report by the Commissioner for the Environment indicated that virtually no progress had been made on meeting emissions targets, especially from the oil sands industry which remains Canada's single largest CO_2 emitter (Auditor General, 2014).

In contrast, however, potential actions at provincial and inter-provincial levels are far more proactive on three fronts:

- Individual provinces are taking unilateral actions on the environment. For example, almost all of the decline in Canadian CO_2 emissions since 2006 is due to successful unilateral action by Ontario to eliminate the use of coal-fired electricity generation (Auditor General, 2014). Similarly, Quebec, Ontario, Alberta and British Columbia have unilaterally imposed or announced carbon taxes in the face of federal opposition.
- Some provinces are now examining the negotiation of inter-provincial agreements on energy infrastructure and environmental mitigation that would effectively bypass the federal jurisdiction. The most significant and perhaps the most achievable of these is the *Energy East Pipeline* proposal that would convert existing gas pipelines to feed Alberta crude into eastern Canadian ports and ultimately to global export markets.
- Most provinces have independent STI-related strategies, policies and institutions that in some cases could compensate for the lack of action at the federal level. In Alberta and British Columbia, for example, proceeds from provincial carbon taxes are diverted into alternative energy R&D funds.

If successful, these initiatives could in effect establish a national energy and environmental strategy independently of the federal government, along with some coordination of STI policies. However, the position of the new federal administration on this issue is not yet settled, and due to Canada's complex constitutional rivalries all of these prospects remain fraught with political and practical challenges.

2.6 Canada as a developer of successful industrial diversification policies

This current situation is entirely atypical of previous Canadian approaches to diversification. However, it is not entirely attributable to any one government, current or past. Rather, it is what has emerged from a fundamental shift in the direction and philosophy of STI policy that began in the 1980s. This reflected a global trend, largely spawned by the information technology revolution of the 1980s and 1990s, to link national and regional economic policies to technology producer goods. This period was characterised also by increasingly intensive government efforts in most industrialised and industrialising countries to transform the 'system of innovation' concept into concrete institutional structures (Smith, 2001).

The systems of innovation concept became fully articulated in the 1980s. In its 'soft' interpretation, it is merely a way to argue that innovation occurs through a confluence of many institutional and organisational factors, mainly through linkages between various public and private sector actors (Freeman, 2004). Originally with reference to Japan in the 1960s, it was noted that different countries and regions displayed different patterns in this respect, leading to observations that different national practices could affect innovation and diversification in different ways; hence, *National Systems of Innovation (NSI)* (Lundvall, 1992; Nelson, 1993).

Eventually, this theoretical construct acquired a 'hard' interpretation as embedded in an upstream-oriented and sector-neutral structure of institutions and instruments, oriented to entrepreneurship and small business development specifically concerning the commercialisation of new technologies and scientific discoveries. This hard NSI model became a putative best practice blueprint for the organisation of national and regional scientific and technological institutions and infrastructures (Mazzucatto, 2013). In large measure the model was patterned after Silicon Valley, whose unique and unarguably productive dynamics were assumed, incorrectly as it turned out, to be both optimal and transferrable to other sectors (Boyer, 2004; Gordon, 2000; Hughes, 2007).

Canada is perhaps an example proving that this hard NSI model has serious flaws. A strong argument can be made that as Canadian policy has become more and more oriented towards building up a horizontal NSI structure – embodied in defined institutional constructs, fixed models of knowledge flows oriented to patent-based models of technology transfer, and formulaic financial models like Venture Capital – the structures so created have become less and less effective in stimulating significant innovation and diversification outcomes. Certainly the Canadian system has become defined by these constructs, at both federal and provincial levels. Certainly also, as all the evidence indicates, the approach would seem to have had little positive effect on any of the standard R&D, innovation and productivity indicators.

A latecomer but an early bloomer

Prior to the 1980s, STI policy in Canada was mostly a matter of opportunity and pragmatism rather than of adopting broad national strategies (Kenny-Wallace and Mustard, 1988). As education has always been a provincial responsibility, federal policy had only weak linkage with the university sector until the 1960s when substantial federal funds began to flow to the provinces in the form of research grants and subsidies for skills development.

Before 1970 Canada had fewer than thirty universities, only a handful of which produced internationally significant research. With federal support the number of universities rose to nearly ninety by 1980. Today, Canada ranks routinely in the top five producers of world science, both in terms of quality and specialisation and in terms of citation impact (CCA, 2006, 2012). On this front at least, federal and provincial policies were to some extent coordinated and demonstrably effective.

The evolution of industry policy has been much less coordinated, and more difficult to assess comparatively. Nevertheless, the 1950–1980 period witnessed several substantial vertical initiatives, most at the federal level but often with provincial cooperation, that resulted in the creation of large-scale industries in specific sectors, mostly oriented to producing very high-value knowledge-intensive products. Most of these initiatives were linked directly to the mandates of specific government Ministries, and typically involved government laboratories, arms-length research agencies, and also universities. All involved substantial direct public investment for considerable periods of time.

Atkinson and Coleman (1989) observe that this situation stemmed from the historically weak constitutional position of Canada's federal institutions, which made it difficult to engineer a programme of industrial policy at an economy-wide level. Instead, the practice had been for different levels of government to intervene in different ways in different sectors according to individual opportunities and conditions. Some intervention was direct through public investment or procurement, and some was indirect through rule making, regulation and fiscal measures.

By looking at shifts in where R&D has been performed in Canada, both between public and private sectors and between Canadian-based and foreign-based companies, Niosi (1990) concluded that there had been a steady evolution since 1919 towards a coherent set of R&D relationships at a national level, which gradually coalesced into a system of federally-based policies and institutions. By 1990 these resembled the NSI model as it had existed since the 1970s in some European countries and in Japan. However, largely by looking at regional distributions of federal research resources in subsequent decades, Salazar and Holbrook (2007) concluded that the ambiguity of federal coordination capabilities resulted in a national system made up of relatively loose regional inter-regional networks, connected in that all leveraged their own resources with federal money and/or linkages to federal institutions (see also Wolfe and Lucas, 2004; Holbrook and Wolfe, 2000).

What is clear is that between 1945 and the mid-1980s, Canadian policies relevant to STI, at both federal and provincial levels, were primarily vertically-oriented and sector based, with few if any of the characteristics of an NSI in its hard interpretation. Policies were oriented to spotting and exploiting specific opportunities in specific sectors by aligning and/or creating specific institutions and competencies that could leverage public and private resources towards turning these opportunities into domestically anchored high value industries.

In these respects, Canada in this period bore many of the hallmarks of Mazzucato's (2013) 'Entrepreneurial State', acting to leverage long-term public sector commitments so as to make new industrial opportunities attractive to private investment, admittedly much of it solicited from foreign investors. Where this involved commitments to early and mid-stage research, this approach had the key advantages of locking in both public and private resources over the long term, thereby spreading the early stage risks, setting managed objectives, and allocating tasks according to the comparative advantages of different stakeholders. Most importantly, the initiatives were aimed at creating sustainable industrial clusters rather than single companies, although where possible they were anchored around the growth of large domestically-based multinationals like Bombardier and Nortel.

The outcomes were impressive. By the late 1950s, Canadian design and engineering capabilities in aerospace were among the most advanced in the world. They would eventually transform the Canadian aerospace cluster into the third largest producer of civil airliners in the world and a major contributor to the NASA effort up to the present day (Niosi and Zeghu, 2010; Story and Isinger, 2007; Handberg, 2003). Atomic Energy Canada pioneered the use of heavy water reactors for civilian use (Cowan, 1990). Digital telecommunications networking is largely a Canadian innovation from this time. By 1985 Canadian companies ranked consistently in the top three global suppliers of digital networking equipment, and Canada hosted the first digitally switched public networks in the world (Babe, 1990; Abramson and Raboy, 1999). Digital satellite imaging and Direct Broadcast Satellites were also Canadian innovations from this period. Much of the foundational work in bio-technology and genomics was conducted in Canada during this time, with major successes like the development of edible Canola oils and the beginnings of the bio-fuels industry (Phillips and Khachatourians, 2001).

Although not all of these initiatives were to become globally competitive in the longer term, most of them were successful in some form or other, and they still constitute the technological backbone of the Canadian economy. Perhaps most significant of all, as shown in Figure 2.6, over this entire period the chronic productivity gap between Canadian and US industrial output narrowed to its smallest extent since the 1950s. Since the mid-1980s, which saw the demise of vertically oriented programmes, this gap has widened again and is currently at its largest extent.

Although mostly a provincial action, the oil sands are also very much a product of this sector-based paradigm. Indeed, it is perhaps the crowning example of this approach. In some way or other, all of the five key elements of the oil sands strategy as outlined above are resident also in most of the major federal initiatives in the same period.

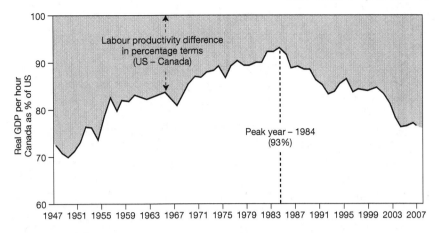

Figure 2.6 Relative Canada/US productivity levels in the business sector.
(CCA 2009 – based on Canadian Center For Living Standards data 2008).

Certainly it is an open question whether the same approach would work as well in the much more globally distributed industrial environment of today. What is beyond doubt, however, is that the approach enabled Canada to develop very substantial and globally competitive new industries in air transport, aerospace, nuclear engineering, telecommunications, computing services and bio-technology, to name only the largest initiatives. With the exception of the oil sands, which followed this model well into the 1990s, no subsequent approach has yielded industrial development and diversification on anything like the scale of these enterprises.

2.7 The transformation from vertical to horizontal STI policy

In 1996 the sitting Liberal government rolled out Canada's first truly comprehensive national STI strategy (Industry Canada, 1996). Apart from establishing the basic structure and mandates of national science and technology institutions, it represented significant evolution in philosophy and approach. Many analysts trace the origins of this shift to the previous efforts of Conservative governments in the 1980s to redefine basic research as a direct input to economic growth (Salazar and Holbrook, 2007; Atkinson-Grosjean, 2002).

Institutions whose specific function was to articulate the space between the university laboratory and industry were mostly absent from the Canadian STI landscape before the Networks of Centers of Excellence (NCE) programme was established in 1989. Its broad mandate was to coordinate university research around specific themes that were deemed to have commercial potential, to attract co-financing from industry, and eventually to establish commercial ventures based on publicly funded research.

Salazar and Holbrook (2007) describe the state of Canadian STI policy at roughly the time that the previous Conservative government first took power.

They characterised it in terms of five major policy-driven shifts that occurred within in the 1996–2006 period. To paraphrase, these were:

- from making direct scientific contributions through government laboratories to financing contributions through arms-length distributive agencies;
- from direct R&D funding in industry to indirect R&D funding, mainly through the tax system;
- from domestic development of scientific talent to importation and repatriation of talent from abroad;
- from domestically-based big science to participation in international big science consortia; and
- from purely curiosity-driven research in universities to research aimed at the practical needs of 'stakeholders'.

All of these changes were indicative of a much more general policy shift from a vertically-oriented focus on building new industries to a horizontally-oriented focus on individual firms, particularly SMEs and start-ups. Accordingly, since the mid-1990s all of the current systems of innovation constructs at both federal and provincial levels have been concerned mainly with research translation, technology commercialisation, and the creation of small firms.

Indeed, it is striking that as the Canadian NSI framework reached its highest point, policy attitudes became more linear than ever before as to the way the relationship between science, technology and industry was perceived. Thus, if the trend has been towards less intervention in industry, it has been counterbalanced by a decisive trend to intervene in the basic and applied research sector. This is decidedly *not* a premise of the NSI concept itself, which is predicated upon the observation that science is *not* related in any linear way to economic development, even though it plays a critical role in some circumstances (Godin, 2006; Pavitt, 1991; Brooks, 1994). Indeed, this is precisely the reasoning behind the systems approach.

The current STI policy environment

The current Canadian approach to STI policy continues to be predicated on the assumption that the problems with the Canadian innovation system lie in getting knowledge to market, rather than in creating industries that can use knowledge investments to leverage a whole range of factor endowments. Furthermore, it is not yet clear that new governments will see things differently although they may well make changes in approach or organisation.

While in power, the Conservative government issued only two official public statements on STI strategy. The 2007 statement was mostly a summary of existing programmes and institutions, most of which had been set up already in the 1996 Strategy. The difference was a much more clearly expressed aversion in principle to any measure associated with interventionist industrial policy (Industry Canada, 2007). The 2014 statement was very similar, differing mainly in that a considerable number of putatively new measures had been implemented or planned (it is often not clear which is which), although with no real increase in funding over normally expected yearly increases (Industry Canada, 2014). The basic non-interventionist philosophy expressed in the 2007 statement was firmly restated.

Both the 2007 and 2014 statements expressed the intention to encourage innovation and diversification, but neither articulated a coherent strategy for pursuing these aims other than to tinker with the structures and mandates of various government agencies and programmes. Priority areas are set out for research – environment and agriculture, health, natural resources and energy, IT, and advanced manufacturing – but with little if any indication of what Canadian comparative advantages might exist in these fields, or of any specific strategies to move discoveries to market. Moreover, during this period most of the key national surveys that monitored Canadian STI performance were terminated, thus eliminating many sources of data that would be necessary to support evidence-based STI policy.

The Conservative position on STI issues tended to be expressed in actions rather than official statements. For example, the Canadian Institutes of Health Research (CIHR) was reoriented such that federal money would be available only to projects that could raise matching funds from the private sector (Globe and Mail, 2014). Likewise, more and more of the Natural Sciences and Engineering Research Council (NSERC) budget was diverted away from basic science and towards industry-centred programmes. Similarly, the National Research Council (NRC) was transformed from a scientific agency to a response mode contract research agency.

As shown in Figure 2.7, federal allocations to specific programmes described in the 2014 statement are dwarfed by the massive indirect wealth transfers that continue to occur via the fiscal route through the Scientific Research and

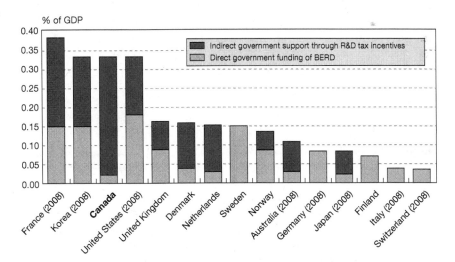

Figure 2.7 Direct and indirect R&D funding in selected OECD countries.
(OECD, 2013).

Experimental Development (SR&ED) tax credit system. In 2011 a federally-appointed Task Force was highly critical of this practice (Canada, 2011). However, their recommendations to rebalance direct and indirect forms of R&D support have been largely ignored.

2.8 A roadmap to a prosperous future – with or without oil

This chapter began with the following question: 'Can current policies for science, technology and industry continue to induce and support diversification as Canada acquires an increasingly specialised profile as an energy exporter?' The short answer is that they are not doing so. However, and with notable exceptions, the deficiency lies not so much in the nature of the individual policies or institutions, any or all of which might be effective in the right circumstances, but rather in the failure at senior policy levels to appreciate that a selection of fiscal and trade measures, supported by the operation of a system of institutions to develop and transfer technology, particularly if focussed mainly on small firms and start-ups, is insufficient to stimulate the creation and growth of new high-value industries.

Although for many the oil sands fact has become the iconic antagonist in the struggle to promote diversity, leading to concerns about the resource curse or the Dutch disease, it is in many respects the last significant artefact to have emerged from a long tradition of activist, mostly sector-based Canadian industrial policies that have also been highly successful in creating globally competitive industries around much higher value-added products and services. On the other hand, those who subscribe to the energy superpower vision have failed to appreciate, or chosen to ignore, the critical role of the public sector and of highly interventionist long-term policies in establishing this industry.

The unfortunate result is that both sides of the argument often fail to see that in the best traditions of Canadian economic development, the ultimate potential of the synthetic oil industry may lie not in extraction and export of the commodity, although this will continue, nor in its upgrading, although this too may be possible. Rather, it will lie in how the knowledge and skills created in this context can be transformed and translated to other endeavours that will persist regardless of the fortunes of oil.

In a diversification context, investments in science and technology are normally seen as a way either to transform raw materials into new kinds of products, or, especially in resource-rich regions, to move the economy away from reliance on the export of low-value resource commodities. The oil sands strategy was and largely continues to be just the opposite – namely, to deploy science and technology to enable the extraction and export of ever greater quantities of a low-value-added commodity. Without these knowledge investments, Canadian bitumen would still be sitting in the ground. Thus, if current practice is continued, Canada runs the risk of focussing its knowledge investments backwards instead of forwards.

A more forward-looking path is not difficult to find. It was shown above that unlike some of the other oil rich jurisdictions – such as the Gulf States, Norway or even the US – Canada's realised oil wealth is actually quite modest (about 8% of

GDP) and most of it is absorbed by the domestic economy in the form of wages and public services. Thus, the option of leveraging entry into high-value industries simply by purchasing significant stakes in them out of massive sovereign wealth funds is not an option. The other option, to create new industries from start-ups, which currently is the focus of virtually every federal and provincial programme, is a possibility, but one with extremely high risks and historically poor efficiency (Tether, 2000; Shane, 2009).

In the best Schumpeterian tradition, the action space for Canada lies more obviously in the very source of volatility in the economy, namely the impending transition away from fossil fuels. Figure 2.8 illustrates a more likely positive scenario. This arrays supply and value chain characteristics orthogonally. Supply chains can require everything from the most standardised commodities that trade mainly on price to the most highly specialised components and systems. Likewise, value chains extend from the lowest levels of value added to the highest.

As indicated by the Canadian case, a strong natural resources sector can create huge positive externalities, in that typically resource exploitation requires inputs from virtually the entire span of both supply and value chain capabilities. Provided of course that the required knowledge investments and industrial capabilities are present in the domestic economy, which in Canada they most certainly are, resources can leverage substantial markets for factors of all kinds and at all levels of value. This dynamic also has the significant advantage of being 'sticky' – anchored permanently in the jurisdiction by the positional nature of the resource.

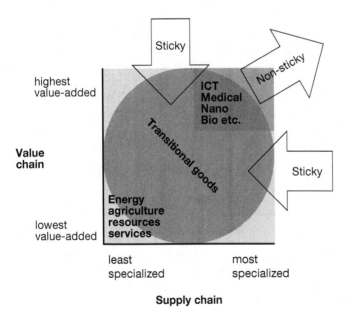

Figure 2.8 Diversification scenario for the Canadian economy.

However, with the increasingly horizontal and generalised orientation of most Canadian STI policy, the focus of public investments in knowledge and enterprise has tended towards those segments that have very specialised and very high-value characteristics, irrespective of whether an industry exists domestically to exploit them. These fields tend to be integrated structurally into global knowledge and production chains, and hence they are non-sticky. Knowledge investments can float away, as has been typical of the fate of Canadian start-ups and investments in basic research. On the other hand, making such investments is absolutely critical, not least because they also feed positively into the resource sectors.

The strategic space lies between the positional and non-positional factors. In Canada, many of these have been exploited for decades – for example, in agriculture, communications, the life-science industries and the geo-physical industries. Historically, all of these have been leveraged successfully by public sector intervention of various kinds to link knowledge investments and the development of industrial capabilities to Canada's positional realities, whether natural resources or locational advantages. The opportunities provided by our experience in non-conventional fossil fuels are more likely to lie in the long run on what follows in their wake. For example, the problems of CO_2 management, land reclamation and water management will be ongoing global problems of ever increasing magnitude. The knowledge, skills, technology and science surrounding non-conventional oil extraction could likely be reoriented to the creation of technology and services industries in these fields, which also would be of high and specialised export value.

Given the unique nature of our primary energy resource, and its special challenges, a credible mark of success for Canada's STI and diversification strategies would be the creation of perhaps half a dozen significantly sized Canadian-based multinationals who have carved out highly specialised global markets for technology and expertise in their fields. That we have created no such entities is yet another sign that our policies need significant re-evaluation. It is a bellwether indicator that as successive Canadian governments have become steadily less interventionist on the downstream industry side, and more interventionist on the upstream research and development side, the emergence of entirely new high-value industries, like those that have always assumed substantive roles in Canada's economic mix, has dwindled from a torrent to a trickle.

References

Abramson, B.D. and Raboy, M. (1999) Policy globalization and the information society: A view from Canada, *Telecommunications Policy*, vol. 23, nos. 10–11, 775–791.

Acha, V. and Cusmano, L. (2005) 'Governance and co-ordination of distributed innovation processes: Patterns of R&D co-operation in the upstream petroleum industry', *Economics of Innovation and New Technology*, vol. 14, nos. 1–2, 1–21.

Alberta Chamber of Resources (2011) *Task force on resource development and the economy*, Edmonton: Alberta Chamber of Resources, February.

AOSTRA (1990) *AOSTRA: A fifteen year portfolio of achievement*, Edmonton: Alberta Oil Sands Technology and Research Authority.

Arundel, A., Bordoy, C. and Kanerva, M. (2008) *Neglected innovators: How do innovative firms that do not perform R&D innovate?: Results of an analysis of the Innobarometer 2007 survey No. 215*, INNO-Metrics Thematic Paper, Maastricht: MERIT.

Atkinson-Grosjean, J. (2002) 'Canadian science at the public/private divide: The NCE experiment', *Journal of Canadian Studies*, vol. 37, no. 3, 71–91.

Atkinson-Grosjean, J. (2006) *Public science, private interests: culture and competition in Canada's Networks of Centre of Excellence*, Toronto: University of Toronto Press.

Atkinson, M. and Coleman, W. (1989) *The state, business and industrial change in Canada*, Toronto: University of Toronto Press.

Auditor General (2014) *Report of the Commissioner of the Environment and Sustainable Development*, Ottawa: Auditor General.

Babe, R. (1990) *Telecommunications in Canada*, Toronto: University of Toronto Press.

Baldwin, J. and Macdonald, R. (2012) *Natural resources, the terms of trade, and real income growth in Canada: 1870 to 2010*, Statistics Canada, Economic Analysis Research Paper Series, April.

Bergerson, J. and Keith, D. (2006) *Life cycle assessment of oil sands technologies*, University of Calgary: Institute for Sustainable Energy, Environment and Economy (ISEEE).

Boyer, R. (2004) *The future of economic growth: As new Becomes old*, Cheltenham, Edward Elgar.

Brooks, H. (1994) 'The relationship between science and technology', *Research Policy*, vol. 23, 477–486.

Canada (2011) *Innovation Canada: A call to action*, Ottawa: Government of Canada.

CAPP (2013) *About Canada's oil sands*, n.p.: Canadian Association of Petroleum Producers.

CCA (2006) *The state of science and technology in Canada: Final report*, Ottawa: Council of Canadian Academies.

CCA (2009) *Innovation and business strategy: Why Canada falls short*, Ottawa: Council of Canadian Academies.

CCA (2012) *The state of science and technology in Canada 2012*, Report of the Expert Panel on the State of Science and Technology in Canada, Ottawa: Council of Canadian Academies.

CCA (2013) *The state of industrial R&D in Canada*, Ottawa: Council of Canadian Academies.

CCA (2014) *Paradox Lost: Explaining Canada's research strength and innovation weakness*, Ottawa: Council of Canadian Academies.

CERI (2005) *Economic impact of Alberta's oil sands*, Study No. 110, Calgary, Canadian Energy Research Institute, October.

CERI (2014) *Canadian economic impacts of new and existing oil sands development in Alberta (2014–2038)*, briefing paper, Calgary, Canadian Energy Research Institute, November.

Chastko, P. (2004) *Developing Alberta's oil sands: From Clark to Kyoto*, Calgary: University of Calgary Press.

Chastko, P. (2012) 'Anonymity and ambivalence: The Canadian and American oil industries and the emergence of continental oil', *The Journal of American History*, doi: 10.1093/jahist/jas049, 166–176.

Cowan, R. (1990) 'Nuclear power Reactors: A study in technological lock-in', *The Journal of Economic History*, vo. 50, no. 3, 541–567.

David, P. and Wright, G. (1997) 'Increasing returns and the genesis of American resource abundance', *Industrial and Corporate Change*, vol. 6, no. 2, 203–245.

Freeman, C. (2004) 'Technological infrastructure and international competitiveness', *Industrial and Corporate Change*, vol. 13, no. 3, 541–569.

Freeman, C. and Soete, L. (2009) 'Developing science, technology and innovation indicators: What we can learn from the past', *Research Policy*, vol. 38, no. 4, 583–589.

Gainor, C. (2007) 'Canada's space program, 1958–1989: A program without an agency', *Acta Astronautica*, vol. 60, no. 2, 132–139.

Gault, F. (2010) *Innovation strategies for a global economy: Development, implementation, measurement and management*, Cheltenham: Edward Elgar.

Getman, C. (1980) 'Canada's National Energy Program: An analysis', *Houston Journal of International Law*, vol. 3, 155–178.

Globe and Mail (2014) *Funding changes usher in a Dark Age for Canadian science*, December 15.

Godin, B. (2006) 'The linear model of innovation: The historical construction of an analytical framework', *Science, Technology, and Human Values*, vol. 31, no. 6, 639–667.

Gordon, R.J. (2000) 'Does the 'new economy' measure up to the great inventions of the past?', *Journal of Economic Perspectives*, vol. 14, no. 4, 49–74.

Handberg, R. (2003) 'Dancing with the elephants: Canadian space policy in transition', *Technology in Society*, vol. 25, no. 1, 27–42.

Hawkins, R. (2012) *Looking at innovation from a uniquely Canadian perspective: The case for a new alliance of practice, policy and scholarship*, discussion paper, Ottawa: Institute for Science, Society and Policy, March.

Hester, A. and Lawrence, L. (2010) *A sub-national public-private strategic alliance for innovation and export development: The case of the Canadian province of Alberta's oil sands*, Santiago, Chile: United Nations Economic Commission for Latin America and the Caribbean (ECLAC), April.

Holbrook, J.A. and Wolfe, D.A. (eds.) (2000) *Innovation, institutions and territory: Regional innovation systems in Canada*, Montreal and Kingston: McGill-Queens Press.

Hughes, A. (2007) *Innovation policy as cargo cult: Myth and reality in knowledge-led productivity growth*, Centre for Business Research, University of Cambridge Working Paper No. 348.

Industry Canada (1996) *Science and Technology for the New Century*, Ottawa.

Industry Canada (2007) *Mobilizing science and technology to Canada's advantage*, Ottawa: Industry Canada.

Industry Canada (2011) *Innovation Canada: A call to action, Expert Panel Report – Review of federal support to research and development*, Ottawa: Industry Canada.

Industry Canada (2014) *Seizing Canada's moment: Moving forward in science, technology and innovation*, Ottawa: Industry Canada.

Innes, H. (1930) *A history of the Canadian Pacific Railway*, revised edition (1971), Toronto: University of Toronto Press.

Innes, H. (1940) *The cod fisheries: The history of an international economy*. Toronto: The Ryerson Press.

Kenny-Wallace, G. and Mustard F. (1988) 'From paradox to paradigm: The evolution of science and technology in Canada', *Daedalus*, vol. 117, no. 4, 191–214.

Lundvall, B.-AÊ (1992) *National Systems of Innovation: Towards a theory of innovation and interactive learning,* London: Pinter.

Mansell, R. and Percy, M. (1990) *Strength in adversity: A study of the Alberta economy*, Edmonton: University of Alberta Press.

Mansell, R. and Schlenker, R. (2006) *Energy and the Alberta economy: Past and future impacts and implications*, paper no. 1 of the Alberta Energy Futures Project, Institute for Sustainable Energy, Environment and Economy, Calgary, December.

Mazzucatto, M. (2013) *The entrepreneurial state: Debunking public vs. private sector myths*, London: Anthem Press.

Mitchell, B. (1984) *Economic development of the British coal industry 1800–1914*, Cambridge: Cambridge University Press.

Munn-Venn, T. (2006) *Lessons in public-private research collaboration: Improving interactions among individuals*, Seventh Annual Innovation Report, Ottawa: Conference Board of Canada.

Nelson, R. (1993) *National Systems of Innovation: A comparative study*, Oxford: Oxford University Press.

Niosi (1990) *Canada's National System of Innovation*, Montreal and Kingston: McGill-Queens University Press.

Niosi, J. and Zhegu, M. (2010) 'Anchor tenants and regional innovation systems: The aircraft industry', *International Journal of Technology Management*, vol. 50, nos. 3/4, 263–284.

OECD (2013) *OECD science, technology and industry outlook*, Paris: Organisation for Economic Cooperation and Development.

Pavitt, K. (1991) 'What makes basic research economically useful?', *Research Policy*, vol. 30, 109–119.

Phillips, P. and Khachatourians, G. (2001) *The biotechnology revolution in global agriculture: Innovation, invention and investment in the Canola industry*, Wallingford UK: CABI Publishing.

Plümper, T. and M. Graff (2001) 'Export specialization and economic growth', *Review of International Political Economy*, vol. 8, no. 4, 661–688.

Pomfret, R. (1993) *The economic development of Canada*, Scarborough: Nelson.

Rainville, A., Hawkins, R. and Bergeson, J. (2014) 'Building consensus in Life Cycle Analysis: The potential for a Canadian product category rules standard to enhance transparency and credibility in GHG emissions estimates for Alberta's oil sands', *Journal of Cleaner Production*, vol. 103, 525–533.

Salazar, M. and Holbrook, A. (2007) 'Canadian science, technology and innovation policy: The product of regional networking?', *Regional Studies*, vol. 41, 1129–1141.

Schaan, S. and Anderson, F. (2002) 'Innovation in the forest sector', *The Forestry Chronicle*, vol. 78, no. 1, 60–63.

Schumpeter, J.A. (1912/1959) *The theory of economic development: An inquiry into profits, capital, credit, interest and the business cycle*, Cambridge: Harvard University Press.

Shane, S. (2009) 'Why encouraging more people to become entrepreneurs is bad public policy', *Small Business Economics*, vol. 33, 141–149.

Smith. K. (2001) 'Innovation as a systemic phenomenon: Rethinking the role of policy', *Enterprise and Innovation Management Studies*, vol. 1, no. 1, 73–102.

Stanford, J. (2012) *A cure for the Dutch Disease: Active sector strategies for Canada's economy*, Ottawa, Canadian Center for Policy Alternatives.

Statistics Canada (2011) *Science and technology data 2011*, Ottawa.

Statistics Canada (2014) *Industrial research and development: Intentions*, Ottawa: Investment, Science and Technology Division.

Story, D. and Isinger, R. (2007) 'The origins of the cancellation of Canada's Avro CF-105 Arrow Fighter Program: A failure of strategy', *The Journal of Strategic Studies*, vol. 30, no. 6, 1025–1050.

Tether, B.S. (2000) 'Small firms, innovation and employment creation in Britain and Europe: A question of expectations', *Technovation*, vol. 20, 109–113.

Thurston, B. and Stewart, R. (2005) 'What drives innovation in the upstream hydrocarbon industry?', *The Leading Edge*, November.

Wolfe, D.A. and Lucas, M. (eds.) (2004) *Clusters in a cold climate: Innovation dynamics in a diverse economy*, Montreal and Kingston: McGill-Queens Press.

Wright, G. (1990) 'The origins of American economic success', *American Economic Review*, vol. 80, 651–668.

Zeller, S. (1996) 'Land of promise, promised land: The culture of Victorian science in Canada', *Canadian Historical Booklet*, no. 56, 1–23.

3   Diversification of the Saudi economy

Challenges and prospects

Hatem Samman and Sheikh Shahnawaz

3.1 Country overview

Saudi Arabia is the largest and most populous of the Gulf Cooperation Council (GCC)[1] countries. The country boasts an area of 2.15 million square kilometres and 2640 kilometres of coastline, and is the wealthiest Arab country by GDP. Indeed, Saudi Arabia's GDP reached more than US$748 billion in 2014 – double that of the UAE, the second highest GDP in the region and the Arab world. Furthermore, in recent years it has ranked among the best G20 economies in terms of GDP growth, fiscal and capital accounts balance, indicating an overall sound economy. Relatedly, a large proportion of the population forms the middle class, and the contribution of nationals to the labour force is higher than other GCC countries.

Saudi Arabia's nationals, unlike those of other GCC countries with a large expatriate population, represent a majority. The population is estimated at 30 million with Saudi nationals representing 68%. An important feature of the Saudi population is its age; young Saudis under the age of 30 represent 60% of the kingdom's population.

Saudi Arabia is the largest world oil producer with a production capacity of 12 million barrels per day and a world-class oil and gas industry. The country is also a major producer of petrochemicals and fertilisers with sixteen plants and petrochemical complexes. The petrochemical industry is dominated by the state-owned SABIC (Saudi Basic Industries Corporation). Current production capacity is estimated at 75 million tons per year with a target of 130 million tons by 2020 (about 10% of the entire global output). Saudi Arabia produces 20% of the world's global methanol, is ranked third in polyethylene, and is the largest producer of ethylene glycol and MTBE and third in urea production.

In addition, energy intensive manufacturing of metals such as steel and aluminium and industrial gases takes place in the kingdom's industrial cities. There are two key industrial cities, Jubail and Yanbu, with expansions of both ongoing since 2004. There are also new industrial zones in Ras Al-Zour hosting an aluminium smelter, and four additional economic cities in Jazan, Rabigh, Medina and Hail.

These developments have contributed to the Saudi economy's growth over the last decade. However, more is needed to provide an evenly balanced growth path going forward. Indeed, the decline of oil prices by more than 50% since June 2014 is poised to represent a major, yet familiar, challenge to Saudi Arabia: The Saudi economy must be sufficiently diversified to face the various economic challenges created by its considerable dependence on hydrocarbons.[2]

3.2 Challenges to the Saudi economy

Despite the apparent strength of the Saudi economy, its dependence on hydrocarbons is unmistakable, putting its economic future at risk. Indeed, Saudi Arabia's GDP is directly correlated to the world's crude oil prices with price fluctuations shaping GDP peaks and dips. With 53% of the Saudi GDP coming from oil and other oil products and with oil prices representing 87% of export earnings and 92% of budget revenues, the Saudi economy is clearly in need of a larger and more diversified economic base (see Figure 3.1).

To ensure robust economic growth, it is imperative for Saudi Arabia to pursue an open trade policy (Sachs and Warner, 1995) and develop resiliency to shocks through a policy of competitive economic diversification (Balassa, 1985), where the former could also be employed in the service of the latter policy goal.

A useful framework in which to examine economic diversification is based on linkages from commodities to the industrial sector (Hirschman, 1981). The three major types of linkages are fiscal, consumption and production, each with its specific channel to the industrial sector. Fiscal linkages refer to resource rents that the government can use to develop sectors unrelated to natural resources. Consumption linkages emerge as a result of incomes earned in the resource sector being spent on goods and services produced in other sectors. However, large portions of these incomes run the risk of leaking out of the Saudi economy due to the country's fledgling domestic manufacturing sector and its penchant for imports. In their original formulation, production linkages come in upstream (or backward) and downstream (or forward) varieties, where the former refers to sectors that produce inputs for the resource sector while the latter uses the resource itself as an input. A third variety is horizontal linkages that are developed based on their relation with the resource sector and are useful for other sectors as well. The logic of horizontally linked sectors is premised on the notion of 'installed capacity', which enables the production of goods that are either similar or rely on existing capabilities for their production (Hausmann et al., 2007). This perspective highlights the incremental nature of structural transformation and growth through linkages between related economic activities (Hidalgo et al., 2007).

Adverse economic shocks

As a result of significant dependency on hydrocarbons and insufficient diversity in the Saudi economy, it is susceptible to adverse shocks through at least three channels. These are macroeconomic volatility, exchange rate overvaluation and underdeveloped institutions.

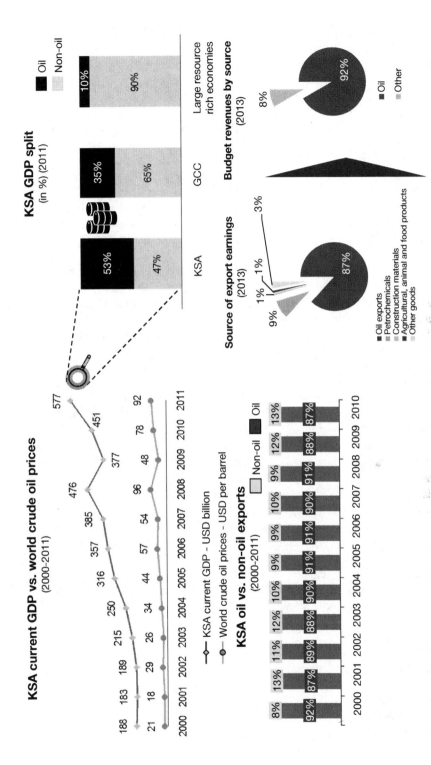

Figure 3.1 Saudi Arabia's economy needs further diversification.

The large swings in oil prices are clearly a source of vulnerability for Saudi Arabia as these can wreak havoc on government budgets and fiscal discipline, which in turn affect economic growth and development. Indeed, without a sufficiently diverse production base economies are bound to experience relatively lower economic growth over the long term, which has significant economic and social implications. Economic diversification ensures a relatively stable revenue stream by reducing susceptibility to terms-of-trade shocks (Ghosh and Ostry, 1994). On the economic side, small differences in economic growth can leave a country's economy less prosperous and less competitive vis-à-vis other nations. For example, at a 2% growth rate a nation's per capita GDP can double in thirty-five years – a length of time much shorter than the average lifespan of an individual (Ray, 1998). On the social side, persistent and diversified economic growth means that new occupations and skills are constantly being created.

Overvaluation of the exchange rate and the associated Dutch disease phenomenon could be the most considerable impediment to economic diversification, particularly in the inchoate export sector. Recent studies, including some from the IMF, have identified short periods of overvaluation of the Saudi Riyal. Other studies have shown long periods of overvaluation. Regardless of the period, however, the risk of overvaluation exists and it negatively affects Saudi export trade, which is critical for the development of small businesses and therefore for diversification efforts and long-term economic growth.[3]

Finally, it is common to observe enclave sectors in natural resource rich economies. These sectors are more advanced in terms of capital and infrastructure development, and tend to have more effective and mature governance institutions. Compared to the enclave sectors, the rest of the economy appears less attractive to investors, which reduces the likelihood of diversification. For example, Figure 3.2 shows that foreign investment in fixed assets in different Saudi economic sectors is much more heavily focussed on manufacturing than on the economy as a whole, of which around 90% is in chemicals and petroleum products.

Since the aim of diversification is to ensure economic growth and job creation, it is imperative that the gains from this process are distributed equitably. This is necessary if the process is to be sustained. Additional risks to sustainability in the form of fiscal imbalance, inflation or unchecked credit growth are likely to be exacerbated by any large-scale effort to diversify the economy. However, these risks must be balanced against additional gains such as transfer of technology and skills from foreign firms, competitive domestic businesses and a rejuvenation of the entrepreneurial spirit. All are drivers of higher productivity and innovation.

Low productivity risk

There is a direct link between diversification and productivity. Indeed, a diversified economy is an innovative and competitive economy through the creation of new products, new processes and the diffusion of knowledge to various economic activities and sectors. This in turn helps improve productivity. On the other hand, natural resource dependency has the potential of creating special economic enclaves and concentrated markets, stifling innovation and reducing economic productivity.

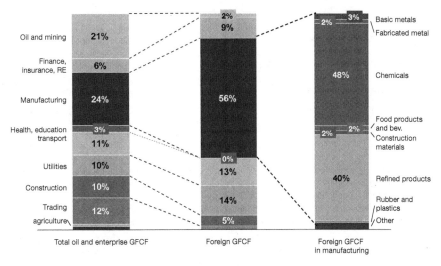

Figure 3.2 Foreign investment focus on enclave sectors in Saudi Arabia.

It is beyond doubt that resource wealth provides countries with a choice: they can invest in efficiency measures that reduce costs (e.g. the use of technology, privatisation) or they can spend their wealth in ways that may exacerbate their dependence on their resources (e.g. energy subsidies, large government employment). This has the potential of locking in low productivity with little if any gains in productivity growth.

Figure 3.3 shows the evolution of Saudi labour productivity and total factor productivity or TFP – a measure of economic efficiency. The lack of productivity gains in the Saudi Arabian economy over such a long period indicates that economic growth is not a result of increased efficiency in the use of production factors – capital and labour. In addition, Figure 3.3 shows little change in efficiency throughout the 1990s and early 2000s, which was a period of economic stagnation. Furthermore, and more disconcertingly, even during the period of high economic growth and increased capital investment there was a decline in efficiency and labour productivity. Indeed, private investment – the main determinant of TFP – declined from 12% of GDP in 2005 to less than 9% in 2010.

The evolution of labour productivity in Saudi Arabia contrasts with that in emerging economies in the rest of the world (as shown in Figure 3.4). In contrast to Asian, Latin American and even sub-Saharan economies in Africa, the Saudi average labour productivity declined by about 10% between 1991 and 2010.

A large government sector and labour market policies that allow for the entry of low-skill expatriate workers, combined with market barriers such as the concentration of markets for goods and services, are the primary reasons that lie behind many of the low productivity activities in the Saudi economy. This can be further verified as oil-related sectors contrast with services sectors in terms of labour productivity.

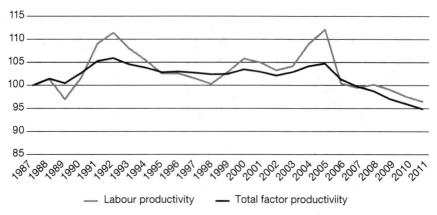

Figure 3.3 Evolution of TFP and labour productivity in Saudi Arabia.

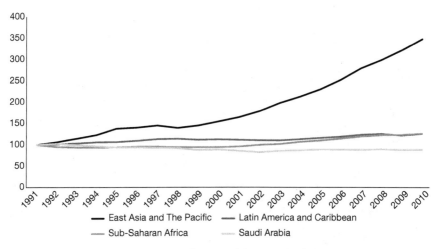

Figure 3.4 International comparison of average labour productivity.

For example, productivity levels attributed to industrial activity (which mainly includes petrochemicals and oil mining industries) are some of the highest in the world, but this is largely driven by the high productivity of the natural resources sector. However, productivity in the services sector (government and private) is low compared to global benchmarks as well as in comparison with regional peers, suggesting an inefficient government services sector as well as insufficient economic diversification into high-value added sectors, such as financial services (see Figure 3.5).

This suggests that the Saudi economy is operating in a sub-optimal environment with significant long-term economic consequences should no action be taken to implement policies that would enact immediate strategies for diversification and provide incentives to businesses and consumers towards that end.

Worker productivity

(GDP USD per worker in each sector)

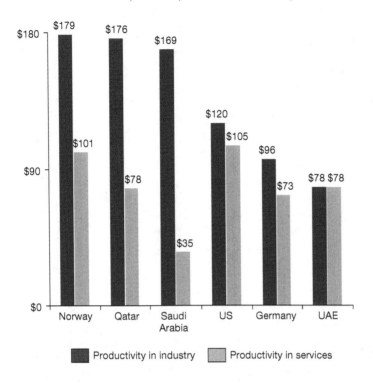

Productivity in industry   Productivity in services

Productivity in industry and services

(GDP USD per worker in each sector)

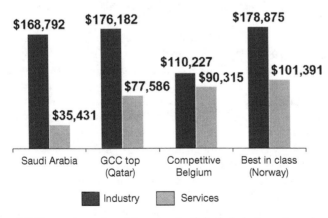

Industry   Services

Figure 3.5 Comparison of workforce productivity in industry and services.

Risk to long-term prosperity

Resource-rich countries, especially those with small populations, have benefited greatly from their oil wealth. For example, Qatar enjoys one of the highest per capita incomes due to that country's rich resources of gas and oil and a small local population. Similarly, when Saudi Arabia's oil income skyrocketed in the 1973 in the aftermath of the oil embargo, the Saudi population was near 6.5 million (including expatriates) and GDP per capita was over 22,000 US dollars – a jump of 47% from the previous year.

However, with a fast growing Saudi population over the past four decades combined with insufficient diversification to expand the sources of national income, Saudi Arabia's GDP per capita has stagnated. Indeed, post the 1980s and throughout the 1990s the evolution of Saudi GDP per capita was characterised by a steep decline and subsequent stagnation lasting until the turn of the century. Furthermore, when compared against a 1980 base value, Saudi Arabia's GDP per capita remains relatively flat compared to other countries such as Norway and New Zealand, and even populous ones such as Malaysia and India (Figure 3.6).

Risk of high unemployment

What is even more pressing for the Saudi economy is the continuous rise in the number of labour market entrants seeking job opportunities. According to Saudi Arabian Monetary Agency figures, in 2013 unemployment among Saudi nationals was near 12% – 28% higher than the world's average. With a young population comprising the majority of Saudis it is no surprise that they suffer the brunt of unemployment, particularly the female working-age population (see Figure 3.7).

The government has invested billions of dollars which has resulted in the growth of new sectors such as healthcare, real estate and hospitality. However, while total jobs in local industries have increased by almost 50% from 2006 to 2012, creating a huge employment opportunity for Saudis, Saudisation – the requirement that private companies must have a minimum quota of Saudis based on a Nitaqat (band) system[4] – has remained at roughly the same level during this time period, indicating possible difficulty by Saudis to gain access to this rapidly growing job market. Reasons include the superior benefits of government jobs (fewer hours, higher benefits), a relatively small private sector that is unable to provide a sufficient number of jobs for Saudi labour market entrants at a rising reservation wage vis-à-vis wages paid to foreign workers, and a mismatch between available jobs and the education of the Saudi labour force.

Indeed, Saudisation varies significantly across local industries: financial services, transportation and telecommunications are already at near-optimal levels, while hospitality and tourism and real estate and business services are far below potential Saudisation levels. For example, based on a business survey conducted by Saudi Arabia's Central Department of Statistics and Information (CDSI), in 2012 the Saudisation level in healthcare and tourism was only 8% compared to 79% in the financial services sector.

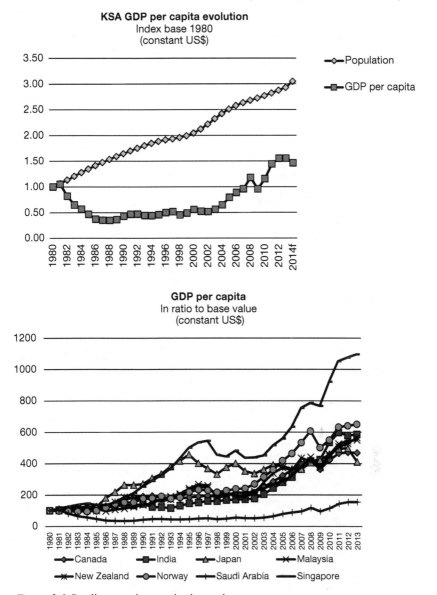

Figure 3.6 Saudi prosperity remains lower than comparators.

Creating a consumer society

The dependence on rich resources such as oil creates another kind of dependency – a consumer society that is dependent on the outside world for its goods and labour. Figure 3.8 shows that while imports over the past two decades have quadrupled in value, the composition of imports remained virtually unchanged.

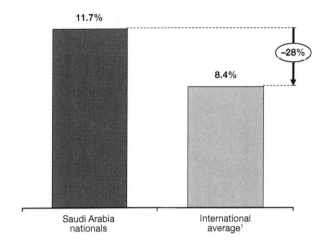

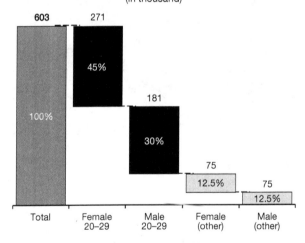

Figure 3.7 Summary of unemployment in Saudi Arabia.

Saudi imports 1995
Total trade $31 B

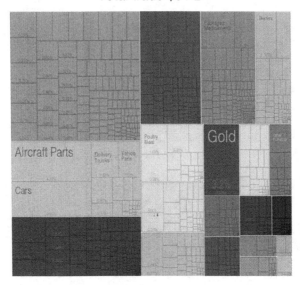

Saudi imports 2012
Total country trade $118 B

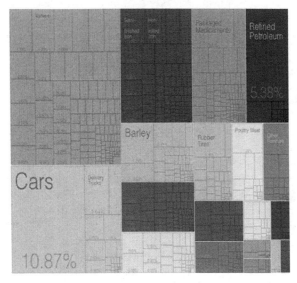

Figure 3.8 Consumption patterns in the Saudi economy.

A clear reason for high consumption of foreign goods is the low level of diversification among local economies and industries and their lack of ability to meet local demand, as well as the weak competitiveness of locally produced goods and services vis-à-vis foreign products and services. An important issue in this respect, linked to low levels of diversification, is the existence of weak value chains in several economic sectors. These have resulted in continued leakage of invested capital from the Saudi economy, despite government investment aimed at stimulating growth and job creation.

One example of such leakage is illustrated in the number of jobs taken by Saudis vis-à-vis those taken by expats and in project-related purchasing. In particular, while government investments have helped to create jobs across the Saudi economic landscape, foreign employment grew at nearly twice the rate of that for nationals over the past decade.[5] Furthermore, purchases of equipment and other CAPEX items divert local investments outwards. In short, the Saudi economy benefits little from major government sponsored projects because a majority of labour and capital spending is leaked out of the Saudi economy – another indication of the need for further economic diversification across sectors.

3.3 The way forward: guidelines for identifying key sectors

While basic economic theory emphasises static gains from trade, attention also has to be given to the dynamic aspects of these gains. The latter can only be realised if country policy is not pinned down by an over-concern for the former. Government policy, guided by the goal of raising productivity, has to play a key role in realising dynamic gains. The Saudi economy, like other typical resource-rich economies, is saddled with the problem of low productivity and high wages. It is therefore no surprise that attracting foreign investment in non-oil sectors to boost the economy has been a considerable challenge. Any set of policies that enhances macroeconomic stability, improves the quality of human capital and considers the needs of the sectors that are closest to being able to stand on their own without necessarily needing close linkages with the oil sector, would make substantial headway in the direction of consistent and long-terms gains from diversification.

The role of the government in giving an initial push to the investment bandwagon when it comes to certain sectors cannot be denied. This role is important because some vital sectors become attractive to private investors only after a critical level of activity or infrastructure becomes available. As mentioned earlier, projects like the Economic Cities, which aim to raise the level of economic activity by providing an enabling business environment, are one way to accomplish this task. However, the government taking a lead by investing in sectors with the lowest-hanging fruit in terms of productivity targets would also provide an alternate approach.

For example, processing raw materials could quickly yield benefits since the technological capacity would likely be replicable from the oil sector, and a ready market would be available in the form of China and other Asian nations where such raw materials are in high demand as an input. Not only would this policy benefit private investors by demonstrating the potential viability and profitability of the chosen sector, it could also generate enough economic activity in the sector to lure in more investors. This might seem like an ode to the strategy of choosing 'champions', and to some extent it is. However, it also means being aware of the dangers inherent in such a tactic, and planning to avoid them is of utmost importance.

In many cases the government leading the way into a non-traditional sector might be the only effective method to subsequently attract private investment. However, policymakers must remain vigilant and actively guard against the possibility of locking precious resources into unproductive activities. While the path is sure to be riddled with difficulties, the government, working together with the private sector, could effectively identify promising investment opportunities, pinpoint stumbling blocks, and release resources from underperforming sectors toward ones that are more propitious. Rather than choosing sectors to champion on its own, the government would need to negotiate with the private sector to determine opportunities that could emerge once impediments to profitability are removed. Any public-private partnership to achieve these goals would require an institutional environment that is supportive of the process.

Another key sector that is a natural candidate for economic diversification is tourism. According to the United Nations World Tourism Organisation (UNWTO), global tourism currently generates close to $1.4 trillion in export earnings and accounts for one in eleven jobs. In terms of business volume, international tourism exceeds world oil exports. UNWTO projects account for up to a 4.5% rate of growth in the industry. While this sector meets the criteria for diversification discussed earlier, and although many countries around the world have focussed on tourism as a vehicle for diversification, the strategy needs to be carried out with a certain amount of caution. In addition to being the home of Islam's two holiest sites, Saudi Arabia is blessed with a variety of natural cultural and historical attractions. There is therefore massive potential to develop both religious as well as more conventional aspects of the tourism sector. In that sense the country has the most important ingredients needed to convert the potential of this sector into real gains as part of a broader economic diversification strategy.

The primary reason for the significant role of the tourism sector in narratives of modern development is the belief that economic growth induced by activity in this sector leads to a diffusion of income, foreign exchange and employment benefits through the rest of the economy. Given the variety of forms that a tourism industry can take, it provides the shortest and most efficient route to economic diversification. For example, the potential linkages that could develop between the tourism industry surrounding the Muslim ritual of the Hajj would, in many ways, be markedly different from those that could arise around tourism centred on the beach resorts of the Red Sea.

This is not to suggest that overlap between the sectors that will be brought into play by the development of the religious and holiday/leisure parts of the Saudi tourism industry is either impossible or undesirable. In fact, complementarities and even redundancies would only help to entrench any growing sectors and contribute to making the overall economy more robust. Hotels and restaurants, health services, retail, farming, construction and even private security services could consequently experience a strong pull from these various segments of the tourism industry. Tourism could even succeed in utilising resources available in the country that might not have any alternative economic use, such as in the case of desert tourism.

Finally, business and conference-related tourism might be a particularly attractive opportunity due to Saudi Arabia's central location with respect to Europe and Asia, and because this type of tourism could fuel intra- as well as international interest in the Saudi economy, leading to further opportunities for diversification. Because the fundamental elements for the promotion of tourism are already in place, the sector can be viewed as one that has some of the lowest barriers to starting up. The Kingdom's experience with intensively developing the sector around Mecca and Medina over the past decade could further facilitate knowledge sharing.

The promise of this sector does, however, need to be tempered. Although global growth in tourism has been impressive, competition to attract visitors remains tough. Ironically, the very weaknesses that the development of this sector is supposed to address in the Kingdom are also the challenges that are likely to make it harder to compete in this arena. Saudi Arabia's lagging position in this sector relative to other countries, and the lack of economic diversity in the country, necessitate a fervently proactive government response. Effective policy formulation and implementation, astute planning and legislation, and strong marketing and promotion are therefore needed if Saudi Arabia is to distinguish itself from its regional competition.

The effectiveness of the tourism sector in spearheading any economic diversification efforts in Saudi Arabia will depend in large part on the depth of commitment to making tourism the linchpin of this strategy. This has been amply demonstrated by Dubai, which in the early 1980s derived two thirds of its GDP from its dwindling supplies of oil. Currently, only 2% of its GDP is accounted for by oil, while well over 60% is derived from the services sector. Dubai devoted itself to enhancing the role of tourism and dedicated the Department of Tourism and Commerce Marketing to realising its goal. Today, travel and tourism account for 8.5% of the emirate's economy. All of this indicates that while developing a highly competitive tourism industry would require a dedicated policy orientation, the challenges along the way are by no means insurmountable. The promise of the depth and density of potential linkages with the rest of the economy make tourism an ideal target sector to cultivate in an effort aimed at economic diversification.

Saudi Arabia would need policies specifically targeted at invigorating the tourism sector if the industry is to take off in any significant way. The policy mix could include the liberalisation of air transport by, for example, adding other regional carriers to selected internal routes. Emphasis on business tourism as it pertains to conferences and meetings, together with significant investments in telecommunications and cyber-technology to develop a modern, cutting edge and reliable communications network, would be other crucial components of this policy strategy. Combined with religious tourism, this would secure a varied mix of visitors to the kingdom that is characterised not only by its levels of income, but also by its desire to visit at different points in a calendar year.

To derive maximum gains from this strategy, it is imperative that policies are put in place to promote a high degree of integration between the tourism sector and the rest of the domestic economy. This is necessary to harness positive spillovers and grow sectors that complement tourism. In short, a dense network of linkages between sectors must be established and nurtured to lock in the promise of growth and employment generation through economic diversification.

Diversification and SMEs

Saudi Arabia ranks a respectable forty-ninth in the world on the World Bank's Ease of Doing Business index. It only lags behind the UAE in the MENA region on the same index. However, when it comes to starting up a new business, Saudi Arabia ranks an alarming 109th in the world. Even its regional rank of eighth among the twenty MENA nations on the list is disappointing given the size of its economy and the resources at its disposal. Any effort to broadly diversify an economy has to rely heavily on start-ups in new sectors. A top priority to let SMEs play their role in the future development of the Saudi economy needs to be the creation of an enabling environment for businesses in general, but for new start-ups in particular. Given Saudi Arabia's high savings rate – its global ranking is fourth in terms of its savings-to-GDP ratio – it should not be difficult to fuel SME growth using domestic investments. Capable financial intermediation could help channel these investments toward target sectors.

While diversification by sectors is an important consideration when it comes to SME activity, the geographic location of these firms plays a critical role as well. Policy guiding the SME portion of a diversification strategy has to examine how a clustering of industries might enhance the effectiveness of SMEs in economic growth and employment generation. It would also be important to design policy that induces firms to locate close to the country's productive capabilities (Hausmann and Klinger, 2006). The government also has to probe the possible effects of linkages between SMEs and up- and downstream firms domestically and in the region. There might even be benefits from forging alliances with industries in other countries in the region in order to capitalise on potential complementarities and regional comparative advantage. Linkages with regional industries could also benefit from possible economies of scale and associated efficiency gains.

The contribution of SMEs to the success of any diversification strategy would rest critically on private sector access to labour that is technologically capable. The internet is perhaps a more important component of this technological mix. An outward orientation of the Saudi economy would only bear fruit if modern technology, including the internet, is leveraged to it maximum advantage. This is particularly important if Saudi Arabia is to diversify into service sectors beyond tourism. Harnessing the benefits of technology is also likely to create a dense network of linkages with other industries, both upstream and downstream. In addition to contributing to growth and job creation, this could benefit the Saudi economy by making it more robust to shocks.

However, none of the possibilities discussed above can be realised without a business environment that empowers and does not impede businesses, a financial services sector that creates access to rather than scarcity of resources, and an institutional structure that supports rather than undermines SMEs. These goals would be made more reachable if necessary legal and institutional reforms are put in place. Examples of steps that would constitute movement in the right direction include the continued relaxation of restrictions on private-sector investment, uniform treatment of domestic as well as foreign investors, and implementation of a property rights regime that promotes predictability. These policies need to be augmented by the removal of ineffective regulatory measures and superfluous constraints to trade openness, both of which are likely to deter private investment. Saudi Arabia's accession to the World Trade Organisation (WTO) should help in making progress toward these ends since WTO requirements and pressure from other member nations will compel the Kingdom to overhaul these policies. With WTO accession and policies aimed at attracting foreign direct investment, access to stock markets has been made easier,[6] corporate tax rates have been lowered, and the process of securing investment approval has been made more efficient. Like the rest of the GCC, Saudi Arabia boasts a banking sector that has been resilient to both oil price volatility and global financial shocks (Samman and Shahnawaz, 2014).

Together with the policies identified here, this means that Saudi Arabia would be well-positioned to realise substantial investment gains in its private sector.

Trade policy and export diversification

An oft-repeated prescription to stimulate economic growth is to expand international trade. To ensure that growth is sustainable, Chenery (1979) and Syrquin (1989) recommend a move away from primary exports toward manufactured exports. Not only does this avenue lead to an increase in trade flows; it also provides countries with the chance for economic diversification. In the past thirty years, almost 60% of developing countries have taken this route to diversification, although many have achieved limited success in terms of gaining entry into new markets (Newfarmer et al., 2009). Even so, export diversification has been associated with raising productivity by 13% in a mix of thirty-four developed and developing countries (Feenstra and Kee, 2004). Productivity gains have been recorded in Sub-Saharan Africa (Ben Hammouda, et al., 2008) and GDP growth observed in Bangladesh and Nepal (Hasan and Toda, 2004). Another example, discussed by Amin Guttierez de Pinres and Ferrantino (1999), is that of Colombia which identifies knowledge spillovers in the form of better management practices and efficient production processes as the reason for that country's productivity gains. In fact, sluggish growth in natural resource-rich countries could be a result of a relatively homogeneous export portfolio rather than being due to any dearth of natural resources.

Resource price volatility can cause macroeconomic instability in resource-dependent economies and may deter domestic firms from making investments. Export diversification would also help Saudi Arabia to increase its resilience against terms-of-trade shocks, stabilise long-run export revenues, and safeguard high growth and investment rates (Bleaney and Greenway, 2001).

Finding the correct mix of sectors to counter export homogeneity is not straightforward. This is in part because of the prevalence of market failures (Hausmann and Rodrik, 2003) as well as due to a missing entrepreneurial culture that aggravates risk aversion (Hoff, 1997). A judicious and careful targeting of sectors with the greatest potential to yield dynamic comparative advantage is necessary to reap the greatest gains from diversification induced by trade policy. The strategy should not, however, focus simply on enlarging the portfolio of exported products. The sectors in which to diversify and subsequently connect to exported products should be the ones where the highest productivity gains for labour and other resources can be realised. Increases in productivity are often most readily attained by focussing on quality improvements in existing exports by increasing the intensive margin. A second component of the strategy is to find newer destinations for existing exports to diversify export markets geographically. The emphasis on existing exports stresses the importance of the processes utilised to ultimately produce the exported products, and therefore highlights backward linkages as channels via which diversification is brought about. In most cases, geographic diversification with existing exports is easier than developing new products to sell in uncharted markets.

Saudi Arabia can also look to the example of a considerable number of countries that have achieved impressive growth outcomes by employing import substitution policies, keeping those imports out that directly compete with existing domestic industries. However, this policy would need to be deployed carefully since the Bretton-Woods institutions that govern the global economy do not favour actions which undercut free trade. Countries like Argentina, Chile and Mexico, at some point in their development process, resorted to import substitution policies to focus on protecting sectors that required relatively simple technology and needed moderate levels of capital per worker. All eventually graduated to the production of more complex consumer goods (Baer, 1972). Many of the constraints that most Latin American economies faced in choosing sectors to protect from foreign competition are likely to be softer in the case of Saudi Arabia. The availability of resource revenues could make it easier to invest in sectors that are higher up in the value chain. However, foreign participation would nonetheless be desirable in higher-value-added sectors due to the benefits it is likely to confer in the form of technology transfer and management know-how. Given the success that Latin American countries had in inviting foreign involvement in sectors with thinner margins, it should not be too difficult for Saudi Arabia to enhance economic diversification by means of this policy. Another possible policy benefit here could come in the form of a competitive business services sector. This was the case in

India and Brazil, where governments made significant investments in higher education to support their policy of import substitution, which ultimately generated comparative advantage in business services.

Another low-hanging fruit for countries like Saudi Arabia would be to concentrate on diversifying into services exports. Services are particularly attractive because these currently account for only about 35% of Saudi GDP – which suggests considerable room for further expansion is this sector – and because sliced up global production chains present the greatest opportunities for entering into value-added service activities. Services growth could be especially effective in improving the quality of merchandise exports by lowering input and transactions costs, and by positively influencing economy-wide levels of competition and efficiency. However, these opportunities remain surrounded by challenges. More than in the case of manufacturing, growth in services requires a robust communications and transportation infrastructure to ensure reliable delivery of many cross-border services, a strong and modern system of higher education to produce graduates with the requisite skills to make the sector globally competitive, and effective regulatory institutions that inspire trust in foreign buyers regarding the quality of the services being exported to them. Like many resource-rich countries, Saudi Arabia has struggled to train a large enough pool of workers with the technical skills needed to succeed in the global marketplace. The kingdom also has only a mixed record in terms of creating institutions that could reassure consumers of service quality and reliability. If the government initially leads private investment into sectors with the most promise, it could not only create broad interest in further exploration of those sectors, but if it is successful it will also aid in leading industrial agglomerations to form and quickly move down their long run average cost curves. Combined with knowledge spillovers from exporters, like insight into production methods, management techniques and even preferences that characterise foreign demand, these can give rise to comparative advantage in previously untapped sectors.

It is important to couple this guiding role of the government in service sector development with an appropriate institutional framework designed to better allocate the economy's resources. Specifically, a business environment that encourages an allotment of capital, land and labour to match Saudi Arabia's dynamic comparative advantage needs to be nurtured and sustained. This is essential to achieve the ultimate goals of diversification policy, namely those of generating numerous and durable employment opportunities. In fact, policies that support an efficient allocation of resources and therefore ensure the long-term viability of high-quality jobs need to be pursued vigorously. Among these are an active role for government in seeking out and going after trade opportunities by, for example, organising trade fairs, setting up export promotion missions and establishing government-to-government and government-to-business arrangements. The importance of a proactive role in this regard can be gauged from an estimate by the World Bank that a dollar spent on export promotion yields a $40 increase in exports. Another policy priority should be to ensure access for businesses to low-cost backbone services such as finance, telecommunications, logistics and energy. While the Kingdom has made considerable headway in improving access to services infrastructure it still lags behind in terms of certain metrics, even compared to the obvious competitors from within the GCC. For example, Bahrain, Qatar and the UAE all have internet penetration that is upwards of 85%. In comparison, Saudi Arabia languishes at just over 60%.

Whether it is services or manufacturing, Saudi Arabia has to encourage support of these efforts by ensuring the availability of cheap credit. Government subsidies to small and medium-sized enterprise, while welcome, could be distracting from the opportunity to deeply embed into the real economy the functions that a financial sector provides in a modern economy. Developing minimal lending requirements for banks and other lending institutions, and giving incentives, credit guarantees and even subsidies to these institutions for lending to manufacturing and services related businesses, would enhance business access to capital. The increased engagement of new entrepreneurs with the financial sector would also positively shift the culture of commerce in a more growth-oriented direction. Start-ups, particularly those aimed at increasing value-addition to exports of primary products already in the Saudi export portfolio, would have the greatest chance of making the positive role of the financial sector common knowledge among entrepreneurs. An added benefit of using the financial sector as a vehicle to grow and diversify exports would be to strengthen the former, as there is growing evidence of economic diversity contributing positively to financial sector strength.

3.4 Concluding remarks

A major goal of developing country policy makers since the 1950s has been to respond to the call by Raul Prebisch among others to diversify out of primary products. Saudi Arabia's diversification has been part of its five-year strategic plans since the 1980s, yet much of this diversification progress has taken place in oil-related industries. Other sectors such as manufacturing and services continue to be relatively small in contribution to local production.

In recent years, however, Saudi Arabia has reprioritised diversification as one of the key growth drivers and seems to be more determined to pursue this path. In 2008 the National Industrial Clusters Programme (NICDP) was launched to catalyse industrial investments across several industrial clusters and through several anchor investment opportunities in each industrial cluster. These clusters include minerals and metal processing, automotive, plastics and packaging, home appliances and solar energy, among others. These industrial clusters are expected to leverage various existing and future industrial and economic zones such as the King Abdullah Economic City and Jubail II industrial zone, to name but two.

Still, the recent deterioration in oil prices – reminiscent of the price declines during the 1980s and 1990s is a stark reminder of the importance of diversification. Technology shocks such as the shale gas revolution or alternative energy uses can also threaten the comparative advantage of Saudi Arabia, not only in terms of the price of oil but also in terms of petrochemical products on which the Saudi economy depends. For example, in the wake of the shale gas boom in the United

Sates the American Chemistry Council identified 110 new investment projects in the US. These investment projects include petrochemical industries that will directly compete with Saudi petrochemical exports.

To make progress in its diversification efforts, Saudi Arabia should support increases in the investment growth rates in high opportunity areas such as machinery and equipment, electrical machinery and equipment and building materials, among others. Such investments will help build the missing or weak value chains in local industries and will help to reduce economic leakage. Investments in services sectors such as tourism and healthcare will also prove critical for expanding the economic base. All such diversification efforts, however, must be done in parallel with continued support for and development of the education system to align education strategies with strategies of the overall economy.

Promoting foreign investments will be key in supporting the diversification goals of the Saudi economy by providing needed funds, helping the transfer of knowledge and technology, and creating jobs for Saudis. Realising this, the Saudi government is moving to open up its economy to foreign investors with a specific focus on investors who will add economic value especially in non-oil sectors. With further easing of regulatory restrictions and improvements of the business and social environments, foreign investments will likely grow and continue to contribute to Saudi diversification efforts.

To that end, diversification will have several important implications at the social and economic levels. These include increased income and higher prosperity for citizens, as well as contributions to innovation and technology through foreign investments, more sustainable job creation through the allocation of jobs across different economic sectors, and long-term economic performance without the frequent volatility that often disrupts economic plans. Saudi Arabia has made great strides in developing its oil economy and petrochemical industries. Now is the time to ensure a healthy economic prospect for the Kingdom by finding creative ways to help the Saudi economy diversify and grow.

Notes

1   The GCC includes the Kingdom of Bahrain, Kuwait, Oman, Qatar, the United Arab Emirates (UAE) and the Kingdom of Saudi Arabia.
2   Salman bin Abdulaziz Al-Saud ascended the throne to become the Saudi King in January 2015. Following a period of falling oil prices, the Kingdom has implemented a number of serious economic reforms including phasing out subsidies for electricity, water and petrol. In April 2016, Deputy Crown Prince Mohammed bin Salman announced an ambitious 2030 Vision with the aim of weaning the Kingdom from its addiction to oil. It remains to be seen whether such economic reforms would bear fruit.
3   See, for example, *Saudi Arabia: 2011 Article IV Consultation – Staff Report; Public Information Notice, IMF, 2011.*
4   Improving private sector employment for Saudis has been a major objective for the government for decades. Many attempts have been made to increase levels of Saudi employment in the private sector and to solve the unemployment challenge for the Saudi youth population. Previously, 'Saudisation' policies were limited to: (i) applying

a set quota in the private sector such that firms were required to maintain a minimum Saudi employment percentage of the overall workforce; and (ii) reserving specific types of jobs for Saudi nationals. Lately the Ministry of Labour has undertaken a number of new initiatives to address Saudi youth unemployment, support Saudisation and provide assistance to unemployed Saudis. These recent measures include, but are not limited to, a new unemployment assistance scheme (Hafiz), the new Nitaqat firm classification system, and an increase in public sector minimum wages. For more details, see the Saudi Ministry of Labour website at www.emol.gov.sa/nitaqat/.
5   The period is from 2002 to 2013, and data is based on CDSI and Ministry of Labour sources.
6   The Saudi Capital Market Authority has recently announced that it has drafted rules that would allow qualified foreign (non-GCC) financial institutions to invest in listed shares in the Saudi stock market (Tadawul) based on certain eligibility criteria.

References

Amin Guttierez de Pineres, S. and Michael Ferrantino, M. (1999) 'Export sector dynamics and domestic growth: The case of Colombia, *Review of Development Economics*, vol. 3, no. 3, 268–380.

Baer, W. (1972) 'Import substitution and industrialization in Latin America: experiences and interpretations', *Latin American Research Review*, 95–122.

Balassa, B. (1985) 'Adjusting to external shocks: The newly-industrialising developing countries', *Weltwirtschaftsliches Archiv*, vol. 122, 1141–1161.

Ben Hammouda, H., Karingi, S.N., Njuguna, A.E. and Jallab, M.S. (2008) *Growth, productivity and diversification in Africa*, Addis Ababa: United Nations Economic Commission for Africa.

Bleaney, M. and Greenaway, D. (2001) 'The impact of terms of trade and real exchange volatility on investment and growth in sub-Saharan Africa', *Journal of Development Economics*, vol. 65, 491–500.

Chenery, H. (1979) *Structural change and development policy,* New York: Oxford University Press.

Feenstra, R. and Kee, H.L. (2004) *Export variety and country productivity*, Policy Research Working Paper 3412, World Bank, Washington DC.

Ghosh, A.R. and Ostry, J. (1994) 'Export instability and the external balance in developing countries', Working Paper 94/8, International Monetary Fund, Washington DC.

Hasan, M.A. and Toda, H. (2004) *Export diversification and economic growth: The experience of selected least developed countries*, ST/ESCAP/2314, United Nations Economic and Social Commission for Asia and the Pacific, Bangkok.

Hausmann R., Hwang, J. and Rodrik, D. (2007) 'What you export matters', *Journal of Economic Growth*, vol. 12, no. 1, 1–25.

Hausmann, R. and Klinger, B. (2006) *Structural Transformation and Patterns of Comparative Advantage in the Product Space*, Working Paper 128, Center for International Development, Harvard University, Cambridge MA.

Hausmann, R. and Rodrik, D. (2003) 'Economic development as self-discovery, *Journal of Development Economics*, vol. 72, 603–33.

Hidalgo, C.A., Klinger, B., Barabasi, A.-L. and Hausmann, R. (2007) 'The product space conditions the development of nations', *Science*, vol. 317, no. 5837, 482–487.

Hirschman, A.O. (1981) *Essays in trespassing: Economics to politics and beyond*, Cambridge: Cambridge University Press.

Hoff, K. (1997) 'Bayesian learning in an infant industry model', *Journal of International Economics*, vol. 43, 409–36.

Newfarmer, R.S., Shaw, W. and Walkenhorst, P. (eds.) (2009). *Breaking into new markets: Emerging lessons for export diversification.* World Bank Publications.

Prebisch, R. (1950) *The economic development of Latin America and its principal problems,* New York: United Nations.

Ray, D. (1998) *Development economics*, Princeton: Princeton University Press.

Sachs, J.D. and Warner, A.M. (1995) 'Economic reform and the process of global integration', *Brookings Papers on Economic Activity*, vol. 1, 1–118.

Samman, H. and Shahnawaz, S. (2014) 'Financial Services and the GATS in the GCC: Problems and prospects', *Review of Middle East Economics and Finance*, vol. 10, no. 3, 293–316.

Syrquin, M. (1989) 'Patterns of structural change', in Chenery, H. and Srinavasan, T.N. (eds.), *Handbook of economic development,* Amsterdam: Elsevier Science Publishers.

4 Diversification in Latin American oil exporters

Was no intervention a better policy option?

Igor Hernandez and Osmel Manzano

4.1 Introduction

Ever since the seminal work of Raul Prebisch (1950) the goal of economic diversification has been in the mindset of Latin American and Caribbean policy makers. Prebisch argued that natural resource abundance could lead to resource dependence and impoverishment. Independently of the merits of this argument,[1] attempts by Latin American countries to develop an export base beyond natural resources do not seem to have been successful. As seen in Figure 4.1, the share of merchandise exports has increased over time in Latin America. However, it is still below the average level of middle income countries or the average for South East Asia, which is considered a success history in diversification.

This quest for economic diversification has seen important changes in the policy tools used. As has been widely documented (e.g. Maloney, 2002; Ocampo and Ros, 2011), Latin America and the Caribbean (LAC) embarked on import substitution (IS) policies during the 1950s. As documented in Maloney (2002) or Crespi et al. (2014), this was not a particular Latin American policy. Most developed countries emerged from World War II with high levels of protectionism. However, the pace of the dismantling of these policies was probably slower in Latin America, and it could be argued that there was sustained government intervention in the region.

Though there is still a debate on the contribution of these policies,[2] it seems that they failed to achieve their objective of reducing dependency on commodities and an improvement of the current account balance. At the same time, they imposed an important fiscal burden on those countries, either through tax exemptions or subsidies. In the 1980s, when the fiscal and external situation was no longer sustainable, programmes for economic stabilisation and structural reform were implemented in the region. These programmes focussed on achieving macroeconomic stability, opening the economy to international markets and reducing the participation of the state in the economy. The view was that the state should focus on keeping macroeconomic stability, fostering an appropriate business climate and providing public goods.

As Figure 4.1 shows, the share of non-resource exports began to increase in the 1980s and continued until the beginning of this century. Clearly, relative prices played a role, since the 1980s and 1990s saw lower relative prices of primary exports. Nevertheless, if we look at recent years, it is clear that most of the gains have been due to an increase in non-resource exports. The recent level of commodity prices has surpassed those of the 1970s, and the share of manufacturing exports has not fallen to the previous level.

It is not the purpose of this chapter to evaluate the success of IS policies compared to structural reform and liberalisation programmes in Latin America. As seen in the figure, LAC has not caught up with other middle income countries even after implementing structural reforms. This is further documented in Crespi et al. (2014). The policies implemented with the reforms programme seemed to have been insufficient to promote productivity and the development of the productive sector.

In this context, in Figure 4.1 we present the weighted average of LAC oil exporters.[3] From the graph it seems that they performed similarly to other LAC countries. Therefore, a priori, it does not seem that the history of LAC oil exporters is different to other Latin American countries. However, the average does not portray the differences among those countries.[4]

In this chapter, we will review the experiences of LAC oil exporters in their pursuit of economic diversification. Section 4.2 will review the stylised facts of the evolution of diversification of these countries, compared to other LAC countries and other oil exporting countries. As we will show, there are no particular characteristics in the patterns of diversification that differentiate LAC oil exporters

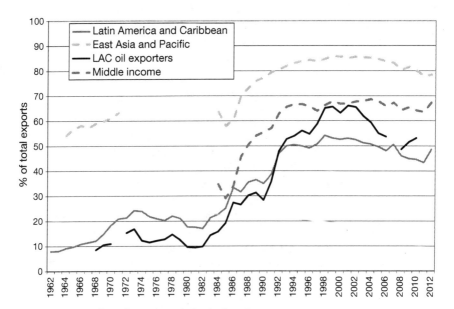

Figure 4.1 Manufacturing exports in Latin America.
(Authors' calculation using World Bank, 2014).

from the other groups, but nevertheless their performance seems to be worse. Therefore, the chapter will shift to look at a long-term account of their performance and change in development approaches over time. Section 4.3 will then review the policies implemented in LAC oil exporters. Section 4.4 will match these policy interventions to the outcomes discussed in the first section. The final section (Section 4.5) presents some concluding remarks.

4.2 Diversification in Latin American oil exporters

Before entering into a discussion of the diversification of oil exporters in LAC, the first question is which of the LAC countries are oil exporters. Since 1980, twenty-six LAC countries have produced oil at some point. Since the focus of this chapter is to understand whether oil abundant countries have faced particular challenges in achieving diversification, we need to determine which of the twenty-six could be considered as such. In this regard, we use the measure of abundance proposed in Leamer (1984), i.e. net oil exports per capita.

Of twenty-six LAC countries that have exported oil, eleven have been net exporters of oil in some years. However, being a net exporter in certain years does not imply consistent abundancy. Therefore, we need to differentiate those countries that have been net exporters over most of the period analysed. Only six countries have exported at least twenty-five years of the thirty-two years since 1980 (75% of the years). Therefore, these six countries could be considered as the consistent Latin American oil exporters – in other words, as oil abundant: Argentina, Colombia, Mexico, Trinidad and Tobago and Venezuela. These Latin American oil exporters have different stories of diversification. In Figure 4.1, we presented manufacturing exports as a way of measuring performance in developing non-oil exports. However, since the focus of this chapter is diversification, a measure more closely tied to economic theory is the Herfindahl index of concentration.[5] In Figure 4.2 we present the evolution of the index for the Latin American oil exporters.[6] We can see that there are different histories.

First we have the case of Argentina, which was diversified even in the 1980s. In a second group we have Colombia, Ecuador, Mexico and Trinidad and Tobago. They started with very concentrated exports in the 1980s[7] but became more diversified over time with different degrees of 'success' – Mexico being the most diversified at the end. Finally we have Venezuela, which has an export basket that has remained concentrated in a few goods.

Given these differences in performance, the next question is how these performances compare to other countries. A first obvious group of comparison is other Latin American countries. A second one is other oil exporting countries. However, for the latter case, it is not clear which oil exporters could be used as benchmarks in a comparative exercise.

To determine the appropriate comparison we ran a cluster analysis with the available data on twenty-three net oil exporters based on net oil exports, income per capita and net manufacturing exports. As we argued before, most Latin American countries underwent important reforms in the 1980s. Therefore we did

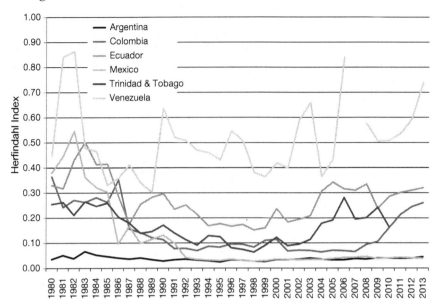

Figure 4.2 Export concentration in Latin America.
(Authors' calculation using United Nations, 2014).

the cluster analysis on data from 1990, as a starting point to evaluate the performance post-IS policies.

The cluster analysis is explained in the Appendix. To summarise, we created eight clusters, six of which are individual countries which are either large producers or developed countries. Venezuela and Trinidad and Tobago are a group. Finally, all other developing countries are in a single group. For this group we chose Egypt, Indonesia, Malaysia, Nigeria and Tunisia. We also chose Oman – which is not in the 'common cluster' – to use as as a possible benchmark for Trinidad and Tobago and Venezuela.

How do LAC oil exporters compare in terms of diversification? Figure 4.3 presents the results. On average, the Herfindahl of this group went from 0.302 in 1990 to 0.261 in 2013. Similar oil countries were more concentrated in 1990 (0.518) but they became less concentrated in 2013 (0.230). If we compare them to other Latin America countries, their concentration went from 0.152 in 1990 to 0.138 in 2013. Therefore, LAC oil exporters became more diversified in the period, similar to other oil exporters and other Latin American countries. LAC oil exporters are today slightly more concentrated than other oil exporters, and they remain more concentrated than other LAC countries.

Since the evolution of the Herfindahl could be driven by the price of commodities – in particular in countries with a concentrated basket – we also looked at non-oil exports. If we do the index for non-oil exports, the concentration of those exports in LAC oil abundant countries went from 0.154 to 0.090. These numbers are in line with the performance seen in other LAC countries. Furthermore, it looks like

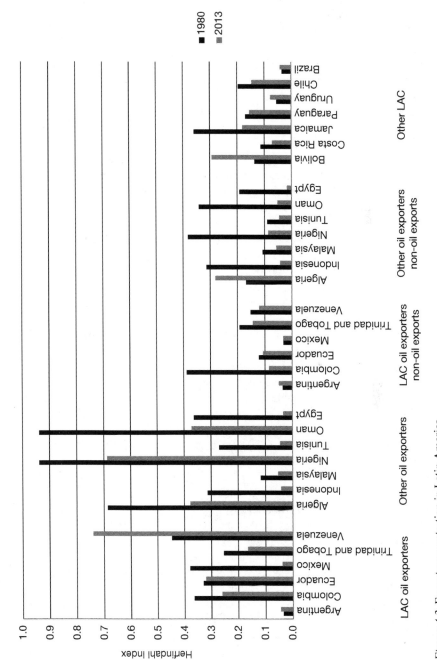

Figure 4.3 Export concentration in Latin America.
(Authors' calculation using United Nations, 2014).

LAC oil exporters have diversified more than other LAC countries when we look at non-oil exports. Nevertheless, some of the other LAC countries are also exporters of a commodity that has a high share of total exports (Bolivia, Chile and Paraguay). Therefore, the comparison might not be appropriate. If we look at Costa Rica, Jamaica and Uruguay, their index went from 0.141 to 0.093, very similar to the pattern seen in LAC oil exporters.

Other oil exporters' non-oil exports were more concentrated than in Latin American in 1990 (0.228) and then became less concentrated in 2014 (0.083). Therefore, again the gains are greater in other oil producers, but the starting points were different. Furthermore, it can be argued that part of the consequence of IS policies is that LAC countries started with a more diversified export basket.

A final question is whether there is a difference in the discovery of new sectors. Part of the diversification process is the appearance of new successful activities. In Figure 4.4, we present the change in the Herfindahl index and its decomposition in two components: the contribution made by the rebalancing of the existing export basket in 1980, and the contribution made by the emergence of new sectors. For oil producing countries we focus on non-oil exports. As seen in the graphs there are important differences between and within groups.

On average, in LAC oil producers 76% of the diversification comes from rebalancing of the 'existing' export basket and 24% comes from new sectors. How do those numbers compare? In other oil producers, the rebalancing of existing exports contributed 69% of the diversification and new products contributed 31%. In other LAC countries 63% came from rebalancing and 37% from new sectors.

At a first glance, it looks like there is little innovation in oil abundant LAC countries. Nevertheless, it is important to reiterate the issue of the starting points of oil abundant LAC countries; they were different from those of other oil abundant countries. Oil abundant LAC countries were more diversified at the beginning. Therefore, this could explain the difference between these two groups.

In this context, the main issue is the difference between other LAC countries. Therefore, it could be argued that there is an 'oil-abundance-related issue' in the role played by new sectors in economic diversification. There is literature that tries to explain this possible pattern in resource abundant countries, and it is a relevant debate in the literature (e.g. see Hausmann and Rigobón, 2003). Nevertheless, for the purpose of this chapter it does not address a particular issue for the countries we are studying.

In summary, on average, oil abundant LAC countries seem to show diversification trends similar to other LAC countries and have shown fewer gains than other oil abundant countries, but their starting points were different. There might be a problem in the incentives to develop new sectors. However, this is a feature shared with other oil abundant countries.

The most salient fact is the difference in performance among oil abundant LAC countries. On one side is Mexico, which started with a very concentrated basket and moved towards a more diversified one, but without much change in non-oil exports. This suggests a shift in the shares of total export from oil to non-oil

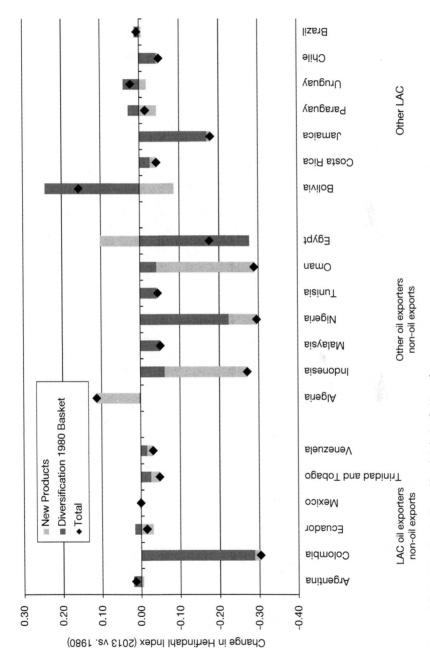

Figure 4.4 Contribution to diversification in Latin America.
(Authors' calculation using United Nations, 2014).

products. At the other extreme is Venezuela, which has become more concentrated in spite of the fact that non-oil exports are slightly more diversified. In this case the shift in the share of total exports is from non-oil to oil.

Similarly, at one extreme we have Colombia, where most of the diversification came from the rebalancing of the existing export basket. On the other hand is Ecuador, where the emergence of new sectors compensated for the concentration of the existing export basket. Therefore, there are significant differences within the group of oil abundant LAC countries.

Can we explain this performance? A first question is to look at the pattern of diversification. There has been a debate in the literature about whether countries should look at natural resources as an opportunity and develop around them, or whether they should develop 'away from' them (see Maloney, 2002). For that purpose we need to have a measure of the relationship between exports and linkages to the oil sector.

We estimated this measure with a correlation. First we estimated the upstream and downstream linkages of the oil and gas sector with other economic sectors. For that estimation we used input-output matrices. We added both linkages for each sector and ranked them. Then we ranked the share of exports in total exports of the same sectors. Finally, we estimated the correlations between these two ranks.[8] A positive and high value of this correlation will imply that exports are more concentrated in products with stronger links to the oil sector. Therefore, the pattern of specialisation would be close to a strategy of diversification 'around' the resource sector. A negative value would imply a strategy of diversification 'away from' the resource sector.

In Figure 4.5 we present the relationship between abundance and the diversification strategy. In the graph, the horizontal axis measures the net oil exports per capita (on a logarithmic scale) as a measure of 'abundance' – i.e. based on Leamer (1984). On the vertical axis we measure the estimated correlation. Each circle represents an oil exporting country. The size of the circle measures the growth in non-oil exports.[9] The blue circles represent Latin American countries and the green ones the other oil exporters. There are two 'special circles'; the first of these is Trinidad and Tobago, which does not have data on linkages in an international database. Therefore, we used a local database, and consequently, comparisons should be interpreted with caution. The second one is Venezuela, where growth is negative.

From the figure, we can get some generalised facts. First, the higher the abundance, the more correlated are exports with linkages to the oil sector.[10] Therefore, in practice the argument of the 'cluster' is happening. Another generalised fact is there seems to be no relation between abundance and non-oil export growth.[11] Therefore, abundance does not seem to hinder non-oil exports. A third fact is that the higher the correlation between exports and linkages, the smaller the growth of non-oil exports.[12] Consequently, even if the 'cluster' is happening, this might not be good. However, if Venezuela is excluded, this relationship is no longer valid.[13]

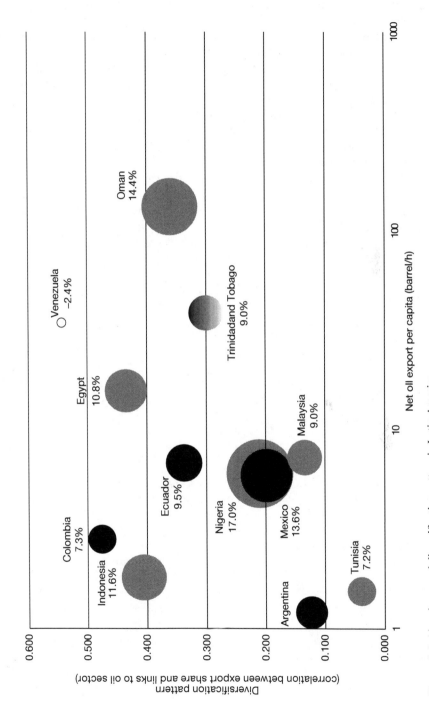

Figure 4.5 Abundance and diversification pattern in Latin America.
(Authors' calculation using United Nations (2014), Center for Global Trade Analysis (2014) and Energy Information Administration (2014)).

As we mentioned before, when we do a cluster analysis, the countries included in the graph are in different clusters. In particular, Oman, Trinidad and Tobago and Venezuela are not in the cluster where the other countries are. When we focus on those countries we find that in that cluster there is no relationship between the correlation of exports with linkages and the growth of non-oil exports,[14] while the other generalised facts remain. Therefore, in this group the 'cluster' diversification seems to have no impact on export performance. For the remaining three countries we cannot draw any conclusions.

When looking at Latin America, a generalised fact is that non-oil exports in oil abundant LAC countries grew less than in other oil abundant countries.[15] This lower growth happens in spite of having a relatively similar pattern of specialisation to other countries[16] and similar 'abundance'.[17]

Therefore, from these analyses we found that resource abundance and specialisation patterns might impact non-oil export performance. However, Latin American countries do not seem to be outliers in terms of how they specialised with respect to their abundance. Nevertheless, non-oil exports grew less than in other oil exporting countries. Consequently, the answer lies beyond abundance and specialisation.

4.3 Diversification policies in LAC countries

Given the results of the previous section we will need to understand the particular process of each country, and therefore we will shift to look at the long-term accounts of their individual performances and changes in development approach. In this section we review productive development polices for the six Latin American oil producers. Our focus is on the period from 1990 to 2013. However, in all cases we will discuss previous policies as a background to the policies that were implemented after 1990.

Argentina

As seen in Figure 4.6, oil has not represented a significant share of exports in Argentina. The Herfindahl indices for total exports and for non-oil exports are almost the same. In fact, the non-oil exports seem to be more concentrated due the role played by agricultural products, particularly soy. If we look at new exports, we see that at the end they contributed to avoiding a 're-concentration' of the Argentine economy. However, in the context of other LAC countries – shown in Figure 4.2 – these are small contributions. The main reason behind the continuous diversification of the Argentine economy is that even before 1990, Argentina was a well-diversified economy. As we will explain below, that trend continued after 1990.

There is ample literature on the evolution of the productive development policies (PDPs) in Argentina. Sánchez et al. (2011) summarises this literature. As in other LAC countries, between the end of World War II and the mid-1970s the main policy was IS. The main policies were tariff and non-tariff barriers to imports, explicit and implicit agricultural export taxes, multiple exchange rate

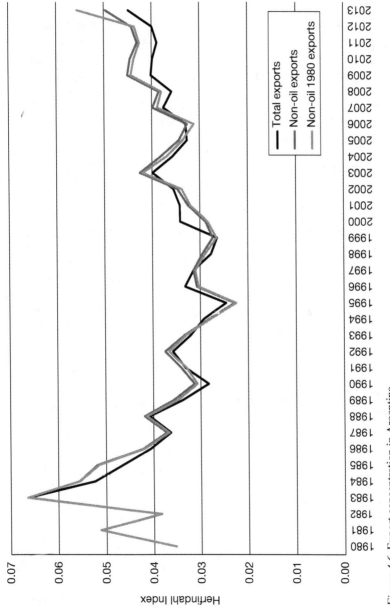

Figure 4.6 Export concentration in Argentina.
(Authors' calculation using United Nations, 2014).

regimes, and subsidies and tax credits for investment in the manufacturing sector. Although protection was granted across the board, certain industries like machinery, automobiles and shipbuilding were targeted.

However, there were different stages. Until the late 1950s, protectionist policies focussed on light, labour-intensive industries. The heavy reliance of these industries on imports of intermediate inputs, together with the neglect of agricultural exports, led to frequent shortages of foreign exchange and to the introduction of barriers to imports of capital goods, which considerably increased the price of these goods and hurt investment. Later, policies geared towards the development of heavy industries through foreign direct investment (FDI) and state-owned enterprises (SOEs) were introduced, which produced intermediate inputs to substitute the imports of petrochemicals, steel, aluminium, pulp and paper, energy, transportation and others.

The creation of SOEs improved the availability of critical inputs, partially reduced the shortage of foreign exchange, solved some coordination failures, and generated some technological learning. However, the prevalence of political criteria to manage these companies led to bloated payrolls and political pricing, which contributed to growing fiscal deficits and to low investment in these firms, together with misallocation of investment. Tariff protection and other PDPs attracted multinational corporations (MNCs) to some strategic sectors as well as to avoid the tariff. These firms acted as providers of technology and capital and contributed to some development of specialised inputs and training of the labour force of local suppliers.

Some authors argued that IS has had both positive and negative effects (e.g. see Chudnovsky and López, 2007). Its pros included productive diversification and some technological learning. In addition, some institutions that will be relevant for the later post-IS stage, such as the National Institute of Agricultural Technology (INTA, by its initials in Spanish) were created during this period (see Cimioli et al., 2009). Its cons included the inherent tendency to cause macroeconomic and external instability, the poor quality and high costs of local inputs, the discouragement and/or lack of incentives for exports, and the embedded incentives to engage in rent-seeking activities rather than innovation.

IS began to experience problems in the mid-1970s, mostly because of the considerable macroeconomic and external instability associated with it. In the late 1970s and early 1980s, the military government initially liberalised imports of final goods but continued to protect critical inputs produced by SOEs. It introduced a negative effective rate of protection for manufacturing activities which, together with a large real exchange rate appreciation, was highly detrimental to manufacturing firms. The military also introduced a national industrial promotion programme that subsidised projects to produce intermediate inputs in large capital-intensive plants.

In the 1990s, with the onset of democracy and the implementation of structural reforms and stabilisation measures, there was a shift towards financial and trade liberalisation, deregulation, privatisation, and the attraction of FDI. PDPs were not abandoned, but there was less emphasis on them, and now they were geared towards enhancing competitiveness in a more open environment, albeit with more faith placed on giving the right market signals. Macroeconomic and regulatory stability and improved access to public utilities were important horizontal public goods until 1997.

The agricultural and service sectors underwent significant technological modernisation, due both to FDI and the provision of important public inputs. In addition, the formation of MERCOSUR in 1995 provided a boost to the manufacturing sector, leading to fast-growing intra-industry trade with Brazil until 1998.

Productivity gains and technological improvements were attained. However, neither those gains nor existing PDPs were enough to compensate for the devaluations in the currencies of Argentina's trading partners (especially Brazil) in the late 1990s, and the costlier and scarcer credit associated with private capital outflows. Macroeconomic conditions deteriorated affecting competitiveness. Industrial relocation towards Brazil, in particular a sizeable firm exit in many sectors characterised by sequential production processes, also weakened the competitiveness of surviving firms.

Throughout the 2000s there has a been a greater emphasis on PDPs, geared towards enhancing competitiveness with an eye to competing in global markets and targeting more sectors and clusters than in the past. However, the overall policy environment has not favoured targeting global markets. Manufacturing exports have grown significantly because of a competitive real exchange rate and world trade growth, but they have also lost world market share. The attitude toward FDI has not been very favourable, causing FDI flows to Argentina to fall significantly.

The most important PDPs, in terms of the number of specific programmes and the allocated budgets, are those that horizontally target SMEs, investment and exports. The most common instruments used to support SMEs are subsidised credits to finance investment, working capital, and exports and guarantee funds.[18] The second most commonly used instruments are subsidies or tax credits for the purchase of capital goods. The most common policies used to support investment are subsidised loans and tax breaks.

There are about twenty-six export promotion programmes. More than half use market interventions, such as subsidised loans, non-reimbursable grants, export processing zones, export drawbacks, VAT reimbursement, temporary admission regimes, long-term post-shipment loans, and other tax break and financing programmes. About one third provide public inputs in the form of marketing information, training of managers for exporting, assistance of managerial reorganisation for exporting, organisation of trade fairs and so on. Other relevant horizontal PDPs support technological innovation and promote cluster formation, mostly through market interventions in both cases.

There are a small but growing number of vertical PDPs that provide market incentives or public inputs depending on sectoral needs. The INTA has provided public inputs in the form of technology transfers to agriculture and to biotechnology applied to plants and animals. INTA transfers some technology to manufacturing firms and certifies compliance with technical regulations. The National Commission on Biotechnology provides key public inputs by certifying the safety of new genetically modified organisms that have led to the vast technological modernisation of agriculture during the past two decades. Finally, non-tariff barriers (antidumping policies, import licenses, technical barriers etc.) continue to be used as defensive PDPs in a number of sectors.

However, as Sanchez et al. (2011) argue, the historical vacillation in attitudes toward PDPs and their rationales, coupled with a large turnover of public officials and a lack of coordination in relevant areas, has led to very little accumulation of learning for formulating the adequate PDPs, and to the lack of an adequate assessment and corresponding strategy behind the PDPs. This has resulted in poor capacity to identify priorities and design and implement adequate policy instruments.

In summary, since 1980 Argentina has been a considerably diversified economy. The role played by IS policies cannot not be discounted from this fact. In addition, it has been a relatively big market (in 1980 it was the twenty-third largest economy in the world), which formed a free trade agreement with another important economy (Brazil was the eighth largest economy in the world). Consequently, the role of scale cannot be ruled out either. Nevertheless, policies have been inconsistent. Tough PDPs have not been abandoned in Argentina, even in the IS period there were constant changes, and this trend continued after that.

Colombia

As shown in Figure 4.7, Colombia is a peculiar case. Non-oil exports were more concentrated than total exports in the 1980s. The reason for this is that coffee was the main export of Colombia until the 1990s. Colombia has been known more as a coffee exporter than an oil exporter, due to its historical roots in coffee production. If we also eliminate coffee from the Herfindahl index, we see in Figure 4.7 a more diversified export basket that has become more concentrated over time. Those exports grew at 8.52% between 1990 and 2013, higher than the number presented in Figure 4.4, but close to the average in Latin America and below the average of all oil producers.

A second salient feature of Colombia is the smaller role played by new sectors. Over the last ten years the export basket of 1980 non-oil exports has become more concentrated, moving from 0.039 to 0.100. However, once new exports are added the index for 2012 becomes 0.085.

As explained in Meléndez and Perry (2010), Colombia, like other Latin American countries, followed an import substitution (IS) strategy from around 1950 up to 1991, although since 1967 the strategy should be rather characterised as a hybrid model that added an active export promotion strategy to IS. The main policy instruments for the execution of the early IS strategy were trade protectionism, subsidised and directed credit, and tax exemptions. A host of institutions and additional intervention instruments were used to protect and promote agricultural development. From 1967 onwards export subsidies, credit

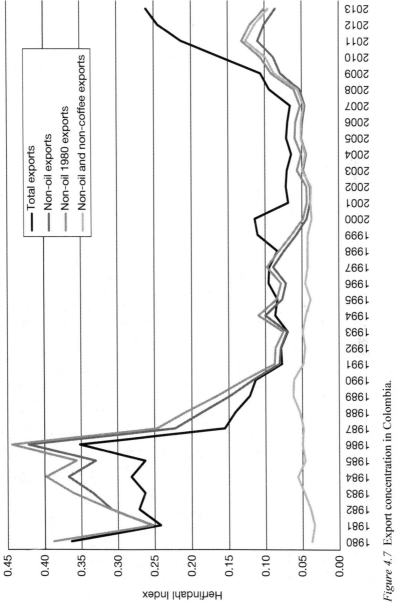

Figure 4.7 Export concentration in Colombia.
(Authors' calculation using United Nations, 2014).

and marketing support, trade agreements to secure market access and an expanded IS strategy through the Andean Community were added to this list of instruments, while tax exemptions were phased out under a commitment to more neutral tax policies. Macro policies were also affected by the paradigm shift: Colombia adopted a 'crawling peg', instead of the previous commitments to fixed exchange rates, in order to avoid overvaluations that discriminated against exports and led to successive currency crises.[19] Subsidised and directed credit was significantly reduced through a comprehensive financial reform in 1974.

In 1991 the Gaviria administration drastically eliminated or reduced much of the trade protection institutions and instruments, opened the capital account, further reduced subsidised and directed credit and many other instruments of support and intervention (notably in agriculture) and initiated the privatisation of public banks and utilities, in what was broadly defined as a new economic model of apertura (opening). It is important to highlight the fact that this was not done under the pressure of a macroeconomic crisis.

The 1991 constitutional reform endorsed this new view (though it also retained significant scope for government intervention), considerably decentralised public finances and services provision, gave autonomy to the Central Bank and reinforced the role of Development Plans, which, proposed by Government in consultation with civil society and approved by Congress, would constitute 'super' laws that gave each Government legal instruments to execute its development strategy and its public investment plan – and would afterwards constrain their policies.

As a consequence of this paradigm shift, the conceptual approach to PDP, as well as its instruments and institutions, underwent a significant change. From the previous traditional 'industrial policies', geared towards promoting industrialisation mostly through trade protectionism and direct support to 'strategic' industries, although also keeping significant protection and support to agriculture – a new concern with 'competitiveness' and institutions and processes to promote it through formal consultation and agreements with the private sector began to emerge.

As explained in detail in Meléndez and Perry (2010), each administration looked to promote this dialogue and competitiveness policy through different mechanisms. The Gaviria Administration, through the Institute for Industrial Promotion, contracted seven sector-level 'competitiveness' studies[20] with the international firm Monitor, composed of previous Porter associates. Though these studies did not lead to significant action, their concept of competitiveness based on 'productive chains' influenced the policy and consultation process for more than a decade.

As soon as it was inaugurated in 1994, the Samper Administration approved a set of policy guidelines on competitiveness (CONPES, 1994), and instituted a more formal structure in the shape of a National Council for Competitiveness with representatives from the private sector, labour, academia and government, which reported directly to the president. Under Council auspices, sector Competitiveness Agreements were negotiated in eleven 'production chains'.[21] However, there was no monitoring of implementation or evaluation of results, so it is difficult to ascertain their effects.

The Pastrana Administration (1998–2002) left the direction of competitiveness policies to the Commission for Foreign Trade and the Ministry of Foreign Trade. The ministry launched a new policy of productivity and competitiveness, somewhat more focussed on export sectors and opportunities, and developed an ambitious ten-year strategic plan for exports. The administration additionally reorganised the previous advisory committees into ten transversal groups, corresponding to the ten competitiveness factors defined by the World Economic Forum, under the coordination of the Red Colombia Compite (RCC).

This organisation survived but languished during the first Uribe Administration (2002–2006). Even more, the first Uribe Administration established a parallel competing process in 2004, as a complement to the launch of negotiations for a Free Trade Agreement (FTA) with the United States: the so called 'Domestic Agenda' (CONPES, 2004). This was a broad process of regional, sector and transversal consultations led by the National Planning Department (DNP), geared to identifying the priority policies and investments required to take advantage of export opportunities under the future FTA, as well as to mitigate the impact of increased import competition from the United States.

Therefore, it was clear that since the main change in PDP's orientation, policies had been changed constantly. Recognising this problem, in 2006 the Government requested an international consulting agency to provide a full assessment of competitiveness policies and processes for the period from 1998 to 2006. The study highlighted major weaknesses in the overall institutional structure: duplication of efforts and consultation activities, excessively informal links with key decision-making bodies and weak participation by entrepreneurs, particularly SMES, as well as by several key agencies. It also concluded that the major process drawbacks were weak execution, followed by weak monitoring of actions and commitments and inadequate impact evaluation.

On the basis of these diagnoses, the Government again reorganised the institutional setup and redefined the strategy.[22] A new institutional structure was set up. A monitoring and evaluation system was designed and is being operated by DNP, with results publicly available through a government webpage (SIGOB). In that context, a new Competitiveness and Productivity Strategy was approved (CONPES, 2008).The main goals would be to guarantee that 'by 2032 Colombia is one of the three most competitive Latin American countries'; to achieve a level of income per capita corresponding to a high middle-income country through an economy exporting goods and services with high value added and technological content and a strong investment climate; and to promote internal regional convergence, increased formal employment and sharply reduced poverty levels. It was further noted that productivity increases would have to come mostly by the development of new products and exports.

The results have shown in the fact that Colombia has won twice in a row the 'prize' of major reformer according to the Cost of Doing Business indicators. Such a strong drive towards achieving improvements in terms ofthese external indicators stimulates activism and compliance and facilitates monitoring and evaluation, but it can also bias efforts towards low-cost actions that may not yield the greatest benefits.

In summary, Colombia has a very different experience than other LAC countries, in a number of respects. First, it was a 'bi-commodity economy'. Second, IS was combined with export promotion. Third, IS was 'reoriented' outside the context of a macroeconomic crisis. When IS was dismantled, Colombia had a relatively well diversified non-oil and non-coffee export basket, probably as a result of these historical conditions. After the dismantling of IS, Colombia continued to pursue diversification and use PDPs, but through a different process, namely dialogue between the private and public sector. This seems to have been a less 'intrusive' approach. However, as seen in this brief summary, policies changed frequently. Though most of the changes were due to the recognition that efforts were not producing the expected results, the experience of Colombia also highlights the problem of continuity and a lack of evaluation in deciding changes. In that context, non-oil and non-coffee exports have actually concentrated and growth has been smaller than in other oil producers.

Ecuador

As seen in Figure 4.8, there have been two periods in the performance of non-oil exports in Ecuador. Prior to the 1990s non-oil exports became more concentrated, while oil exports fell. Then, in the 1990s there was increased diversification of non-oil exports in a context where oil exports also grew due to reforms in the oil sector. Furthermore, new sectors made an important contribution to this diversification. This performance of non-oil exports reflects fundamental changes in economic policy.

As argued in Arteta et al. (2006), there have been several versions of sectoral policies in Ecuador's economic history. These policies began with the Industrial Development Act 1957, strengthened by the creation of the National Planning Board in 1962 and the entry of Ecuador to the Andean Pact in 1966. The policies reached their greatest effect when the state achieved abundant oil revenues, since 1973.

The sectoral policy of greatest impact prior to 1957 was the development of the banana sector. Galo Plaza's government (1948–1952) introduced a range of successful policies to support this sector, including credit, exchange and promotion policies that allowed Ecuador to go from being a marginal producer in 1948 to the world's largest exporter of bananas in 1954.

Both the promotion policies for bananas in the 1950s and later industrial development policies were supported by implementing pro-export exchange rate policies. In the case of bananas, product competitiveness was associated with devaluations without specific reasons. For the promotion of industrial development, the exchange rate policy always sought to benefit the import of raw materials as ordered by the Industrial Development Act. The exchange rate of the free market was almost always higher than that of the regulated one, which remained overvalued. On the other hand, large trade restrictions persisted until the early 1990s. The aim of the high import tariffs was to promote the consumption of domestic goods to protect domestic producers. There was also a series of non-tariff barriers such as quotas or import bans, and highly complex mechanisms of permits and licenses that demotivated imports.

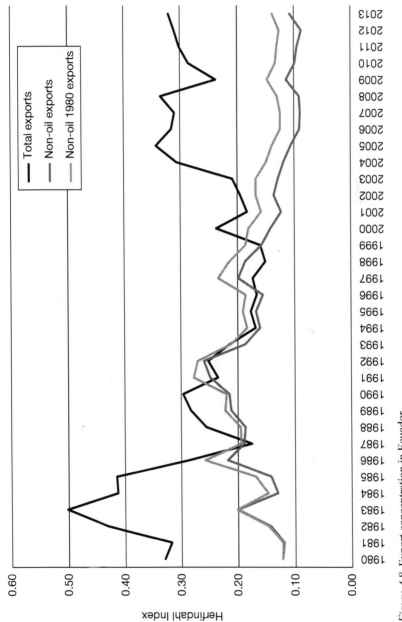

Figure 4.8 Export concentration in Ecuador.
(Authors' calculation using United Nations, 2014).

Furthermore, two types of PDPs of a financial nature were applied: direct public credit, applied in the context of the import substitution model, and mechanisms for second-tier banking. Direct public credit used different instruments: directed credit, rates lower than market remissions (explicit or implicit), and nationalisation of private debts through various government financial institutions. Finally, the policy framework also contained multiple incentives that were expanded in subsequent years. There were exonerations of the sales tax, allowances for accelerated depreciation and investment credits. Finally, certain subsidies were also granted.

In the 1970s, thanks to oil resources the state could reinforce these industrial development policies. The government then removed a number of taxes and increased levels of sectoral credit available through the National Development Bank (BNF) and the National Finance Corporation. The state size also increased, from thirty-five state agencies and institutions in 1965 to 163 in 1976. Finally, all incentives were expanded in the extensive and/or intensive margins.

All these policies created countless distortions that undermined the competitiveness of the economy, and at the same time caused a severe fiscal problem with an unsustainable increase in external debt. Accumulated problems reached their limit when the two funding sources mentioned (external debt and oil) were exhausted.

In the early 1990s, much of the fabric of the protectionist policies was dismantled. Import duties, permits and red tape were gradually reduced. The new direction favoured exports. Tariff reduction, simplification of red tape in exports and participation in the common external tariff scheme in the sub-market of the Andean Community of Nations (CAN) between Ecuador, Colombia and Venezuela were emphasised. In addition, the distortion of the exchange rate was reversed in 1993.

Similarly, tax incentives and subsidies fell significantly after 1982 due to the debt crisis, and almost all exemptions were repealed between 1986 and 1989. The only subsidies that remained – in a far smaller amount – were subsidies on utility rates for telecommunications, energy and others. Additionally, coinciding with the dismantling of the import substitution model, export promotion credit policies were partially altered. Finally, development banks were restricted in their budgets and the National Finance Corporation (CFN) became a second-tier bank only focused on exporting firms. However, this was the only instrument that remained to carry out PDPs.

This liberalisation is credited with much of the increase in the number and variety of items exported, from less than two hundred in 1989 to over 1,300 in 1993 to 1,733 today. These benefited from the lower cost of importing capital goods and intermediates as well as access to public financial resources. Non-traditional exports grew from 8% of total exports in 1990 to 30% in 2002. However, public credit generated enormous fiscal costs, either through bailouts or the need for repeated capitalisations of banks to cover losses due to the subsidy on the interest rate.

In the early 2000s there was a growing momentum to build a policy to promote competitiveness. In 1998 the Corporation for the Promotion of Exports and

Investments (CORPEI), a private sector entity, was created. In 2000 the private sector and the government agreed on the National Competitiveness Agenda. In 2001, the National Competitiveness Council (CNC) was created with the aim of improving competitiveness, and an agenda that included promoting policy reforms and the study of market and technological conditions in different sectors with potential for export.

However, as argued in Martín-Mayoral (2009), the post-dollarisation period (2000–2006) was plagued by frequent changes of government and continuous policy instability. Therefore, none of these ideas and policies were fully implemented. From a macroeconomic point of view, however, price stability was achieved after five years. Between 2000 and 2005, the country grew at real rates above 4% – higher than those observed in the previous period and also higher than the average for Latin American economies in the previous decade. The lending and deposit rates were also reduced. The current account balance recovered and from 2004 began to register a surplus.

From 2008 there was a new shift towards a greater role of the state. However, this role has focussed on the provision of public goods. Gross capital formation increased from 4.6% of GDP to 8.6% between 2007 and 2008, and focussed on strategic sectors such as transport infrastructure, communications, energy, housing, education, health and agriculture. Additionally, the state has assumed greater control over energy and mining resources; the reform to the Hydrocarbons Law in October 2008 established new conditions for the exploitation and export of oil.

In summary, non-oil exports in Ecuador became more concentrated between 1980 and 1990. Ecuador applied the well-known stock of IS policies, and began a slow process of dismantling them in the 1980s. After 1990 credit from second-tier public banks was almost the exclusive instrument used for productive development. Non-traditional export flourished in this period. Although there was pressure from the private sector to work with the government on a competitiveness agenda, macroeconomic pressure and political instability did not allow for the setting of new productive development policies. Consequently, PDPs were not used extensively. Since 2008 there has been a change in public policy towards more government intervention, but it is still too early to see the impact that this change has had.

Mexico

As seen in Figure 4.9, the Mexican non-oil economy was well diversified in 1990 and it was diversified even before that. As the figure shows, overall exports actually converge in the diversification of the non-oil sector. This shows the combination of two trends: the decline in the oil sector, not only due to prices but also production, and the important increase of non-oil exports. With regard to new sectors, they contribute to diversification only slightly. In the margin, the export concentration of Mexico has not changed, and the contribution of new sectors has offset the concentration of the 1980 export basket.

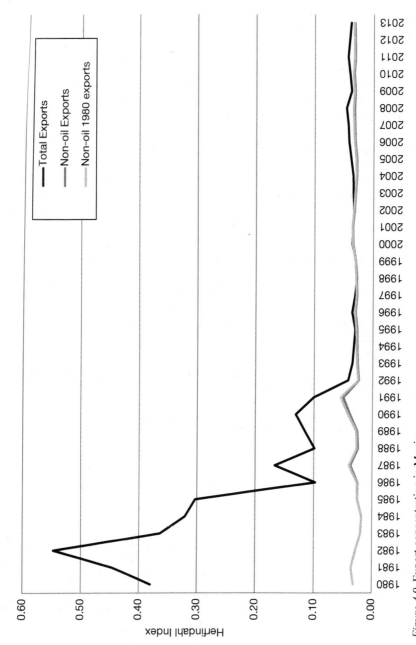

Figure 4.9 Export concentration in Mexico.
(Authors' calculation using United Nations, 2014).

As explained in Baz et al. (2010), like most of Latin America from the 1950s to the mid-1980s, Mexico based its economic policies on the IS model. PDPs implemented during this phase ranged from limited import quotas and high tariffs, to price controls for public inputs, to subsidies for specific products, to limitations on the money supply. While these policies accelerated growth in the industrial sector at the expense of the primary sector (e.g. agriculture), this new industrial sector was characterised by firms with low and inefficient economies of scale and high unit costs, incapable of competing in international markets.

The IS model created distortions in the economy as well as an anti-export bias, a reduction in the total value of agricultural production, and ultimately a productive structure less intensive in labour and biased toward the use of capital. After the 1982 financial crisis the government had no option but to begin reforming the system, shifting its economic policies to structural reforms and macroeconomic stabilisation. These policies implied the end of the government stranglehold over the country's productive sectors.

In this context PDPs shifted toward export and investment promotion, focussing mostly on the manufacturing industry through the maquila model. In addition, second-tier banks, such as Nacional Financiera (NAFIN), continued operations. Though most sectors were liberalised, very important ones remained closed to competition, including telecommunications and energy. In addition, the failure to reform the country's regulatory framework resulted in remaining entry barriers for the whole economy, such as onerous financial and labour market regulation.

After facing a major financial crisis in 1994, which resulted from a mixture of rapid high-risk credit expansion, a fixed exchange rate and a depletion of foreign reserves, achieving macroeconomic stability became the main priority. From 1995 to 2000, economic policies were directed at stabilising the economy and creating solid macroeconomic conditions to prevent another economic debacle. Mexico's entry to the North American Free Trade Agreement (NAFTA) marked the end of the closed economy but also highlighted large inefficiencies in the Mexican private sector.

Since 2000 the government has maintained its focus on macroeconomic stability. Public finances are healthy and monetary policy has remained stable, creating good conditions for attracting increasing levels of investment. However, a multiplicity of new interest groups and a strong political opposition, particularly in Congress, has often resulted in a stagnant policymaking process (e.g. see Stein and Tommasi, 2008). There is no consensus on the development path Mexico wants to follow, or on what it needs to do in order to achieve specific goals. The policy debate remains ideological and lacks pragmatism. Discussion keeps focussing on whether to protect the agricultural sector from NAFTA competitors, who should own the country's energy resources, or the role of labour unions. The Mexican government has not been able to articulate a development strategy that can be subscribed to by all relevant actors (Rubio, 2001). As a result, PDPs are often incongruent with each other, redundant and uncoordinated.[23]

Interestingly, there is a formal process. The government outlines its objectives for industrial policy in its National Plan for Development (NDP), and more specifically in the sectoral plan of the Ministry of Economy (SE). The strategies contained in the economic sectoral plan target the development of SMEs as a general activity, as well as support for specific sectors based on their weight in economic terms or their potential to increase value added.[24] The NDP and sectoral plans are intended to serve as an all-encompassing vision for the country's development path including a prioritisation of the sectors and activities the government should support in order to encourage higher rates of economic growth. In practice, however, the NDP and sectoral plans represent little more than a legal requirement containing very few operational recommendations. This in turn makes it difficult for stakeholders – i.e. civil society and Congress – to evaluate the impact of PDPs on the country's productive structure.[25]

Other ministries, including those for the areas of Agriculture, the Environment and Tourism, design and implement – independently – their own PDPs similar to those of the SE. In addition, several states have implemented their own PDPs. While PDPs should not necessarily be concentrated in one agency, coordination is important. It is not clear whether objectives and strategies from these different plans are discussed and coordinated between the different government actors.[26]

In summary, since 1980 Mexico has been a considerably diversified economy. The role played by IS policies cannot be discounted. In addition, it has been a relatively big market (in 1980 it was the tenth largest economy in the world), which entered into a free trade agreement with the biggest economy in the world. Consequently, the role of scale cannot be ruled out either. In the context of a highly diversified economy, new sectors have contributed only marginally to keeping the economy diversified. Finally, the main policy driver in Mexico since the 1990s has been macroeconomic stability. The lack of clear objectives and coordination among actors does not seem to have allowed the definition of a framework for PDPs.

Trinidad and Tobago

As seen in Figure 4.10, export diversification in Trinidad and Tobago has been unstable. Part of the issue has been the volatile price of gas and oil. However, non-oil exports have also shown volatility. In part, this is due to the fact that the diversification strategy of Trinidad and Tobago has been skewed to the energy sector. In addition, new products have contributed little to export diversification.

As described in Moya et al. (2010), historically the Government of Trinidad and Tobago has played an active role in several economic sectors (vertical policies), often involved as a provider or a key decision maker, taking these responsibilities away from the private sector. Since the mid-1950s Trinidad and Tobago has applied diverse industrial policies that have changed over time.

The People's National Movement (PNM) government elected in 1956 pursued economic development through the 'industrialisation by invitation' model. According to Mottley (2008), in its first years the country sought to industrialise following the example of Puerto Rico. In this initial stage, the government actively sought to attract investment using a newly created agency called the Industrial

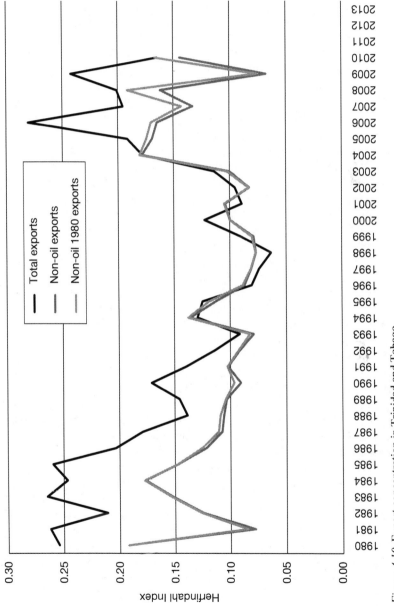

Figure 4.10 Export concentration in Trinidad and Tobago.
(Authors' calculation using United Nations, 2014).

Development Corporation (IDC). However, this policy was not successful, as the country could not match the benefits granted to US investors by the Puerto Rican government. In those years (1958 to 1973), there were three five-year development plans following a policy of state-directed economic planning.

Beginning in the mid-1960s, the government implemented a policy of industrialisation by IS. The main instrument of protection was the Negative List: items on this list would require an import license that was not easily acquired. The IDC additionally began to construct service industrial parks during this period. In the 1970s there was an explosion of assembly-type industrial production. Goods assembled locally in response to the IS strategy included (but were not limited to) mattresses, garments, radios, TVs, car batteries, motor cars, home appliances, light bulbs, processed foods and furniture. In addition, Trinidad and Tobago began a broad process of public ownership before independence (in 1962) with the acquisition of the Telephone Company of Trinidad and Tobago (Telco) and British West Indian Airways (BWIA) in 1960.

In the third development plan, from 1969 to 1973, the government outlined the need for investment in heavy industry, specifically the petroleum industry. In addition, the plan stated that the public sector would not 'hesitate to enter either alone or in partnership with foreign or local private capital into the productive fields of industry, tourism or agriculture' (Bernal and Leslie, 1999).

From 1973 onward, oil production was an enormous source of revenue for the government.[27] During this boom, the State of Trinidad and Tobago embarked on a broad-based programme of industrialisation, spending part of its revenues on acquiring corporate assets. The policy basically followed a state-led rather than a private-led approach (Mottley, 2008). At its peak, sixty-two enterprises were owned by the state, covering sectors of activity as diverse as airlines, cement, telecommunications, hotels, food processing and, most importantly, energy. This policy might be seen as signifying a distrust of market mechanisms and the ability of the private sector to serve as an engine for development.

In the early 1980s the fall in the international price of oil and in domestic production caused a severe decline in government revenues, and this circumstance forced the country to adjust to a lower level of income. After 1984 the Negative List was replaced by high import tariffs amid accusations of corruption in the granting of import permits. From the mid-1990s the authorities began to scale down the highly protective tariffs, unwinding the old IS policy. In order to avoid a new swing due to the dependence on oil, the new government elected in 1986 attempted a policy of industrial development based on the non-energy sector. Since then, several policies have been implemented to diversify the industrial fabric.

A process of privatisation began in 1987 with a partial divestiture of some public companies. However, this process has not been quick or continuous. The Government continued acquiring equity in various companies until the early 1990s. In 1991, the newly appointed Government outlined the need to let the private sector take the lead in the economy. Nevertheless, the State would keep its stakes in strategic sectors such as oil and gas, telecommunications and other utilities.

According to Bernal and Leslie (1999), by 1993 the Government had identified thirty SOEs for divestment and twelve for liquidation, and by mid-1995 several companies had been either fully or partially privatised. As for the energy sector, the exploration and production activities of the Trinidad and Tobago Oil Company (TRINTOC) and the Trinidad and Tobago Petroleum Company (TRINTOPEC) were merged into a new company, the Petroleum Company of Trinidad and Tobago Ltd. (PETROTRIN). The new petroleum assets of both TRINTOC and TRINTOPEC were divested. Finally, it is worth mentioning that the water and sewage authority, WASA, was handed over in a contract of concession to a private company in 1996 but lasted for only three years under this regime.

In 2002 the Government issued a policy statement declaring the divestment of management and ownership of State Operated Enterprises (SOEs) as a top priority, with preference given to local investors. Fairbanks et al. (2007) see these movements as being related more to fiscal management than to any explicit connection to private-sector development, stressing that 'moving the locus of responsibility to the private sector requires a shift in the Government of Trinidad and Tobago's approach'.

After 2007 there seems to have been a change in the main vision of the Government about PDPs (Ministry of Trade and Industry, 2007). The main strategy is to diversify the economy away from its dependence on the petroleum sector by developing non-oil manufacturing activities as well as services. The first choice of targeted sectors was based on an economic report elaborated by an international consultancy firm. In proposing what sectors should be promoted they consider several variables, such as contribution to GDP, employment and so on. The report identifies some problems and provides a set of eventual policies the Government might adopt. Most of these policies are Government-intensive in the sense that the problems are intended to be solved through Government institutions rather than market-oriented reforms, which is evidence that there is little or no change in Trinidad and Tobago's approach to developing private business. There is, however, a change in the traditional approach, since these plans have been formulated in part through collaboration with private sector representatives. However, different sets of incentives would be recommended for the promotion of each sector, and no single policy works for all sectors. Therefore, it seems that authorities would assume that policies should be basically vertical rather than horizontal in nature.

In summary, in the case of Trinidad and Tobago we have a case where IS was not only heavily used, but where there were also several state-owned and operated enterprises in different sectors, even before independence. However, after 1990 a programme of divesture of firms was implemented that was completed around the beginning of the new century in a process that was slow and non-linear. These continuous changes in policies could be reflected in the volatility of export concentration, and the slow pace could explain the small contribution of new sectors. Later, around the midpoint of the first decade of the new millennium the government began considering a new set of interventions, with a movement towards a more market-based industrialisation. In this new framework there is no explicit attempt to integrate to a specific trading group in the context of a relatively small economy.

Venezuela

As seen in Figure 4.11, the evolution of export diversification in Venezuela is driven mostly by the oil sector, which reflects the low level of development of non-oil exports. Diversification of non-oil exports was slowly improving and new sectors seemed to be contributing to this diversification, especially after 1989, but after 2000 non-oil exports have become more concentrated and in general they contribute little to the diversification of the country. This reflects the different changes in policy orientation in the period.

As explained in Manzano (2013), parallel to the discovery and boom of the oil sector was the relationship between the oil sector and the rest of the economy. Since its appearance at the beginning of the twentieth century, oil has been seen as a 'temporary' productive sector. Most Venezuelan intellectuals of the time warned about the problems that this temporary boom could cause for other productive sectors, saying that it would be impossible to restore these sectors to their former state once the supply of oil had been exhausted.[28] This perception that the productivity of the oil sector was only temporary led to one of the guiding principles of the Venezuelan oil policy: the 'sowing of oil'. According to this principle, given that oil is an industry that can last only for a certain period, the income from it should be invested in other sectors of the economy in the service of diversification.[29]

Although some industrial policies were implemented during this period, this does not necessarily reflect a particular orientation towards one sector. Moreover, there was no perception that oil could be a productive sector that could be integrated with the other sectors of the economy; therefore, there was no policy towards such integration. Nevertheless, it is important to note that there was a perception that Venezuela should capture a greater share of the oil market. To this end, steps were taken to increase oil production. The Hydrocarbons Law of 1943 encouraged the domestic refining of oil and was central to the development of the current refining network in Venezuela.

In 1958, the installed refining capacity was 883,000 barrels a day and the total amount of crude oil refined in that year was ten times higher than in 1943. In addition, in 1956 the government established the Venezuelan Institute of Petrochemicals, with the idea of fostering the development of a petrochemical sector. However, although the construction of a petrochemical complex started, in 1958 Marcos Perez Jimenez, the dictator of that time, was ousted and the democratic era began.[30] Though the petrochemical complex was finalised by the democratic governments, as will be pointed out later, priorities changed.

This vision did not change with the advent of democracy. Even though the refining capacity continued to grow until 1965, the growth was due mostly to the completion of the refineries whose construction started after the Hydrocarbons Law of 1943. A second petrochemical complex was started, but was based mostly

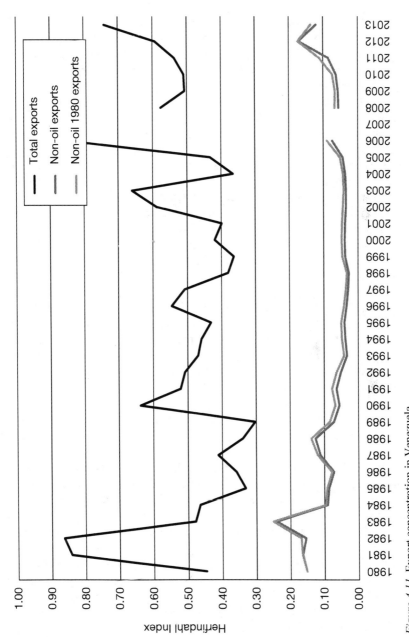

Figure 4.11 Export concentration in Venezuela.
(Authors' calculation using United Nations, 2014).

on state-owned firms or joint ventures in which the state held the majority of the capital. During this time, import substitution policies were in full swing in Latin America (Maloney, 2002). Therefore, rather than reflecting a 'cluster vision' of the sector, these attempts at industrialisation around oil were just part of a wider set of policies that had the goal of producing most of the goods imported by the country.[31]

This policy was reinforced by the oil price shocks of the seventies. The windfall generated was spent in other sectors with the intention of further diversifying the economy away from oil. Big state-owned companies were established in a variety of sectors, ranging from basic metals to tourism. Therefore, in this period, not only was the idea of diversifying the economy present, but also the idea that the state should carry out that task. To 'foster' the private sector, this policy was accompanied by the decree to 'Buy Venezuelan', whereby state firms favoured local production over imports.

In the 1990s Venezuela embarked upon a programme of structural reform, similar to those followed by other Latin American countries. These programmes proposed the opening of the economy to international markets, the removal of distortions, and the establishment of institutions needed to achieve macroeconomic stability (such as central bank independence), among other measures. The macroeconomic adjustment policies included the unification and flotation exchange rate, the release of prices and interest rates and the renegotiation of external debt. Structural reforms were referred to areas of taxation, financial, commercial and government reform.

As explained in Barrios and Genua (2006), the policy also included a component of export promotion.[32] Despite these efforts, the petroleum and petrochemical industries as well as basic industries such as iron, steel and aluminium continued to be the only real sources of export activity. Other non-traditional exports, such as those in the automotive sector, also recorded some development, but this was relatively marginal in its ability to generate foreign exchange. These results can be explained by the concentration of efforts in support of exports, rather than in generating new exports.

With the reform, many of the state companies were privatised, including the national telephone company, the flagship airline and basic iron and steel production, as well as several smaller companies like hotels and tourism companies that the state had inherited from insolvent firms to pay for public financed loans. In addition, the 'Buy Venezuelan' decree was repealed, and a training programme of suppliers linked to the main state industry Petroleos de Venezuela (PDVSA) was implemented

However, these reforms could not be implemented fully due to the political crisis that began in 1992. This crisis, combined with the financial crisis in 1994, even reversed some of the policies of macroeconomic and financial adjustment, reversing the liberalisation of prices and the exchange rate but without altering the course of trade reforms and international policy.[33]

Furthermore, these programmes lacked instruments such as monitoring and sunset clauses that nowadays are seen as necessary in the process of diversifying the economy (Hausmann and Rodrik, 2003). Balza and Manzano (2014) used the Manufacturing Survey of Venezuela to find productivity spillovers from the resource sector, and found that there are some negative productivity effects of using oil as an input, as well as some negative horizontal spillovers – in the same sector – from oil consumption in productivity and from being a supplier of PDVSA. The paper argues that this is the result of policy decisions of forcing PDVSA to buy locally and sell oil at subsidised prices, without any target on outcomes of these policies.

After 1998 Venezuela changed its insertion policy, looking for a deepening integration with the Mercosur bloc and withdrawal from the Andean Community. The government also started to create a South American unit that could counteract the economic and political power of the United States. In that sense, the government chose not to participate actively in the FTAA negotiations that the US had with other Andean countries. At the same time, there is an important orientation towards achieving treaties and agreements with oil-consuming countries, intended to establish strategic alliances between energy companies and agreements to exchange oil for food, among other things.

Also, since 2001 government policy has reversed again to a controlled foreign exchange market. Venezuela currently maintains an exchange control regime, with different fixed official exchange rates and a commission defining priority lists of import application mechanisms, granting currencies and amounts authorised. There is a parallel currency market, but it has been criminalised.

In addition, there is a revival of the concept of SOEs covering aviation sectors and the manufacturing, distribution and sale of food, among others. The high purchasing power of the state, together with an overvalued currency, discourages exports, and the small domestic market has meant that decisions within the private sector are highly influenced by the state. Price, exchange and interest rate controls, investment authorisations, the establishing of employment conditions, as well as the implementation of control mechanisms for trade policy, all confirm this pattern.

Finally, there has been an expansion in public financial institutions of finance oriented productive activities and projects on public and private infrastructure. The Investment Fund is now the Venezuela Bank of Economic and Social Development of Venezuela (BANDES), oriented in theory to provide resources to finance productive development projects and agriculture. However, credit has been mostly directed to other government entities.

In summary, Venezuela has had a relatively diversified non-oil sector that has remained stagnant over the last thirty years, and it has recently become more concentrated. After 1990 Venezuela embarked on a liberalisation process and was part of the Andean Pact. However, the process was cut short. Furthermore, policies implemented were not targeted to develop new exports. This process was fully reversed after 1998 and the policies again were more in line with the state in control of the economy; even the international insertion policy changed, by switching to a different trading block and looking for 'barter' agreements with other Latin American countries. In this context, there has been little development of non-oil sectors.

4.4 Policies and outcomes

As we explained in Section 4.1, Latin American oil exporters do not seem to be different from other oil exporters in terms of abundance and diversification patterns. However, it seems that in terms of results, they perform worse. Between 1990 and 2003, on average non-oil export grew less in Latin America than in other oil exporters. Therefore, it is important to understand the policies followed.

All Latin American countries more or less followed the same pattern. Prior to 1980 all of them embarked on IS policies. During the 1980s and the 1990s all of them embarked on structural reform programmes and liberalisation of the economy. However, the speed and adoption of complementary policies varied. To summarise thirty years of history in six countries runs the risk of oversimplification; we therefore try to summarise these experiences in three groups, as shown in Table 4.1.

In the first group is Argentina and Mexico. As we reviewed, both countries started with considerably diversified economies and were large economies. In the 1990s these countries were in the middle of a liberalisation process and concerned more with macroeconomic stability. Both countries signed trade agreements with big trade partners, and these agreements clearly influenced the development of the non-oil sector. However, in Argentina PDPs were still used in that period. At the beginning of this century they followed different paths. Mexico continues with

Table 4.1 Policies and outcomes in Latin America

	Non-oil export growth	Change in non-oil export concentration	Post IS policies	Market size	
				Relevant trade agreements	Rank of economy
Argentina	8.1%	=	Constant changes. Mix of PDPs and liberalisation	Mercosur	23
Mexico	13.6%	=	Minimum	NAFTA	10
Colombia	7.3% (8.5% w/o coffee)	– (+ w/o coffee)	'Competitiveness' with constant changes	Andean Pact	34
Ecuador	9.5%	–	Minimum/ 'Competitiveness'	Andean Pact	53
Trinidad and Tobago	9.0%	–	Still high intervention	Caricom	67
Venezuela	–2.4%	–	Liberalisation, followed by reversal to command and control	Andean Pact, later Mercosur	27

little or no intervention, while in Argentina the government tried to reintroduce some forms of intervention. In both countries non-oil exports are almost as concentrated today as they were in 1990. Of the countries presented in Figure 4.3, only Brazil was more diversified than both of them. In addition, in both countries non-oil exports grew, but they grew more in Mexico.

A second group is Trinidad and Tobago and Venezuela. In these countries, during the IS period the state was heavily involved in the economy, becoming the owner of productive firms in a variety of sectors. They also embarked on a process of reform. However, in the case of Trinidad and Tobago the process was slower than in other Latin American countries. After 2000 they followed different paths. While Trinidad and Tobago continued its process of slow liberalisation and after 2007 began to consider a new set of productive development policies oriented towards competitiveness, in Venezuela reforms were reverted and there has been a return of an economy with a strong presence from the state, even as an owner of productive firms. In both countries, non-oil exports in 2013 were more diversified than in 1990. However, in the case of Trinidad and Tobago they began to change the total diversification of the economy while in Venezuela the total diversification of the economy is still being driven by the oil sector. As a result of the expansion of non-oil exports in Trinidad and Tobago they grew close to the average of Latin American countries, while they fell in Venezuela.

The third group is Colombia and Ecuador. These countries are not as resource dependent as Trinidad and Tobago and Venezuela, and they did not have an IS policy as 'state-oriented as those countries. However, neither did they have the opportunity to integrate themselves with a big trading partner. Both countries negotiated a FTA with the US in the mid 2000s, but it is too early to measure the impact of these agreements, and they clearly lack the geographic advantage the Mexico has with the US and Argentina has with Brazil.

In that context, Colombia, which has been characterised by macroeconomic stability, embarked earlier on a process of policies to foster competitiveness. However, as explained above, there were constant changes of the process along the way. On the other hand, Ecuador was plagued by macroeconomic and political instability. Therefore, government efforts were directed towards that front. Only recently has there been a new look at competitiveness and increased participation by the state. In these different policy environments both countries increased their diversification of non-oil exports. However, export growth was higher in Ecuador.

Given this result, the first instinct will be to say that the most successful cases in terms of diversification and growth of non-oil exports liberalised their economy and reduced state intervention. However, this does not take into account other external factors such as the important devaluation in Brazil in 1998 and its adverse effect in Argentina, or the impact of the Venezuelan collapse and retirement from the Andean block on Colombia, which was its main trading partner. Similarly, Crespi et al. (2014) highlight the positive impacts of policies in Colombia and Argentina.

However, these results do raise the question as to whether no intervention is better than constant changes in policy. Argentina, Colombia and Venezuela experienced changes in productive development policies. Changes in Colombia were in a positive direction and underpinned by a strategic vision. Changes in Argentina and Venezuela were more reactive. However, in all three countries, including Colombia, there were constant revisions which were not related to an evaluation of the policies applied to date and their impact.

On the other hand, Ecuador, Mexico and Trinidad and Tobago were focussed on achieving macroeconomic stability. Only Trinidad and Tobago produced strategic documents on the role of the state in the economy; most of these outlined their drawn-out process of the liberalisation of the economy. The private sector tried to call for a review of policies in Ecuador, but political instability prevented this dialogue. Some of the PDPs of the 1980s were kept and used after the reforms of the 1990s, but on a smaller scale.

However, this does not imply that these are successful cases. As argued before, LAC countries have underperformed in terms of diversification and non-oil export growth. Furthermore, in all three countries there have been calls to review policies and think about a new framework of PDPs, either to reduce the reliance on oil and gas (Trinidad and Tobago) or to generate exports with more value added or more sophisticated (Ecuador and Mexico). This shows the dissatisfaction with the current situation and the interest of looking towards alternative policy goals.

4.5 Concluding remarks

Economic diversification has been a desired outcome of Latin American policy makers since the 1950s. Nevertheless, the performance of Latin America has not been in line with expectations. When looking at Latin American oil exporters, they seem to show diversification trends similar to other LAC countries and have shown fewer gains than other oil abundant countries, but their starting points were different. The most salient fact is the difference in performance among oil abundant LAC countries.

This performance of Latin American oil producers seems not to be related to their pattern of diversification. When compared with other oil producers they behave similarly: more abundant countries tend to diversify around sectoral clusters, and abundance does affect non-oil export growth. However, non-oil export growth is still lower in Latin America. Therefore, the cause of this poor performance goes beyond the issue of abundance and the pattern of specialisation.

The next issue is policies. A first look at policies might suggest that no intervention is preferred to any intervention. However, we find that constant changes in productive development policies might affect export performance. In particular, Argentina, Colombia and Venezuela experienced more frequent changes in productive development policies. On the other hand, Ecuador, Mexico and Trinidad and Tobago had more stable policies. Consequently, policy stability might explain the differences in performance between Latin American oil producers. However, this does not imply that any of the countries are successful cases. As argued before, LAC countries have underperformed in terms of diversification and non-oil export growth. Therefore, the quest for diversification continues to be a policy challenge in the region.

Acknowledgements

We thank Yasser Al-Saleh, Danny Bahar, Juan Blyde, Graham Davis, Richard Price, anonymous reviewers and workshop participants at INSEAD Abu Dhabi for their helpful comments on this chapter. We also thank Maria Gabriela Salazar for excellent research assistantship. All remaining errors are ours.

Notes

1 See Manzano (2014) for a review on the economic research around the issue of extractive industries and development.
2 See Stallings and Peres (2000), Bielschowsky, R. (2009), and Ocampo and Ros (2011), for a different perspective on the issue.
3 Argentina, Colombia, Mexico, Trinidad and Tobago and Venezuela. In the next section we will explain how we chose these countries.
4 For example, in 2010 the weighted average of manufacturing exports as a share of merchandise exports in Latin American oil exporters was 53%. However, the simple average was 29%.
5 The Herfindahl index (also known as the Herfindahl-Hirschman Index, or HHI) is a measure of the size of firms in relation to the industry, and an indicator of the amount of competition among them. The index is from 0 to 1, with 1 being a market with just one firm and 0 a market with infinite firms. Given its construction, it could also be used to measure the relative size of export sectors and the degree of concentration of the export basket of a country. In this case, 1 will represent an export basket with just one product and 0 with infinite products. See Lederman and Maloney (2007) for a discussion of measures of export patterns.
6 The index was constructed using United Nations (2014) at the 4-digit level.
7 We have to remember that a Herfindahl of 0.5 would be equivalent to the country exporting two goods with the same share.
8 We use ranks to avoid the impact that outliers could have in the correlation. In the Appendix we present in detail how we calculated this correlation.
9 The number is the average annual growth of nominal exports from 1990 to 2013. Though there might be some concerns about changes in relative prices and their impact on nominal growth, given the relative low value of the non-oil Herfindahl indexes, these differences should have little impact.
10 The correlation is 0.27 and the p-value 0.201.
11 The correlation is 0.13 and the p-value 0.339.
12 The correlation is -0.33 and the p-value 0.166.
13 The correlation is 0.12 and the p-value 0.370.
14 The correlation is 0.04 and the p-value is 0.458.
15 The average growth of non-oil exports for all countries is 9.58%. However, the average for Latin America is 7.50% and the average for other countries is 11.65%. Both are different to the mean at the 10% level.
16 The correlation between shares of exports and linkages to the oil sector is 0.33 in LAC countries, while in other countries it is 0.26. They could only be considered different at the 25% level.
17 The ratio of exports (in barrels) per habitant is 14.9 in Latin America and 27.4 in other oil abundant countries. However, given the high variance they could only be considered different at the 28% level.
18 Support to SMEs receives a large amount of resources. Almost US$100 million were allocated in the 2008 national budget to this end to more than twenty programmes. There are several government offices (both at the national and provincial levels) that have programmes to support SMEs.

19 See Perry (2008) for an analysis of the motivations and conceptual structure behind these policy changes.

20 For petrochemicals, flowers, leather, textiles, fruit juices, graphic arts and metal mechanics.

21 Textiles and apparel; leather and leather products; ironworks, metal mechanics and automobile industries; software; pulp, paper and graphic industries; aquiculture; maize, sorghum, cassava, poultry and pork; milk and milk derivatives; oleaginous products, oils and fats; and rice. See Flórez and Misas (2008).

22 CONPES (Consejo Nacional de Política Económica y Social) (2006).

23 As this chapter is being written, an attempt to achieve coordination inside the government was being tested with a new law for competitiveness and productivity.

24 The list of 'strategic sectors' includes the following: automotive, aerospace, electric/electronic, energy, biotechnology, software, IT and BPO services, logistics and tourism. See 'Política Sectorial' section of the economic sectoral plan in Secretaria de Economia (2007).

25 Behind this reality is the fact that any commitment to meet certain specific objectives derives from legal commitments that can then be enforced by the Office of the Comptroller (Auditoría Superior de la Federación). Thus, officials have little incentive to avoid specificity in programme goals.

26 As this book was being edited an ambitious reform programme was being implemented in Mexico. The goal was to remove microeconomic inefficiencies and also to foster better coordination among government institutions. The impact of these reforms will have to be evaluated in the future.

27 In 1969 the Amoco Oil Company found a substantial oil reserve off Trinidad's east coast; the following year, Amoco discovered an important natural gas reservoir; and finally there was an increase in oil prices after the Arab/Israeli war of 1973. These events let to an increase of the share of oil production in the GDP.

28 Basically, they used the argument that is currently referred to in the literature as the Dutch disease. Adriani (1931), Mayobre (1944) and Peltzer (1944) discussed the problems of an appreciated exchange rate for the agricultural sector and the industrialisation of Venezuela.

29 The name of the principle came from an editorial published in 1936 by Arturo Uslar Pietri, an influential writer and intellectual.

30 Further evidence of the relative lack of a comprehensive policy towards the integration of the oil sector in the Venezuelan economy is provided by the state of technical education related to oil. Most of the technical expertise in the sector had to be provided by foreigners. Geology as a career was not introduced until 1937, and petroleum engineering not until 1952. It is important to note that, by that time, most of the universities in the country were run by the government.

31 According to OCEPRE (1988), between 1964 and 1973 from 9% to 13% of the budget went on supporting productive sectors net of infrastructure spending, which indicates an active intervention of government in the economy. However, more than 60% went to agriculture, which indicates that government priorities were in other economic sectors.

32 The Institute for Foreign Trade (ICE, from its initials in Spanish) and the Bank for Foreign Trade was created, with the functions of advising, promoting and financing exports. The Law of Export Incentive, as well as other tax credit policies, were also created to promote exports.

33 For a complete description of reform programmes in Venezuela and their successful or failed implementation, see Gonzalez et al. (2004).

References

Adriani, A. (1931) 'La Crisis, los cambios y nosotros', in Valecillos, H. and Bello, O. (eds.), *La Economía Contemporánea de Venezuela*, Caracas: Banco Central de Venezuela.

Artana, D. et al. (2007) 'Trinidad and Tobago: Economic growth in a dual economy', Washington DC, United States: Inter-American Development Bank. Available at: http://sta.uwi.edu/salises/pubs/workingpapers/16.pdf (accessed 21 April 2016).

Arteta, G. and Albornoz, V. (2005) 'Políticas sectoriales en Ecuador: revisar el pasado y proyectar al futuro', in Castilla, L.M., Manzano, O. and Nagel, J. (eds.), *Políticas sectoriales en la región andina*, Venezuela: Publicaciones CAF.

Balza, L. and Manzano, O. (2011) 'Productivity spillover of resource exploitation: Evidence from Venezuelan industrial surveys', *Paper presented at EcoMod 2011 Conference, Azores, Portugal.* Available at ecomod.net/system/files/Balza_Manzano_ Industrial_Productivity.pdf (accessed 21 April 2016).

Barrios, A. and Genua, G. (2005) 'Políticas sectoriales en Venezuela: historia y propuestas', in Castilla, L.M., Manzano, O. and Nagel, J. (eds.), *Políticas sectoriales en la región andina*, Venezuela: Publicaciones CAF.

Baz, V., Capelo, M.C., Centeno, R. and Estrada, R. (2010) 'Policies in Latin America and the Caribbean: The case of Mexico', *IDB Working Paper Series No. IDB-WP-168*, Washington DC: Inter-American Development Bank.

Bernal, R.L. and Leslie, W.J. (1999) 'Privatization in the English-Speaking Caribbean: An Assesment', *Policy Papers on the Americas*, Volume 10, Number 7. Washington DC: Center for Strategic and International Studies. Available at csis.org/files/media/csis/ pubs/1999_bernal,_leslie.pdf (accessed 21 April 2016).

Bielschowsky, R. (2009) 'Sixty years of ECLAC: Structuralism and neostructrualism', *ECLAC Review*, vol. 97.

Center for Global Trade Analysis (2014) *Global Trade Analysis Project (GTAP)*, database. West Lafayette, Indiana: Purdue University. Available at https://www.gtap.agecon. purdue.edu/GTAP (accessed 2 May 2015).

Chudnovsky, D. and López, A. (2007) *The elusive quest for growth in Argentina*, Hampshire, UK: Palgrave Macmillan.

Cimoli, M., Ferraz, J.C. and Primi, A. (2009) 'Science, technology and innovation policies in global open economies: Reflections from Latin America and the Caribbean', *Globalization, Competitivenes, and Gobernability*, vol. 3, no. 1. Georgetown University-Universia.

CONPES (Consejo Nacional de Política Económica y Social) (1994) 'Por una Colombia Competitiva', *Documento CONPES 2724*, Bogota, Colombia: CONPES.

CONPES (Consejo Nacional de Política Económica y Social) (2004) 'Agenda Interna para la Productividad y Competitividad', *Documento CONPES 3297*, Bogota, Colombia: CONPES.

CONPES (Consejo Nacional de Política Económica y Social) (2006) 'Institucionalidad y Principios Rectores de Política de Productividad y Competitividad', *Documento CONPES 3439*, Bogota, Colombia: CONPES.

CONPES (Consejo Nacional de Política Económica y Social) (2008) 'Política Nacional de Productividad y Competitividad', *Documento CONPES 3527*, Bogota, Colombia: CONPES.

Crespi, G., Fernández-Arias, E. and Stein, E. (2014) *Rethinking productive development: Development in the Americas 2014*, IDB and Palgrave.

Crespi, G., Fernández-Arias, E. and Stein, E. (eds.) (2014) *Development in the Americas (DIA) 2014: Rethinking productive development*, New York: Palgrave McMillan.

Energy Information Administration (2014) *Energy Information Administration Statistics*, database. Washington DC: US Department of Energy. Available at www.eia.gov/ (accessed 26 April 2016).

Fairbanks, M. et al. (2007) 'Building competitive advantages', in Rojas-Suárez, L. and Elías, C. (eds.), *Policy perspectives for Trinidad and Tobago: From growth to prosperity*, Washington DC: Inter-American Development Bank.

Flórez, L.B. and Misas, G. (2008) *La Competitividad y el Plan del Salto Social*, Bogota, Colombia: Universidad Nacional de Colombia.

Gonzalez, M., Monaldi, F., Rios, G. and Villasmil, R. (2007) 'The difficulties of reforming an il dependent economy: The case of Venezuela', in Fanelli, J.M. (ed.) *Understanding market reforms in Latin America: Similar reforms, diverse constituencies, varied results*, New York: Palgrave Macmillan.

Hausmann, R. and Rigobón, R. (2003) 'An alternative interpretation of the 'Resource Curse': Theory and policy implications', *NBER Working Paper No. 9424.* Cambridge, MA: National Bureau of Economic Research.

Hausmann, R. and Rodrik, D. (2003) 'Economic Development as Self Discovery', *Working Paper 8952*, National Bureau of Economic Research, Cambridge, MA.

Leamer, E. (1984) *Sources of international comparative advantage: Theory and evidence*, Cambridge, MA: Massachusetts Institute of Technology Press.

Lederman, D. and Maloney, M. (eds.) (2006) *Natural resources and development: Neither curse nor destiny*, Stanford: Stanford University Press and World Bank.

Maloney, W. (2002) 'Missed opportunities: Innovation and resource-based growth in Latin America', *Economía*, vol. 3, no. 1, 111–151.

Manzano, O. (2013) 'Venezuela after a century of oil exploitation', in Hausmann, R. and Francisco, R. (eds.) , *Venezuela Before Chávez: Anatomy of an economic collapse*, State College, PA: Penn State University Press.

Manzano, O. (2014) 'From dependency theory to local governance: Evolution of the research on extractive industries and development', in Cruz Vieyra, J. and Masson, M. (eds.), *Transparent governance in an age of abundance: Experiences from the extractive industries in Latin America and the Caribbean*, Washingtpon: Inter-American Development Bank.

Martín-Mayoral, F. (2009) 'Estado y mercado en la historia de Ecuador. Desde los años 50 hasta el gobierno de Rafael Correa', *Revista Nueva Sociedad*, no. 221.

Mayobre, J.A. (1944) 'La paridad del Bolivar', in Valecillos, H. and Bello, O. (eds.), *La Economía Contemporánea de Venezuela*, Caracas: Banco Central de Venezuela.

Meléndez, M. and Perry, G. (2010) 'Industrial Policies in Colombia', *IDB Working Paper Series No. IDB-WP-126*, Washington DC: Inter-American Development Bank.

Ministry of Trade and Industry (2007) *Green paper on the Trinidad and Tobago Investment Policy 2007–2012*, Trinidad and Tobago: Ministry of Trade and Industry.

Mottley, W. (2008) *Trinidad and Tobago: Industrial Policy 1959–2008*, Kingston, Jamaica: Ian Randle Publishers.

Moya, R., Mohammed, A.-M. and Sookram, S. (2010) 'Productive development policies in Trinidad and Tobago: A critical review', *IDB Working Paper Series No. IDB-WP-115*, Washington DC: Inter-American Development Bank.

Ocampo, J.A. and Ros, J. (2011) 'Shifting paradigms in Latin America's economic development', in Ocampo, J.A. and Ros. J. (eds.), *The Oxford Handbook of Latin American Economies*, Oxford: Oxford University Press.

OCEPRE (Oficina Central de Presupuesto) (1988) *Cuarenta Años de Presupuesto Fiscal*, Caracas: OCEPRE.

Peltzer, E. (1944) 'La industrialización de Venezuela y el alto tipo de cambio del Bolívar,' in Valacillos, H. and Bello, O. (eds.), *La Economía Contemporánea de Venezuela*, Caracas: Banco Central de Venezuela.

Perry, G. (2008) *El Legado Económico del Gobierno Lleras Restrepo*, Bogota, Colombia: Fedesarrollo.

Prebisch, R. (1950) The economic development of Latin America and its principal problems, Economic Commission for Latin America and United Nations Department of Economic Affairs.

Rubio, L. (2001) *Políticas Económicas del México Contemporáneo*. Mexico City, Mexico: Editorial CIDAC.

Sánchez, G. and Butler, I. (2008) 'Competitiveness and growth in Argentina: Appropriability, misallocation or disengagement?' Washington DC: Inter-American Development Bank.

Sanchez, G., Rozemberg, R., Butler, I. and Rufo, H. (2008) 'The emergence of new successful export activities in Argentina: Self-discovery, knowledge niches, or barriers to riches? Case study of biotechnology applied to human health', *Research Network Working Paper R-548*. Washington DC: Inter-American Development Bank.

Sánchez, G., Butler, I. and Rozemberg, R. (2011) 'Productive Development Policies in Argentina', *IDB Working Paper Series No. IDB-WP-193*, Washington DC: Inter-American Development Bank.

Secretaria de Economia (2007) *Diez Lineamientos de la Subsecretaría de Industria y Comercio para incrementar la Competitividad 2008–2012*, Mexico: Secretaria de Economia.

Stallings, B. and Peres, W. (2000) *Growth, employment and equity: the impact of economic reforms in Latin America and the Caribbean*, Santiago, Chile: The Brookings Institution Press and ECLAC.

Stein, E. and Tommasi, M. (eds.) (2008) *Policymaking in Latin America*, Washington DC: United States Inter-American Development Bank and David Rockefeller Center for Latin American Studies.

Taylor, A. (2003) 'Capital accumulation', in Dellapaolera, G. and Taylor, A. (eds.), *A new economic history of Argentina*, Cambridge, United Kingdom: Cambridge University Press.

United Nations (2014) *UN Comtrade*, database. Geneva: United Nations. Available at http://comtrade.un.org/ (accessed 21 April 2016).

Williamson, J. (1989) 'What Washington means by policy reform', in Williamson, J. (ed.), *Latin American readjustment: How much has happened?* Washington DC, United States: Institute for International Economics.

World Bank (2014) *World Development Indicators*. Database, Washington DC: World Bank. Available at http://data.worldbank.org/data-catalog/ (accessed 21 April 2016).

Appendix

Cluster analysis

As explained in Section 4.1, to compare the performance of Latin American oil exporters we wanted to have a benchmark, besides other Latin American countries. For that purpose we used cluster analysis. We use three variables: GDP per capita, as a measure of the level of economic development; net manufacturing exports per capita, as a measure of diversification; and net oil exports per capita, as a measure of abundance.

As we explained, we measured all these variables at the 'starting point' of our analysis in 1990. Latin America embarked on import substitution (IS) policies that imposed an important fiscal burden on those countries. In the 1980s when the fiscal and external situation was no longer sustainable, they began structural reform programmes. In this chapter, we are analysing the performance after those programmes were implemented. On the thirty-six oil exporters, only twenty-five have the full set of data.

To do the cluster analysis we started with the estimation of the principal components. Since all components explain at least 5% of the variance, we used three. With the scores of this analysis we did average-link clustering. The results are shown in Figure 4.12. We wanted to determine the optimal number of clusters, but the Calinski/Harabasz test did not give a conclusive result. However, the Duda/Hart test supported the argument for eight clusters. The clusters were:

1   Canada
2   United Kingdom
3   Brunei, Tunisia, Bolivia, Indonesia, Algeria, Ecuador, Iran, Colombia, Egypt, China, Argentina, Cameroon, Malaysia, Peru and Mexico
4   Trinidad and Tobago and Venezuela
5   Bahrain
6   Oman
7   Saudi Arabia
8   Norway

Linkages and trade pattern

For the analysis presented in Figure 4.4, we use three sources of data. For the linkages of the non-oil sector to the oil sector we used the input-output matrices developed by the Center for Global Trade Analysis (2014). The most recent matrices developed are for 2007. The matrices have fifty-seven sectors. For each sector backward and forward linkages were estimated.

Backward linkages are measured by the following formula:

$$Backward_k = \Sigma_{j \neq k} \delta_{jk} Oil\ Consumption_j \tag{1}$$

where δ_{jk} represents the fraction of sector j output supplied to sector k. The information is taken from the input-output matrix.

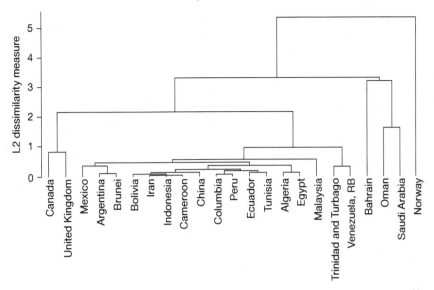

Figure 4.12 Dendrogram for clavg1990 cluster analysis.
Source: Authors' calculation using World Bank (2014).

Similarly, forward linkages are measured by the following formula:

$$Forward_k = \Sigma_{j \neq k} \delta_{kj} Oil\ Consumption_j \qquad (2)$$

where δ_{kj} represents the fraction of sector k output supplied to sector j. This information is also taken from the input-output matrix.

Once both linkages were estimated, we added them and ranked the sectors from higher to lower linkages. We then took the rank of the thirty-eight tradable sectors.

For the exports, we used data from the United Nations (2014). We took the exports from 2007, to be consistent with the matrix. The data at the 3-digit level was reclassified in terms of the thirty-eight sectors represented in the input-output matrices. We then ranked the sectors from higher to lower exports.

Once we had the rank in exports and the rank in linkages, we estimated the correlations that are represented by the vertical axis of Figure 4. The horizontal axis was constructed using net oil exports (in barrels) based on data from the Energy Information Agency (2014). Finally, the growth rate of non-oil exports was estimated with information from the United Nations (2014).

5 Economic diversification in Malaysia

Timing, path dependence and increasing returns

Abdillah Noh

5.1 Introduction

The steep drop in global oil prices in the last quarter of 2014 sent the Malaysian ringgit reeling against the greenback and gave investors little comfort about the state of the Malaysian economy, given that Malaysia is a net exporter of petroleum and the traditionally high correlation between the ringgit and oil prices gave investors good reasons to worry. To help quell the market, Abdul Wahid Omar, the Minister in charge of the country's economic planning, cited Malaysia's strong fundamentals, highlighting the country's current account surplus that stood at RM 41 billion in the first nine months of 2014 and its national saving rate of 32% of its GDP. He also pointed out Malaysia's good growth momentum, where GDP growth has averaged 5.5% for the past ten years. More importantly, Wahid cited Malaysia's highly diversified trading economy as the prime reason for his optimism (The Malaysian Insider, 7 December 2014).

While market fear is not entirely misplaced, Malaysia's varied economic structure does provide reasons to stay optimistic. The oil and gas sector contributed only 30% of Malaysia's total revenue even though Petroliam Nasional Berhad or Petronas – the national oil company – remains the country's largest tax payer. In fact, the oil and gas sector contributed only 19% of GDP (Pemandu, 2010). Services formed the bulk of the country's output, making up 55% of Malaysia's GDP with manufacturing contributing a quarter. Mining and agriculture make up 7% and 8% respectively (IMF, 2015). Malaysia's exports also remain varied. They include electronics (34.5%), petroleum related products (9.9%), palm oil (9.3%) and chemical products (6.9%). In addition, the country's national debt stood at RM 596.8 billion (USD 166 billion) or about 52% of GDP (The Sun Daily, 2015b) with domestic debt forming 97% of total debt. Given such numbers, it is not surprising that Malaysia remains an attractive investment destination and one of the world's most open economies. The Institute for Management Development (IMD) ranks Malaysia as the fourteenth most competitive nation in its recently released World Competitiveness Yearbook 2015 (The Sun Daily, 2015a). It is ranked in the top twenty most competitive economies and the six most competitive economies in Asia (Global Competiveness Report, 2014–2015).

For a country that has abundant natural resources Malaysia's achievements in developing a vibrant multi-sector economy do not match conventional wisdom. The common narrative is that resource-rich states often find it difficult to move away from primary sectors and develop durable sectors like manufacturing and services. These countries often struggle to develop a vibrant private sector and the state often ends up as the largest employer (Mehlum, Moene and Torvik, 2006). Resource-rich countries also often distort existing economic structures, employing suboptimal distributive policies that do damage to the economy in the long run. Abstaining from addressing long-term imperatives, these states often resort to subsiding fuel and apportioning funds to social services like education, health and welfare which – while good – would often result in suboptimal allocation of resources. Such states are also prone to develop extractive institutions (Acemoglu, 2012). For instance, competition among elites for control of natural resources could lead to a predatory state (Evans, 1995), which promotes patronage, rent seeking and makes economic diversification a huge challenge. The quest for control of natural resources could also see elites resisting much-needed reform, often preferring to employ populist and creative policies to appease the public than to undertake privatisation of the natural resource sector. To safeguard their interests and mute public demands, elites would also resort to redistributing natural resource receipts in the form of direct transfer to key areas like education, food and transportation. In sum, resource-rich states – particularly developing countries – often experience an under-developed private sector, a lack of financial depth, a high incidence of rent-seeking activities and low domestic and foreign investment (Gylfason, 2004).

While Malaysia's ability to diversify its economy proves an exception to the rule, it should not really be so. When taken into perspective, Malaysia has all the right ingredients to be an economic failure – a classic case for what could possibly go wrong with a state having abundant natural resources. To start with, it has huge natural resources reserves, being the third largest producer of rubber, the third largest holder of natural gas reserves and the fourth largest oil reserve holder in Asia (US Energy Information Administrative Report, 2014). Its plural society could also be prone to wanton abuse of resources by elites who could be out to secure rents and patronage. Its society is also highly fractured, with ethnic groups developing almost mutually exclusive political, economic and social institutions and making competing claims over resources.[1] To complicate things even further, Malaysia's federal system provides individual states with exclusive rights over land – a condition conducive to potentially intractable elite capture, patronage and political bargaining.[2] In addition, the state assumes a dominant role in Malaysia's development process; this is unsurprising because the current regime has ruled Malaysia since the country's independence in 1957. The government is led by the Barisan Nasional (BN), a coalition of fourteen mainly ethnic-based parties where the largest component is the UMNO (United Malays National Organisation), the largest Bumiputera (Malay) political party. Given such combinations – abundant natural resources, a fractured plural society, a federal system, a strong state presence, a politically dominant Malay (Bumiputera) class and a political party that has ruled since independence, one would expect Malaysia to have succumbed to unrestrained state patronage, uncontrolled rent-seeking behaviour, elite capture and unmitigated extractive state institutions that would debilitate its economic effort. Logically, fifty-eight years of independence would be enough time to turn Malaysia into economic basket case.

Why didn't the Malaysian state suffer from unrestrained state patronage and rent seeking? How is it possible that the economy continues to diversify and grow at a respectable rate? Paul Collier explains that Malaysia's ability to develop a varied economic structure and avoid the resource curse lies in its ability to keep its macroeconomic policies on the right course, employ liberal market ideas and show competence in handling conflict in a plural society (Collier, 2006). In a slightly different vein, Islam and Chowdury (1997) argue that Malaysia's ability to develop a vibrant multi-sector economy lies in its successful management of a plural society and its exercise in consensual democracy. Malaysia's economic success, they explain, is the result of a tacit agreement between Malaysia's politically dominant Malay actors and economically dominant Chinese actors. Under such an agreement the state (being Malay dominated) agrees not to over indulge in productive activities (the Chinese domain), and in return the state is allowed to disburse resources to invest in the economic and human capital of the Malay majority.

The two arguments both hold some truth. There is little doubt that Malaysia's ability to diversify its economy is largely due to its adoption of appropriate macroeconomic policies and the state's ability to handle a highly fragmented and fractious plural society. For instance, Malaysia has not veered away from adopting liberal economic policies. Malaysia understood the merits of a liberal market economy and the need to maintain an open trading regime and take advantage of its geography. In fact, being located at the heart of Asia Pacific and the busy Straits of Malacca facilitated the right policy option.

However, while there are truths in Collier's (2006) and Islam and Chowdury's (1997) arguments, there is a need to supplement them. Malaysia's success at economic diversification inevitably demands that we provide a fuller appreciation of the idiosyncratic character of Malaysia's political economy. While there are various policy remedies to promote economic diversification there is also no one size-fits-all policy prescription for diversification efforts (Malik and Temple, 2009). Adopting such a perspective, this chapter argues that Malaysia's successful economic diversification strategy is a function of its institutional character and historical process. In other words, Malaysia's diversification story is a function of its idiosyncratic institutional qualities – a product of its political, social and economic character.

To demonstrate this, the chapter will explain three areas that contribute to Malaysia's ability to diversify its economy. It will first explain the path dependent nature of Malaysia's economic policy (during both the colonial and the post-colonial periods) and the increasing returns from the development of other economic sectors that have made the oil and gas sector only an add-on to the country's already varied economic production structure. It will explain that the

Malaysian economy was already diversified with major revenues coming from tin, rubber and palm oil before oil and gas production became commercially viable. The chapter will also explain that Malaysia's success in diversifying its economy is due to the character of its political and economic trajectory. It will argue that the path dependent nature of Malaysia's political economy unwittingly limits Malaysia's economic policy option as it attempts to adhere to a consociational arrangement. It will demonstrate that the affirmative nature of Malaysia's New Economic Policy (NEP) unintentionally gives the state little choice but to continue to adopt an economic diversification strategy in the bid to expand the economy and provide legitimacy to redistributive policy. Finally, the chapter will demonstrate how the state has deftly instituted the economic diversification story, readying its population to look beyond natural resources for economic sustainability.

The chapter is divided as follows. Section 5.2 provides the theoretical background by introducing the concepts of historical institutionalism, path dependence, increasing returns and timing. Section 5.3 will describe the Malaysian economy and show how a diversified economy has paved the way for relying less on natural resources, especially oil and gas. Section 5.4 will describe the NEP and how it forces the state to expand and diversify, because failure to do so would challenge the legitimacy of Malaysia's affirmative action policies. Section 5.5 will also describe Malaysia's response to its economic crisis in the 1980s, the 1990s and in the year 2008. The chapter describes Malaysia's response to crisis for two reasons: first, to demonstrate the state's determination to keep to a liberal and expansive economy; and second, to stress Malaysia's willingness to change the terms of reference for affirmative action in a bid to diversify and keep to an expanding economic story. The final section (Section 5.6) will describe how the state has consistently instituted the economic diversification that has cognitively prepared the public to look beyond natural resources for economic sustainability.

5.2 Historical institutionalism and path dependence

Historical institutional analysis seeks to explain large outcomes and asks 'big' questions. A historical institutionalist believes that 'detailed investigation' of carefully chosen case studies can provide a 'powerful tool for uncovering the sources of (policy) change' (Pierson, 1993). This approach believes that institutional processes can best be understood if they are studied over time. In explaining policy outcomes, works on historical institutionalism place a premium on context, historical moments and processes (George and Bennet, 2005). An integral part of historical institutional work is process tracing, where historical episodes are linked in a sequential and meaningful way to offer explanation of a particular case (Goldstone, 2005).

Central to historical institutionalism is the concept of path dependence. There are various definitions of path dependence. Levi (1997) provides a clear description, stating that once a state 'has started down a track, the costs of reversals are very high'. She believes that path dependence entrenches certain institutional arrangements that effectively 'obstruct an easy reversal of the initial choice'. Sewell (1996) defines path dependence as the fact that 'what happened at an earlier point in time will affect the possible outcomes of a sequence of events occurring at a later point in time'. Mahoney (2000) sees path dependence as 'specifically those historical sequences in which contingent events set into motion institutional patterns or event chains that have deterministic properties'.

Given the above definition, the natural question to ask is why social, political and economic processes get stuck in a path dependent mode. Historical institutionalists think that making an initial choice counts. Once a particular choice is made, self-reinforcing mechanisms set in where 'each step in a particular direction makes it more difficult to reverse course' (Pierson, 2004: 21). However, reversing a course is not impossible, but reversal is made increasingly difficult because the cost of reversal increases over time as the actors invest resources in the choice made. There are two important works that deconstruct the logic of path dependence, carried out by economic historians Paul David (1985) and Brian Arthur (1994). Arthur suggests that path dependence is due to self-reinforcing mechanisms. He describes four such self-reinforcing mechanisms that encourage path dependence. These are: large set up costs; learning effects, coordination effects, and adaptive expectations. Put simply, the initial choice gets hardwired within an institutional setting and thus makes it harder for existing institutions to adopt alternative technology (Thelen, 2006; Pierson, 2000; Krasner, 1988; North, 1990). As an example, we are hardwired to use Microsoft applications in all our dealings and having to move to open source, though not impossible, is highly unattractive simply because we will have to invest time and effort in learning the new application.

David's and Arthur's works are extensively borrowed by social scientists. One effort at incorporating David's and Arthur's works in public policy is the work by Paul Pierson (2004). Pierson argues that the source of path dependence and self-reinforcing mechanisms lies in the nature of public good. He explains that the non-excludable and non-rivalrous nature of public good gives rise to collective action problems and the development of institutional density, which results in self-reinforcing mechanisms. In the Malaysian case, the collective action dilemma of public policy and the increasing returns nature of economic activities act together to produce a dense institutional network that sees the state remaining on the economic diversification path. We will elaborate on this below.

While it is true that path dependence gives the impression that the state is limited by the type of institutions it inherits, in reality it does not necessarily mean that states are caught in institutional stasis. Changes do happen when there are inherent ambiguities and gaps that exist, either by design or emerging over time between formal institutions and actual implementation (Streeck and Thelen, 2005). However, change, according to historical institutionalism, is incremental in nature. Streeck and Thelen (2005) do not see change as drastic: 'rather than abrupt and discontinuous, transformative change often results from an accumulation of gradual and incremental changes.' In other words, change can be gradual and unexciting in the short term – small gradual steps – but when viewed from a longer term perspective change is nothing short of transformational. The Malaysian economy during colonialism in the 1800s, for instance, is very different from the sophisticated multifaceted economy that we see today.

The historical institutional narrative fits this chapter's explanation of Malaysia's diversification effort. The ensuing pages will demonstrate that Malaysia's economic diversification effort is a function of timing, sequence and path dependence. Its success in diversifying the economy rests on the timing of the state's discovery of oil and the path dependent nature of Malaysia's economy, which has never been reliant on a single economic resource. This character of Malaysia's political economy, which is itself the result of historical processes, facilitates the diversification process. Malaysia's power sharing arrangement – which Arendt Lijphart (1996) termed consociationalism – is also highly institutionalised. Governing elites understand the perils of political, social and economic fragmentation. They understand the need to maintain cohesion and stability among political constituents, as only then can there be a successful and expansive economy and a higher chance of economic survival (Lijphart, 1996).[3] In fact, existing institutions provide Malaysia's policy actors with the mental maps of economic, social and political realities that encourage path dependence and the maintenance of economic diversification (David, 1985; North, 1990; Pierson, 2004). To understand Malaysia's historical path we now look at the Malaysian economy.

5.3 Timing and path dependence: the economy and the late entry of the oil and gas industry

Historically, the Malaysian economy has never been dependent on a single source of economic production. During the British colonial period the Malayan economy was one of the most laissez-faire economies and among the world's freest trading economies. In the nineteenth century the Malaysian economy relied on exports of primary products like tin, rubber and palm oil. Tin especially dominated Malaysia's (then called Malaya) economic output. Malaya became the world's largest exporter of tin. In the early twentieth century Malaya's tin output contributed more than half the global tin production. Even as late as 1979, Malaysia accounted for 31% of the world's tin output, producing 63,000 tonnes of tin ores. Malaysia now hardly exports any tin. The drop in production, due to dwindling tin deposits, low tin prices and high operating costs, has meant that tin is now only used for domestic electronic and tinplating industries (Drabble, 2000).

After independence, manufacturing increasingly became the dominant sector with the economy still relying on tin, rubber and oil palm receipts. At the time of independence the manufacturing sector only accounted for 11% of GDP, but by the late 1960s the sector began to emerge as Malaysia's main industrial output. The early 1970s saw Malaysia aggressively targeting foreign manufacturing firms and employing a string of investment incentives. It set up five export-processing zones to promote cluster production networks and reduce costs. It also made efforts to reduce tariffs and non-tariff barriers. In the 1970s Malaysia's effective rates of protection (ERPs) stood between 35–40% – still far less than in most developing economies – and these rates declined to 23% in 1982 and dropped further to 17% in 1987 (Ghee and Woon, 1994; Auty, 2000).

Throughout the 1980s Malaysia's industrialisation plan took advantage of the surge in global production output, incentivising firms with the right perks. The 1960s saw Malaysia's industrial output making up a mere 6.3% of GDP, but by 1980 the country's industrial activities rose to about one fifth of total GDP. By 1990 manufacturing made up almost 60% of Malaysian exports, a sharp contrast to the figure of 12% in 1970 (Drabble, 2000). In 1968 manufacturing made up 13%of Malaysia's GDP, but by 2007 manufacturing contributed more than 30% of the GDP. Given the varied economic structure and the increasing returns that the state was reaping from the boom in manufacturing, it is not surprising that the state in the 1970s was less reliant on natural oil and gas receipts. In other words, diversified economic production gave Malaysia the flexibility and room to be less reliant on natural oil and gas.

The timing of the commercial production of oil entrenches the diversification story. Oil and gas were late entrants to Malaysia's industrial output. Prior to 1970, oil and gas were discovered in Sarawak as early as 1911 (Sarawak only became a member state of Malaysia in 1963), but there was little commercial interest given the high cost of extraction. Even when oil and gas was discovered in substantial quantities off the east cost of Peninsular Malaysia in the 1970s, initial interest in Malaysia's oil deposits was tepid given the lack of technological capabilities and low oil prices. A senior official of a continental oil company remarked: 'it would appear that we do not have another Middle East, or even another North Sea, but an area where relatively small discoveries are the norm' (Gale, 1981). When we put together Malaysia's diversified economic production structure and the late entry of oil and gas industry to the economy, path dependence and timing ensured that the state relied less on oil and gas as sources for economic growth. The diversified nature of the economy prior to the discovery of commercially viable oil and gas also meant that the state was not in a rush to invest overwhelming resources in developing the sector at the expense of other sectors of the economy.

The varied economic structure prior to the discovery of oil meant that Malaysia had the luxury of being able to map a comprehensive oil management strategy. In 1974 Malaysia introduced the Petroleum Development Act that gave birth to Malaysia's Petroleum Nasional Berhad, or PETRONAS. Under the Act PETRONAS was given custodial rights to Malaysia's petroleum resources, retaining ownership and management control of the exploration, development and production of oil resources. Malaysia also mapped out a sustainable oil management strategy when it introduced the National Depletion Policy in 1980, the purpose of which was to manage oil production. Under the policy oil production at the time was limited to no more than 270,000 barrels per day.

The important point here is that increasing returns from earlier economic diversification efforts have made relying only on oil and gas a non-option. Further, it would be costly and unproductive for Malaysia to unwind its diversification strategy. An entrenched diversified economy and the insurance that came from a lucrative oil and gas sector might also provide added luxury for policy makers to embark on greater and more ambitious industrialisation strategies.[4]

The discovery of oil and gas in the 1970s coincided with an important milestone in Malaysia's political economy – the introduction of Malaysia's New Economic Policy. To many, the New Economic Policy was seen as a step backwards in terms of Malaysia's economic growth. However, as we will show below, ironically the introduction of the NEP imposed further discipline on Malaysia's economic diversification effort. We turn to this next.

5.4 The New Economic Policy: part of Malaysia's problem or part of Malaysia's answer to maintaining a diversified economy?

An appraisal of Malaysia's economy in the post-colonial period would not be complete without mentioning the New Economic Policy (NEP). Even though it was termed an economic policy, the NEP is an economic document meant to serve Malaysia's larger social and political objectives.[5] Implemented in 1970 following a bloody racial riot on 13 May 1969, the NEP had two objectives. The first was to restructure the economy and society and eliminate the identification of economic function with a particular ethnic group. The second was to eradicate poverty irrespective of race. The NEP set a target that by 1990 equity distribution among the *bumiputeras* (Malays), non-*bumiputera* (non-Malays) and foreigners must be in the ratio of 30:40:30 respectively, which stands in contrast to the equity distribution in the 1970, where the ratio of *bumiputeras* (Malays) to *non-bumiputera* (non-Malays) and foreigners stood at 1.9:23.5:60.7.

There is no shortage of literature that details the distortionary capacity of the NEP (Gomez and Jomo, 1997; Lee, 2010). It is indeed true that state intervention and the affirmative nature of the NEP only encouraged suboptimal allocation of economic and political resources. However, rather than turning its back on pro-market qualities, what was equally confounding was that the affirmative action nature of the NEP did little to compromise Malaysia's liberal economic arrangement. Despite having an interventionist policy in the form of the NEP, Malaysia stands among the top twenty most competitive nations, suggesting that the state has managed to maintain a competitive economic regime with an open and diversified economy. Equally perplexing is how it was possible that the NEP, given its so-called distortionary qualities, allowed Malaysia to raise the wealth of all ethnic groups, not just the *bumiputeras*. The drop in poverty among Chinese and Indians is just as impressive as the drop in poverty among *bumiputeras* (see Table 5.1). In 1970 26% of Chinese were considered poor, but by 1990 only 6% of Chinese were deemed poor.

While not dismissing the distortionary character of the NEP, this chapter argues that the raison d'étre and the terms of reference of the NEP ensure that Malaysia continues to maintain a liberal and diversified economic regime. This is because the legitimacy of the NEP rests on the regime's ability to keep to the NEP's redistributive promise, which could only come from an expanding and diversified economy. It is indeed ironic that the NEP imposes discipline on the state to

Table 5.1 Incidence of poverty (%) by ethnic group in Malaysia, 1970 and 1990 (Drabble, 2000)

	1970	*1990*
Bumiputeras	65.0	20.8
Chinese	26.0	5.7
Indian	39.0	8.0
Overall	49.3	15.0

continue to expand the economic cake in order to maintain consociational democracy and preserve social and political peace.

Malaysia's policy makers understand this logic. The NEP must be built on fairness – a policy that is meant to alleviate poverty and improve the living standards of all Malaysians, not just the *bumiputeras*. The state spent considerable effort to convince the investing community that the NEP was an attempt at expanding the economy and empowering local capacities. It also spent considerable effort to make it clear that the NEP was not an outright nationalisation strategy because it only targeted 30% *bumiputeras* ownership, with the remaining 70% of total assets being held by non-*bumiputeras* and foreigners. Elites know that they must employ liberal economic policies and not place excessive restrictions on non-*bumiputeras* and foreign investors, because failure to do so would result in a shrinking economic pie that could potentially destroy the social and political peace. It is indeed helpful that the path dependent nature of Malaysia's economic production structure has made it easy for the Malaysian economy to stay on its diversified course. We will demonstrate below how the state tweaked the terms of the NEP in an attempt to maintain an expanding economy.

5.5 The financial crises and willingness to improvise the sacred cow

Since the introduction of the NEP the state has time and again indicated that it was prepared to amend terms of the NEP to make room for economic expansion. The economic crises in the 1980s and 1990s and the recent global crisis in 2008 tested Malaysia's resolve to expand and diversify the economy, while at the same time keeping to the terms of the NEP. On all three occasions, Malaysia showed that it was prepared to tweak the conditions of the NEP to allow for economic recovery. We look now at the three economic episodes.

The 1980s

The recession in the 1980s tested Malaysia's resolve to keep to a liberal and diversified economy as the crisis threatened, for the first time, Malaysia's commitment to the NEP's redistributive character and the relevance of the NEP. The Malaysian economy contracted by 1% in 1985, hurt by falling commodity prices of tin, petroleum and rubber (Doraisami, 2012). In 1986 growth was a mere

1.2%, with unemployment hitting a high of 8.1%. Also in that year, Malaysia's debt stood at 112% of its GDP.

These economic woes saw the state reviewing existing economic policies and the terms of the NEP. A review of the NEP invited strong political reactions that caused bitter fights between members of the dominant ruling Malay party UMNO. The UMNO was split into two camps; the first advocated the 'pro-growth' strategy, calling for less state intervention and a review of some aspects of the NEP, while the second was 'pro-distribution', promoting the preservation of Malaysia's economic restructuring process. In the end the 'pro-growth' team, under the then Prime Minister Mahathir Mohamed, won the political contest.

In an effort to restore economic growth the Mahathir administration made changes to the NEP. It modified the highly unpopular Industrial Coordination Act (1975), which required small Malaysian firms to provide for 30% *bumiputera* (Malay) ownership and foreign firms to have no more than 30% equity, imposing new rules that relieved smaller firms from such quota imposition.[6] The Mahathir administration also introduced the Promotion of Investment Act in 1986 that created added incentives for foreign investment by excluding foreign investors from NEP quotas. Foreign firms were also exempted from adhering to the 30% bumiputera equity ownership, on condition that 50% of their output was exported or sold to companies in the newly established Free Trade Zones (FTZs) (Leete, 2007).

The changes in the NEP produced the desired results. Exemptions from the NEP rules drew foreign manufacturing industries in electrical and electronics, metals, chemical and petroleum (Leete, 2007). By the end of the 1980s Malaysia had established ten Free Trade Zones (FTZs), and most of the companies that operated within them were foreign-owned companies – mainly Japanese and American. Manufacturing remained the prime driver of the economy, contributing substantially to employment, export and industrial output.

The 1980s also saw further diversification in the Malaysian economy. This was the period when Malaysia rode the privatisation wave that was sweeping most parts of the world. By the early 1990s thirteen state enterprises had been privatised, involving companies from telecommunications, television, utilities and airlines. Privatisation boosted the stock market, which saw some 201 billion ringgit in market capitalisation. By 1996, total market capitalisation in KLSE was sixteen times that in 1987 (Doraisami, 2012).

The 1980s also saw Malaysia embarking on the development of heavy and chemical industries (HCI). The promotion of HCI was part of the state's effort to broaden the economic base and emulate the economic success of developmental states like Korea and Japan. Under its 'Look East' policy, Malaysia introduced heavy industries like automobile manufacture, steel manufacturing, cement, machinery and equipment and petrochemical industries. The state also set up the Heavy Industry Corporation of Malaysia (HICOM) which allowed the flow of foreign funds, specifically from Mitsubishi and Honda, to spearhead the new industrialisation drive.

Even though Malaysia's decision to move into heavy industries drew heavy criticism, as Sanjay Lall points out, one cannot take away the fact that the development of this sector – unproductive as it may be – has added depth and width to the Malaysian economy. Indeed, in times to come embarking on high industries may well hold Malaysia in good stead as such industries involve the acquisition of high technology, the injection of huge capital investment and the development of skilled labour – factors that would give Malaysia a comparative advantage especially in heavy industries (Lall, 1995).

The tweaking of the NEP and the introduction of a new economic structure in the 1980s had the desired results. After recording sluggish growth of just 1.2% in 1986, the next few years saw Malaysia posting impressive growth. Between 1988 and 1990 the economy grew at the impressive rates of 8.9%, 8.8% and 9.8%. Malaysia's response to its economic condition in the 1980s was not an anomaly. The 1990s would also see the state tweaking the economic structure further to ensure growth and diversification in the economy as well as maintaining the legitimacy of the NEP.

The 1990s and Malaysia's response

The Asian financial crisis in late 1997 threatened to undo Malaysia's promising growth. The early 1990s saw the Malaysian economy thriving with an impressive average annual growth rate of 8%. Between 1990 and1995 Malaysia's manufacturing exports grew at an annual rate of 20%. Unemployment was also at its lowest level for many years; in 1995 Malaysia's unemployment rate stood at 3.1%, the lowest since independence (Leete, 2007).

The Asian crisis threatened the relevance of the NEP (now called the New Development Policy, NDP) and tested Malaysia's commitment to maintaining a liberal economy. The Malaysian economy began to fall apart in the summer of 1997. In 1998 the country's real GDP fell by a massive 7.5%. By the middle of 1998 the Malaysian stock market had lost more than 50% of its value with the Malaysian ringgit falling to its lowest point against major currencies. By the middle of 1998 the ringgit had depreciated by some 40% against the US dollar (Leete, 2007).

In response to the crisis the state did little to move away from its liberal market economy. However, instead of following the IMF's full prescription, Malaysia acted on its own initiative. The then Prime Minister Mahathir Mohamad feared that adopting the full IMF solution would seriously threaten the economy and tear at Malaysia's social and political fabric, as well as making the state's defence of the NEP increasingly tenuous (Mahathir, 2000).

Malaysia's immediate concern was to resuscitate the economy, keep to the tried and tested economic structure and at the same time safeguard Malaysia's fragile social and political conditions. In the summer of 1998 the government introduced the highly unpopular capital control, which made offshore trading of the ringgit illegal – all part of an effort to improve credit ratings, reduce any further weakening of the ringgit, curb inflation and prevent the outflow of capital. In a bid to stabilise the economy and make a speedy recovery, Malaysia set up two state asset and credit managing companies – *Danaharta* and *Danamodal*. Both companies were tasked to do a corporate rescue of local firms and financial houses – both *bumiputeras* and non-*bumiputera* owned – to provide liquidity and stabilise domestic companies' credit positions.

Despite heavy criticism from the international community, Malaysia's unorthodox approach worked. In the three years after the crisis the electronic sectors, petroleum and palm oil sectors recovered (Lau, 2005). Diversification grew apace. By the year 2000 Malaysia's GDP had grown by 9% spearheaded by an increase in manufacturing output, specifically in electronics. After 1998 Malaysia began to accumulate a huge surplus with its external current account making up 13% of GNP. Though Malaysia's handling of the crisis had its fair share of critics, Kaplan and Rodrik (2001) argue that 'Malaysia would have fared even better if they had imposed capital controls sooner'. We turn now to another episode, the 2008 global financial crisis that entrenched Malaysia's diversification strategy even further.

The 2008 global crisis

Malaysia's response to the global financial crisis of 2008 demonstrates yet again its commitment to maintain an open, diversified economy. The crisis threatened Malaysia's growth momentum. In 2009 the economy contracted by 1.7%, a far cry from the average annual growth rate of more than 5% in the five years prior to the crisis. The year 2009 also posed an added challenge to the ruling Barisan Nasional (BN), whose rule of more than fifty years came under serious threat from Malaysia's opposition law makers after the opposition pact denied the incumbent BN party its two-thirds majority in the 2008 election.

In the face of yet another crisis, Malaysia continued to be persuaded by the overriding need to keep the growth momentum, with the state knowing very well that only with continued expansion of the economy could it justify the relevance of the NEP. More importantly, however, the crisis again shows that Malaysia is prepared to make further changes to the NEP so long as the overall objectives of the NEP remain intact.

Despite the gloomy economic outlook in combination with a fragile political scene, the state made further efforts to liberalise the economy, undertaking further changes to the NDP in a bid to maintain Malaysia's growth trajectory. To jump start the economy, in 2009 Malaysia announced two fiscal stimulus packages that gave greater attention to construction and infrastructural projects. There was further tweaking of existing NDP guidelines to attract foreign investments. Foreigners are now allowed to buy commercial properties above RM 500 000 without approval from the state's Foreign Investment Committee (FIC). The services sector also saw further liberalisation. By 2015, the state allows 70% foreign ownership of the sector. The state has agreed to remove the 30% *bumiputera* equity requirements for twenty-seven services sectors. In addition, the state has also set aside some RM 2 billion to be made available to private companies for capacity building projects in new growth sectors like biotechnology, healthcare and education.

Thus far, the economy seems to be responding well to the stimulus packages. In 2010 the economy registered growth of 7.2% before slowing down a little in 2011 when it posted growth of 4%. During the full year 2012 the economy grew by more than 5%. A more important point here is that the economy has become more varied, since it is spearheaded not only by traditional sectors like manufacturing and construction but increasingly by the services sector, specifically finance and insurance. In 2011, for instance, services made up more than half of total GDP with finance and insurance contributing 17% (Department of Statistics and Ministry of Finance, 2012).

Malaysia's adroitness in reacting to economic crisis and its ability to craft new terms to the NEP without further fragmenting its plural society shows its commitment to keep to a liberal economic regime, and its willingness to restructure its economic production given changes in factors and conditions. In fact, the state has been consistent in instituting economic diversification, which we will turn to now.

5.6 Instituting the diversification story

Since independence the state has been consistent in propagating the diversification narrative. Path dependence, timing and increasing returns have contributed in no small ways to this appetite for economic diversification. The increasing returns from sectors like manufacturing and services, the late entry of the oil and gas sector to the economy and the nature of the NEP that forces continued economic expansion made it easy for Malaysia to institute diversification and the need for continuous reform. Equally important, having the same ruling regime since independence also helps reinforce the diversification story and give policy consistency.

Malaysia has been consistent in instituting economic change and a diversification narrative. The 1970s, for instance, saw the introduction of a series of policies that sent the message about the need to diversify. In 1979 it introduced the National Energy Policy, the purpose of which was to develop alternative sources of energy to ensure adequate and cost effective energy supply. The National Energy Policy was supplemented by the National Depletion Policy in 1980 that focussed on the need to conserve finite and non-renewal resources. There were two other policy documents, both dealing with fuel diversification. The first was the four-fuel diversification policy in 1981, and the second was the five-fuel diversification strategy in 2001. However, the fuel diversification policy has not produced a varied mix of energy resources. The only consolation is that other than natural gas and oil, Malaysia now depends on coal for its energy needs. In fact, 80% of the country's energy comes from coal and natural gas (see Figures 5.1 and 5.2).

The past ten years also saw the state consistently repeating the need for Malaysia to trim its fiscal deficit – which stood at 3.5% of GDP in 2014 – and create new sources of economic growth. In February 2006 the government raised the price of fuel by 60%. This huge hike triggered public unrest and caused the Barisan Nasional (BN), the ruling party, to suffer its biggest electoral defeat in

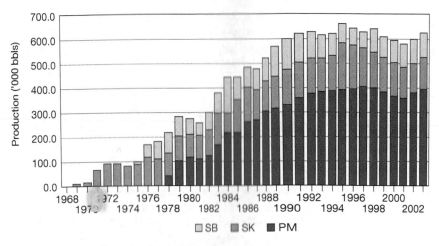

Figure 5.1 Crude oil production in Malaysia.

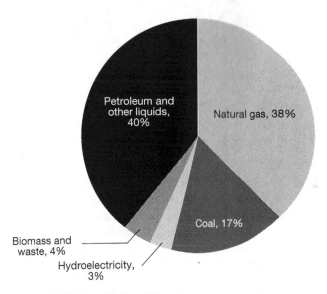

Figure 5.2 Malaysia's electricity mix.

March 2008. Undeterred, the regime continues to make a series of unpopular but necessary policy moves to impress the need to rationalise fuel subsidies. Subsidy rationalisation was given significant consideration under the Tenth Malaysia Plan (2010–2015) – the state's five-year development plan (Bridel and Lontoh, 2014). In 2010 the government produced a schedule to reduce subsidies for fuel, sugar and other products. In September 2013, four months after losing its two-thirds majority in the polls, the BN-led government announced a 20-sen rise for RON95 petrol and diesel fuel, the first increase since 2010. Days later it announced a 15-sen rise for RON 97 petrol. To press home the need to reinvigorate the economy the Najib administration announced, in late October 2013, that it would abolish the subsidy on sugar. To further drive the momentum of economic restructuring, Malaysia again announced in November 2014 that it would abolish subsidies for gasoline and diesel from December 2014.

The administration also took another political gamble when it announced the introduction of the goods and services tax (GST) starting in April 2015. To narrate the need for reform, it cited slow economic growth and the prospect of Malaysia losing out to foreign investment. Rating agencies' negative outlook on Malaysia also gave the administration added impetus to introduce the GST. To institute reform, the state went on a publicity drive to educate the public. It took great pains to point out that the GST would improve the fiscal position and help address tax leakages. The GST would go some way towards enabling fiscal flexibility and providing the state with greater luxury to improve corporate tax and provide investment incentives. To ameliorate public concerns the administration announced several policy measures to buffer any shocks from the introduction of the GST – from expanding the exclusion list to providing direct transfer payment (Noh, 2014a,b).

The series of tough but necessary policy measures have indeed impressed on the public about the need for pragmatic solutions and continued economic reform, which inadvertently adds to Malaysia's economic diversification story. However, instituting the diversification story and convincing the public to take on economic reform and move away from subsidies was never going to be easy. What has stood in Malaysia's favour is the state's track record at building a diversified and competitive economy, and its continued adoption of liberal economic principles.

5.7 Conclusion

While other resource-rich states have struggled to move away from their high dependence on natural resources, Malaysia seems to have made light work of the state's ability to drive economic diversification. To be fair, however, idiosyncrasies have had a hand in the Malaysian story. Timing, path dependence and increasing returns have made it easy for Malaysia to embark on a diversification strategy. The prior existence of a thriving private sector and the late development of commercial oil production facilitated the country's economic diversification efforts. Increasing returns from a thriving manufacturing and services sector made relying on oil and gas a less attractive option. Instituting the diversification story has also proven to be less onerous as the Malaysian public has developed an appetite for economic reforms. Having a ruling regime that has been in power since 1957 has also provided continuity and consistency in policy, which has further institutionalised the diversification story. Finally, Malaysia's consociational arrangement and the NEP provided unintended consequences; rather than limiting Malaysia's diversification effort, the NEP only served to promote it further. The redistributive nature of the NEP forces Malaysia to diversify as it is the only sure way to expand the economic cake – failing which the NEP and the regime would lose its legitimacy. Put differently, the constant pressure to conform to consociationalism and redistributive

Table 5.2 Malaysia's per cent share of GDP

Year	Agriculture	Forestry	Mining	Industry	Services
1960	47	n.a.	7.3	6.3	43.5
1970	30.8	17.6	6.3	13.4	51.3
1980	22.8	n.a	10.0	20.0	47.2
1990	19.4	n.a.	9.8	26.8	44.2

Sources: Drabble (2000); Ministry of Finance (1990).

policies helps ensure that the economy stays expansive, even if it demands crafting new terms of reference to the NEP/NDP. A neo-liberal would argue that the NEP is evil because it promotes economic distortion and creates a suboptimal allocation of resources (Gomez and Jomo, 1997). However, one could also argue that the NEP is a necessary evil because it disciplines Malaysia to maintain its diversification story. As Drabble (2000) points out, without the NEP and its target of eradicating poverty and tackling income inequality, 'it is unlikely that Malaysia's development experience would have been anywhere near as successful as we have seen'.

Notes

1   Malays or Bumiputeras form almost 60% of its population, with the economically successful Chinese community forming a quarter of the population and Indian, sub-ethnic and indigenous groups forming the remainder.
2   In fact, from time to time, proceeds from oil and gas still remain a contentious issue between federal and state government.
3   Lijphart's (1996) consociationalism refers to the presence of multiple ethnic groups of equal proportion in terms of their political power, which are prepared to come together in a political arrangement despite retaining their identities through agreements reached between leaders of these groups who act with the support of their ethnic communities.
4   In fact, in the 1980s official views held that Malaysian oil reserves could be exhausted in thirteen years if the state maintained oil production at 200,000 barrels per day.
5   The NEP was replaced by another document, the New Development Policy (NDP). However, analysts tend to use the two terms interchangeably.
6   Under the ICA of 1975, firms with over $100,000 in shareholder funds and more than twenty-five workers must obtain a license where they had to reserve at least 30% equity for bumiputeras. Under the revised scheme, only firms with over $2.5 million in shareholder funds and more than seventy-five workers would have to reserve 30% bumiputera equity.

References

Acemoglu, D.R.J.A. (2012) *Why nations fail: The origins of power, prosperity, and poverty*, New York, Crown Publishers.

Arthur, W.B. (1994) *Increasing returns and path dependence in the economy*, Ann Arbor: University of Michigan Press.

Auty, R. (2000) 'How natural resources affect economic development', *Development Policy Review*, vol. 18, 347–364.

Auty, R. (2001) 'The political economy of resource driven growth', *European Economic Review*, vol. 45, 839–846.

Bloomberg (2014) *Malaysia scraps fuel subsidies as Najib ends decades-old policy*, available online at www.bloomberg.com/news/2014-11-21/malaysia-scraps-fuel-subsidies-as-najib-ends-decades-old-policy.html (accessed 21 April 2016).

Bridel, A. and Lontoh, L. (2014) *Lesson learned: Malaysia's 2013 fuel subsidy reform*, Research Report, March, International Institute for Sustainable Development.

Collier, P. (2006) *Angola: Options for prosperity*, Oxford: University of Oxford.

David, P.A. (1985) 'Clio and the economics of QWERTY', *The American Economic Review*, vol. 75, no. 2, 332–337.

Department of Statistics and Ministry of Finance (2012) *In Malaysia Economic Report 2012/2013*, Kuala Lumpur, Malaysia.

Doraisami, A. (2012) 'Economic crisis and policy response in Malaysia: The role of the new economic policy', *Asian Pacific Economic Literature*, vol. 26, no. 2, 41–53.

Drabble, J.H. (2000) *An economic history of Malaysia, c. 1800–1990: The transition to modern economic growth*, New York and Canberra: St. Martin's Press (in association with the Australian National University).

Evans, P.B. (1995) *Embedded autonomy: States and industrial transformation*, Princeton, NJ: Princeton University Press.

Gale, B. (1981) 'Petronas: Malaysia's national oil corporation', *Asian Survey*, vol. 21, no. 11.

George, A. and Bennett, A. (2005) Case studies and theory development in the social sciences, London: MIT Press.

Ghee, L.T. and Woon, T.K. (1994) *Industrial restructuring and performance in Malaysia: Trade policy and industrialisation in turbulent times*, London: Routledge.

Global Competitiveness Report 2014–2015, World Economic Forum(WEF), Geneva, available online at www.weforum.org/gcr (accessed 21 April 2016).

Goldstone, J.A. (2006) 'Comparative historical analysis and knowledge accumulation in the study of revolutions', in Mahoney, J. and Rueschemeyer, D. (eds.), *Comparative historical analysis in the social sciences*, Cambridge: Cambridge University Press.

Gomez, E.T. and Jomo, K.S. (1997) Malaysia's political economy: Politics, patronage, and profits, Cambridge, New York: Cambridge University Press.

Gylfason, T. (2004) *Natural Resources and Economic Growth: From Dependence to Diversification*, Centre for Economic Policy Research (CEPR), Iceland: University of Iceland.

IMF (2015) *Favourable Prospects for Malaysia's Diversified Economy*, IMF Survey, March 3. Available at: www.imf.org/external/pubs/ft/survey/so/2015/car030315c.htm (accessed 21 April 2016).

Islam, I. and Chowdury, A. (eds.) (1997) *Asia Pacific economies*, London: Routledge.

Kaplan, E. and Rodrik, D. (2001) *Did the Malaysian capital control work?* NBER Working Paper 8142. Cambridge, MA: National Bureau of Economic Research.

Krasner, S. (1988) 'Sovereignty: An institutional perspective', *Comparative Political Studies*, vol. 21, 66–94.

Lall, S. (1995) 'Malaysia: Industrial success and the role of the government', *Journal of International Development*, vol. 7, no. 5, 759–773.

Lau, B.T. (2005) *Capital control and the Malaysian economy*, Kuala Lumpur: Pelanduk Publications.

Lee, K.H. (2010) Multiethnic Malaysia: Past, present and future, Kuala Lumpur: Strategic Information and Research Development.

Leete, R. (2007) *Malaysia: From Kampung to Twin Towers*, Kuala Lumpur: Oxford Fajar.

Levi, M. (1997) 'A model, a method, and a map: Rational choice in comparative and historical analysis', in Lichbach, M. and Zuckerman, A. (eds.), *Comparative politics: Rationality, culture, and structure,* Cambridge: Cambridge University Press: 19–41.

Lijphart, A. (1996) 'The puzzle of Indian democracy: A consociational interpretation', *The American Political Science Review,* vol. 90, no. 2, 258–268.

Mahathir, M. (2000) *Krisis matawang Malaysia: Bagaimana dan mengapa ia berlaku,* Kuala Lumpur: Pelanduk Publications.

Mahoney, J. (2000) 'Path dependence in historical sociology', *Theory and Society,* vol. 29, 507–48.

Malaysian Insider (2014) *Ringgit slide won't affect the economy, Wahid says,* 7 December, available at www.themalaysianinsider.com/malaysia/article/ringgit-slide-wont-affect-economy-adversely-says-wahid-bernama (accessed 21 April 2016).

Malik, A. and Temple, J. (2009) 'The geography of output volatility', *Journal of Development Economics,* vol. 90, no. 2, 163–178.

Mehlum, H., Moene, K.O. and Torvik, R. (2006) 'Institutions and the resource curse', *Economic Journal,* vol. 116, no. 508, 1–20.

Mehlum, H. et al. (2006) 'Cursed by resources or institutions', *The World Economy,* 1117–1131.

Noh, A. (2014a) 'Historical institutionalism and economic diversification: The case of Malaysia', *Asian Social Science,* vol. 10, no. 9, 40–51.

Noh, A. (2014b) 'Malaysia's dilemma: Economic reform but politics stay the same', in Singh, D (ed.) *Southeast Asian Affairs,* Singapore: Institute of Southeast Asian Studies.

North, D.C. (1990) *Institutions, institutional change, and economic performance,* Cambridge: Cambridge University Press.

Pemandu (2010) *Economic transformation programme: Oil and gas sector.* P.M.s.O. Malaysia. Kuala Lumpur, Government Press.

Pierson, P. (1993) 'Review: When effect becomes cause: Policy feedback and political change', *World Politics,* vol. 45, no. 4, 595–628.

Pierson, P. (2000) 'Increasing returns, path dependence, and the study of politics', *American Political Science Review,* vol. 94, 251–67.

Pierson, P. (2004) *Politics in time: History, institutions and social analysis,* Oxford: Princeton University Press.

Rahim, K.A. and Audrey, A. (2012) 'Oil and gas trends and implications in Malaysia', *Energy Policy,* vol. 50, 262–271.

Razalli, R. (2005) 'The Malaysian oil and gas industry: An overview', *Jurutera,* vol. 2005, no. 1.

Sewell, W.H. (1996) *Three temporalities: Toward an eventful sociology,* Ann Arbor: University of Michigan Press.

Streeck, W. and Thelen, K. (Eds.) (2005) *Beyond Continuity, Institutional Change in Advance Economies,* Oxford: Oxford University Press.

Thelen, K.A. (2006) 'How institutions evolve', in Mahoney, J. and Rueschemeyer, D. (eds.), *Comparative historical analysis in the social sciences,* Cambridge: Cambridge University Press.

The Sun Daily (2015a) *Malaysia ranked 14ᵗʰ most competitive nation,* 28 May.

The Sun Daily (2015b) *National Debt at RM 596.8 billion,* 19 May.

US Energy Information Administration Report (2014), available online at www.eia.gov/countries/cab.cfm?fips=my (accessed 21 April 2016).

Yudha, P. and Nakano, M. (2012) Exploring Malaysia's transformation to net oil importer and oil import dependence, *Energy 2012,* vol. 5, 2989–3018.

6 Diversification, Dutch disease and economic growth

Options for Uganda

Thorvaldur Gylfason and Jean-Pascal Nguessa Nganou

6.1 Introduction

Now that Uganda has discovered significant amounts of oil within its territory, there is a need to assess the experiences of other countries that have made similar natural resource discoveries in the past. Some of those countries have disappointingly little to show for their resource riches, while others – Botswana and Mauritius, for example – have fared quite well. Abundant natural resources sometimes tempt politicians to team up with rent-seekers focussed on the transfer of wealth rather than creation of wealth, often imparting a false sense of security, a feeling that abundant natural resource wealth somehow makes it unnecessary to accumulate human capital and social capital to lay a lasting foundation for inclusive economic growth.

According to Henstridge and Page (2012), Uganda's oil reserves are neither enormous nor trivial (Table 6.1). They will not catapult Uganda to quick success, but neither do they seem likely, on their own, to create serious macroeconomic trouble should things go awry. The oil discoveries announced in 2006 are expected to generate rather modest revenues equivalent to between 3% and 9% of GDP each year, over a period of twenty-five years (ending in 2045 or thereabouts). According to the new World Bank Country Economic Memorandum (World Bank, 2015), the Government estimates total oil reserves of Uganda at around 6.5 billion barrels, with recoverable reserves averaging 1.3 billion barrels. Based on this picture and assuming a long-term oil price of US$90/barrel, oil production in Uganda is expected to generate US$57 billion in government revenue between 2017/18 and 2044/45, through the government share of oil profits, royalties, income taxes, dividends and interest on the 15% government equity in oil fields. Additional government revenue will average US$2.1 billion per year (two thirds of domestic revenue in FY2013/14) and will reach US$4 billion in peak production years (2025 and beyond).

Recent economic growth literature suggests several ways of increasing GDP by comparable amounts or more, by encouraging saving, investment, social efficiency, and sound institutions (Acemoglu, 2009). Empirical evidence suggests that realistic increases in domestic saving and investment rates, school enrolment rates, foreign trade and investment, democracy, good governance and so on can

Table 6.1 Oil production in selected countries*

Country	Population (mil)	Oil Reserves (mil bbl)	Oil Reserves per capita (bbl)	Oil Production (mil bbl)	Oil Prod per capita (bbl)	Refined Petrol Production (mil bbl)	Refined Petrol Consumption (mil bbl)
Algeria	38.5	12,200	317	1.88	0.05	0.57	0.32
Angola	20.8	10,470	503	1.87	0.09	0.04	0.08
Chad	12.4	1,500	120	0.10	0.01	0.00	0.00
Congo	50.0	1,600	32	0.29	0.01	0.01	0.01
Egypt	80.7	4,400	55	0.72	0.01	0.60	0.82
Eq. Guinea	0.7	1,100	1,494	0.32	0.43	0.00	0.00
Gabon	1.6	2,000	1,225	0.24	0.15	0.02	0.02
Libya	6.2	48,010	7,801	1.48	0.24	0.39	0.31
Nigeria	168.8	37,200	220	2.52	0.01	0.10	0.27
Qatar	2.0	25,380	12,377	1.58	0.77	0.29	0.17
South Sudan	10.8	3,750	346	0.09	0.01		
Sudan	37.2	1,250	34	0.03	0.00	0.12	0.10
Uganda	36.4	6,500	179	0.00	0.00	0.00	0.02

Sources: Various, including World Bank, *World Development Indicators*, and CIA.
(*) Data years vary from 2010 to 2013 depending on country and indicator.

significantly encourage long-run economic growth (Spence et al., 2008). The revolution of living standards in several Asian countries since the 1960s seems by and large to support these findings. Recent evidence from Africa also points to significant progress, illustrated more clearly by various social indicators (decreasing child mortality and fertility, for example) than by standard economic indicators such as per capita GDP (Young, 2012). This suggests that, ideally, Uganda would need to make an all-out effort on many fronts at once, including strong, industry-standard emphasis on judicious management of its newfound oil wealth within an appropriate institutional setup.

Uganda's recent development and its initial position with oil production in its infancy are illustrated in Figure 6.1. Compared with Kenya, Tanzania and Ghana, the purchasing power of Uganda's gross national income (GNI) has lagged behind

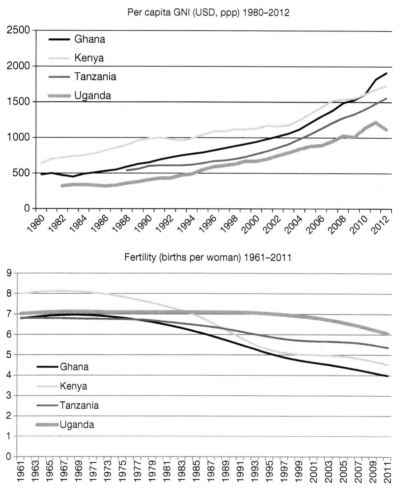

Figure 6.1 Uganda: incomes and family size.
(World Bank, World Development Indicators).

the other three countries over the past thirty years. The slow reduction in fertility in Uganda confirms this impression. Reduced fertility is a strong indicator of economic and social advances and of human capital formation in particular. This is explained by the fact that, in large families, relatively fewer children have full access to the education opportunities that their parents would like them to have if they could afford it. At fifty-eight years in 2012, life expectancy at birth in Uganda remains two to three years below that in Kenya, Tanzania and Ghana, just as it was in 1961 (except Tanzania and Uganda were then about even at forty-four years). Among many other things, economic progress means moving from short lives in large families to long lives in small families. Reduced fertility is both a cause and a consequence of rising incomes. This explains why social policies, including family planning, have taken centre stage on Uganda's growth agenda, in addition to economic policies aiming to promote saving and investment, as well as increased efficiency through more and better education, infrastructure, foreign trade and institutional reforms (Gylfason, 2012).

With many remaining opportunities still to be exploited in full, Uganda faces bright prospects for economic growth. How can Uganda assess and emulate the experience of those countries that have successfully managed their oil discoveries? How can Uganda avoid the mistakes made by those that did less well? This chapter addresses these questions selectively by emphasising economic and political diversification away from excessive dependence on oil and other natural resources, as well as aspects of the Dutch disease and how to stay clear of it.

6.2 Diversification and the Dutch disease

Concerning diversification, including the need to transform oil wealth into other types of growth-friendly wealth including human resources and social capital, there exists no universally acknowledged blueprint for such a transformation. Even so, a number of influential ideas about economic diversification have emerged from the academic literature, as well as from policy debates. These ideas are derived from economic analysis, and from the experience of several countries around the world that have managed to successfully diversify their economies and support sustainable and equitable management of the extractive sector for human development. These economies have also emphasised the need for transparency in the management and disbursal of natural resource rents (see e.g. Gelb, 2011; Hausmann et al., 2014).

Mauritius is a case in point. Frankel (2012) shows how Mauritius managed to reduce its reliance on its main export commodity (sugar), mainly by expanding foreign trade as well as improving education. The share of manufactures in merchandise exports increased from a minuscule amount in 1970 to about 60% in recent years, compared with 35% in Uganda and Kenya and 25% in Tanzania. Exports of goods and services from Mauritius are at present equivalent to more than half of its GDP, compared with 25% to 30% in Uganda, Kenya and Tanzania. Mauritius has kept inflation under control, which is a sign of essentially sound fiscal and monetary policies. From 1981 to 2012, inflation in Mauritius was 7%

per year on average, compared with 38% in Uganda, 13% in Kenya and 19% in Tanzania (World Bank, *World Development Indicators*). These efforts have paid off. Since 1980 the economy of Mauritius has grown in tandem with that of Botswana, Africa's richest country in terms of the purchasing power of its per capita GNI. Those comparisons and experiences are relevant to Uganda.

Transparency is fundamental to natural resource management, and is fostered by openness – 'glasnost', for example. This could be achieved through the involvement of international expert groups – e.g. independent NGOs such as Revenue Watch or other trusted advisors – who may be asked to guide the government on methods of resource management and ways to stave off rent seeking and corruption that otherwise, without appropriate checks and balances, might be difficult to avert. In this context, capacity development and institution building are key, including legal safeguards for a free press and an independent judiciary. Full and unfettered transparency can be to natural resource management what effective financial supervision can be to the banking sector. In other words, it is an essential complement, without which natural resource rents may be dissipated without benefitting the state or the people, the rightful owners of the resources by international law. The 'old economic geography', emphasising the economic and strategic importance of abundant natural resources, now shares the stage with the 'new economic geography' that acknowledges the fact that many countries have managed to prosper without any natural resource possessions (land-locked Switzerland is a case in point, as is Austria), while other countries have languished for long periods despite significant, sometimes even huge, natural resource endowments and discoveries. This observation gave rise to the literature on the 'resource curse', by which is meant the possibility that natural resource wealth, if not well managed, may prove to be a mixed blessing (Sachs and Warner, 1995; for a review, see Van der Ploeg, 2011). The resource curse works through various mechanisms, not least the Dutch disease in its different guises, including an overvaluation of the currencies of resource-rich countries, and the volatility of exchange rates, export revenues and output, in addition to other channels of transmission to be discussed below.

The exchange rate channel of the Dutch disease is clear. A boost to foreign exchange earnings following a natural resource discovery increases the supply of foreign exchange in the domestic market, thus driving down the price of foreign exchange and making the local currency appreciate in real terms. This means that total exports – that is, resource plus non-resource exports – will rise mainly as a result of the increase in resource exports. Meanwhile, non-resource exports will fall, as they cannot compete as easily in foreign markets when the currency rises in value, since a higher value of the currency translates into fewer local currency units (e.g. Uganda Shillings) earned from each foreign currency unit (e.g. dollar or euro) of export earnings. Therefore, rising currency values in natural resource-rich countries may undermine the exports of manufactures and services, weakening the long-run economic growth potential of the resource-rich country even as a boost to total export earnings can fuel economic activity in the short term. There is no inconsistency involved here. Just as increased consumption at the expense of national saving tends to increase output in the short run and reduce its rate of growth in the long run, a natural resource discovery – or, for that matter, a commodity price boom – can boost economic activity in the short run while undermining efficiency and economic growth potential over the long haul.

If it takes hold, the Dutch disease may impact Uganda through both the agriculture and tourism sectors. As elsewhere, agriculture in Uganda is bound to contract over time in terms of both manpower use, currently at about two thirds of total employment, and its share of GDP, currently about a quarter, as modern farming methods necessitate fewer and fewer working hands to feed the population, a process that would be accelerated by a rising real exchange rate reducing the profitability of farm exports. On the other hand, tourism faces no natural constraints apart from environmental considerations, but may also suffer from reduced profitability due to an appreciation of the shilling in real terms as well as from price hikes for services triggered by expatriate workers in the oil sector. Tourism, the oil sector and emerging industries (Hausmann et al., 2014) need to be positioned to train and absorb unskilled workers leaving the agriculture sector. To this end, the CEM argues that Uganda should scale up its diversification efforts by focussing its diversification strategy on light manufactured exports (garments, leather and wood products) as these products do not require sophisticated skills, which are not readily available in Uganda, and would use the large pool of unskilled and semi-skilled workers available in the country. Other opportunities include agriculture-related processing industries (cereals, dairy products, more types of cooking oils and new sugar products) and the existing chemicals and metal product industries (World Bank, 2015).

In another guise, the Dutch disease often manifests itself through import protection or subsidies which reduce the demand for foreign exchange, thereby lowering the price of foreign currencies and contributing to an appreciation of the local currency, with deleterious consequences for export firms as well as local industries competing with imports. Often, the same political forces favour the protection of selected domestic industries against foreign competition and the indirect subsidisation of the natural-resource-based industries by not charging them enough for their extraction rights. In addition, taxing the resource revenues of these domestic industries too lightly could lead to significant overvaluation of the currency and associated balance of payments and external debt problems as a result. This aspect of the Dutch disease brings fiscal policy into the story because it often takes a fiscal correction to create conditions for establishing a competitive value of the local currency.

The advent of oil will confront Uganda with an even greater need than before to exercise fiscal and monetary restraint for the purpose of keeping inflation in check, while at the same time countering the tendency toward overvaluation of the shilling. This may be quite a challenge because an appreciation of the currency in real terms reduces inflation in the short term, creating a policy bias in favour of appreciation as an auxiliary instrument in the fight against inflation. Therefore, keeping inflation under control by other means, i.e. with fiscal and monetary restraint, without resorting to real appreciation of the shilling, becomes even more important than before. This is a relevant consideration in view of the fact that the Ugandan shilling has depreciated in nominal terms by 18% per year on average since 1986, compared with 6% in Kenya and 14% in neighbouring Tanzania.

Volatility is a separate issue. Volatility of commodity prices produces fluctuations in exchange rates, export earnings, output and employment, thereby discouraging investment and growth (Aghion and Banerjee, 2005). For this reason as well, natural-resource rich countries may be prone to sluggish investment and slow growth due to export price volatility. In like manner, high and volatile exchange rates tend to slow down investment and growth.

Since 1960 oil exporting countries have withstood sharp price volatility, which can be attributed to several exogenous factors including political events in oil-producing countries, hurricanes in the Gulf of Mexico, and increasing global demand for petroleum products. Matovu and Nganou (2015) present a brief survey of empirical studies discussing how pro-cyclical fiscal policies are in OPEC states. Budget financing constraints are often mentioned among the main factors underlying pro-cyclical fiscal policies. Frankel (2011) argues that an inflation-targeting monetary policy that emphasises export commodities (Product Price Targeting) could render countercyclical fiscal policies more effective. As proposed by Frankel (2011), countries should adopt fiscal policies that emulate the Chilean example. Chile has been successful in avoiding over-spending in boom times while only allowing deviations from a target surplus in response to permanent commodities price changes (Matovu and Nganou, 2015).

6.3 From natural capital to diverse kinds of capital

Several further channels through which natural resource wealth may prove to be a mixed blessing independently of exchange rates have been identified in recent growth literature. These channels can be placed under the headings of human, physical, social and financial capital.

Human capital

Countries rich in natural resources may lose sight of the need to build up human capital through education and training. There is some evidence that resource-rich countries tend to allocate a smaller share of their national income to education and send fewer children and adolescents to school than do countries which have fewer natural resources but are at the same general income level (Gylfason, 2001, 2012). One possible explanation for this observed pattern is that in resource-rich countries a false sense of economic security may be created, causing the authorities and perhaps also some segments of the population to lose sight of the need to build up human capital. This phenomenon is well known in human affairs. Wealthy parents sometimes have difficulty convincing their children to acquire an education or even to work. Why work if you can play? Even so, for the majority of the poor population, access to education continues to be constrained by low income. Education and job training are always beneficial and desirable, and should therefore always be a high priority. This is even more relevant for a country like Uganda where only 20% of the labour force has completed at least secondary education, compared with 50% in Ghana (Figure 6.2). Moreover, UNESCO's school life expectancy[1] for Uganda is eleven years (as in Kenya), compared with twelve years in Tanzania, Ghana and Botswana, fourteen years in Mauritius, and seventeen years in the United Kingdom.

Physical capital

If this is so, the argument can be extended to other kinds of investment, for example, in physical capital. The quality of physical capital is hard to gauge, however. National income accounts do not yet distinguish between productive and unproductive investment expenditures because investment, like other expenditure, is measured by input rather than by output. The point is simple: natural-resource-rich countries may be less careful about the quality of the investments they make in real capital than countries with few resources, because resource-poor countries can ill afford to make mistakes. Many resource-rich countries are littered with white elephants. Clearly, improving the efficiency of public investment management (PIM) in terms of the appraisal, selection, implementation and evaluation of projects could enlarge the fiscal space for developing countries to invest in the infrastructure much needed for their growth and development. However, the 2011 Public Investment Management Index (PIMI) of the World Bank and the IMF, which ranks countries in terms of the quality of public investment, is a good indicator of the quality of physical capital. For a new resource-rich country such as Uganda, the efficiency of public expenditure will be crucial in order to prepare for the advent of resources from oil and other extractives.

Social capital

The same argument applies to social capital in its many guises. Here, social capital is the societal infrastructure that keeps economic activity humming along efficiently, including governance, independent judiciaries, freedom of the press, trust, equality and the absence of corruption and political oppression (for a review, see Paldam, 2000). There is some evidence that just as natural capital, if not judiciously managed, tends to crowd out human and physical capital, it can also crowd out social capital in several dimensions. For example, countries rich in natural resources tend to be awarded lower governance scores according to the Ibrahim index of African governance. Of the twelve African countries that produce oil in commercial quantities, six are among the bottom 20% in the Ibrahim ranking of governance that includes Safety and Rule of Law, Participation and Human Rights, Sustainable Economic Opportunity, and Human Development (Ampratwum and Ashon, 2012). Of the fifty-two African countries ranked by the Ibrahim index in 2013, Uganda ranks at eighteen, compared with twenty-one for Kenya, seventeen for Tanzania and seven for Ghana. On a scale from eight (Somalia) to eighty-three (Mauritius), Uganda scores fifty-six, Kenya fifty-four, Tanzania fifty-seven and Ghana sixty-seven. Table 6.2 provides some further figures on aspects of the oil sector, physical capital, and social capital in thirteen African countries, including Uganda.

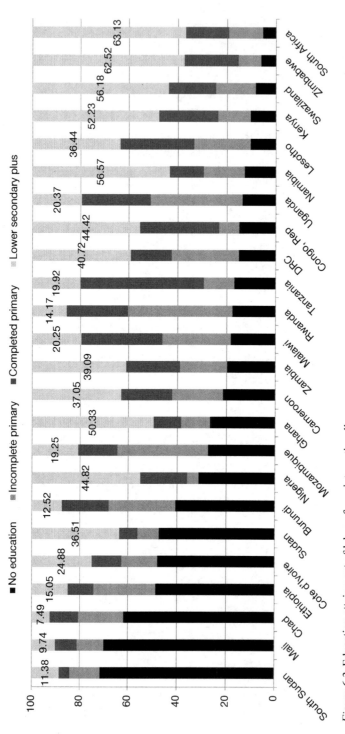

Figure 6.2 Education attainment of labour force internationally.
(Uganda Bureau of Statistics. 2010).

Table 6.2 Oil, physical capital and social capital in selected countries*

Country	GNI (Bn USD)	Gov Oil Rev (% of GDP)	Headcount Poverty ratio (%)	Public Inv (% of GDP)	Private Inv (% GDP)	FDI (% of GDP)	Rail	% Paved Roads	Urban Population growth (%)	Global Competitiveness Index (Rank out of 148)
Algeria	203.6	25.2	23.0	14.4	26.3	11.1	3,973	77.1	3.0	100
Angola	102.6	34.4	40.5	9.0	6.0	14.9	2,764	10.4	4.4	142
Chad	9.8	15.6	80.0	12.5	16.3	34.9	0	0.5	3.4	148
Congo	10.8	2.1		0.0	0.0	0.0	886	5.0	3.3	
Egypt	256.4	0.0	20.0	0.0	0.0	29.4	5,083	92.0	2.0	118
Equ. Guinea	11.0	18.5		19.6	31.4	0.0	0	0.0	3.2	
Gabon	16.4	16.5		13.8	17.2	0.0	649	12.0	2.8	112
Libya	0.0	69.2	33.0	4.9	11.6	20.6	0	57.2	1.1	108
Nigeria	241.3	21.5	70.0	6.4	16.1	28.4	3,505	15.0	4.0	120
Qatar	0.0	24.2		14.4	14.0	16.7			7.2	13
South Sudan	9.3	0.0	50.6	0.0	0.0	0.0	236	0.0	5.4	
Sudan	56.4	2.8	46.5	0.0	0.0	0.0	5,978	36.3	2.5	
Uganda	16.8	1.4	24.5	7.6	12.7	…	1,224	16.3	6.0	129

Sources: Various, including WDI and IMF.
(*) Data years vary from 2010 to 2013 depending on country and indicator.

Countries rich in natural resources also tend to be awarded lower corruption perception rankings, suggesting more corruption, according to Transparency International. Examples abound. Further, there is evidence that resource-rich countries tend to be less democratic than countries with fewer natural resources, if democracy is measured by the Polity IV index compiled by political scientists at the University of Maryland, for instance. Further, there is some empirical evidence to suggest that income inequality as measured by the Gini coefficient, for example, is generally greater in resource-rich countries than in countries with fewer natural resources (Gylfason and Zoega, 2003). Quantitative indicators of trust – e.g. the confidence that people say they have in their countries' institutions such as banks or courts or media – are quite recent and have not yet been included in statistical research on the relationship between natural resources and economic growth, but they are gaining ground.

Financial capital

Abundant natural resources may also crowd out financial capital by holding back the emergence of a well-developed financial system, and producing an inefficient allocation of savings across industries and firms by weakening incentives to save and invest. When a significant part of a country's national wealth takes the form of natural resources, whether renewable or non-renewable, there is less need for banks and other financial institutions to facilitate everyday transactions. The country can save through less rapid depletion or more rapid renewal with renewable natural resources, or it can spend through more rapid depletion of the natural resource (Arezki and Gylfason, 2011; Gylfason and Zoega, 2006). Empirical evidence suggests that financial development is a significant source of economic growth, physical capital accumulation, and improvements in the efficiency of capital allocation (King and Levine, 1993a, 1993b). If so, natural resource dependence may go along with financial backwardness, thereby hindering efficient capital deepening and economic growth.

All in all, natural capital differs from other kinds of capital – human capital, physical capital, social capital, and financial capital – in one key fashion: the other types of capital never give rise to calls for diversification away from them. No country has ever felt economically challenged by its abundance of or dependence on its human or social capital. Natural capital is different because experience seems to suggest that it sometimes sets in motion processes – the Dutch disease through overvalued and volatile currencies, rent seeking, plundering, lack of respect for democracy, and neglect of the need for accumulating other kinds of capital and for economic diversity essential for social efficiency and growth – that may undermine long-run economic growth.

6.4 Rent seeking, subsidies and transparency

A further channel through which plentiful natural resources may hamper economic efficiency and growth is rent seeking (Krueger, 1974). Output produced from natural resources differs from many other commodities in that it costs very little to produce relative to the earnings it generates. For example, an oil shipment that can be sold for a million dollars may have cost only $200,000 to produce, leaving a rent of $800,000 in the pocket of the producer. This helps explain why, if the property rights of the people to their natural resources are not well protected, natural resource wealth may attract unscrupulous people to politics.

An example may help. Citing a report from Citigroup, the *Financial Times* reported on 9 July 2011 that the retail value of Russia's natural resources amounted to about $650 billion per year while the cost of production amounted to roughly $150 billion. If so, Russia's natural resource rent amounts to about $500 billion each year, an amount equivalent to around a fifth of Russia's annual GDP measured in terms of purchasing power. Clearly, it matters greatly to whom the rent accrues and how it is divided among the recipients. According to the Citigroup report, more than 60% ($310 billion) of Russia's natural resource rent originates in the oil sector, about a third ($160 billion) in the natural gas sector, and the rest in the minerals sector. The report states that 58% of the rent accrues to the state through taxes and that another 18% accrues to consumers through subsidies on gasoline, among other things. That makes a total of 76% of the rent. A sixth of the rent, or 16%, is devoted to investment, according to the report, and the rest, 8%, accrues to shareholders, including oligarchs. These figures are cited here only to give a ballpark idea of the amounts and proportions involved; other studies may well arrive at different figures. For comparison, about 80% of the oil rent in Norway has accrued to the state over the years through taxes, royalties etc., with minimal subsidies involved.

Many if not most oil-rich countries choose to subsidise gasoline at a high cost in terms of inefficiency and associated deadweight losses (Aguinaga et al., 2014). Selling fuel at cost price at home rather than on the world market price, even including taxes, is tantamount to a subsidy on fuel. Subsidising fuel is inherently inefficient because selling domestically produced fuel at home at a lower price than could be fetched in the world market deprives producers of revenues, thereby reducing national income. Artificially inexpensive fuel discourages firms and households from conserving energy, inviting waste.

Further, the indirect subsidy involved discriminates against those recipients who might have preferred other things had the subsidy been paid out in cash rather than in kind as cheap fuel, as well as against those who do not use much fuel, perhaps because they cannot afford a car. A tax on petrol aimed at bringing its price at the pump closer to world market prices would raise revenue to finance education, health care and infrastructure. If the tax proceeds are used to bolster the education system, the fuel subsidy is, in effect, replaced by a subsidy to education. Prices at the pump span a wide range, even across oil producing states. In 2012, gasoline at the pump cost 16c/litre in Saudi Arabia, 23c in Kuwait, 62c in Nigeria, and $2.53 in Norway compared with 97c in the United States and $1.23 in Botswana. In Uganda, the price of gasoline per litre was $1.31, $1.37 in Kenya, $1.42 in Tanzania, and 92c in Ghana (World Bank, World Development Indicators).

Resistance to the temptation to divert part of the newfound oil to the domestic market to reduce energy prices at home – for example, to impress voters – signals a strong commitment to sound natural resource management and to socially efficient macroeconomic policies.

Rent seeking, especially when accompanied by ill-defined property rights, imperfect or missing markets and lax legal structures, tends to divert resources away from more socially fruitful economic activity. This is where transparency can be helpful by increasing public awareness of counterproductive behaviour patterns, thereby providing incentives for rent seekers to put their best foot forward. Recent international initiatives to raise transparency have proved encouraging in many countries, including the Extractive Industries Transparency Initiative (EITI) which aims to set a global standard for transparency in oil, gas and mining, the Revenue Watch Institute (RWI) which promotes responsible management of oil, gas and mineral resources, and the Natural Resource Charter (NRC) which has set out principles for how to manage natural resources for development. Like Ghana and Tanzania, Uganda must become an EITI compliant country, meeting all the requirements in the EITI standard. According to Revenue Watch, Uganda needs to do more to promote transparency to 'provide citizens with substantial amounts of information about revenue from the extractive sector'.

As yet, Uganda has not been included in the Revenue Watch's Revenue Governance Index (RGI), which measures the quality of governance in the oil, gas, and mining sectors of fifty-eight countries, only eleven of which are reported to have satisfactory standards of transparency and accountability. The RGI scores and ranks countries based on a detailed questionnaire completed by researchers with expertise in the extractive industries, assessing the quality of four key governance components: Institutional and Legal Setting, Reporting Practices, Safeguards and Quality Controls, and Enabling Environment. The index also reflects information on state-owned companies, natural resource funds, and subnational revenue transfers; three special mechanisms commonly used to govern oil, gas and minerals. Opening the doors to and collaborating with the aforementioned international non-government organisations is an essential aspect of the checks and balances needed to foster the best possible natural resource management regime.

Rent seeking is often closely linked to corruption, a serious issue in many resource-rich countries as evidenced by the corruption perceptions index issued by Transparency International, using a scale from 1 (corrupt) to 100 (clean). Of the twenty-two largest oil-producers around the world, only four (the United States, the United Kingdom, Canada and Norway – the sole full-fledged democracies in the group) have corruption perceptions indices above 70, while the remaining eighteen countries range from 16 (Iraq) to 69 (the United Arab Emirates). A similar pattern is observed in the numbers reported recently by Gallup (2013). Asked in 2012 whether corruption is widespread throughout the government of their country, 25% of the roughly one thousand adults aged fifteen years or older said yes in Norway, 43% in the United Kingdom, 46% in Canada, and 73% in the United States compared with 62% to 92% for all other oil producing countries.

Both sets of figures suggest that corruption generally thrives less well under democracy than under autocracy, presumably because democratic rule is more conducive to the establishment of institutional structures and mechanisms and international cooperation which act to restrain corruption (Gylfason, 2012). Without adequate checks and balances, despots usually find it more alluring than democrats to engage in corrupt practices, and often manage to do so with impunity. Even so, corruption is rampant in some democracies. Even before the advent of oil corruption is a serious macroeconomic concern in Uganda, rated 26 by Transparency International, as compared to 27 for Kenya, 33 for Tanzania and 46 for Ghana (higher scores suggest less corruption). Gallup projects a slightly different picture, reporting that 81% of Ugandans think that corruption is widespread throughout the government of their country, compared with 93% in Kenya, 95% in Tanzania and 89% in Ghana. These results bring home the crucial importance of transparency as an effective remedy against corruption in business and government, and its potentially corrosive effects on growth.

Figure 6.3 provides a snapshot of the cross-country evidence linking corruption to natural resources and economic growth in a large group of countries (an increase in the corruption perceptions index means less corruption, or more honesty; hence, the positive correlation between the corruption perceptions index and income shown in Figure 6.3 suggests that honesty is good for growth).[2]

Each country is represented by a bubble, the size of which is proportional to the country's population in 2012, making China and India easy to identify in the figure.[3] Notice that in the figure, and in the others to follow, Uganda is generally positioned close to (i.e. not too distant from) the trend line.

In the top panel of Figure 6.3 we see that corruption, as measured by Transparency International in 2013, is directly correlated across 140 countries with the share of natural capital in tangible capital in 2005 (World Bank, 2006). The Pearson correlation between the corruption perceptions index and the natural capital share is -0.75. The slope of the unweighted regression line through the scatter on the left suggests an economically as well as statistically significant relationship between corruption and natural capital's share of tangible capital. This matters because corruption is inversely correlated to per capita GNI across the 151 countries shown in the rightmost panel, where growth is represented by the log of purchasing power parity (PPP) of per capita GNI in 2012 on the grounds that the level of current income reflects its rate of growth in the past. The use of only the end-of-period value of per capita GNI for each country rules out reverse causation from growth to corruption.

The Pearson correlation between corruption and income is significant at 0.74, a finding that corroborates the econometric results of Mauro (1995), among others. If countries could be viewed as moving up or down along the regression line, the slope of the line would suggests that a decrease in corruption by 40 points, corresponding roughly to the difference between Angola (23) and Botswana (64), would make per capita GNI rise by a factor of three, *ceteris paribus*. The effect would in fact be smaller than this because of the two-dimensional nature of the chart which does not reflect other relevant determinants of growth, thus assigning

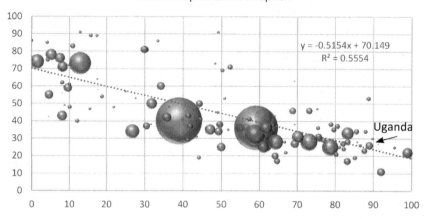
Natural capital and corruption

$y = -0.5154x + 70.149$
$R^2 = 0.5554$

Uganda

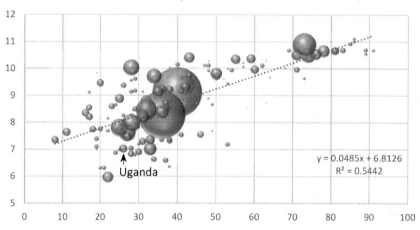
Corruption and income

$y = 0.0485x + 6.8126$
$R^2 = 0.5442$

Uganda

Figure 6.3 Uganda: corruption, natural capital and income.
(Authors' computations based on World Bank, World Development Indicators and Transparency International).

too much weight to corruption, the one determinant shown. The same caveat applies to the remaining bivariate correlations to be presented in what follows. Incidentally, in 2012 there was a threefold difference between purchasing-power-parity-adjusted per capita GNI in Botswana and Angola.

The take-away in this scenario is that if a large share of natural capital in total tangible capital creates temptations that prove conducive to corruption, and if corruption hurts growth, then this constellation of mechanisms may help explain part of the resource curse – that is, why a high natural capital share may be detrimental to growth.

6.5 Two dimensions of diversification

Specialisation in production for export is one of the keys to realising gains from domestic and foreign trade. However, there can be too much of a good thing, for two reasons. First, excessive specialisation can increase risk. Should the specialised sector be hurt, if it is too dominant, its problems may then inflict extensive damage on the rest of the national economy, causing economic collateral damage. This is why economic diversification is a useful tool to mitigate risk. Second, the specialised sector needs to be one without significant adverse spillover effects on other sectors. No country has ever felt the need to diversify away from excessive reliance on human capital, but natural capital is another story. Its negative externalities are manifest in many countries, and include rampant rent seeking, environmental degradation and repeated bouts of the Dutch disease.

As a general principle diversification is good for growth, in part because it reduces the risk of Dutch disease (Page, 2008). For example: economic diversification encourages efficiency and growth by channelling economic activity away from primary production in agriculture or excessive reliance on a few natural-resource-based industries, thus helping workers or their sons and daughters to transfer from low-paying jobs in low-skill-intensive farming or mining to more lucrative employment in more high-skill-intensive occupations in manufacturing and services. This is how countries become rich: technological advances release workers from agriculture, because in modern societies technological progress has meant that it takes only a tiny proportion of the workforce to feed the population, a task that not so long ago occupied virtually the entire labour force.

As an example, South Korea's export-oriented diversification strategy helped catapult the country from rags to riches in fifty years, in stark contrast to the import substitution strategies followed by several Latin American countries which yielded less impressive results. In 1960 Korea's exports of goods and services amounted to 3% of GDP, compared with 8% in Argentina. In 2012 Korea's exports of goods and services amounted to 57% of GDP, compared with 20% in Argentina. Further, manufactured goods constituted 85% of Korea's merchandise exports compared with 32% in Argentina. As a result, Korean manufacturers know how to produce things that households and firms in other countries demand, and today the purchasing power of Korea's per capita GNI is more than twice that of Argentina.

The impressive record of Botswana is also relevant here. Botswana gained independence in 1966, having only twelve kilometres of paved roads, twenty-two college graduates and one hundred secondary-school graduates. Today, diamonds (discovered in 1967) provide tax revenue equivalent to 33% of GDP, giving Botswana sub-Saharan Africa's highest per capita GNI. How did Botswana manage to achieve the world's highest rate of economic growth over the past fifty years?

The short answer is good policies, good institutions and democracy. Botswana assigned mining rights away from the tribes toward the state to head off tribal contestation for revenue, paid civil servants well, and hired foreign experts where needed (Gelb, 2011). Furthermore, Botswana has emphasised quality appraisals of public investment projects. Even so, Botswana's economy is not yet well diversified. At present manufacturing accounts for only 6% of GDP, while 30% of the workforce remains in agriculture which accounts for only 2% of GDP, suggesting low productivity in agriculture. Services, including government services, employ 55% of the labour force and account for 52% of GDP. Botswana spends more money on education relative to GDP and is less corrupt according to Transparency International than any other African country (Botswana 64, Mauritius 52).

Other relevant examples of diversification include: Indonesia, where the authorities provided help to the low-cost textiles and footwear industry with good results; Thailand, which diversified its agriculture; Malaysia, which opened its arms to foreign direct investment to become a successful producer of manufactured goods, including electronic equipment and cars; and Chile, where the authorities encouraged farmers to branch out into wine and salmon production as New Zealand had done in the 1980s, also with good results. These examples of success suggest that industrial policy is not always doomed to failure (Rodrik, 2004). Picking winners seldom works, but even so, cutting losses can be fruitful. Industrial policy is prone to political capture and corruption, but so is privatisation. Corrupt privatisation is a symptom of corruption, not of privatisation. The same applies to industrial policy. Generally, it pays to encourage new industries in line with the country's comparative advantages and available expertise in public administration rather than try to break new ground; to follow the market rather than try to take the lead. A promising industrial policy strategy needs to be based on general principles and tailored to specific circumstances, not one-size-fits-all; simply more of the same is unlikely to succeed (Hausmann et al., 2014).

There is more to diversification than meets the eye. Economic and political diversification can be viewed as two sides of the same coin (Gylfason and Wijkman, this volume). Just as economic diversification spurs growth by transferring labour from low-paying jobs in low-skill-intensive farming and mining to more lucrative jobs in more high-skill-intensive occupations, political diversification spurs growth by redistributing political power from narrowly based ruling elites to the people, giving way to political competition, democracy and pluralism. Put differently, political diversification through democratisation, exemplified by the promotion of electoral competitiveness, openness and popular participation, can be viewed as an investment in social capital, including strong civil society, good governance and societal institutions that people can trust (Paldam, 2000).

The essence of the argument is the same in both cases. Diversity pays by redistributing risk. Modern mixed economies need broadly-based manufacturing, trade and services to be able to offer the people steady improvements in their standard of living. An important part of a country's economic success is defined by its ability to produce goods and services that it can sell abroad – that is, goods and services that households and firms in other countries want to buy. Hence the need to find ways to diversify economic activity away from once-dominant agriculture that tends to keep the rural population in poverty, and also from too much dependence on a few natural resources that sometimes (but not always) stifle or delay the advance of modern manufacturing and services. To function smoothly and grow at a rapid pace, national economies generally need broad political participation and a broad base of power in order to be able to offer all citizens an efficient and fair way of exercising their political will and civic rights through free elections, freedom of information, free assembly and so on. Without political democracy, bad governments tend to become heavily entrenched, and the resulting damage becomes nearly insurmountable.

There is some evidence that the positive effects of democracy on long-run economic growth may outweigh the negative effects which may arise from political dissent derailing economic activity. The latter argument has been and still is used in China and some other countries to this day, as in South Korea before the country became a democracy in the late 1980s (Gylfason, 2012).[4] The need for diversification may be especially pressing in many resource-rich countries because they often face a double jeopardy – that is, natural-resource wealth concentrated in the hands of small groups that seek to preserve their own privileges by opposing both economic and political diversification that would disperse their power and wealth. Rent-seekers often resist reforms – economic diversification as well as democracy – that would redistribute the rents more evenly among the population (Auty, 2001; Ross, 2001).

The structure of exports with regard to manufactured goods and other products is important for long-run economic growth, among other things. The top panel of Figure 6.4 illustrates the strong inverse cross-country relationship between manufactured exports, measured by the average share of manufactured goods in total merchandise exports (from 1962 to 2012) and natural capital in 126 countries (Pearson correlation = -0.82). In the right panel, as before growth is represented by the log purchasing power of per capita GNI in 2012 to rule out reverse causation from growth to manufactured exports. The relationship across 139 countries is significant in a statistical sense (Pearson correlation = 0.63) as well as in an economic sense. The slope of the regression line (0.029) means that a twenty-point increase in the manufacturing share (e.g. from 40% to 60%) goes along with an increase in real per capita GNI by well over a half (*viz.*, by 58%).

A similar pattern emerges if economic diversification is represented directly by the diversification of exports as measured by one minus the Herfindahl index, which shows whether the structure of exports by product of a given country differs from the world average. The index ranges from zero to one, with values closer to one indicating a larger difference from the world average. Hence, one minus the Herfindahl index rises with diversification. In Figure 6.5, the top panel shows an inverse cross-country relationship between export diversification on average from 1996 (the earliest year available from UNCTAD) to 2012 and natural capital, measured as before in a group of 126 countries (Pearson correlation = -0.70). The right panel shows a strong positive link between export diversification and income per capita across 147 countries (Pearson correlation = 0.66). The slope of the regression line (5.58) means that a twenty-point increase in the export diversification index, corresponding roughly to the difference between Norway's 0.61 and Nigeria's 0.78, would more than double per capita GNI.

Natural capital and manufacturing

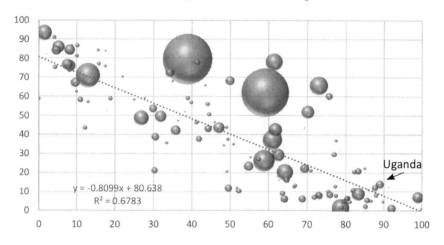

Manufacturing and income

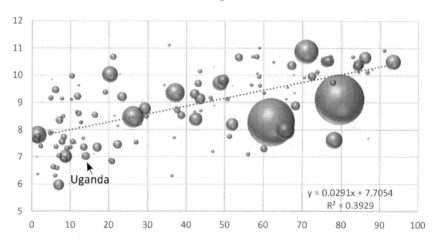

Figure 6.4 Uganda: from manufactured exports to growth.
(Authors' computations based on World Bank and World Development Indicators).

With expanding trade, economic diversification is on the rise around the world. In sub-Saharan Africa, the share of manufactured goods in total merchandise exports increased from 12% in 1974 to 27% in 2012, which is down from 32% in 2002 (World Bank, World Development Indicators). In Latin America and the Caribbean, for comparison, the share of manufactured goods in total merchandise exports increased from 8% in 1962 to 46% in 2012. Likewise, the world average share of manufactures in total exports rose from 59% to 69% over the same period (same source). In Uganda, the share of manufactured goods in total merchandise exports rose from 2% in 1994 to 34% in 2012, which is a good sign for growth. For comparison, the manufacturing share of exports in 2012 was 35% in Kenya,

Natural capital and diversification

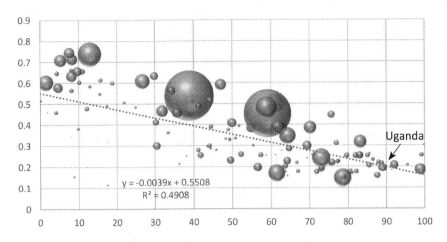

Export diversification and income

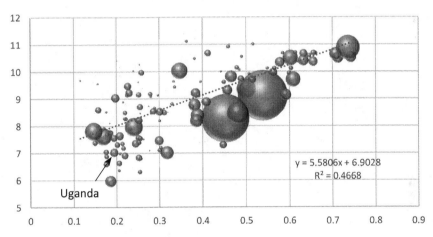

Figure 6.5 Uganda: from export diversification to growth.
(Authors' computations based on World Bank, World Development Indicators and the UNCTAD).

25% in Tanzania, and 9% in Ghana. Clearly, the composition of exports can be quite volatile, and volatility negatively impacts growth.

Political diversification is also on the rise in Africa, where the number of autocracies has plunged since 1990 (Gylfason, 2013). The left panel of Figure 6.6 illustrates the inverse cross-country relationship between democracy and natural capital in 123 countries (Pearson correlation = -0.59). Democracy is measured by the average of the Polity2 variable in each country over the sample period of 1960 to 2012, a variable that covers a spectrum of governing authority that spans fully institutionalised autocracies, through mixed or incoherent authority regimes to fully institutionalised democracies on a twenty-one-point scale ranging from -10

Natural capital and democracy

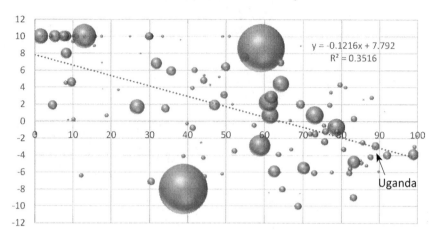

Democracy and income

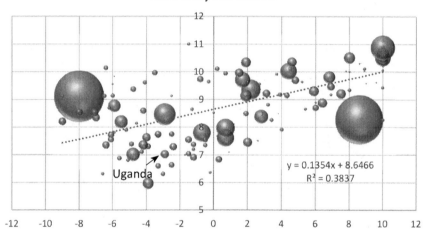

Figure 6.6 Uganda: from democracy to growth.
(Authors' computations based on World Bank, World Development Indicators and the Polity IV Project).

(hereditary monarchy) to 10 (consolidated democracy). The rightmost panel of the figure illustrates the cross-country relationship between growth and political diversification through democracy in 139 countries from 1960 to 2012. As before, growth is represented by the log purchasing power of per capita GNI in 2012 to rule out reverse causation from growth to democracy. The relationship is significant in a statistical sense (Pearson correlation = 0.62) as well as in an economic sense. The slope of the regression line (0.136) suggests that a six-point increase in Polity2 (e.g. from 0 to 6) would increase per capita GNI by about 80%. Democracy can be a powerful catalyst for growth, and so can high-quality leadership. Based on a new dataset on the education of public officials covering 178 countries from 1981 to 2011, Arezki et al. (2012) report a positive association between education attainment in public administration and government effectiveness (e.g. higher tax revenue mobilisation, limiting corruption, better public finance management and private market support).

Notice the resemblance between the bottom panels in Figures 6.4 and 6.5, shown again in Figure 6.7. Economic diversification and political diversification are both good for growth and they go hand in hand across countries, whether economic diversification is measured by the share of manufactured goods in total merchandise exports or by the Herfindahl export diversification index (Figure 6.8).

Diversification and income

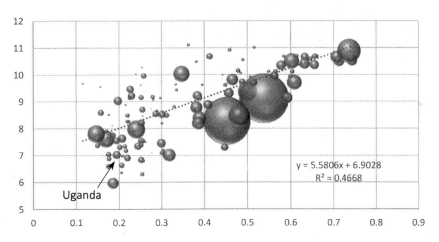

Democracy and income

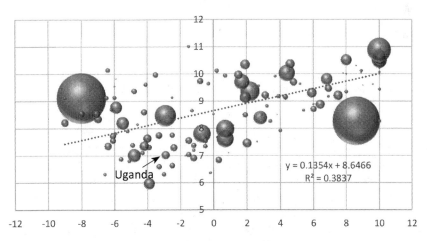

Figure 6.7 Uganda: recap – from double diversification to growth.
(from Figures 6.4 and 6.5).

Democracy and manufacturing

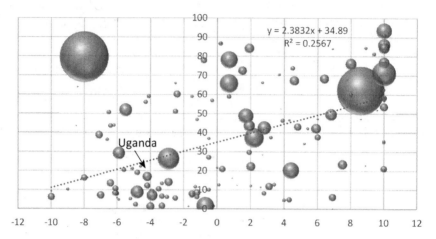

Democracy and diversification

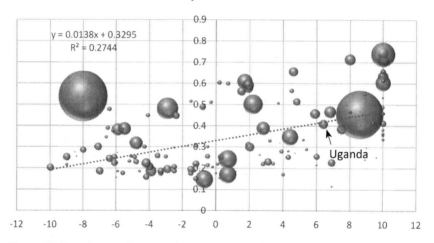

Figure 6.8 Uganda: complementarities.
(Authors' computations based on World Bank, World Development Indicators, UNCTAD and the Polity IV Project).

In Figure 6.8 the Pearson correlation between the share of manufactured goods exports in total merchandise exports and democracy is 0.51 (143 countries), and between the export diversification index and democracy is 0.52 (142 countries). If the absence of democracy enables rent seekers to hold back economic as well as political diversification, the advance of democracy – that is, political diversification – seems likely to create conditions for economic diversification, among other things. The left panel of Figure 6.9 shows how democracy and low corruption go hand in hand across countries (Pearson correlation = 0.64, 141 countries). The relationship works both ways: democrats are less likely than autocrats to tolerate

Democracy and corruption

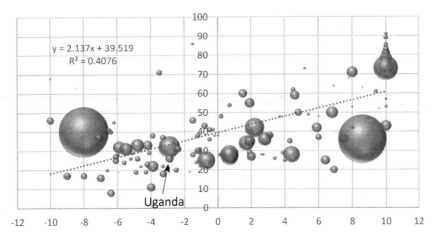

Diversification and manufacturing

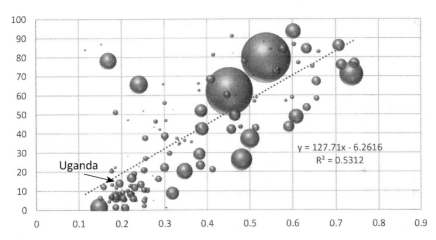

Figure 6.9 Uganda: further complementarities.
(Authors' computations based on WB, World Development Indicators, Transparency International, UNCTAD and the Polity IV Project).

high levels of corruption. Corrupt rulers typically resist democracy, and may use low taxes and generous transfers and subsidies to weaken popular demand for democracy, even if they amount to only a small fraction of each citizen's fair share of the nation's oil wealth. Democratisation through institutional reform and the fight against corruption can be viewed as complementary investments in social capital. The right panel of Figure 6.9 illustrates the fairly close correspondence between manufactured exports and export diversification (Pearson correlation = 0.73, 140 countries).

Taken together, Figures 6.3 through to 6.6 suggest a qualitative pattern, even if the quantitative slopes of the regression lines need to be interpreted with care. In summary: first, if a high share of natural capital in total tangible capital tends to go along with corruption, and if corruption is bad for growth, we have identified a channel through which a high natural capital share may (if left unattended) slow down growth (Figure 6.3). Second, if a high natural capital share discourages manufactured exports and export diversification, and if manufactured goods and diversification are good for growth, then we have an additional channel through which a high natural capital share may slow down growth (Figures 6.4 and 6.5). Third, if a high share of natural capital tends to weaken democracy and if democracy is good for growth, then we have yet another channel through which a high natural capital share may hurt growth (Figure 6.6).

When these possibilities are considered along with various other forms of rent seeking as well as the Dutch disease, plus the possibility that natural resource wealth may weaken incentives to build up human as well as social capital (Gylfason, 2001), it is not surprising to see a fairly strong inverse relationship between natural capital and economic growth across the 129 countries for which we have data on both variables, with a Pearson correlation of -0.83 (Figure 6.10). If taken at face value, the slope of the regression line (-0.038) means that a thirty-point decrease in the natural capital share, corresponding to the difference between India's 0.59 and Uganda's 0.89, would more than double per capita GNI.

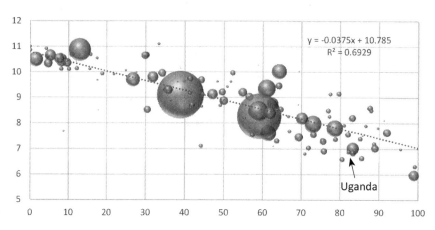

Figure 6.10 Uganda: natural capital and income per capita.
(Authors' computations based on World Bank and World Development Indicators).

6.6 Concluding remarks

The need to develop a strategy to sustainably transform natural capital into human capital and social capital is evident even if the road map on the table remains somewhat unclear. In other words, there is no one-size-fits-all blueprint available to guide Uganda or other countries to a sustainable path of successful economic diversification and growth. It seems natural to conclude from other countries' experiences that what is good for long-run growth is generally conducive to economic diversification. The build-up of human resources through education and training is good for growth, and also for diversification since manufacturing, and especially many modern services, depend on a well-educated labour force. The same argument applies to the construction of essential infrastructure – schools, hospitals, roads, bridges, telecommunications facilities and electrification – that passes the test of benefit-cost appraisals: it is always good for growth and generally helps promote a wide range of economic activities. In keeping with the principle that diversification along existing lines of comparative advantage is more likely to succeed than entering unknown territory, construction of oil pipelines and technical assistance to less experienced oil and gas producers has worked well for Norway, whose Statoil operates in over thirty countries around the world.

Generally, investment in social capital, including sound institutions that people can trust as well as good governance, is important in itself, benefits to growth and diversification notwithstanding. The Legatum Institute has recently published a comprehensive prosperity index, designed to include subjective dimensions such as trust and transparency in an overall assessment of prosperity. Comprised of eight different categories including Economy, Entrepreneurship and Opportunity, Governance, Education, Health, Safety and Security, Personal Freedom, and Social Capital, the prosperity index suggests that in Uganda, 34% of those surveyed have confidence in the judicial system. This is compared with 48% in Kenya, 41% in Tanzania, 75% in Ghana, and 82% in Botswana. At 41%, confidence among Ugandans in their government is about the same as in Kenya and Tanzania, but less than in Ghana (75%) and Botswana (69%). Trust is important. Public and private investments in human and social capital, including trust, need to be given high priority to foster both diversification and growth.

Foreign trade and investment benefit diversification and growth as illustrated by the examples of Mauritius and South Korea, among others. One reason for this is that foreign and domestic competition helps make domestic producers more competitive. In brief, the promotion of competition, domestic as well as foreign, encourages efficiency, diversification and growth. However, this is not always easy to accomplish, because those who benefit from barriers to trade and competition (such as cartels), may resist liberalisation. Another time-honoured way to promote growth is through regional trade initiatives as exemplified by the East African Community. This is a fully-fledged customs union comprising Burundi, Kenya, Rwanda, Tanzania and Uganda. Like charity, trade promotion begins at home.

With so many issues to be addressed to promote diversification and growth, there is no presumption that some things ought to be prioritised. In other words, there is no presumption derived from theory or country experiences that any particular sequencing of actions is to be preferred. This means that, as a practical matter, it may be advisable to seek the path of least resistance, doing the easy things first; climbing up the ladder rung by rung. This approach suggests that as oil revenue begins flowing in, a big effort to boost education, infrastructure and institution building, including good governance, subject case by case to benefit-cost analysis, ought to be given high priority, since such efforts are not likely to generate much opposition. Such efforts can be driven by the government or by the private sector with government encouragement and support, or by autonomous oil funds. The promotion of free trade, competition and full transparency may be harder to accomplish among strong political opposition, and should probably not be attempted up front in such instances.

Exchange rates also have an important part to play. While depreciating currencies accompanied by inflation can be an important catalyst of currency unions as, for example, in Europe and parts of Africa, overvalued and volatile currencies accompanied by slow export diversification and sluggish growth can also constitute a potentially important justification for fixing exchange rates through currency unions in natural resource rich economies. In countries prone to the Dutch disease, a currency union requires flexible fiscal and structural adjustment facilitating vigorous export activity in lieu of nominal currency appreciation aiming to contain inflation at the cost of stagnant non-resource exports. Even so, real exchange rates always float through domestic and foreign price adjustment regardless of nominal exchange arrangements. These considerations need to enter into existing plans for currency cooperation within the East African Community.

Sovereign wealth funds can play an important role in the process of economic diversification by protecting the management of oil revenues from the vicissitudes of the political process and by resisting short-sighted political demands for cash injections into the government's coffers to meet current needs. Clearly, with its modern infrastructure, Norway can afford to be patient and to stash away virtually all of its oil revenues in foreign accounts for future use, thus using the interest earned to finance future pensions while keeping the principal intact. In view of their more pressing needs, emerging economies cannot be expected to show such patience; it is more desirable to use some of the oil revenues to finance investments in human and social capital, and infrastructure, and to save the rest for future use through sovereign wealth funds (Collier, 2011).

Acknowledgements

The authors are indebted to Andreas Ebenhart, Arne Jon Isachsen, Samuel Wills, Gylfi Zoega and an anonymous reviewer for their helpful comments on earlier drafts. The excellent research assistance provided by Travis Wiggans is also appreciated.

Notes

1 School life expectancy from UNESCO is the total number of years of primary to tertiary schooling that a child can expect to receive, and can be taken as a proxy for the evolution of educational attainment over time because the advance of school life expectancy is a gradual process.
2 Depending on data availability, there is a slight variation in the number of countries covered by each chart in the text. Data for corruption and natural capital exist for 142 countries. Liberia and the Republic of Congo were not included in the left panel of Figure 6.3 because of their extremely high values for the natural capital share, well above 100%. Natural capital estimates exist for 1995, 2000, and 2005.
3 We present each observation as a bubble proportional to country size rather than as a weightless dot, a practice originated by Fischer (2003). Like Fischer, we do this to allow the visual impression conveyed by the figure to reflect people rather than countries, giving larger weight to large countries than to small ones. Even so, the regression estimates presented are unweighted by population size. Throughout the chapter, weighted regressions (not shown) would convey a similar qualitative pattern as the unweighted ones shown.
4 In an early econometric study, Helliwell (1994) found that while higher incomes helped democracy, the data did not allow him to conclude that more democracy was conducive to subsequent economic growth.

References

Acemoglu, D. (2009) *Introduction to Modern Economic Growth*, Princeton, NJ: Princeton University Press.

Aghion, P. and Banerjee, A. (2005) *Volatility and growth*, Oxford: Oxford University Press.

Aguinaga, P., Ncho-oguie, C. and Nganou, J.-P.N. (2014) 'Review of oil-price subsidies: Lessons for Uganda', working paper (forthcoming).

Ampratwum, E.F. and Ashon, M.A. (2012) *Governance in Africa's oil and gas exporting countries: Evidence from the Ibrahim Index of African governance*, Ghana Center for Democratic Development Briefing Paper, Vol. 10, No. 4, May.

Andrews, M. and Bategeka, L. (2013) *Overcoming the limits of institutional reform in Uganda*, ESID Working Paper No. 27, ESID Policy Paper No. 1, November.

Arezki, R. and Gylfason, T. (2011) 'Commodity price volatility, democracy and economic growth', in de la Grandville, O. (ed.), *Frontiers of Economic Growth and Development*, Bingley, UK: Emerald.

Arezki, R., Lui, H., Quintyn, M. and Toscani, F. (2012) *Education attainment in public administrations around the world: Evidence from a new dataset*, IMF Working Paper WP/12/ 231, September.

Auty, R.M. (2001) 'The political economy of resource-driven growth', *European Economic Review*, vol. 45, May, 839–846.

Collier, P. (2011) *The plundered planet: Why we must – and how we can – manage nature for global prosperity*, Oxford: Oxford University Press.

Fischer, S. (2003) 'Globalization and its challenges', *American Economic Review*, vol. 93, no. 2, 1–30.

Frankel, J. (2011) 'A solution to fiscal procyclicality: The structural budget institutions pioneered by Chile', *Fiscal Policy and Macroeconomic Performance*, Fourteenth Annual Conference of the Central Bank of Chile. NBER WP No. 16945.

Frankel, J. (2012) 'Mauritius: African success story', CID Working Paper No. 234, April, also in Edwards, S., Johnson, S. and Weil, D. (eds.), *African successes, volume IV: Sustainable growth*, Chicago: University of Chicago Press.

Gallup (2013) 'Government corruption viewed as pervasive worldwide', Sonnenschein, J. and Ray, J., available at www.gallup.com/poll/165476/government-corruption-viewed-pervasive-worldwide.aspx (accessed 9 April 2016).

Gelb, A. (2011) 'Economic diversification in resource-rich countries', in Arezki, R., Gylfason, T. and Sy, A. (eds.), *Beyond the curse: Policies to harness the power of natural resources*, Washington DC: International Monetary Fund.

Gylfason, T. (2001) 'Natural resources, education, and economic development', *European Economic Review*, vol. 45, May, 847–859.

Gylfason, T. (2012) 'Development and growth in resource-dependent countries: Why social policy matters', in Hujo, K. (ed.), *Mineral rents and the financing of social policy: Opportunities and challenges*, UK: Palgrave.

Gylfason, T. (2013) 'Democracy in Africa', *Vox*, 17 November, available at www.voxeu.org/article/democracy-africa (accessed 9 April 2016).

Gylfason, T. and Zoega, G. (2003) 'Inequality and economic growth: Do natural resources matter?' in Eicher, T. and Turnovsky, S. (eds.), *Inequality and growth: Theory and policy implications*, Boston, MA: MIT Press.

Gylfason, T. and Zoega, G. (2006) 'Natural resources and economic growth: The role of investment', *World Economy*, vol. 29, no. 8, August, 1091–1115.

Gylfason, T. and Wijkman, P.M. (this volume), 'Double diversification with an application to Iceland.'

Hausmann, R., Matovu, J., Osire, R. and Wyett, K. (2014) 'How should Uganda grow?', ESID Working Paper No. 30, ESID Policy Paper No. 2, January.

Helliwell, J.F. (1994) 'Empirical linkages between democracy and economic growth', *British Journal of Political Science*, vol. 24, no. 2, April, 225–248.

Henstridge, M. and Page, J. (2012) 'Managing a Modest Boom: Oil Revenues in Uganda', OxCarre Research Paper 90.

King, R.G. and Levine, R. (1993a) 'Finance and growth: Schumpeter might be right', *Quarterly Journal of Economics*, vol. 108, August, 717–737.

King, R.G. and Levine, R. (1993b) 'Finance, entrepreneurship and growth: Theory and evidence', *Journal of Monetary Economics*, vol. 32, 513–542.

Krueger, A. (1974) 'The political economy of the rent-seeking society', *American Economic Review*, vol. 64, no. 3, 291–303.

Matovu, J. and Nganou, J.-P.N. (2015) 'Fiscal policy stance, oil revenues, growth and social outcomes for Uganda', working paper (forthcoming).

Mauro, P. (1995) 'Corruption and growth', *Quarterly Journal of Economics*, vol. 110, no. 3, August, 681–712.

Page, J. (2008) *Rowing against the current: The diversification challenge in Africa's resource-rich economies*, Global Economy and Development Working Paper 29, Brookings Institution, Washington DC, December.

Paldam, M. (2000) 'Social capital: One or many? Definition and measurement', *Journal of Economic Surveys*, vol. 14, no. 5, December, 629–653.

Rodrik, D. (2004) *Industrial policy for the twenty-first century*, CEPR Discussion Paper No. 4767, November.

Ross, M. (2001) 'Does oil hinder democracy?' *World Politics*, vol. 53, April, 325–361.

Sachs, J.D. and Warner, A.M. (1995, revised 1997, 1999), *Natural resource abundance and economic growth*, NBER Working Paper 5398, Cambridge, Massachusetts.

Spence, M. et al. (2008) *The Growth Report: Strategies for Sustained Growth and Inclusive Development*, Commission on Growth and Development, Washington DC: World Bank.

Van der Ploeg, F. (2011) 'Natural resources: Curse or blessing?' *Journal of Economic Literature*, vol. 49, no. 2, 366–420.

World Bank (2006) *Where is the wealth of nations? Measuring capital for the 21st century*, Washington DC: World Bank.

World Bank (2015) *Economic Diversification and Growth in the Era of Oil and Volatility*, Uganda Country Economic Memorandum (CEM). Report No: 97146-UG.

Young, A. (2012) 'The African Growth Miracle', *Journal of Political Economy*, vol. 120, no. 4, 696–739.

7 Economic diversification in Australia

John Phillimore and Kenneth Leong

7.1 Introduction

Australia has been a stand-out economic performer for more than two decades, having enjoyed uninterrupted economic growth since 1991. During this time it has sailed through the Asian financial crisis of the late 1990s, the 'dot com bubble' of the early 2000s and the global financial crisis in 2008–09 with solid economic and income growth, low unemployment, low inflation and sound public finances. It has moved up the international country rankings of income and wellbeing (see Figure 7.1) and been lauded by international organisations (Australian Financial Review, 2012) and prominent economists (Krugman, 1998; Stiglitz, 2013).

Thirty years ago this outcome would have surprised observers both in and outside Australia (Parkinson, 2014). A severe recession in 1981–82 had seen the loss of more than 100,000 manufacturing jobs and Australia was regarded

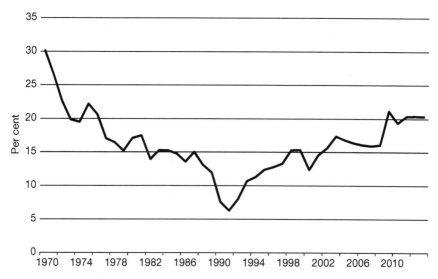

Figure 7.1 Percentage deviation of per capita GDP: Australia and OECD.
(OECD, National Accounts statistics).

generally as having a rigid, unresponsive, inward-looking and uncompetitive economy, protected behind a high tariff wall with high input costs, poor management skills, a narrowly educated and skilled workforce and adversarial, unproductive labour relations. From being the richest country in the world in the 1880s, it had fallen to around twentieth place; analogies were drawn between Australia's decline and that of Argentina, another resource-rich country (Duncan and Fogarty, 1984), and Singapore Prime Minister Lee Kuan Yew famously commented that unless it changed its ways, Australia would become 'the poor white trash of Asia'.

There are two broadly accepted explanations for the change in Australia's fortunes and its prolonged period of prosperity. The first is that Australia undertook an extensive suite of economic reforms over a decade or more from the mid-1980s, which led to a more flexible and competitive economy as well as much improved macro-economic performance. The second is that Australia benefited greatly from 2003 onward as demand for its iron ore and coal skyrocketed in the wake of China's industrialisation.

Both periods were driven by major changes in Australia's terms of trade, which in turn were closely linked to Australia's traditional resource dependence. Interestingly, though, the directions of the changes in the terms of trade were diametrically opposed. The first period saw a large drop in the price of Australia's commodity exports, and this provided the political, economic and intellectual justification for the swathe of economic reforms that were undertaken. By contrast, the second period saw Australia's terms of trade soar to their highest level in 140 years and led to a massive investment boom in iron ore, coal and liquefied natural gas (LNG). During each period the question of whether – and if so, how – Australia's economy should become more diversified has been asked. Two broad and somewhat competing answers can be identified.

The dominant narrative has been that Australia's success has been, and will continue to be, based on economic liberalisation and the adoption of sound economic policy fundamentals. Protectionist policies have been reversed and replaced with an emphasis on openness, flexibility and competitiveness. This has allowed comparative advantage to operate and enabled Australia to negotiate the economic ups and downs visited upon it by international markets and, in particular, by global shifts in demand for Australia's commodity exports. This perspective dominates economic policy thinking in both major political parties, the key agencies of government, leading business groups, the media and most economic commentators. Under this policy regime, both Labor and Coalition governments have adopted a 'kind of agnosticism about economic structure' (Bell, 1997: 227), and only rarely resorted to explicit policies of economic diversification or active industry policy. They have preferred instead to rely on competitive pressures, moves towards a more competitive cost structure, and Australia's natural advantages to build companies and sectors able to participate successfully in domestic and global markets. While there have been many diverse industry and innovation policy initiatives, these have generally been 'sector blind', offering generic support for research, development and innovation primarily from a 'market failure' perspective. Departures from these principles have at best been tolerated as necessary for sensitively managing the decline of a few politically or regionally important sectors or companies, and at worst regarded as examples of inefficient and unproductive 'rent seeking' against which policy makers need to be vigilant.

A second, contrasting approach to this dominant view has been more critical of economic and industry policy, although its analysis and policy prescriptions are more varied. The main advocates of this alternative have been academics (e.g. Ewer et al., 1987; Marceau et al., 1997; Conley, 2009; Hampson, 2012), unions, some manufacturing interests, and for a while, even some elements within government industry departments. While acknowledging the impressive performance of the economy, and accepting that tariffs needed to be brought down and competitiveness enhanced, this interpretation has been suspicious of the reliance on comparative advantage and the market failure approach to policy interventions. While China's economic miracle undoubtedly boosted Australia's economic fortunes, it also entrenched the country's resource dependence and lack of preparedness for addressing climate change. As the terms of trade revert closer to their historic average and the resources boom subsides, Australia now faces questions about whether and how it can continue to generate sustainable economic growth. According to this interpretation, diversifying the economy through active support measures for non-resource industries is once again – and indeed always has been – an urgent priority.

7.2 Australia: a vulnerable but successful natural resource-based economy

Australia's economic history is peppered with references to 'riding on the sheep's back' and 'the [gold] rush that never ended' (Blainey, 2003). One commentator notes that 'Australia is a quarry with a view, a first world consumer and services economy, serviced by a third world commodities base' (Megalogenis, 2006: 286). Yet employment in mining (including oil and gas), agriculture, forestry and fishing comprises only around 5% of Australia's national workforce (see Figure 7.2). In what way then can it be considered a resource-based economy?

The underlying justifications for considering Australia as a resource-based economy are historical and international (McLean, 2013). Historically, the discovery and exploitation of primary commodities were crucial to initially stimulating British settlement of the continent and promoting economic development and population growth. Whaling, timber, and in particular wool were vital to early prosperity, while gold discoveries stimulated rapid population increases in Victoria and New South Wales in the 1850s, and in Western Australia in the 1890s.

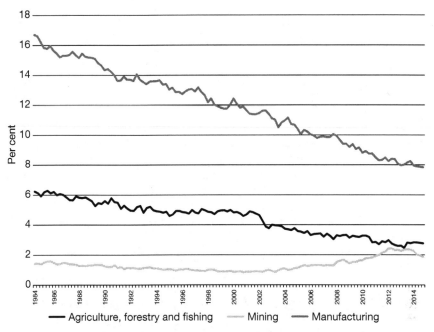

Figure 7.2 Employment share of major Australian industries.
(Australian Bureau of Statistics, Cat No 6291.0.55.003).

Just as important has been the crucial role that commodities have played in Australia's international economic relations. As Fenna (2013: 90) notes:

> Australian economic development has always been predicated on the exploitation of its natural resource endowment to generate foreign income through commodity exports. That export income finances both ... extensive manufactured imports ... and the substantial overseas capital investment that has underpinned its economic development.

McLean's (2013: 242) influential recent account of *Why Australia prospered* notes that the commodity mix of exports has always been quite diverse, and subject to both continuity and change. Wool, copper and gold were leading exports from well before 1890, while wool, wheat and beef were prominent from 1945. Since the 1960s diamonds, aluminium, natural gas, iron ore, coal, oil, nickel and uranium have been added to the list of mineral exports. Moreover:

> Our mineral wealth is globally significant ... Australia has a staggering 19 per cent of the world's total known mineral wealth ... beyond minerals, we have large assets of timber-yielding forest, farmland, coast and wilderness, as well as energy.

> (Charlton, 2014: 16–17)

Therefore, despite their relatively small share of employment, primary industries have always constituted a huge share of Australian exports (see Figure 7.3) and foreign investment, and had a large impact on other sectors of the economy.

While well aware of this natural bounty, Australians have also had a keen sense of 'the perceived vulnerabilities inherent in the resource-based economy' (McLean, 2013: 242), relating both 'to changes in international commodity demand and international financial supply' (Conley, 2009: 119-120). After a depression in the 1890s and following federation in 1901, governments in the early twentieth century established policies of 'domestic defence' (Bell, 1997: 65–69; Castles, 1988), sometimes referred to as the 'Australian settlement' (Kelly, 1992), aimed at fostering domestic manufacturing as a buffer against the fluctuations of the internationally-exposed rural and mining industries. The core components of this strategy were: protective tariffs to support local manufacturing industry; immigration controls ('the White Australian Policy') and industrial arbitration to boost wages and win the support of workers; a major role for

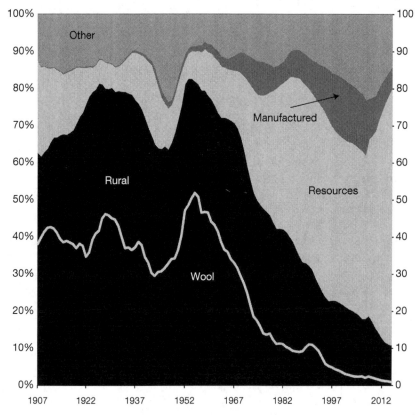

Figure 7.3 Australia's goods exports: share of the value of total goods.
(Reproduced from Atkin et al., 2014).

government in providing infrastructure such as ports, railways and utilities; and dependence on Britain in providing privileged market access for Australian commodity exports and for foreign policy and defence. Later, agricultural price support schemes for farmers were added in what was described as a system of 'protection all round'. As a consequence, Australia developed a substantial and diverse manufacturing sector (much of it foreign-owned), but it was essentially closed to the outside world, with trade having a very low share of the total economy for many years (see Figure 7.4).

Even though the trade share is now increasing, Australia's economy is still much less trade-driven than comparable rich, less populous countries (see Table 7.1).

The impact of these domestic defence policies has received much attention, in particular the extent to which they were responsible for consigning Australia to long-run relative economic decline. Charlton (2014: 12) attributes this decline to the understandable but ultimately unfortunate adoption of policies favouring manufacturing in which Australia was not globally competitive. This view has been highly influential among political leaders, government agencies, economists and commentators.

More recently, others (e.g. Fenna, 2012; McLean, 2013) have criticised this view as somewhat naïve and defended the policy framework of the Australian settlement as reasonable in the difficult international circumstances of the times, and not so different from comparable countries. They note that Australia did not suffer from a 'resource curse' to anywhere near the same degree as other resource-dependent economies, and remained one of the richest countries in the world. This

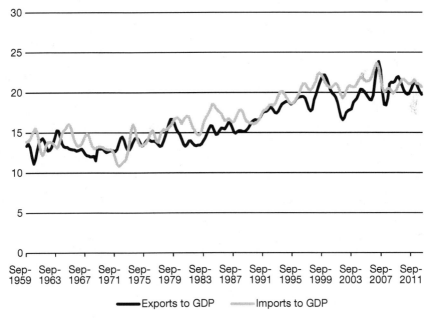

Figure 7.4 Australia's per cent ratio of exports and imports to GDP.
(Australian Bureau of Statistics, Cat No 5206.0).

Table 7.1 Per cent ratio of exports and imports to GDP in 2013 (World Bank, World Development Indicators)

Country	Import to GDP ratio (%)	Exports to GDP ratio (%)
Republic of Korea	49	54
Germany	40	46
Norway	28	39
Canada	32	30
United Kingdom	32	30
France	30	28
New Zealand	28	30
India	28	25
China	24	26
Australia	**21**	**20**
Japan	19	16
United States	17	13
Brazil	15	13

was largely attributable to the quality of its institutions and governance, which included a respect for property rights, sound public administration, low levels of corruption, and relatively equitable distribution of income across regions, industry sectors and between workers, farmers and employers. In addition, commodity export sectors received active government support (for example, through public support for agricultural research and extension, and for geological exploration), enabling them to continually increase their productivity even while efforts were being made to diversify the economic structure and increase employment through manufacturing. According to this view, Australia's fall in the international pecking order was more due to a general post-war convergence in incomes among industrialised economies and an apparently long-term secular decline in commodity prices and hence in Australia's terms of trade.

Whichever interpretation one held, there is no doubt that commodities – mainly wool, but from the 1960s also minerals and energy – have been crucial to the Australian economy, and in particular to its trading position. More recently, massive investments in coal, iron ore and LNG over the past decade have reinforced this, not just in trade terms but also as a catalyst for higher incomes and faster domestic growth more generally. This most recent growth period has once again raised issues of whether the Australian economy is too dependent on natural resources and needs to diversify.

7.3 1980s–1990s: liberalising the economy to ward off the 'banana republic'

In 1983 a new Labor Government was elected, led by Prime Minister Bob Hawke and Treasurer Paul Keating. The economic situation they inherited was bleak. A short-lived 'resources boom' had led to a wages blowout followed by a recession, so that both inflation and unemployment were over 10%. Over the next twenty years successive governments introduced wide-ranging changes to economic policy and governance, which liberalised and transformed the Australian economy. In doing so, the 'Australian settlement' of an inward-looking, protectionist economy was overturned. Initiated by Labor these reforms were retained, and in certain respects extended, by the conservative Coalition government led by Prime Minister John Howard from 1996.

The economic reforms involved both market liberalisation ('microeconomic reform') aimed at increasing economic efficiency, and internationalisation (or 'opening up' the economy) to expose the domestic economy to international competition and integrate it more closely into the world economy, rather than insulating it – as had been the modus operandi for the previous eighty years (for more details, see Kelly, 1992; Megalogenis, 2006; Parkinson, 2014).

Internationalisation measures included the floating of the dollar in 1983, easing restrictions on foreign banks, deregulation of the financial sector and, most notably, the decision to end Australia's long experiment with protective tariffs, which occurred substantially in two main tranches of unilateral tariff reductions in 1988 and 1991.

Microeconomic reforms included corporatisation and privatisation of government business enterprises in banking, transport, water, telecommunications and postal services; a national competition policy involving state and federal governments to create national markets (and associated institutions) for electricity and gas; a national competition regulatory regime; and competitive reforms to state-based industries and business enterprises. New public management and other changes were introduced into the public sector, and budgetary stringency was pursued across the board.

Corporate and personal income tax rates were reduced while taxes on capital gains and business perks, and (in 2000) a goods and services tax, were introduced. Important macroeconomic changes included granting independence to the central bank (the Reserve Bank of Australia) and other financial regulators, while setting inflation and balanced budget targets. The labour market was also progressively deregulated and decentralised, initially in the early 1990s under Labor through the introduction of enterprise bargaining, and further still under the conservative Coalition government with more individualised employment being encouraged. Unionisation rates fell sharply and the structure of employment shifted towards services, contract, part-time and temporary work.

Unlike the combative economic policies of the Thatcher and Reagan administrations in the UK and the US respectively, the radical reshaping of the Australian economy under Hawke and Keating followed a more consensual, inclusive, social democratic approach, based on a prices and incomes *Accord* between the Labor Government and the peak trade union body (Singleton, 1990). The Accord provided for supportive social policies in return for wage restraint. Initiatives such as a compulsory superannuation scheme, a national health system, large increases in childcare provision and support for lower income families bolstered the 'social wage' in return for restricting real wage rises, while reforms to skills and training policy were implemented alongside industrial relations changes. The Accord formed a vital backdrop to the economic policy changes undertaken over the Labor period. It helped build a consensus that Australia needed to become an efficient, export-oriented economy built around the value-added production of quality goods and services that would enable Australia's high wages and living standards to be maintained (Phillimore, 2000).

An important catalyst for building this new consensus was a radio interview by the Federal Treasurer, Paul Keating, in May 1986, in which he said:

> In the 1970s ... we became a third world economy selling raw materials and food and we let the sophisticated industrial side fall apart ... If ... Australia ... doesn't deal with these fundamental problems ... Then you are gone. You are a banana republic.
>
> (Keating, in Conley 2009: 106–7)

Keating's 'banana republic' warning galvanised discussion among policy makers, business groups and unions about the need to reconsider Australia's economic and industrial situation. The statement by the Treasurer was itself precipitated by a large fall in the terms of trade in 1985–86 following a sharp downturn in commodity prices, and came on the back of what was seen at the time as a long-term secular decline in real commodity prices and in the share of world trade accounted for by commodities as opposed to manufactured goods and services (see Figure 7.5).

In short, 'it was clear that Australia had the wrong mix of industries and the wrong type of economy for the world trading conditions of the late twentieth century' (Bell, 1997: 80). As a major ministerial statement accompanying the tariff reductions in 1991 said:

> The days of our being able to hitch a free ride in a world clamouring, and prepared to pay high prices, for our rural and mineral products, are behind us. *From this fact flows everything else.*
>
> (Hawke et al., 1991, emphasis added)

This was the context underlying the reforms of the 1980s and 1990s. Opening and liberalising the economy was designed to spur competitive behaviour by firms and industries and the development of a more broadly-based economy that was engaged with the world rather than protected from it. There was, however, a paradox here. While the terms of trade crisis suggested a need to *diversify away* from Australia's over-reliance on commodities, the floating of the dollar, tariff

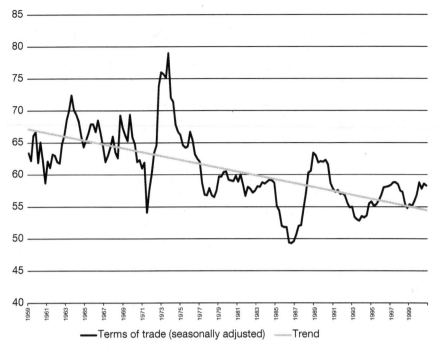

Figure 7.5 Australia's terms of trade – pre 2001, Index (2012/13 = 100).
(Australian Bureau of Statistics, Cat No 5206.0).

cuts and competition reforms *actually supported* the commodity export sector. Intense debates were waged during the 1980s about the extent to which economic restructuring and reform alone could succeed in promoting globally competitive industries outside of the commodity sector, or whether to pursue policies specifically aimed at encouraging and supporting particular companies and sectors. Unions and some elements within government urged a more interventionist approach (Ewer et al., 1987). However, advocates of economically liberal policies generally held sway at the most senior levels of government. Despite this, there were a number of policy interventions aimed, in one way or another, at diversifying the economy both by supporting manufacturing and by pursuing new opportunities.

During the 1980s, the introduction of competition and the cut in tariffs placed significant pressure on mature manufacturing sectors. In response (and urged on by its trade union allies), the Labor government introduced a number of industry plans in the most affected sectors such as heavy engineering, steel, shipbuilding, the automotive industry, and textiles, clothing and footwear (TCF) (Ewer et al., 1987; Bell, 1997). These plans usually involved a combination of financial support for companies to assist with rationalisation in order to achieve greater economies of scale (e.g. Australia had five car manufacturers, thirteen automotive plants and a large number of vehicle models basically servicing a small domestic market), changes to work and management practices, export assistance, skills and training packages, and in some instances, capital investment. The aim was to rationalise the industry, manage the transition for those companies and workers forced to exit while building more competitive, innovative and export-oriented capabilities in those that remained. In addition, decisions to build key defence assets such as submarines in Australia, rather than purchase them from overseas, were partly justified on the grounds of strengthening Australian manufacturing capability.

Efforts were also directed at promoting new technology sectors (Bell, 1997: 222). Plans were established in pharmaceuticals, telecommunications, biotechnology and aerospace. These generally involved a much lower commitment of public resources than plans for the mature manufacturing sectors, and focussed on export assistance, improved regulation and – in the case of sectors dominated by large multinationals, such as pharmaceuticals and IT – facilitating access to public procurement and price support in return for investment in R&D and linkages with local industry.

In addition to these sector-specific policies, government introduced a range of initiatives aimed at boosting research and innovation (Dodgson, 1989; Bell, 1997: 223). Australia's innovation system was characterised by low levels of R&D, with particularly low levels of private sector R&D, a high proportion of government-performed and funded R&D (in particular in rural industries), and a high dependence on foreign technology (Gregory, 1992). A range of generic support schemes aimed at tackling these problems was established. They included an R&D company tax concession, export promotion services, venture capital support, and industry extension services. After initially reducing public expenditure on science and government research agencies as part of general budget cutbacks and a desire to increase industry's share of total R&D spending, the government delivered a major science and technology policy statement in 1989, accompanied by a Prime Ministerial exhortation for Australia to become 'the Clever Country'. This statement restored much of the public research funding that had been lost, established new science advisory institutions, and funded a series of Cooperative Research Centres involving industry, government and universities.

Over time, selective industry assistance lost favour and a more consistently non-interventionist approach was adopted. Key government agencies such as Treasury and the Industry Commission (later renamed the Productivity Commission) strongly opposed interventionist policies, and argued instead for microeconomic reform, free trade and sound macroeconomic policy as the best ways for industry to restructure and become competitive in the global economy.[1] Interventionists were considered to be 'new protectionists' who were proposing 'the same discredited policies that had isolated our national economy from the rest of the world' (Hawke et al., 1991: 1.7).

Such policies were broadly continued under the Coalition government of John Howard, whose Treasurer, Peter Costello, remarked in 1998 that 'we do not need an industry policy, we have got the fundamentals right' (quoted in Roberts, 1998). This attitude was reinforced by Australia's success in navigating the Asian financial crisis of 1997. Nevertheless, under the Howard government, ad hoc assistance packages were provided for a number of politically sensitive industries, such as TCF, sugar, magnesium and ethanol. The car industry continued to receive substantial financial support.

There was evidence of success in certain areas (Edwards, 2000). The share of trade in the economy began to increase measurably, reflecting its much greater openness to global markets. Productivity growth in the 1990s was significantly above the OECD average and historical trend growth in Australia. Perhaps most significantly, even though manufacturing continued to decline as a share of the total economy, exports of manufactures doubled as a proportion of all exports, and were equal to farm exports by the end of the 1990s (Figure 7.6). Exports of services (primarily tourism) also rose. In addition, business expenditure on R&D (BERD) as a percentage of GDP increased, albeit from a low base.

Critics, however, were not convinced (Bell, 1997). While noting that tariff reductions and competition had been necessary to shake industry out of its complacency, they feared that the remaining companies and industries were not necessarily well prepared to compete internationally, while insufficient support was being provided to create new industries. Although manufacturing exports had indeed increased, imports had increased at a faster rate, meaning that Australia's balance of trade in manufactured goods was actually growing. Australia was still a predominantly commodities-based exporter.

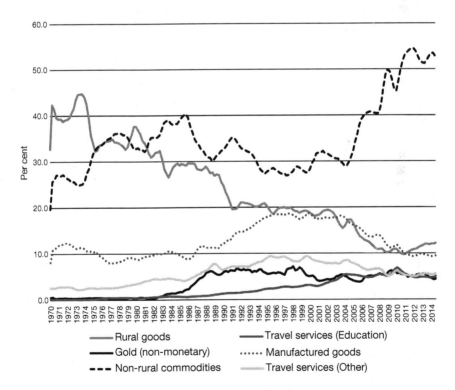

Figure 7.6 Share of Australia's goods and services exports.
(Australian Bureau of Statistics, Cat No 5302.0).

In addition, most Australian manufacturing was in relatively low and medium technology sectors rather than the higher value added areas, and was still highly dependent on foreign multinationals. This was deemed to be important by those influenced by ideas associated with new growth theory and evolutionary economics (Department of Industry, Science and Resources, 1998), which stressed that in a world where technology, knowledge, learning and innovation were becoming central to economic growth and competitiveness, some industry structures generate more positive knowledge externalities and spillovers than others. Thus, 'structural agnosticism' risked Australia becoming stuck on a 'low road' of growth built on sectors competing based on low exchange rates, wages and costs, rather than a 'high road' based on technology, knowledge, and skills (Marceau et al., 1997).

Furthermore, there was some evidence that productivity and business R&D growth were beginning to slow as the effects of the initial tariff and competition shocks began to wear off (Garrett-Jones, 2007). One of the Howard government's first actions had been to cut the R&D tax concession from 150% to 125% and reduce funding for universities (including research), while government R&D expenditure in its own agencies was also targeted. Another large fall in the Australian dollar in the early 2000s and the country's relative lack of capacity in new technology industries such as ICT led many to consider Australia as an 'old economy', still wedded to commodities.

Partly in response to these concerns the Coalition government produced an Innovation Statement in 2001, which provided a significant injection of funds into research, including increasing the R&D tax concession for smaller companies and reversing some of the cuts to higher education and public sector research agencies. A follow-up statement was delivered in 2004.

Around the same time, several states saw the election of Labor governments who were keen to openly encourage economic diversification in the face of perceived problems in relying on their traditional strengths. The government of Queensland, for example, adopted the slogan 'The Smart State', and injected large amounts of funds into bio-medical and ICT research institutes in an effort to broaden its economy from its traditional reliance on mining, agriculture and tourism (Dodgson and Staggs, 2012). In South Australia, whose large manufacturing sector had been adversely affected by tariff cuts and industry rationalisation, the new government provided financial support to encourage international universities to establish branch campuses in Adelaide in an attempt to turn that city into an 'education city'.

By 2000, retired Treasurer and Prime Minister Keating (quoted in Conley 2009: 202) echoed the thoughts of most policy makers and commentators when he said:

> The global terms of trade will not suddenly flow back in the direction of commodity producers. So even if we wanted to, we can never again rely on export wealth generated by Australian farmers and miners to pay for the preservation of tariff walls to protect our manufacturing and services sectors from competition.

The main debate centred on whether the situation required active and strategic policy to help existing industries to restructure and new ones to grow, or if continued attention on increasing competition and cost reduction – which would support Australia's traditional world-class commodity exporters – would provide sufficient incentive and opportunity for other companies and industries to thrive. Writing in the late 1990s, Bell argued that:

> Australia has tried to carry both these policies; but the commitment to restructuring has been less than full-blooded ... Australia can no longer afford to run policies that harm our key export sectors, yet, at the same time, those traditional export sectors can no longer pay our way in the world.
>
> (Bell, 1997: 232)

As it turned out, both Bell and Keating (and many others) could not have been more mistaken in their prognosis about the terms of trade and the capacity of the traditional export sectors to carry the Australian economy. From 2003 onwards, China's industrialisation led to the greatest boost in Australia's terms of trade in its history. The debate about whether Australia had the 'wrong' industry structure was largely suspended while Australia dealt with this new reality.[2]

7.4 2003–2014: the resources boom

The resources boom had three distinct phases: prices, investment and production. First, commodity prices rose rapidly in response to increased demand, from China in particular; this reversed more than forty years of secular decline in Australia's terms of trade, which had been a prime justification for much of the previous twenty years of economic reform. Beginning in 2003 and with only a short-lived dip during the global financial crisis, the terms of trade rose to their highest level in 140 years (see Figure 7.7), increasing domestic incomes substantially while the rest of the world was suffering from the global financial crisis and its after-effects.

Two commodities – iron ore and coal – were mainly responsible for this increase in the terms of trade. Iron ore prices had been flat at around US$12–15 per tonne for twenty years; at one stage in 2011 they reached US$192 per tonne (see Figure 7.8). The Governor of the Reserve Bank of Australia (Stevens, 2010) put it in simple terms in 2010 when he commented that 'five years ago, a ship load of iron ore was worth about the same as about 2,200 flat screen television sets. Today it is worth about 22,000 flat-screen TV sets – partly due to TV prices falling but more due to the price of iron ore rising by a factor of six'. And this was said before the iron ore price peak was reached.

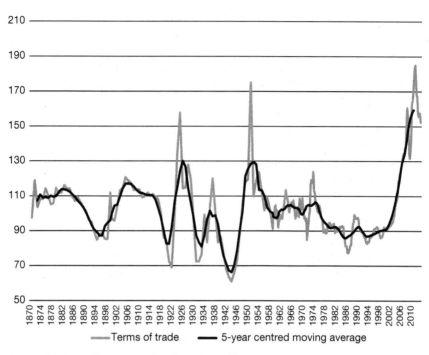

Figure 7.7 Australia's terms of trade, Index (1900–01 to 1999–00 = 100).
(Reproduced from Gruen and Wilcox, 2014).

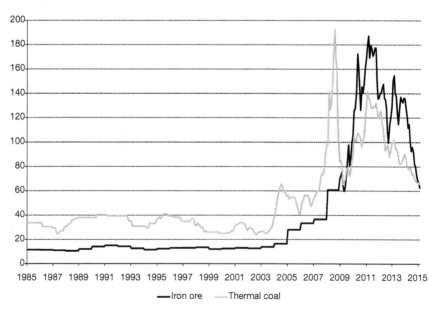

Figure 7.8 Iron ore and thermal coal prices, in USD per metric tonne.
(Indexmundi, Commodities data – Energy and Metals).

The rise in prices was sustained for far longer than previous terms of trade spikes. Moreover, the prospects of ongoing economic growth, industrialisation and urbanisation in China and India made it likely that levels of demand for Australian commodities would remain buoyant for years to come. As a senior Treasury official (Gruen, 2011) said, the current boom 'seems like a generational change in Australia's comparative advantage'. Although the iron ore price dropped from over US$120/ tonne to US$50/tonne in just over twelve months from February 2014, the price in 2016 was still more than four times its long-run average from 1985–2004.

As prices rose, investment in iron ore and coal increased markedly. In addition, as global oil and gas prices also rose, investment in Australia's world-class LNG assets also took off. Resources investment increased from less than 2% of GDP in 2002–3 to 7.5% in 2012–13, or from AUS$14 billion to over AUS$100 billion a year (see Figure 7.9).

The resulting economic activity helped reduce unemployment to below 5% – a level not seen since the early 1970s. An extra 180,000 workers were employed in the resources sector and mining doubled as a share of GDP over the decade (Gruen and Wilcox, 2014: 3).

As investment in new facilities came to fruition, commodity production and export volumes increased rapidly. New companies entered both the iron ore and coal sectors, while existing companies ramped up production. By 2013–14 iron

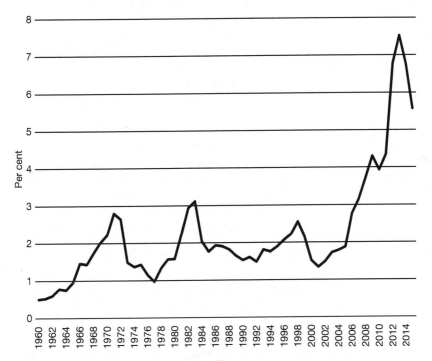

Figure 7.9 Resources investment in Australia.
(Reproduced from Gruen and Wilcox, 2014).

ore exports from Australia were over 650 million tonnes with plans to increase even further, compared to around 200 million tonnes ten years earlier. Similarly large increases in coal production were registered.

The impact of this multi-staged resource boom on economic outcomes has been broadly very positive, with increased incomes, employment and government revenues. At the same time, numerous policy challenges have arisen about how to sustain the boom while simultaneously dealing with its effects on government finances and the rest of the economy.

For mining and energy and related construction companies, attracting labour has been a key issue. Virtually all mining projects are in regional areas, many of which are quite remote from large population centres. Attracting labour led to higher wages and skill and labour shortages in these and competing sectors and regions. Temporary and permanent skilled migration increased rapidly, leading to criticisms from many unions and workers. With families often reluctant to leave their homes in the major urban centres, 'fly in fly out' arrangements for workers in mining and gas projects became commonplace, causing consternation among regional communities and leaders as well as concern at the health impacts on the workers themselves (House of Representatives, 2013).

Fiscal aspects of the resources boom were contentious as well. Governments responded to growing company and income tax revenues with a mix of tax cuts and increased welfare spending programmes. Proposals for a sovereign wealth fund to be established along the lines of Norway were rejected (Cleary, 2011; Prime Minister's Manufacturing Taskforce, 2012). Efforts to capture more of the economic rents arising from increased global commodity prices led the federal Labor government to move to introduce a Resource Super Profits Tax on mining companies in 2010. This was fiercely opposed by the industry and the conservative parties, and was instrumental in the replacement of Labor leader Kevin Rudd as Prime Minister (Marsh et al., 2014). His replacement, Julia Gillard, negotiated a much narrower Mineral Resource Rent Tax which raised much less revenue than expected and was later repealed by a new Coalition government in 2014.

Healthy public finances during the pre-global financial crisis (GFC) years of the boom – even with regular income tax cuts – gave the federal government the fiscal capacity to undertake a classic (and successful) Keynesian response to the GFC in 2008–09. However, post-GFC revenues have been subdued and substantial budget deficits are now being experienced. State governments which benefited most from the boom – primarily Western Australia, the locus of the iron ore industry – experienced booming revenues which have recently been punctured by collapsing iron ore prices and resulting falls in mineral royalties. This has led several influential observers to wonder if Australia 'wasted the boom', in fiscal policy terms at least (Garnaut, 2013; Charlton, 2014).

In addition, concern has been expressed at whether Australia might experience Dutch disease – i.e. where a short-term increase in the terms of trade leads to a long-term decline in manufacturing and tradeable services through an appreciation in the currency and competition for labour and capital, eventually leaving the economy in worse shape.

There is no doubt that currency and cost pressures have been evident in Australia over the past decade. The Australian real exchange rate rose relentlessly from 2003 (with a short reversal in 2008) to levels 35% or more above its average since the dollar was floated in 1983 (Figure 7.10). Against the US dollar, it rose from just $0.48 in 2001 to $1.10 in 2011. This put enormous pressure on manufacturers, farmers and sectors such as tourism and international education. However, key policy leaders (Henry, 2006; Gruen, 2011) were firm in resisting calls to prevent or slow the flow of labour and capital to mining companies and regions, arguing that this would reduce economic welfare and efficiency.

Analysis by the Treasury (Gruen, 2011; Gruen and Wilcox, 2014) has shown that, at a macro-economy level, evidence of Dutch disease has been quite modest, especially in view of the size of the terms of trade 'shock' and resulting investment boom. Across the decade real GDP growth was relatively steady, the unemployment rate remained around 5% and was fairly evenly dispersed geographically, while inflation was kept within the Reserve Bank's targeted band. Consumption declined as a share of GDP and savings and investment increased. Much of the credit for these outcomes is due to Australia's greater flexibility in product and labour markets, as well as the floating currency and independent monetary policy, all of which allowed the economy to adjust much more quickly than during previous booms and their aftermath (Parkinson, 2014). Whether the non-resources sector can 'pick up the slack' as commodity prices fall, the currency declines and resources investment tapers off, is now a key question facing the economy.

While earlier debates about industry policy and Australia's economic structure have not been at the centre of political and economic discussions during the resources boom, they have not been absent either. Labor Prime Minister Kevin Rudd, before

Figure 7.10 Australian dollar exchange rate against the US dollar.
(Reserve Bank of Australia, historical data – exchange rates).

being elected in late 2007, had explicitly stated that he was 'a long-term believer in industry policy ... we have a future as a manufacturing country ... we have a future with new knowledge-intensive industries ... where the government must be engaged, not just sitting idly by' (in Hart and Lewis, 2006). In government, Labor set up reviews of the car and TCF industries, trade and innovation policy (Conley and van Acker, 2011). Significantly, these reviews were conducted outside the auspices of the Productivity Commission, which was the usual expert group to which government turned for advice – and was well-known for its scepticism and antagonism to industry policy and government intervention, beyond accepting the need for support for R&D on the grounds of market failure.

With a small number of significant exceptions (see below), the Labor government focussed most policy attention on innovation, because 'in today's economy, innovation policy is industry policy' (Carr, 2008). Its *Powering Ideas* statement (Australian Government, 2009) increased the budget for science and innovation by 25% in one year to AUS$8.6 billion, and by another AUS$1 billion over the next four years. Consistent with previous practice, the primary emphasis of this increased investment was on basic science and university research, scientific infrastructure and commercialisation programmes. However, added emphasis was placed on boosting non-R&D innovation in business, with the government declaring the ambition to increase the proportion of businesses engaging in innovation by 25% over the next decade. Innovation through collaboration was encouraged by initiatives such as industry innovation councils, a new network of business advisory services, and a commercialisation institute.

Some criticised these initiatives for being ''soft' proposals ... set within an innovation perspective, shorn of the tough politics of interventionist industry policy' (Hampson, 2012: 48). As *Powering Ideas* noted, the role of government was still largely seen as being to 'create the conditions for innovation by managing the economy responsibly, regulating effectively, and making specific investments in education, research and infrastructure' (Australian Government, 2009: 18). Nevertheless, three areas that explicitly aimed at diversifying the economy received substantial financial support under the Labor government: the automotive sector, broadband and climate change.

The car industry has been the principal recipient of government industry support throughout the past thirty years, reflecting its political and regional influence, but also its direct and indirect linkages to other industry sectors such as plastics, steel, glass and electronics. An AUS$6 billion fund was announced by the new Labor government in 2008 to support the industry with investment in plant and equipment, R&D, structural adjustment and supply chain development. The plan included AUS$1.3 billion for a ten-year 'Green Car Fund' aimed at building the capacity for fuel-efficient, low emission vehicles. By comparison, support for other manufacturing industries was much more modest. The TCF programme, for example, was allocated around AUS$140 million over five years (Conley and van Acker, 2011).

The ongoing dominance of the car industry as the recipient of most industry support was controversial, with even supporters of industry and innovation policy considering it to be excessive (Conley and van Acker, 2011), while neoliberal critics regarded the government's continued financial support as propping up an uncompetitive industry. As budget conditions deteriorated the Labor government was forced to cut back the Green Car Fund, while the high dollar, increased global competition and reduced willingness to provide financial support by the new Coalition government eventually resulted in each of the three car manufacturers (Toyota, GM and Ford) announcing their intentions to cease automobile construction in Australia by 2017. While a transition support package has been devised, this represents the end of an era in Australian industry and industry policy.

Another major development under Labor was the government's decision to invest in a national high-speed broadband network (NBN) at an initial estimated cost of over $40 billion over ten years. This was by some accounts potentially Australia's largest ever infrastructure project and was intended as a key element in preparing the economy – and society more generally – for the future, including supporting new knowledge and creative industries. The NBN's cost, design and ownership was politically controversial and it suffered financial and rollout problems. The Coalition government elected in 2013 has since scaled back the NBN's cost, ambition and timetable.

A third area where significant resources were applied by the Labor government was climate change and promoting low emission industries and projects. This was undertaken through setting a renewable energy target, introducing a carbon tax, and investing in low carbon technologies. Again, some of these initiatives were overturned by the Coalition government, which has shown limited interest in reducing Australia's reliance on coal and gas.

The new Coalition government introduced its own *Industry Innovation and Competitiveness Agenda* in 2014 (Australian Government 2014). While reducing expenditure compared to Labor, the policy contained many familiar themes promoting competitiveness, productivity and stressing comparative advantage. Its specific ambitions were classic 'business environment' ones, such as lower costs, business friendly regulation and better economic infrastructure. The *Agenda* rejected interventionist industry policy and giving "money to big international corporations or to struggling businesses". The government also announced a modest $188 million program over four years to establish 'Industry Growth Centres' in food and agribusiness, mining equipment, oil and gas, medical technologies, and advanced manufacturing. This choice of resource-linked sectors where Australia has recognised competitive strengths, along with niches of science-based industries, was broadly consistent with past policy.

Following a change in leadership, new Coalition Prime Minister Turnbull released as his first major policy a new, more expansive *National Innovation & Science Agenda* in December 2015 (Australian Government 2015) with $1.1 billion worth of initiatives over four years. This policy aims to assist early stage venture capital, start-up companies and entrepreneurs; co-investment in commercialising research; increased investment in research infrastructure and collaboration between universities and business; support for digital literacy and science, technology, engineering and maths education; and a role for government as an 'exemplar' in terms of procurement and the use of big data.

While a significant advance on the previous innovation statement, the policy broadly maintained the non-sector specific nature of support inherent in industry and innovation policy. Furthermore, much of the 'new' funding only restored previous cuts made by the Coalition government to science and higher education. In that sense, it followed a trajectory similar to the Hawke government on science policy in the late 1980s.

In a further echo of the Hawke era, the Coalition has also agreed to major expenditure on defence related industries, including a $50 billion commitment over 20 years to build the next fleet of submarines in Australia, with much of the work located in South Australia, the state hit hardest by the closure of the car industry.

One success story that has tended to be ignored in most accounts of economic diversification has been international education – primarily, foreign students attending Australian universities. With export earnings of $18.3 billion in 2014-15, international education has grown from almost nothing to overtaking LNG as Australia's third largest export item, behind only iron ore ($54 billion) and coal ($39 billion). Australia is the fifth largest destination for international students in the world (with 5.5% of the global market), with almost 650,000 foreign student enrolments in 2015. The industry emerged almost unintentionally from a major restructure of the university sector in the late 1980s and subsequent budget cuts which led universities to seek alternative sources of funding. A combination of entrepreneurial universities, supportive government regulations (including the opportunity for foreign students to emigrate), coupled with Australia's status as an English-speaking country with high quality education, enabled the sector to grow rapidly. It too experienced a downturn in 2009–11 as the dollar rose, but has since recovered.

7.5 Future prospects

After showing signs of diversification in the wake of the liberalisation reforms of the 1980s, the Australian economy (unsurprisingly) increased its resource dependence in the decade after 2003. Mining and energy exports have increased as a share of total goods exports (see Figure 7.11).

Given the huge increase in the terms of trade and the massive scale of Australia's resource commodities, the bounce back in mining was inevitable. Perhaps more surprising – and encouraging from a diversification perspective – is that while primary processed and manufacturing exports have declined as a share of the total, they have managed to broadly maintain or even (in the case of processed primary products) increase their total value, despite the pressure of the rising dollar and higher input costs (Figure 7.12). Also, as noted above, the international education sector has grown rapidly to become a significant exporter, as has tourism.

Mining and construction have also increased their share of the economy while manufacturing has continued its long decline, although services continue to dominate overall (see Figure 7.13).

The question now being asked is: how prepared is Australia for transitioning away from the resources boom? At least three responses can be observed in current debates, which in many respects pick up from the situation existing immediately prior to the boom in the early 2000s.

The first response is one expressed by many liberal economic commentators and leading policy figures, who argue that the transition will be painful because of a combination of fiscal laxity and reform complacency (Garnaut, 2013; Richardson, 2014). According to this view, the terms of trade-induced boom boosted private incomes and government revenues which led to increased government spending, lower taxes and unaffordable public expectations of government. Productivity growth slowed dramatically. Now that commodity prices have fallen back, budget deficits have grown and economic, income and employment growth is slowing. On this reading, the primary task now is to reinstate fiscal discipline and reinvigorate liberal economic policies (such as the privatisation of utilities and further labour market deregulation) which can boost productivity and reduce input costs for industry. Beyond arguing for a lower dollar, however, few specific measures are suggested that actively promote industry diversification. On the

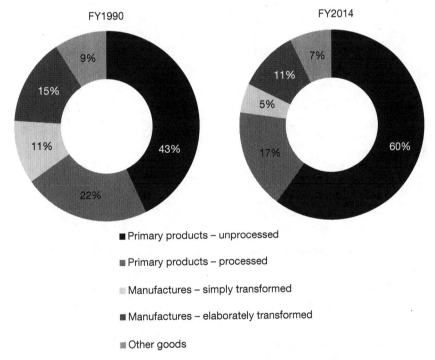

Figure 7.11 Australia's goods export by category.
(Department of Foreign Affairs and Trade, Composition of Trade – Australia 2013–14).

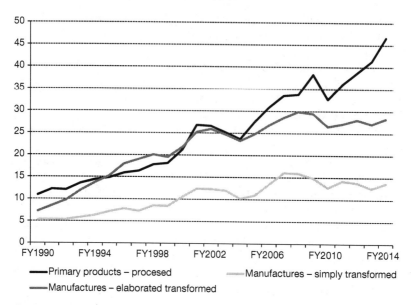

Figure 7.12 Australia's exports of primary and manufactured products, in $AUD billions. (Department of Foreign Affairs and Trade, Composition of Trade – Australia 2013–14).

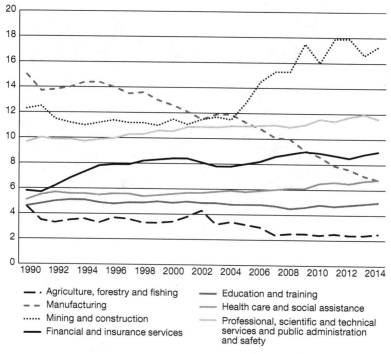

Figure 7.13 Australia's per cent sectoral share of total gross value added. (Australian Bureau of Statistics, Cat No 5204.0).

contrary, this view argues that 'corporate welfare' needs to be cut back. Indeed, the Coalition government rejected further calls for assistance from the car industry and other leading companies.

While generally agreeing with these policy prescriptions, senior levels of government appear more confident that the Australian economy is resilient and flexible enough for other sectors to grow as the resource industries fall back – not as a result of active targeting, but because Australia's economic fundamentals will provide space for them to emerge and thrive. For example, Edwards (2014), a former economic adviser to Prime Minister Keating and current member of the Reserve Bank Board, believes the Australian economic model of a low tax, low spending, liberal market economy, underpinned by a commitment to social equity, is basically sound and that the impact of the resources sector has been exaggerated. Sensible and modest tweaking of policy is all that is required to continue twenty-four years of uninterrupted prosperity. In an interview, the Governor of the Reserve Bank (Stevens, 2012) appeared confident that no special measures are necessary: 'we always get this question, where will the growth come from? And most of the time it comes'. Treasury officials (Gruen and Wilcox, 2014: 9) argue that in terms of transitioning from the resource investment boom, the situation is 'so far, so good' and that Australia's economic prospects remain promising given its proximity and complementarity to Asian markets, not only in resource industries but in related sectors such as agri-food, mining and environmental services, tourism and education.

There remains a third perspective which is much more critical of the continued role that the resources sector – mining, oil and gas (rather than agriculture) – plays in the Australian economy and society more generally, and expresses concern at the apparent lack of government attention being given to non-resource industry sectors. Conley and van Acker (2011) have asked 'whatever happened to industry policy?', arguing that Australia is once again faced with the problem of finding sources of growth and prosperity as the resources sector slows. Conley (2014) has also expressed concern at Australia's dependence on China, with China's share of Australian exports having grown from 8.5% of all exports in 2003–4 to 28.3% in 2014–15. This view also considers a 'hard landing' more likely than a smooth transition. Innovation advocates (Dodgson et al., 2012) acknowledge that advances have been made since the 1980s in terms of R&D spending by business and in some measures of innovation. However, they also note that Australia has very low levels of collaboration between companies and universities; a preponderance of small companies without any great interest in innovation; and a government bureaucracy which generally refuses to move beyond a static market failure policy perspective. Other observers (Cleary, 2011, 2012; Pearse, 2009) are critical of the disproportionate political power of the mining and energy sectors, as demonstrated by their successful opposition to the mining and carbon taxes and by government's continued support for fossil fuel industries, which they believe leave Australia vulnerable to any shifts in global demand for iron ore and coal which might occur due to technological change or breakthroughs in international climate negotiations. These disparate voices are urging for more concerted attention to be paid to economic diversification and for future resource booms to include measures such as higher resource taxation and establishment of a sovereign wealth fund.

As the investment and price phases of the boom have only recently reversed direction, it is still too early to say which of these views is likely to be more accurate. However, Australia's policy history strongly suggests that economic liberalism – with a nod to sector-blind innovation policy – is more likely to guide government policy is more likely to guide government policy than an active attention to economic diversification.

Notes

1   Australia was strongly supportive of free trade in international forums such as GATT (later WTO), helping establish the 'Cairns Group' of agricultural exporting nations to push for reductions in agricultural subsidies. It was also a prime mover in establishing the Asia-Pacific Economic Partnership, designed to promote free trade in that fast growing region (Conley, 2009: 207–09).
2   Not all observers considered Australia's terms of trade trends to be inherently negative. In a prescient speech given in 2002, the Governor of the Reserve Bank of Australia (Macfarlane, 2002: 9) said: 'A lot of people would say … because resource-based goods are 'commodities' … this means their prices will fluctuate widely in a cyclical sense, but more disturbingly, their trend will continue to show a long-run decline … [and] our terms of trade will continue to decline. But I think we have to doubt this assumption. The products whose prices will show long-run declines are likely to be those whose production can be expanded most easily. And nothing fits this description better than large areas of manufacturing … These are precisely the sorts of things that we in Australia import, and increasingly what developing countries export.'

References

Atkin, T., Caputo, M., Robinson, T. and Wang, H. (2014) *Macroeconomic consequences of terms of trade episodes, past and present*, Research Discussion Paper 2014-01, Reserve Bank of Australia, Sydney.

Australian Financial Review (2012) 'IMF praises Australian economy', *Australian Financial Review*, 16 November.

Australian Government (2009) *Powering Ideas: An innovation agenda for the 21st Century*, Canberra.

Australian Government (2014) *Industry Innovation and Competitiveness Agenda: An action plan for a stronger Australia*, Canberra

Australian Government (2015) *Welcome to the Ideas Boom: National Innovation and Science Agenda*, available online at www.innovation.gov.au/ (accessed 3 May 2016).

Bell, S. (1997) *Ungoverning the economy: The political economy of Australian economic policy*, Melbourne: Oxford University Press.

Blainey, G. (2003) (first published 1963) *The rush that never ended: A history of Australian mining*, Melbourne: Melbourne University Press.

Carr, K. (Minister for Innovation, Industry, Science and Research) (2008), *Government announces review of national innovation system*, media release, 22 January.

Castles, F. (1988) *Australian public policy and economic vulnerability*, Sydney: Allen & Unwin.

Charlton, A. (2014) 'Dragon's tail: The lucky country after the China boom', *Quarterly Essay*, vol. 54.

Cleary, P. (2011) *Too much luck: The mining boom and Australia's future*, Melbourne: Black Inc.

Cleary, P. (2012) *Mine-Field: The dark side of Australia's resources rush*, Melbourne: Black Inc.

Conley, T. (2009) *The vulnerable country: Australia and the global economy*, Sydney: UNSW Press.

Conley, T. (2014) 'Australia's China dependence: do we need a Plan B?', *The Conversation*, 9 December, available online at https://theconversation.com/australias-china-dependence-do-we-need-a-plan-b-34976 (accessed 22 April 2016).

Conley, T. and van Acker, E. (2011) 'Whatever happened to industry policy in Australia?', *Australian Journal of Political Science*, vol. 46, no. 3, 503–518.

Department of Industry, Science and Resources (1998) *A New Economic Paradigm? Innovation-based Evolutionary Systems*, Canberra, Commonwealth of Australia.

Dodgson, M. (1989) 'Research and technology policy in Australia: Legitimacy in intervention', *Science and Public Policy*, vol. 16, no. 3, 159–166.

Dodgson, M., Hughes, A., Foster, J. and Metcalfe,S. (2011) 'Systems thinking, market failure, and the development of innovation policy: the case of Australia', *Research Policy*, vol. 40, no. 9, 1145–1156.

Dodgson, M. and Staggs, J. (2012) 'Government policy, university strategy and the academic entrepreneur: The case of Queensland's Smart State Institutes', *Cambridge Journal of Economics*, vol. 36, no. 3, 567–585.

Duncan, T. and Fogarty, J. (1984) *Australia and Argentina: On Parallel Paths*, Melbourne: Melbourne University Press.

Edwards, J. (2000) *Australia's economic revolution*, Sydney: UNSW Press.

Edwards, J. (2014) *Beyond the boom*, Melbourne: Lowy Institute for International Policy/ Penguin.

Ewer, P., Higgins, W. and Stevens, A. (1987) *Unions and the future of Australian manufacturing*, Sydney: Allen & Unwin.

Fenna, A. (2012) 'Putting the 'Australian Settlement' in Perspective', *Labour History* vol. 102, 99–118.

Fenna, A. (2013) 'The economic policy agenda in Australia, 1962–2012', *Australian Journal of Public Administration*, vol. 72, no. 2, 89–102.

Garnaut, R. (2013) *Dog days: Australia after the boom*, Melbourne: Redback.

Garrett-Jones, S. (2007) 'Marking time? – The evolution of the Australian national innovation system, 1996–2005', in Turpin, T. and Krishna, V.V. (eds.), *Science, technology policy and the diffusion of knowledge: Understanding the dynamics of innovation systems in the Asia-Pacific*, Cheltenham: Edward Elgar.

Gregory, R.G. (1992) 'The Australian innovation system', in R.R. Nelson (ed.), *National Innovation Systems: A Comparative Analysis*, Oxford: Oxford University Press.

Gruen, D. (2011) 'The resources boom and structural change in the Australian economy', paper presented to Committee for the Economic Development of Australia, Economic and Political Overview 2011, Melbourne, 24 February.

Gruen, D. and Wilcox, R. (2014) 'After the resources investment boom: seamless transition or dog days?', speech to the Australian Conference of Economists, Hobart, 3 July.

Hampson, I. (2012) 'Industry policy under economic liberalism: Policy development in the Prime Minister's Manufacturing Task Force', *The Economic and Labour Relations Review*, vol. 23, no. 4, 39–56.

Hart, C. and Lewis, S. (2006) 'New team pledges a future for industry', *The Australian*, 5 December.

Hawke, R., Keating, P. and Button, J. (1991) *Building a competitive Australia*, Canberra: Australian Government Publishing Service.

Henry, K. (2006) 'Managing prosperity', address to the 2006 Economic and Social Outlook Conference, Melbourne, 2 November.

House of Representatives Standing Committee on Regional Australia (2013) *Cancer of the bush or salvation for our cities? Fly-in, fly-out and drive-in, drive-out workforce practices in Regional Australia*, Canberra: Parliament of the Commonwealth of Australia.

Keating, P. (2000) *Engagement: Australia faces the Asia-Pacific*, Sydney: Macmillan.

Kelly, P. (1992) *The end of certainty: The story of the 1980s*, Sydney: Allen & Unwin.

Krugman, P. (1998) 'I know what the Hedges did last summer', *Fortune*, December.

Macfarlane, I. (2002) 'The Australian economy: past, present and future', *RBA Bulletin*, April.

McLean, I. (2013) *Why Australia prospered: The shifting sources of economic growth*, Princeton: Princeton University Press.

Marceau, J., Sicklen, D. and Manley, K. (1997) *The high road or the low road? Alternatives for Australia's future. A report on Australia's industrial structure*, Sydney: Australian Business Foundation.

Marsh, D., Lewis, C. and Chesters, J. (2014) 'The Australian mining tax and the political power of business', *Australian Journal of Political Science*, vol. 49, no. 4, 711–725.

Megalogenis, G. (2006) *The longest decade*, Melbourne: Scribe.

Parkinson, M. (2014) 'Reflections on Australia's era of economic reform', address to the European Australian Business Council, Sydney, 5 December.

Pearse, G. (2009) 'Quarry vision: Coal, climate change and the end of the resources boom', *Quarterly Essay*, vol. 33, 1–122.

Phillimore, J. (2000) 'The Limits of Supply-Side Social Democracy: Australian Labor, 1983–96', *Politics & Society*, vol. 28, no. 4, 557–587.

Prime Minister's Manufacturing Taskforce (2012) 'Report of the Non-Government Members', *Smarter Manufacturing for a Smarter Australia*, Canberra: Commonwealth of Australia.

Richardson, C. (2014) 'Boom to gloom: why the budget is bad news', *Australian Financial Review*, 8 May.

Roberts, P. (1998) 'Fundamental Weakness in Canberra's Values', *Australian Financial Review*, 13 February.

Singleton, G. (1990) *The Accord and the Australian Labour movement*, Melbourne: Melbourne University Press.

Stevens, G. (2010) 'The challenge of prosperity', address to the Committee for Economic Development of Australia (CEDA) Annual Dinner, Melbourne, 29 November.

Stevens, G. (2012) 'Full transcript of interview with RBA's Stevens', *Australian Financial Review*, 19 December.

Stiglitz, J. (2013) 'Australia, you don't know how good you've got it', *Sydney Morning Herald*, 2 September.

8 Economic diversification in Russia

Nuclear to the rescue?

Li-Chen Sim

8.1 Introduction

Russia has made commendable economic progress since the start of the twenty-first century, as a quick glance at some data will testify:

- Gross domestic product (GDP) per capita increased two-and-a-half times from US$7,700 to US$18,100 between 2000 and 2013, making Russia a leader among its peers in the BRICS group of countries (CIA, n.d.);
- Unemployment has halved from 12% to 6%, which is below the 10% rate in the European Union (EU) and that of the top oil-producer Saudi Arabia (CIA, n.d.);
- Poverty levels have declined from 35% of the population in 2000 to 11%;
- Russia is now the ninth largest economy in the world with a nominal GDP of US$2.1 trillion, up from twentieth position in 1999 with a GDP of US$200 billion. In fact, Russia surpasses Germany as the fifth largest economy if GDP is measured in purchasing power parity;
- Public debt levels among the lowest in the world with a debt-to-GDP ratio of 13% in 2013, down from 70% a decade ago (Ernst and Young, 2013), which compares favourably to 91% in the Euro area and 20% in China;
- Healthy international reserves of more than US$380 billion as at April 2016, a level which places it among the ten countries with the largest reserves in the world (IMF, 2014).

Part of the credit for Russia's economic record must go to its resource-abundance, and indeed, its resource-dependence. As the world's second largest oil producer (11% of global production in 2013) and second largest oil exporter (14% of global exports), it is particularly and increasingly dependent on oil, on the rents that oil generates, and on the knock-on effects of oil on the wider economy, as evidenced below:

- Oil production grew by over 60% from 323 million tonnes to 531 million tonnes between 2000 and 2013. During the same period the price of oil increased from US$28 to US$108 (BP, 2014). Unsurprisingly, President

Putin has been referred to as 'Vladimir the Lucky' (Kuchins, 2006) because he became and remains President in a time of high oil prices.

- Oil and gas account for almost 70% of export revenues (the same as GCC), up from 30% in 2000. Oil and gas account for 52% of the federal budget, up from 30% in 1996, and for 17–25% of Russian GDP (Simola et al., 2013).
- Oil is by far the most important export commodity at 55% of total export revenue, up from 35% in 2000, and gas at 12% (EBRD, 2012). While 75% of oil production is exported, the comparative figure for gas is one third.
- Almost everything in Russia tracks the fluctuations in the price of oil. This includes the annual average sales of Russia's top companies by sales outside the oil and gas sectors, the production rates of railway freight cars, and the value of Russia's imports (Gaddy and Ickes, 2010; Hedlund, 2014).
- Every 1% change in oil prices results in an almost 0.5% change in real GDP growth (Ito, 2012). A US$10 drop in oil prices translates into a 5% loss, or about US$20 billion in annual budgetary revenues (Naymushin, 2014).
- High oil prices in the 2000s allowed Russia to pay off its entire debt to the International Monetary Fund (IMF) in 2005, three and a half years ahead of schedule.

In this regard, the deluge of advice for Russia to diversify its economy seems counter-intuitive. The IMF, for instance, has noted that 'Russia is still a resource-dependent economy that must take meaningful steps to diversify in a market-friendly way' (Berglof et al., 2009). Rabobank, a top international bank, cautioned that 'Russia must diversify its economy away from the hydrocarbon sector, especially by improving the business climate' (van der Molen 2014). Anders Aslund, a prominent scholar, has argued that membership in the World Trade Organisation 'can help Russia diversify and move toward a knowledge-based economy' (Aslund, 2010). Russian leaders themselves are leading this charge to diversify – as far back as 2005, President Vladimir Putin admitted that 'we know that one of our main tasks is the diversification of the economy. That it is essential to depart from a model based on raw materials is obvious' (Rutland, 2008). The puzzle, then, is whether the hydrocarbon sector, and oil in particular, is a locomotive or an obstacle to modernisation and diversification.

This chapter will be organised as follows. Section 8.2 examines the rationale for economic diversification by identifying the conventional wisdom for this policy choice and then appraising its applicability to Russia. In so doing, it argues that diversification in Russia is driven more by fears about political or regime longevity than by concerns about the sustainability of economic growth. Section 8.3 focusses on the country's attempt to diversify its export profile through exports of civilian nuclear reactors to produce electricity. An evaluation of the strengths and challenges of this strategy concludes that Russia's success in diversification is hostage, for the most part, to reforms that need to be implemented in the wider economic policy landscape in Russia.

8.2 Why diversify?

To reap the benefits of manufacturing

A key reason for the almost unequivocal support for economic diversification in resource-dependent countries concerns its role as a panacea for various aspects of the so-called 'resource curse' or 'Dutch disease'. The latter is a term that broadly refers to the undesirable consequences of a commodity export boom, in particular a change in the structure of production that results in the contraction of non-resource tradables such as agriculture or manufactured goods.[1] This displacement of the manufacturing sector is considered a negative development because engaging in manufacturing appears to result in gains that raise productivity, income, job creation and global competitiveness (Hesse, 2008; Lederman and Maloney, 2007). The success of the Asian 'Tiger' economies with their export-led growth strategy seemed to suggest that manufacturing a diverse range of products was one of the keys to achieving high income and economic development levels (Birdsall et al., 1993; Imbs and Wacziarg, 2003). Hence, deliberate policy-induced diversification out of commodities and into manufacturing could be justified and useful.

In the case of Russia there is inconsistent evidence of the 'Dutch disease', although some symptoms are present (Dobrynskaya and Turkisch, 2010; Oomes and Kalcheva, 2007). On the one hand, the manufacturing sector has experienced a sharp contraction. In 1990, for example, industry accounted for almost 50% of GDP while services contributed only 35%, whereas in 2013, services make up two thirds of GDP while manufacturing comprises 16% (EBRD, 2012). There has also been a corresponding fall in employment in the manufacturing sector. However, this is the result of a 'transition effect': in other words, the slowdown in manufacturing is due less to high oil prices associated with the 'curse of oil' than to an adjustment to the implosion of the curse of the Soviet hyper-industrialised command economy (Gustafson, 2012). Today Russia's manufacturing sector is, in fact, on par with its peers in the developed and developing world, and among oil-rich countries (Figure 8.1).[2]

On the other hand, and contrary to the expected outcome of Dutch disease, some manufacturing sub-sectors in Russia have experienced output and productivity growth in spite of the boom in the oil/gas sectors. The previously mentioned example of the production of railway cars is one example. Other examples of growth in manufacturing may be found especially after the Russian economic crisis of in 1998. These so-called 'gazelles' are fast-growing small and medium-sized companies with an annual turnover of up to US$400 million each, boasting average annual revenue growth of over 20% for at least five consecutive years. Many of them are privately-owned, rely for the most part on private funds, and have some level of foreign ownership (Kolodnyaya, n.d.; Yudanov, 2008). They include companies such as Ralf Ringer (footwear), Gloria Jeans (clothing), Splat (cosmetics), Konfael (confectionery), Vimpelcom (wireless telecommunications goods and services), and Kaspersky Lab (anti-virus software and services). Their target audience tends to be the lower-middle and middle-income Russian professionals who form the backbone of small/medium-sized companies. As the post-Soviet

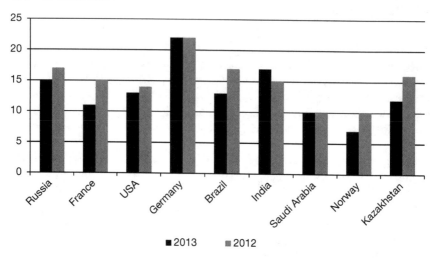

Figure 8.1 Size of the manufacturing sector in selected countries, as a % of GDP.
(World Bank).

transition progressed in the 1990s they were offered either very cheap products or high-quality goods at prohibitive prices; consequently, 'gazelles' stepped in to fill the intervening niche.

In this regard, some Russian economists have counselled that the current practice of identifying and supporting 'national champions' must go hand-in-glove with improving business conditions for these 'hidden champions' which are 'more resilient and have a greater capacity for relatively low-cost growth' (Kuznetsov et al., 2011). The Agency for Strategic Initiatives, which was proposed in 2011 and chaired by then-Prime Minister Putin, represents an attempt to support entrepreneurs of medium-sized businesses.

Moreover, there is some ambiguity about whether and when Russia should indeed diversify away from its current comparative advantage in energy exports. This is, firstly, because a U-shaped pattern informs the diversification of exports (Cadot et al., 2011; Imbs and Wacziarg, 2003). According to such research, developing countries initially export a few basic products such as wheat or crude oil, then move on to a bigger range of products that may include light processing such as food processing, and after a higher income is reached seek to specialise again particularly into selling services such as financial services. The issue here is two-fold; one, that the threshold where diversification ends and specialisation begins is thought to be a GDP per capita of US$13,000 (EBRD, 2012), and Russia is just on that cusp. Secondly, Russia is atypical of a resource-dependent country: thanks to the Soviet model of development, Russia is not a developing economy with a large agrarian sector, low rates of urbanisation and rudimentary levels of education. Hence, much of the literature on diversification may, at best, not apply to it, and at worst be contra-indicative.

To reduce economic and financial volatility

A second reason that explains the popularity of economic diversification stems from its role in reducing the volatility of growth and of state revenue in resource-dependent countries. Prices of commodities are notoriously volatile, and all the more so for oil where the coefficient of variation of prices is 0.7 (Figure 8.2). In contrast, the price of manufactured goods is much less volatile, which explains why it is often included as a key component of diversification for resource-dependent countries.

Oil prices are also extremely difficult to predict; indeed, 'since the start of the 1970s none of the major turning points in the oil market has been widely predicted' (Gelb, 2011), including the recent 50% slump in oil prices since mid-2014. Together, these characteristics make it difficult for policy-makers and private businessmen alike to initiate decisions with regard to growth, savings, investment in physical assets, income distribution, poverty and educational attainment, all of which require large upfront outlays and long gestation periods. For example, the oil production capacity of the Organisation of Petroleum Exporting Countries in the mid-2000s was lower than 1978 levels because production expansion had been held back by the low oil prices of the 1980s and historically unpredictable real prices (Kochhar et al., 2006).

In the case of Russia, as noted earlier, government budget revenues, absolute GDP, GDP growth, and almost everything else in the economy rise and fall in tandem with the price of oil, including even the non-resource tradables. As noted by Gaddy and Ickes (2010), 'every single non-oil sectoral index in the benchmark Russian stock market, the RTS, fell more than the oil and gas sector index after the market's mid-2008 peak. The oil and gas index fell 68% from peak to trough ... the telecom and consumer goods indexes fell by around 80%, and the manufacturing and financial sectors by over 90%.' Among its peers in the BRICs, Russia also

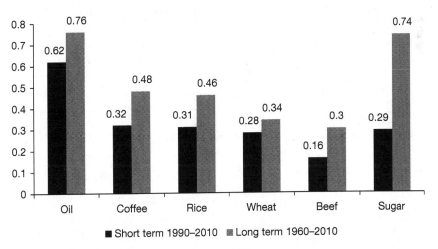

Figure 8.2 Coefficients of variation for commodities.
(Maurice and Davis, 2011).

fares badly in terms of volatility: it outperformed them in terms of GDP per capita prior to the 2008 crisis, but suffered much more during the recovery when its GDP contracted by 8% in 2009 compared to a smaller decline of 0.5% in Brazil and growth levels of 8.7% and 5.7% in China and India respectively.

Consequently, despite suffering through two financial crises within a decade – in 1998 and 2008 – the European Bank notes that 'Russia has not done enough to inoculate itself from recurring crises which stem, in large part, from a sharp drop in the price of oil' because 'diversification away from oil, gas, and other commodities remains a key long-term challenge' (Berglof et al., 2009). While diversification is certainly one way to reduce volatility, identifying a non-oil sector whose fluctuations is not correlated to oil prices is challenging in Russia's case. More significantly, the political will to sustain genuine economic diversification – and associated reforms to transparency, corporate governance, and rule of law – is lacking since the existing partial reform equilibrium is in the interest of political elites, as will be explained below. Hence, diversification by itself will not reduce volatility in the absence of other complementary reforms.

To reduce corrosive impact on governance

A third reason to embark on economic diversification is that it may minimise the impact of resource-dependence on the quality of a country's public institutions and standards of governance. In resource-rich countries, state and private actors engage in repeated struggles to wrest, secure and control an ever-larger share of these rents. Such conflicts detract from improvements in governance and provide little incentive for elites to invest in the long-term development of the country (Caselli, 2006; Hodler, 2006). In Russia, the struggles over oil companies such as Sibneft, Russneft and most infamously Yukos underline the complicity of state officials, private businessmen and law enforcement agencies in appropriating privately-owned and highly profitable oil companies (see Gustafson, 2012; Sakwa, 2009; Sim, 2008). Gaddy and Ickes (2011) have surmised that in exchange for loyalty to Putin and doing his bidding, Putin, as patron, will offer his clients protection and advancement.[3] For 'Putin's Protection Racket' to work well, clients must feel that they are always vulnerable to accusations of criminal behaviour should the patron choose to bring forth such allegations. Hence, 'grabber friendly' institutions (Mehlum et al., 2006), including ambiguities in the criminal and tax codes as well as pliable enforcement agencies, are retained in this system. Russia also shares the distinction, along with its oil-dependent counterparts in Nigeria and Kazakhstan for instance, of playing host to higher than average levels of corruption and lower than average levels of governance (e.g. see the annual surveys and datasets from Transparency International and Worldwide Governance Indicators). For these reasons, diversifying away from energy could, in theory, reduce the rents it generates, and hence minimise opportunities for corruption by public officials, thereby improving the business environment in Russia.

Tompson (2006), however, reminds us that while struggles over Russia's resource wealth have fuelled corruption, Russia would have had very high levels of corruption anyway. In the first place, the fact that corruption levels are appallingly similar in many post-Soviet states (Transparency International, 2016, regardless of whether they are resource-dependent or not, suggests that there may be a cultural dimension to the tolerance of corruption, as exemplified by the Soviet-era practice of an exchange of favours known as 'blat' (Filippov, 2011; Ledeneva, 1998; Orttung, 2014). Second, corruption may also be a result of low levels of remuneration among law enforcement agents (Schulze et al., 2013). Third, it could reflect the absence of or poorly-enforced property rights (Bhattacharyya and Hodler, 2010). This is because while high-profile cases of corruption and illegal corporate raiding seem to proliferate in the natural resource sector in Russia, it occurs in industries as diverse as telecommunications, steel and confectionery, and is also the bane of small and medium-sized enterprises (Freeland, 2000; Khilji, 2005; Kuznetsov et al., 2011; Rochlitz, 2014). Since there is no clear linear relationship between resource-dependence and corruption, diversification per se may not lead to an improvement in the quality of governance in Russia after all.

To build a modern economy

Apart from economic rationale discussed above, diversification may also be driven by political ends. According to one variant of this perspective, a diversified economy is the *sine qua non* for a modern, industrialised and powerful country, a source of national pride and prestige. The US, Germany and the UK, for example, have high per capita incomes and are the world's largest, fourth and sixth largest economies respectively, and boast a very diversified range of exports. In contrast to scores of 1.6–1.7 on the Herfindahl-Hirschmann index for the three countries above, Russia recorded a level of over 3.5 in 2010, up from 2.9 in 2000 (Gill et al., 2014). This is higher than even China (just under 2) and Brazil (2.5), an indication that the range of exports from Russia is shrinking.

In addition, high-technology exports in Russia account for only 8% of its total manufacturing exports in 2012, which is very low by international standards, and puts it on par with Madagascar, Paraguay and Tunisia; whereas the comparable figure for the G7 countries is 16% on average (World Bank dataset).[4] Globally, high-tech exports from Russia account for less than 0.3% of the world's total (Vercueil, 2014): its ranking of twenty-eighth in the world has not improved since 1996 (Table 8.1). Since exports of high-tech products are projected to grow more quickly (9% per annum) than exports of other goods including mineral fuels (5%) over the next fifteen years, Russia's dismal performance provokes concern (HSBC, 2014).

For a country like Russia, whose self-image is that of a world power, being relegated to the periphery of the economic world is unacceptable. To this extent, 'either Russia will be a great power, or she will not exist at all. There is no alternative' (Blank, 2012). The Russian embrace of '*derzhavnost*' or 'greatpowerness' reflects this deep-seated, persistent and widespread belief in the existence of a manifest destiny, 'a natural right to the role and influence of great

Table 8.1 Per cent global share of high-tech exports (Source: HSBC, 2014)

Rank	Country	2013
1	China	36.5
3	USA	9.6
8	Germany	4.4
9	Malaysia	3.3
13	Canada	0.9
14	Poland	0.9
16	India	0.4
22	Saudi Arabia	0.1

power whether they have the wherewithal or not' (Levgold, 2006), by virtue of its size, geography, resource and history (for a more comprehensive analysis of 'derzhavnost' and other concepts that inform Russian foreign policy, see Blank, 2012). The insistence that Russia be regarded as a great power is 'an important theme in foreign policy statements and discussions and it remains an important driver of foreign policy' as well as domestic policy (Light, 2010). In this connection, 'accustomed to being regarded as citizens of a great power, the country's decline to Third World status has been traumatic' (Pipes, 1999).

It is little wonder, therefore, that Russia's top leaders have repeatedly emphasised the need for modernisation and diversification. In 2009, for example, then-President Dmitri Medvedev argued that the 2008 crisis hit Russia especially hard because of the country's energy dependence and its failure to move to a diversified economy that exports a variety of high-technology goods (Robinson, 2011). His solution – the creation of a high-technology incubator park called Skolkovo modelled on the USA's Silicon Valley, in order to address the fact that 'twenty years of tumultuous change has not spared [Russia] from its humiliating dependence on raw materials' (Medvedev, 2009). This sentiment of being on the receiving end of a neo-colonial arrangement with Western countries is exacerbated by Russia's relationship with China, which has been described as 'a modernising China exploiting a backward Russia for its energy and timber resources and as a market for low-grade goods unsalable in the discerning West' (Lo, 2008). Agreements in 2013 and 2014 locking Russia into long-term oil and gas supply deals with China merely reinforce this perception of an asymmetric relationship.

However, as alluded to earlier, a modern, prosperous, and industrialised economy is not always synonymous with a diversified one. In fact, natural resources can drive modernisation through investments in collective learning, technological progress and economy-wide linkages. Examples include the resource origins and contributions of the US Geological Survey, the Columbia School of Mines, and horizontal drilling/hydraulic fracturing techniques (Wright and Czelusta, 2007). The experience of countries like the USA, Norway, Australia and Sweden are also commonly highlighted. In this regard, Russia can and should continue to leverage its revealed comparative advantage in oil exports while minimising the negative impact that may arise from rents by altering the ownership structure of oil companies. This is because Russia is not cursed by oil per se, but rather by the state ownership of oil companies (Luong and Weinthal, 2010). During 2000–2004, for instance, almost all the remarkable growth in the production and export of Russian oil was accounted for by privately-owned oil companies, whereas state-controlled companies barely figured (Ahrend, 2005). Reflecting on this issue, Aslund concludes that 'rarely has the superiority of private ownership over state companies been as clearly displayed as in the Russian oil industry from 2000 to 2004 when Yukos, Sibneft, and TNK emerged as clear winners' (Aslund, 2005). In this connection, the fact that the Russian state today directly controls more than 50% of oil production (up from 30% in 2000), a share that rises to 60% if Kremlin-loyal oil companies are included, is a worrying sign for Russian oil production and economic stability.

To increase resources for patronage

Finally, a country may choose to embark on economic diversification because this policy creates new channels for rents, cements and expands patronage, and therefore enhances regime longevity in oil-dependent illiberal democracies, authoritarian regimes and monarchies. One reason why alternative avenues of rent may be desirable is that high rates of population growth dilute the long-run level of rents per capita. Hence, new sources of rents are required to sustain prosperity and political stability in a country with a growing population. In Saudi Arabia, for instance, the oil rents available per capita in the 2000s are half of what they were in the 1970s and 1980s, partly because the population has increased from almost 10 million in 1980 to 27.3 million in 2010 (ESCWA, n.d). Even if Saudi Arabia reduces spending levels to 3% of annual growth – the state budget has actually increased by 15% each year over the past decade – and assuming oil prices remain at 2006 levels, Saudi Arabia's official financial reserves will be depleted by 2026 (Hertog, 2013). A second reason to create new sources of rent through diversification is that technology shocks may threaten an oil-dependent country's only source of comparative advantage. Abu Dhabi's renewable energy initiatives, such as Masdar, for example, were adopted as 'a hedge in favour of a new technology for the future. In case there was a global multilateral carbon regime, we did not want to be latecomers to the game' (Sim, 2012). By creating a class of new, non-oil rentiers, the regime strengthens its legitimacy among a wider swath of the population (Davidson, 2009).

A third reason to establish a new channel for rent via diversification is to compensate for the depletion of a key commodity such as oil. This is because resource depletion, particularly if it is irreversible, may imperil rents used to dole out patronage. In Russia, for example, there is widespread agreement that a repeat of the heady growth in oil production during the late 1990s and 2000s is unlikely; consequently, oil production in Russia is expected to reach a peak in 2015 and thereafter fall by 50 million tonnes to around 440 million tonnes by 2030

(Kononczuk, 2012). One reason has to do with geology, namely that much of the oil being produced is from 'old oil' or 'legacy' oilfields in western Siberia (Dienes, 2004; Gustafson, 2012). The giant Samotlor oil field, for instance, was for many years the leader in Soviet and Russian oil output until 2007; today it produces 82% less than its record high because its reservoir is largely depleted (BNP, 2011). New oil fields, however, such as those in the Arctic region, are technologically harder to recover, located in geographically inhospitable areas, and largely devoid of existing transportation facilities (Simola et al., 2013). All these factors raise costs, reduce export rents and thereby shake the foundations of 'Putin's Protection Racket'. Since Western companies are the source of much of the technological expertise with regard to developing offshore oil fields, and since Russia's leaders envisage an increasingly hostile external operating environment unconducive to east-west co-operation, success in developing new oil reserves could be elusive.

Therefore, 'Russia's dilemma is that any serious attempt to convert the economy into something resembling a modern, Western, non-oil economy would require dismantling the rent distribution system' (Gaddy and Ickes, 2011) that underpins Putin's regime. This would be highly destabilising economically, socially and politically, which in turn reduces the incentive for Russian elites to embark on meaningful diversification. The fact that Russia has actually taken tentative steps towards diversification, as discussed in the next section, could reflect Putin's expectation of political longevity, which increases his incentive to do something to stem the diminishing pool of rents through economic reform and diversification. Unfortunately, this gets mixed in with the desire for a quick and tangible result, which explains why diversification and modernisation in Russia proceeds in fits and starts.

8.3 The nuclear industry as a diversification strategy

Why nuclear?

In 2009, then-President Medvedev identified the nuclear industry – together with space, medical, nanotechnology and information technology – as a strategic vector to spearhead the diversification of the economy away from hydrocarbon dependency (Medvedev, 2009). Subsequently, in March 2010 Putin set the goal of capturing at least 25% of the world's nuclear plant construction and operating needs, from a 16% market share (Baev, 2010). Rosatom, the Federal Agency for Atomic Energy, has also been given the right to set up representative offices within Russian embassies abroad. The elevation of the nuclear industry is surprising, given that it had been suffering from benign neglect for much of its post-Soviet existence. During the 1990s, state-owned nuclear entities not directly responsible for nuclear power reactors and nuclear weapons were basically left on their own to find means of survival with little financing or support from their principal, the Ministry of Atomic Energy or Minatom. Many latched themselves onto other more viable parts of the bureaucracy or onto private owners. In 2001 the head of Minatom, Yevgeny Adamov, was sacked for embezzlement and illegal stock transfers (Bellona, 2008), and in 2004, Minatom reached its nadir when it was abolished and reconstituted as Rosatom. The simultaneous downgrade from a Ministry into a federal agency meant that it no longer had an automatic place in the federal Cabinet (which was reserved only for Ministries), and it occupied one of the lowest rungs on the totem pole of federal state bodies, alongside the agencies for tourism and sports.

Rosatom's re-emergence into the spotlight began at the end of 2005 with the appointment of a career bureaucrat and former Prime Minister, Sergei Kiriyenko, to head the agency. His determination to turn Rosatom around, combined with favourable global conditions – high oil prices and the renewed interest in nuclear energy, particularly among countries in Asia and the Middle East – largely conspired to engineer Rosatom's revival. Having replaced many of the directors of Rosatom's units with more business-oriented managers, he presented and received approval for his plan for the nuclear industry. According to the US$55 billion Federal Target Program for the Development of the Nuclear Power Industry Complex for 2007 to 2010 and Further to 2015 (henceforth FTP), Rosatom will build new reactors in Russia and extend the lifetime of existing reactors so that nuclear energy will account for 23% of electricity, up from 16% in 2000. The state will allocate US$25 billion for the FTP up to 2015; thereafter the remaining US$30 billion required to fulfil the FTP would come from Rosatom's retained earnings and its own revenue streams, especially from the construction of new reactors internationally. To facilitate implementation, Rosatom was converted into a state corporation under Russian law in 2007, a status also held by Gazprom, the Russian gas behemoth.

Essentially this means that Rosatom is a creation of the state, rather than of private individuals, and that it is the legal owner of assets donated by the state. These include all possible structures of the atomic industry, including the semi-independent entities that had operated in grey-zones for more than a decade, and those entities that had been 'lost' to other Ministries – all of which amounted to over three hundred enterprises and scientific institutes. As a state corporation, Rosatom has more flexibility with respect to human resources and can keep and reinvest earnings since it is a non-commercial entity. Moreover, it is not part of the Government but reports directly to the President. Alongside its new status, it was also revamped into four branches, namely the civilian nuclear energy complex, the nuclear weapons complex, oversight of nuclear safety, and research (Bellona, 2007; Mukhatzhanova, 2007; Voss, 2008).

Kiriyenko had clearly engineered a spectacular bureaucratic coup for himself and Rosatom, and also for the wider goal of diversification – after all, Rosatom was but one of eight state corporations created between 2006 and 2007.[5] The primary objective of state corporations was to manage capital resources for public investments to modernise the economy, while avoiding the red tape, theft and overlapping lines of authority that plagued federal programmes. Another objective was to consolidate ownership and management of the numerous enterprises in strategic sectors, especially the atomic and defence industries, so that these sectors would become globally competitive. For Russia, the stellar performance of similar parastatals in Singapore and the Persian Gulf countries (Hertog, 2012; Sim et al., 2014) appeared to suggest that such arrangements represented the best possible arrangement for those sectors deemed to be strategic for the state, and which could be efficiently endowed with resources in order to advance economic diversification and modernisation.[6]

Another factor that explains Rosatom's high-profile role in economic diversification is that the nuclear industry ticks most of the boxes with regard to advice from scholars and practitioners, discussed earlier. Nuclear reactors and enriched uranium are clearly high-technology exports that will enhance the vitality of the manufacturing sector. For example, Rosatom is a world leader in developing and commercialising small modular reactors as well as new kinds of reactors that can use reprocessed uranium. Such exports also appeal to the 'prestige' factor alluded to earlier; paraphrasing a former Prime Minister, Yevgeny Primakov, 'Russia's foreign *economic* policy cannot be the foreign *economic* policy of a second-rate state. We must pursue the foreign *economic* policy of a great state' (Blank, 2012; words in italics are author's own). Also, the nuclear sector is not an 'artificial' construct but is one of Russia's comparative advantages. It suffices to note that the first reactor in the world used to produce electricity was Russia's Obninsk reactor in 1954. Nuclear power also played a huge role in fulfilling one of the slogans that had guided Soviet development for over seventy years, namely, 'Communism equals Soviet power plus electrification of the whole country'. In addition, the educational bedrock of the nuclear industry – mathematics, science, physics and engineering – while not as outstanding as during the Soviet days, is nevertheless still among the world's best.

The fact that the nuclear industry has important linkages to the rest of the economy, and is not simply an 'island of innovation', also makes it a useful driver of diversification. A good example is the role of the world's largest and most powerful nuclear-powered icebreakers in the largely ice-bound Northeast Passage in the Arctic (Bellona, 2011; Ragner, 2008).[7] Apart from supplying and maintaining the isolated military and industrial settlements there, the Russian icebreakers also enable highly profitable cargoes of ore and processed minerals mined in the north to be shipped elsewhere. They have also been used to collect crucial data on Russia's continental shelf to bolster its claim of sovereignty over the Arctic seabed and its alleged oil and gas reserves (Conant, 2012). The construction of a Liquified Natural Gas (LNG) terminal at Yamal to harness the gas-rich deposits there, along with the melting and thinning of the sea-ice, could increase the popularity of the Northeast Passage as an international maritime route, where nuclear icebreakers would be required to keep the route open all year round.

The nuclear industry may also help to diversify the source of rents and sustain patronage opportunities, elements which are integral to Putin's regime. The reduction in the growth rate and flow of oil rents, as previously noted, has turned the spotlight on gas as the source of rents. Currently, gas is the source of 50% of electricity production in Russia, with nuclear, coal and hydro power each accounting for 16% of total electricity (WNA, 2015). Therefore, the higher the contribution of nuclear energy (and other sources) to electricity production, the more gas will be available to supply the lucrative export market, thereby enriching Gazprom's officials and patrons. Gazprom produces three quarters of the natural gas in Russia and controls one sixth of the world's reserves of natural gas. Over 55% of Gazprom's revenues comes from European sales alone, even though Europe consumes only 30% of the company's total volume of gas production (Nazarov, 2015).[8] Should Russia fail to replace nuclear power plants that will be shut down due to their age, nuclear power will, by 2030, only account for at most 2% of overall electricity output (Voss, 2008), with gas having to take on a larger burden in electricity production. In other words, building new nuclear reactors and extending the lifetime of existing reactors in Russia itself – which will be partly funded through international sales of reactors and nuclear fuel – will facilitate the enhanced role of gas in underwriting rents, patronage and regime survival in Russia.

Gazprom, however, will be hard-pressed to meet such expectations. This is partly because Russia's output of gas, which has trailed that of oil since 1992, is projected to grow at an annual average of only 0.9% until 2030 (Hanson, 2008). This is because the low domestic price of gas acts as a disincentive for production increases. Gazprom is also beset with internal weaknesses, including corruption and management quality, which impact on growth strategies and profits.[9] Moreover, the company has not responded well to the availability of alternative gas supplies for Europe in the form of LNG gas from the Middle East and shale gas from the USA. Relative to Gazprom, these new sources are less likely to lock customers into pricey long-term contracts, and they have less undesirable geostrategic implications (Dickel et al., 2014; Vavilov, 2015).

Finally, the choice of Rosatom as a driver to diversify the economy may be justified on the basis that alternative options – manufacturing/services, arms exports and nanotechnology – are hardly more attractive. Although the manufacturing and service sectors can rightly boast of 'gazelle' companies, the latter are outliers and are the exceptions that have thrived in a difficult operating environment. Given that much of their success has been due to their nimbleness in satisfying pent-up demand for light consumer goods and IT goods/services, they are vulnerable to a downturn in this same demand as a result of satiety or a reduction in disposable income due to falling oil prices and a depreciating rouble.[10]

Russia's state-controlled weapons industry has been touted as a possible contender to drive economic growth.[11] Russia is the world's second largest (27% of global share) arms exporter after the USA (31%), and its arms exports increased by 37% between 2006–2009 and 2010–2014 (Wezeman and Wezeman, 2015). The value of its exports exceeded US$15 billion in 2014 and it claims an order book of over US$30 billion (Dunai and Forrester, 2015). Russia's arms industry also forms the basis for the development of some of the products in the high-technology sector – such as precision, optical, and electronic equipment – thereby contributing to economic diversification and modernization (Koshovets, 2014). However, the continued growth of Russia's arms exports will face significant constraints. Foremost among these are funding cuts to the US$600 billion state armaments programme for 2011–2020, which aims to upgrade the country's military and which underpins the surge in arms exports. This is due to the pressure on the state budget in view of falling oil prices and international sanctions. Another reason is Ukraine's termination of defence cooperation with Russia, a fallout from the current Russian-Ukrainian conflict. Given that the defence sectors of both countries have been closely intertwined since Soviet times, it will take some time for Russia to replace key Ukrainian-sourced components and service expertise for Russian weapons and other military exports (Weir, 2014). In addition, China is expected to reduce its future imports of Russian arms as it builds up its own military procurement/manufacturing capabilities. At this time, China is Russia's second largest market for its arms export (11%) and the third largest arms exporter in the world.

As for the Russian nanotechnology sector, its promise of economic diversification through innovation was introduced with great fanfare in 2007. However, its achievements have been modest (Connolly, 2013; Westerlund, 2011). Compared to the indigenous nature of the Russian nuclear industry, the key actors in the nanotechnology sector are foreign firms who have taken advantage of access to co-financing from Rusnano, the Russian state corporation for nanotechnology, to enter the Russian market. The demand for nanotechnology products is also very muted due to the correspondingly low levels of high-technology goods produced in Russia. There is therefore an absence of linkage to the rest of the economy; unlike the situation with the nuclear industry with its links to electricity production and shipping. In this regard, while Rosatom was recently singled out for praise because of its 'stability' at a time of economic malaise in Russia, Rusnano is being investigated for misappropriation of funds (Gregory, 2015; Medetsky, 2013). The profile of the wider policy of innovation is also under siege. Skolkovo, for instance, is increasingly perceived by Russian experts as 'just another testing area for modernization ideology or at most a new money and time-consuming project with vague prospects' (Klochikhin, 2012).

Evaluating the success of the nuclear strategy

Having analysed how and why Rosatom is perceived to be an important part of Russia's attempt to diversify its economy, it is time to examine the extent of its success. Rosatom has had a mixed bag of results. At home, most of its thirty-three operating reactors have been licensed for life extensions of fifteen to twenty-five years following extensive refurbishment. Most have also been upgraded – for example, by replacing the turbine generators – by an average of 5% in order to produce more power. With regard to new nuclear capacity, Rosatom's initial plan of commissioning two plants per year for 2011–2014 and then three per year until 2020 has been scaled back; this is partly the result of reductions in domestic demand after the 2008 crisis and decreases in state revenues as a result of lower oil and gas prices since 2012. Nevertheless, it is currently building nine nuclear plants in Russia. Rosatom is also in the process of constructing smaller-capacity floating nuclear plants mounted on barges to service the power and water needs of remote areas with projects in the uranium, aluminium, oil and gas sectors.

Rosatom has enjoyed more success with its export of reactors, building nineteen of the fifty reactors currently under construction outside Russia, including in Iran, China and India. It has also won contracts to build reactors in countries that have never had nuclear energy before, most notably in Turkey, Vietnam, Bangladesh and Jordan (see Figure 8.3). Foreign orders had increased by 60% to US$66.5 billion by 2012, and by 25% to over US$100 billion by the end of 2014, up from a modest US$2 billion in 2000. By 2030, Rosatom expects to build a further nineteen reactors abroad (de Carbonnel, 2013; WNA, 2015). This frenzy of activity has led to wariness about Russia's new nuclear empire (Conant, 2013), as well as warnings that reactor sales to the USA's erstwhile allies in Europe and the Middle East may, in fact, be Trojan horses aimed at enhancing Russia's geopolitical power (Hornat, 2013; Traynor, 2014). In addition to building reactors, Rosatom also has long-term contracts to supply nuclear fuel and to train the local population in host countries on nuclear management and safety techniques.

One reason for Rosatom's success in the export market is that it is a one-stop shop for all things nuclear from start to finish: mining and processing/enrichment of uranium, power plant construction, waste management, and plant decommissioning. Today, Russia supplies 17% of the nuclear fuel used around the world and has by far the largest global uranium enrichment capacity (almost 50%), while URENCO, a European consortium, has the second largest uranium enrichment capacity in the world with a 27% share (WNA, 2015). This means that Rosatom can offer the complete fuel cycle supply, along with a discount on fuel, to clients who buy its reactors. Only Areva of France comes close to offering the full range of services, but even it does not take back the spent fuel from foreign reactors. In explaining why Bangladesh chose to turn to the Russians to build the country's first-ever nuclear power plant, its ambassador explained that 'they will take back the spent fuel – no other country has agreed to do that' (de Carbonnel, 2013). In so doing, Rosatom is continuing the Soviet practice of taking back spent fuel if it is of Russian origin and if it was irradiated in Soviet or Russian-built reactors.

Nevertheless, Russia does have some weakness with respect to the uranium industry – it produces only 5.3% of the world's natural uranium (the sixth largest producer in the world) and owns 9% of global uranium reserves (the third largest stockpile). Determined to 'change the situation and eliminate this imbalance' (Terentieva, 2010), Rosatom has bought stakes in uranium mines in Kazakhstan, Canada and the USA, and it also co-operates closely with Kazakhstan – the world's largest producer – on uranium mining (Oxenstierna, 2010). This has led to warnings that Russia is attempting to lock-up supplies of uranium and enrichment capabilities, a policy that has been dramatically described as the 'Putinisation of uranium' (Katusa, 2014). In this regard, the fact that Russia is the third-largest source of enriched uranium – 13% of total supply – for nuclear power plants in the USA is perceived as a threat to the latter's security (Krancer, 2015; Wellen, 2014).[12] However, this ignores the fact that much of the uranium from Russia is the result of a bilateral agreement concluded in 1993 to extract highly-enriched uranium from Russian nuclear warheads and down-blend it into

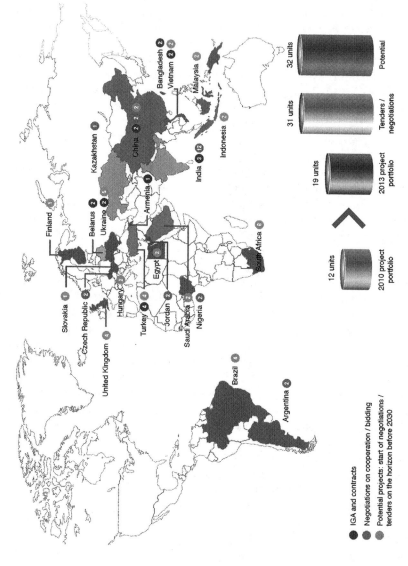

Figure 8.3 Russia's foreign sales of nuclear reactors, as at end 2013.
(Rosatom Annual Review: International Business 2013).

low-enriched uranium for use in US nuclear power plants. The 'Megatons to Megawatts' programme, which safely reduced the size of Russia's nuclear arsenal and provided post-Soviet Russia with much-needed hard currency of US$12–17 billion, ended in 2013 (Pavlov and Rybachenkov, 2013; WNA, 2014), and with it a probable reduction in Russia's role as a fuel supplier to the USA. Australia's announcement in September 2014 of an embargo on sales of natural uranium in response to Russia's actions in Ukraine[13] is a further reminder of the limits to Russia's ambition on the nuclear front.

Second, Rosatom has been able to offer extremely attractive financing terms, thanks to its status as a state corporation and the backing of the Russian state. Apart from building and operating nuclear plants (which typically comprise two or more reactors), Rosatom also offers to finance such projects. Financing is a massive undertaking given that nuclear reactors cost an average of US$4–5 billion each. In Vietnam, for instance, Russia extended a loan guarantee of US$8 billion for the US$10.8 billion project. In Finland, Russia will finance at least 75% of the cost of the €6–7 billion new Hanhikivi-1 nuclear plant, a sum which will come from the country's National Welfare Fund, which is in turn derived from profits from oil and gas exports.[14] As for Hungary, Russia has agreed to lend up to US$13.7 billion or about 80% of the cost of construction of two new reactors. As a possible sign of financial belt-tightening, Rosatom announced in March 2015 that it will finance only 49.9%, rather than the bulk, of the US$10 billion nuclear power plant construction in Jordan. Moreover, Jordan is obliged to buy reactor fuel from Rosatom for at least the first decade. It is worth noting here that Jordan discovered a large domestic supply of uranium in 2007 but has yet to mine/ develop these deposits.

The sustainability of this financing model is, arguably, Rosatom's biggest challenge. Given that the cost effectiveness of Rosatom's nuclear power plants depends on allocations from the state budget, which is in turn tied to oil revenues, Russia's current economic malaise may limit the amount of funding for new projects abroad. Salary and general budget cuts of 10% have been announced for 2015 and the Russian government is expected to draw over US$50 billion from the country's oil-funded Reserve Fund – thereby depleting over half of the Reserve Fund – to reduce the budget deficit for 2015. This depletion of the Reserve Fund is likely to continue for two reasons.[15] First, banks and companies are lining up for handouts because they cannot easily access debt markets in the West due to the sanctions over Ukraine, and because the cost of debt servicing has increased due to the depreciation of the rouble. As patron of 'Putin's Protection Racket', Putin will be under pressure to reprise his role in 2008 with regard to protecting Kremlin-connected companies from financial ruin.[16] Second, with real wages projected to fall by 9% in 2015 for the first time since Putin became President in 2000 (Aslund, 2015), there may be pressure to subsidise basic necessities.[17] Even prior to the drawdown for 2015 the amount in the Reserve Fund was already well below the 7% of GDP mandated by the authorities. In short, therefore, additional state financing for Rosatom's foreign projects is uncertain since competition for financial resources is fierce.

Even if Russia is able to bounce back fairly quickly from the current crisis should the oil price slump be short-lived, the fact that economic crises reoccur every decade or so in Russia, partly due to unresolved problems in the economy, is detrimental to Rosatom's prospects. This is because the nuclear industry requires a long and stable time horizon: it takes a minimum of ten years to conceptualise and actualise a nuclear power plant. Moreover, while costs for nuclear power plants tend to rise in the course of construction, those for renewable energy, particular solar, have decreased significantly and made solar a viable option.[18]

What differentiates and worsens this current crisis from previous ones in 1998 and 2008 is the impact of the financial and trade sanctions levied against Russia since March 2014 over its policy in Ukraine. These have put the brakes on access to the Western debt markets and technology necessary to modernise the energy and manufacturing sectors, as illustrated by the suspension of BP's and ExxonMobil's exploration for crude in Russia's shale and Arctic formations respectively. Any widening of the sanctions to include the nuclear industry will badly affect Rosatom. Such sanctions will limit its growth strategy of building global alliances with other nuclear vendors (Gorst and Simon, 2010). They will also significantly reduce its earning from commercial exports and deliveries of enriched uranium products and services, of which 80% originate from customers in Europe and North America (Rosatom, 2014). Rosatom's success is, therefore, partly hostage to Putin's willingness to reintegrate Russia into the global economic system through the pursuit of a less confrontational foreign policy.

A third reason for Rosatom's success abroad is that Kiriyenko has modernised much of its Soviet-era management, even bringing in Western personnel. For instance, Jukka Laaksonen, the former head of Finland's nuclear regulator, is Rosatom's face of overseas sales, and his appointment 'speaks of how much significance we do attach to effectiveness and safety of our projects' (Rosatom, 2012). Rosatom has also worked hard to overcome the Soviet Union's Chernobyl legacy, when a reactor in Ukraine exploded in 1986, spewing tons of radioactive particles into the air; to this day the once-thriving town of Pripyat, 3 kilometres away from the power plant, remains eerily devoid of human inhabitants. Russia has, in fact, been using Chernobyl to emphasise its unique understanding of nuclear safety in reactor design (Conant, 2012). The fact that the same reactors which are marketed overseas are also being built in Russia itself has dampened criticism of Rosatom for using foreign 'test subjects', a criticism that American nuclear vendors are not spared from given that no new nuclear plant has been built in the USA since the 1970s.

Nevertheless, questions about safety and oversight in Russia are valid since Rosatom functions as both regulator and vendor, unlike nuclear industries in France or the USA. They are also especially pertinent since Rosatom may have over-committed itself in building a large number of reactors domestically as well as abroad, and may be tempted to cut corners. As the scandals in South Korea's nuclear industry have demonstrated, a corporate culture of secrecy and opaque transactions between regulators and state-owned companies is unhelpful in building trust among domestic and foreign audiences (Davis, 2014; Patel, 2013).

Management issues at Rosatom are, in fact, part of a bigger wariness about its principal, Russia. Declarations by Kiriyenko that Rosatom wants 'to make profits out of nuclear energy. We want to power the world' (de Carbonnel, 2013) and that nuclear energy 'should be out of all political discussions, all temporary disagreements' (Chestney, 2014) suggest commercial ambition above all. However, this is tempered by Russia's repeated demonstrations of its willingness to use the 'gas weapon' – foreign gas sales and pipeline ownership by Gazprom – to pursue political ends, for example in Ukraine since 2005.

Unsurprisingly there are concerns that Turkey and Finland, which already depend on Russia for 55% and 100% respectively of their natural gas imports and which have concluded nuclear plant construction contracts with Rosatom, will be even more vulnerable to the vicissitudes of Russian foreign policy. Likewise, the tender in the Czech Republic to increase the number of reactors at the Temelin nuclear power plant was, to a large extent, a sideshow amid the geostrategic jockeying between consortiums led by Rosatom and Westinghouse of the USA (Hornat, 2013; Wesolowsky, 2013). Nevertheless, the tender was eventually cancelled in 2014. In fact, with Rosatom as the source of one third of the European Union's enriched uranium, the bloc's Energy Security Strategy adopted in 2014 still warned that 'particular attention should be paid to investments in new nuclear power plants to be built in the EU using non-EU technology, to ensure that these plants are dependent not only on Russia for the supply of the nuclear fuel' (Bershidsky, 2015). The privatisation of the civilian nuclear energy division of Rosatom, as is the case with German and US nuclear companies, will help to address such fears on the part of host countries. However, this solution is highly unlikely given Russia's historical and current political pathologies.

Finally, Rosatom's success may have been a consequence of cooling relations between the host country and Western governments. A few examples of Rosatom making nuclear inroads into countries that had been pro-Western should suffice. In Turkey, the 2002 electoral victory of the moderate Islamist AKP party in Turkey resulted in a noticeable reduction in commitments to secularism, and a rapprochement with Russia as part of the government's 'zero problems with neighbours' policy.[19] All of this has strained relations between the North Atlantic Treaty Organisation's most loyal member in the Muslim world and the USA/EU. As for Jordan, it was keen to escape its dependence on foreign oil and gas, which was costing it US$3 billion annually. However, its refusal to cede its right to enrich local uranium ore by concluding a 'gold standard' 123 Agreement prior to nuclear cooperation with the USA meant that American vendors could not legally participate in the tender for a nuclear plant in 2013 (El-Anis, 2012). Meanwhile, the increasingly authoritarian behaviour and policies of the government in Hungary led by Prime Minister Viktor Orban – including high-level corruption, limits to judicial independence and praise for Putin's illiberal model of politics – has earned him stern rebukes from his EU counterparts. According to one commentator, 'Hungary has gone so far as to actually reject explicitly by the Prime Minister the very values that guide the European Union and NATO. This has never happened before. This is a unique event' (Jovanovski, 2014). It cannot be a coincidence that in all three countries cited above, Rosatom was awarded nuclear contracts ahead of bids by Western-led consortiums. In the same way, however, Russia's close ties with nuclear Iran and the Assad regime in Syria could mean that Rosatom has little hope of securing nuclear contracts with oil-rich countries in the Gulf, such as Saudi Arabia. The latter, who has announced plans to build nuclear power plants, is implacably opposed to what it perceives as a regional power grab by Shia-ruled countries.

8.4 Conclusion

The case study of the nuclear industry implies that Rosatom possesses the raw material, human talent, marketing savvy and technological wizardry for success. Can this be extrapolated to suggest that diversification writ large will be a successful endeavour for Russia? Diversification will proceed, albeit in fits and starts; it will be primarily driven by political considerations rather than economic arguments, and financed largely by oil revenues. As a rational political leader, Putin will want to maximise political longevity. This will require him to perpetuate his rent-management system for the purpose of instrumental legitimacy and to satisfy popular aspirations for a modern economy befitting a great power as a nod to ideological legitimacy.

Diversification, however, will be circumscribed by three interlocking considerations. First, diversification takes time, costs money, and is hence highly dependent on a continuous flow of oil revenues; Russia will therefore remain oil-dependent for the foreseeable future. Second, diversification requires not just financial commitment but also institutional reforms to the way the economy is managed in Russia. These include the introduction and implementation of a more secure property rights regime to encourage long-term investment, business-friendly regulations to encourage the growth of 'gazelle' companies and other businesses, and transparency of the rent management system to increase accountability and reduce corruption. After all, sound macro- and microeconomic policies are futile without the relevant supportive institutional structures. Third, the two tasks noted above will need to be complemented by the existence of a more benign global operating environment. Mikhail Gorbachev and Boris Yeltsin, the last President of the Soviet Union and the first President of post-Soviet Russia respectively, were able to focus on urgent economic reforms partly because the world at that time was relatively stable and unthreatening to Russian interests. Western countries and global institutions had also been willing and able at that time to provide assistance, and to try to integrate Russia into the world economy. Today, Russia also has to play its part in creating a conducive external environment, namely by respecting international law and being a generally cooperative member of the world community. These three conditions, taken together, hold the keys to the sustainability of Rosatom and to successful economic diversification in Russia.

Notes

1 Al-Sabah (1988) has suggested that 'Dutch disease' also affects countries that are neither rich nor dependent on natural resources. He cites the example of Japan, where the technology boom in the country's manufacturing sector in the 1960s adversely affected its less dynamic agriculture sector.

2 It is worth noting that manufacturing may not be a perfect proxy for diversification away from a hydrocarbon economy since, in Russia, it includes oil-related activities such as oil refining.

3 Jonathan Stern, an expert on Russia's gas industry, describes the following situation: 'People at Gazprom are not stupid... But Putin is forcing them into all kinds of crazy projects and refusing to allow them to adapt to market conditions. If you look at all the major announcements that Gazprom has supposedly made about projects, they're all Putin's announcements. They are all things that Putin has led in the public domain' (Balmforth, 2013). In return, Putin has protected Gazprom's gas export monopoly from rival Russian gas companies, and from being broken up into separate production and distribution entities.

4 Exports of military weapons and armaments are not captured in the World Bank's data on manufactured goods (author's personal communication). High-technology products produced by the Russian military-industrial complex but with civilian applications are also excluded because they do not conform to the OECD/ISIC classification based on non-military sectoral origins (Koshovets, 2014).

5 The other state corporations were the Bank of Development, the Russian Corporation for Nanotechnologies (Rusnano), the Communal Services Reform Fund, Olympstroi (which spearheaded the construction and management of the 2014 Olympic Games venue in Sochi), Russian Technologies (which gathered together defence industry assets as well as chemical and automotive enterprises), the United Shipbuilding Corporation, and the United Aircraftbuilding Corporation.

6 The experience of Singapore's parastatals suggests that monopolies like Rosatom and Gazprom may not reap similar successes. This is because in Singapore there are multiple and competing government-linked companies within each industry, rather than a single monopoly as is the case in Russia.

7 The nuclear icebreaker fleet had, in fact, been managed by the Murmansk Shipping Company since 1994, even though the fleet was under state ownership. Although the MSC is mostly privately-owned, the state maintains a 25% share in the company. The official transfer of the fleet to Rosatom took place in 2008, despite objections from MSC.

8 Revenue from domestic gas sales accounts for only 25% of Gazprom's total gas sales, since domestic gas is highly subsidised.

9 For example, although Gazprom posted net profits of US$45 billion in 2011, it may have lost US$40 billion to corruption and inefficiency (Aslund, 2012).

10 Gevorkyan (2013), Baranov (2014), and Koshovets (2014), however, argue that the focus must be on Russia's domestic market and operations rather than on exports, despite the institutional and policy barriers within the business environment. This is partly because they expect Russia to face a hostile international environment.

11 It is represented by the Rosoboronexport company and is an integral part of the Russian Technologies state corporation. The latter was created at the same time as Rosatom.

12 If countries closely associated with Russia are included, namely Kazakhstan and Uzbekistan, then former Soviet countries are the largest source (28%) of enriched uranium for nuclear plants in the USA (EIA, 2013).

13 Australia has the world's largest reserves (29%) of uranium (WNA, 2014), but does not use nuclear power.

14 Russia has two sovereign wealth funds funded by tax revenues from oil and gas sales. The Reserve Fund is used to support government finances when the economy is weak

– it was last tapped in 2009. The National Welfare Fund was expressly created to finance pension expenditures, but has been used to support infrastructure projects during economic crises.

15 The values of the Reserve Fund and National Welfare Fund were US$76 billion and US$74 billion respectively at the end of March 2015 (Simola, 2015).

16 Putin's crisis management plan in 2008, which included raiding the Reserve Fund of US$100 billion, was perceived as tantamount to a de facto privatisation of a good part of the country's foreign currency reserves by highly-leveraged and highly-connected businessmen (Hedlund, 2013).

17 In February 2015 the government mandated a 16% reduction in the price of vodka, a key commodity in Russia.

18 The cost of the Areva-built Olkiluoto 3 nuclear plant in Finland has increased from €3 billion to a potential €8.5 billion, and actual operation has been pushed back to a decade later to 2018. In comparison, the cost of solar panels and electricity from solar has fallen by 50–75% since 2009 (IRENA, 2014).

19 This policy is known as the Davutoglu doctrine, named for its originator and Turkey's foreign minister, Ahmet Davutoglu. For conflicting evaluations on the sustainability of Turkey's rapprochement with Russia, see Warhola and Bezci (2013), Trenin (2013) and Flanagan (2013).

References

Ahrend, R. (2005) 'Can Russia break the resource curse?' *Eurasian Geography and Economics*, vol. 46, no. 8, 584–609.

Al-Sabah, M. (1988) 'The Dutch disease in an oil exporting country: Kuwait', *OPEC Review*, 129–144.

Aslund, A. (2005) 'Russian resources: Curse or rents?' *Eurasian Geography and Economics*, vol. 46, no. 8, 610–617.

Aslund, A. (2010) 'Why doesn't Russia join the WTO?' *The Washington Quarterly*, vol. 33, no. 2, 49–63.

Aslund, A. (2012) 'Why Gazprom resembles a crime syndicate', *The Moscow Times*, 28 February.

Aslund, A. (2015) 'Russia in free fall', *Capital*, 25 February.

Baev, P.K. (2010) Russia abandons the 'energy superpower' idea but lacks energy for 'modernisation', *Strategic Analysis*, vol. 34, no. 6, 885–896.

Balmforth, T. (2013) *At 20, Russia's Gazprom struggle to stay dominant*, Radio Free Europe/Radio Liberty, 20 May.

Baranov, A.O. (2014) 'A macroeconomic analysis of the main outcomes of Russia's economic development in the post-Soviet period', *Problems of Economic Transition*, vol. 56, no. 10, 21–38.

Bellona (2007) *Rosatom state corporation*, Bellona, 26 November.

Bellona (2011) *Rosatom to incorporate nuclear-powered icebreakers – how transparent is the move?* Bellona, 11 October.

Berglof, E., Plekhanov, A. and Rousso, A. (2009) 'A tale of two crises', *Finance and Development*, June, 15–18.

Bershidsky, L. (2015) 'Be glad about Russia's nuclear setback', *Bloomberg View*, 13 March, available at www.bloombergview.com/articles/2015-03-13/be-glad-about-russia-s-nuclear-setback (accessed on 14 April 2016).

Bhattacharyya, S. and Hodler, R. (2010) 'Natural resources, democracy, and corruption', *European Economic Review*, vol. 54, no. 4, 608–621.

Birdsall, N. et al. (1993) *The East Asian miracle: Economic growth and public policy - A World Bank policy research report*. New York: Oxford University Press.

Blank, S.J. (2012) 'The sacred monster: Russia as a foreign policy actor', in Blank, S.J. (ed.), *Perspectives on Russia foreign policy*, Carlisle, Pennsylvania: US Army War College.

BP (2014) *BP Statistical Review of World Energy*, London: BP.

Cadot, O., Carrere, C. and Strauss-Kahn, V. (2011) 'Export diversification: What's behind the hump?' *Review of Economics and Statistics*, vol. 93, no. 2, 590–605.

Caselli, F. (2006) 'Power struggles and the natural resource curse', in *LSE Research*. London: London School of Economics.

Chestney, N. (2014) *Nuclear energy should be kept out of politics: Russia's Rosatom*, Reuters, 11 September.

CIA (n.d.) Russia: The World Factbook. Available online at www.cia.gov/library/publications/the-world-factbook/geos/rs.html (accessed 7 November 2015).

Conant, E. (2012) 'Russia uses lessons of Chernobyl as a selling point for its reactor technology', *Scientific American*, 18 September.

Conant, E. (2013) 'Russia's new empire: Nuclear power', *Scientific American*, vol. 309, no. 4, 88–93.

Connolly, R. (2013) 'State industrial policy in Russia: The nanotechnology industry', *Post-Soviet Affairs*, vol. 29, no. 1, 1–30.

Davidson, C. (2009) *Abu Dhabi: Oil and beyond*, Oxford: Oxford University Press.

Davis, W. (2014) 'South Korea nuclear power: Are the dark times over?' 6 February, American Nuclear Society.

Deak, A. (2014) *The Putin-Orban nuclear deal: A short assessment*, Berlin: Heinrich Boll Stiftung.

de Carbonnel, A. (2013) *Russian nuclear ambition powers building at home and abroad*, Reuters, 22 July.

Dickel, R., Hassanzadeh, E., Henderson, J., Honore, A., El-Katiri, L., Pirani, S., Rogers, H., Stern, J. and Yafimava, K. (2014) *Reducing European dependence on Russian gas: Distinguishing natural gas security from geopolitics*, Oxford: Oxford Institute of Energy Studies.

Dienes, L. (2004) 'Observations on the problematic potential of Russian oil and the complexities of Siberia', *Eurasian Geography and Economics*, vol. 45, no. 5, 319–345.

Dobrynskaya, V. and Turkisch, E. (2010) 'Economic diversification and Dutch disease in Russia', *Post-Communist Economies*, vol. 22, no. 3, 283–302.

Dunai, P. and Forrester, C. (2015) 'Russia reveals defence orders, order backlog', *IHS Jane's Defence Industry*, 18 March.

EBRD (2012) *Diversifying Russia: Harnessing regional diversity*, London: European Bank for Reconstruction and Development.

EIA (2013) 'The US relies on foreign uranium, enrichment services to fuel its nuclear power plants', *Today in Energy*, Washington DC: US Energy Information Administration.

El-Anis, I. (2012) 'The political economy of energy security and nuclear energy in Jordan', *The Central European Journal of International and Security Studies*, vol. 6, no. 1, 13–35.

Ernst and Young (2013) 'Ernst and Young's Attractiveness Survey: Russia 2013 – Shaping Russia's Future', Ernst and Young.

ESCWA (n.d.) *The Demographic Profile of Saudi Arabia*, UN Economic and Social Commission for Western Asia, available online at http://www.escwa.un.org/popin/members/SaudiArabia.pdf:

Flanagan, S.J. (2013) 'The Turkey-Russia-Iran nexus: Eurasian power dynamics', *The Washington Quarterly*, vol. 36, 1, 163–178.

Filippov, P. (2011) 'Is corruption in Russia's DNA?' *Open Democracy*.

Freeland, C. (2000) *Sale of the century: The inside story of the second Russian revolution*, London: Little, Brown and Company.

Gaddy, C.G. and Ickes, B.W. (2010) 'Russia after the global financial crisis', *Eurasian Geography and Economics*, vol. 51, no. 3, 281–311.

Gaddy, C.G. and Ickes, B.W. (2011) 'Putin's protection racket', in Korhonen, I. and Solanko, L. (eds.), From Soviet plans to Russian reality: Essays in honor of Pekka Sutela, Helsinki: WSOYpro Oy.

Gelb, A. (2011) 'Economic diversification in resource-rich countries', in Amadou, N.R.S, Arezki, R. and Gylfason, T. (eds.), *Beyond the curse: Policies to harness the power of natural resources*, Washington DC: International Monetary Fund.

Gevorkyan, A. (2012) 'Is Russia still a BRIC?' *Challenge*, vol. 55, no. 6, 88–116.

Gill, I.S., Izvorski, I., van Eeghen, W. and de Rosa, D. (2014) *Diversified development: Making the most of natural resources in Eurasia*, Washington DC: The World Bank.

Gorst, I. and Simon, B. (2010) 'Rosatom launches global charm offensive', *Financial Times*, 1 September.

Gregory, P. (2015) 'Rosatom: Russia's one bright spot (thanks to Hillary?)', *Riccochet*, 27 April, available online at https://ricochet.com/rosatom-russias-one-bright-spot-thanks-to-hillary/ (accessed 21 April 2016).

Gustafson, T. (2012) *Wheel of fortune: The battle for oil and power in Russia*, Cambridge, MA: The Belknap Press of Harvard University Press.

Hanson, P. (2008) 'State-led, oil-fueled development: Is that good for Russia's future?' in CESifo Forum, vol. 9, no. 2, Munich: Ifo Institute for Economic Research.

Hanson, P. and Teague, E. (2013) *Liberal insiders and economic reform in Russia*, London: Chatham House.

Hedlund, S. (2013) 'Economic reform under Putin 2.0: Will petrodollars suffice to keep the ship afloat?' in Blank, S.J. (ed.), *Politics and economics in Putin's Russia*, Carlisle, Pennsylvania: Strategic Studies Institute and US Army War College Press.

Hedlund, S. (2014) *Putin's energy agenda: The Contradictions of Russia's resource wealth*, Boulder, Colorado: Lynne Reiner.

Hertog, S. (2012) 'Public industry as a tool of rentier economy diversification: The GCC case', in Luciani, G., Hertog, S., Woertz, E. and Youngs, R. (eds.), *The Gulf region: Economic development and diversification*, Berlin: Gerlach Press.

Hertog, S. (2013) 'The evolution of rent recycling during two booms in the Gulf Arab states: Business dynamics and social stagnation', in Legrenzi, M. and Momani, B. (eds.), Shifting geo-economic power of the Gulf: Oil, finance, and institutions, Farnham, Surrey: Ashgate.

Hesse, H. (2008) *Export diversification and economic growth*, Washington DC: Commission on Growth and Development/The World Bank.

Hodler, R. (2006) 'The curse of natural resources in fractionalized countries', *European Economic Review*, vol. 50, no. 6, 1367–1386.

Hornat, J. (2013) 'Czech nuclear power in the shadow of geopolitics', *Open Democracy*, 9 January, available online at www.opendemocracy.net/jan-horn%C3%A1t/czech-nuclear-power-in-shadow-of-geopolitics (accessed 21 April 2016).

HSBC (2014) *HSBC Global Connections Report: March 2014*, London: HSBC Bank plc.

Imbs, J. and Wacziarg, R. (2003) 'Stages of diversification', *American Economic Review*, vol. 93, no. 1, 63–98.

IMF (2014) *IMF Data Template on International Reserves and Foreign Currency Liquidity*, International Monetary Fund, available at www.imf.org/external/np/sta/ir/IRProcessWeb/colist.aspx (accessed on 14 April 2016).

IRENA (2014) 'Falling costs drive record solar and wind growth', *IRENA Quarterly*, Abu Dhabi: International Renewable Energy Agency.

Ito, K. (2012) 'The impact of oil price volatility on macroeconomy in Russia', *The Annals of Regional Science*, vol. 48, no. 3, 695–702.

Jovanovski, K. (2014) 'Hungary eyes Russia's 'illiberal' model', *AlJazeera*, 18 August.

Katusa, M. (2014) *The Colder War: How the global energy trade slipped from America's grasp*, Hoboken, New Jersey: John Wiley & Sons.

Khilji, E. (2005) *Corruption in Russia: Reiman's telecommunication empire (a case study)*, New Jersey: Institute of Modern Russia, available online at http://imrussia.org/en/research/2005-corruption-in-russia-reiman%E2%80%99s-telecommunication-empire-a-case-study (accessed 21 April 2016).

Klochikhin, E.A. (2012) 'The challenges of fostering innovation: Russia's unstable progress', *International Journal of Economics and Business Research*, vol. 4, no. 6, 659–678.

Kochhar, K., Ouliaris, S. and Samiei, H. (2006) *What hinders investment in the oil sector?* Washington DC: International Monetary Fund.

Kolodnyaya, G. (n.d.) *Foundation factors of the growth of fast growing 'Gazelle Firms'*, unpublished manuscript.

Kononczuk, W. (2012) *Russia's best ally: The situation of the Russian oil sector and forecasts for its future*, Warsaw: Center for Eastern Studies OSW.

Koshovets, O.B. (2014) 'Financial performance and technological modernization of Russian hi-technology complex and their role to boost economic development', *Journal of International Scientific Publications*, vol. 8, 633–640.

Krancer, M. (2015) 'What's more dangerous than Iran enriching uranium? America enriching none', *Forbes*, 3 March 2015, available at http://onforb.es/ICpp9cX (accessed 14 April 2016).

Kuchins, A. (2006) *Vladimir the Lucky*, 25 July 2006: Carnegie Endowment for International Peace.

Kuznetsov, B., Dolgopyatova, T., Golikova, V., Gonchar, K., Yakovlev, A. and Yasin, Y. (2011) 'Russian manufacturing revisited: Industrial enterprises at the start of the crisis', *Post-Soviet Affairs*, vol. 27, no. 4, 366–386.

Ledeneva, A.V. (1998) *Russia's economy of favors: Blat, networking, and informal exchange*, Cambridge: Cambridge University Press.

Lederman, D. and Maloney, W.F. (eds.) (2007) *Natural resources: Neither curse nor destiny*, Washington DC: World Bank.

Levgold, R. (2006) 'Russian foreign policy during state transformation', in Levgold, R. (ed.), *Russian Foreign Policy in the 21st Century and the Shadow of the Past*, New York: Columbia University Press.

Light, M. (2010) 'Foreign policy thinking', in Malcolm, N., Pravda, A. and Light, M. (eds.), *Internal Factors in Russian Foreign Policy*, Oxford: Royal Institute of International Affairs and Clarendon Press.

Lo, B. (2008) *Axis of convenience: Moscow, Beijing, and the new geopolitics*, London: Royal Institute of International Affairs.

Luong, P.J. and Weinthal, E. (2010) *Oil is not a curse: Ownership structure and institutions in Soviet successor states*, New York: Cambridge University Press.

Maurice, N.E. and Davis, J. (2011) *Unraveling the underlying causes of price volatility in world coffee and cocoa commodity markets*, New York and Geneva: UNCTAD Special Unit on Commodities.

Mcdctsky, A. (2013) 'Auditors lay into Rusnano following criticism by Putin', *The Moscow Times*, 29 April.

Medvedev, D. (2009) *Go Russia!* Available online at http://archive.kremlin.ru/eng/speeches/2009/09/10/1534_type104017_221527.shtml (accessed 7 November 2015).

Mehlum, H., Moene, K. and Torvik, R. (2006) 'Institutions and the resource curse', *The Economic Journal*, vol. 116, no. 508, 1–20.

Mukhatzhanova, G. (2007) *Russian nuclear industry reforms: Consolidation and expansion*, James Martin Center for Nonproliferation Studies, available online at www.nonproliferation.org/russian-nuclear-industry-reforms-consolidation-and-expansion/

Naymushin, I. (2014) *Global oil glut sends prices plunging to 4-year low*, Reuters, 15 October.

Nazarov, I. (2015) 'Overview of the Russian natural gas industry', in Vavilov, A. (ed.), *Gazprom: An energy giant and its challenges in Europe*, Houndmills, Basingstoke: Palgrave Macmillan.

Oomes, N. and Kalcheva, K. (2007) 'Diagnosing Dutch disease: Does Russia have the symptoms?' IMF Working Paper, Washington DC: International Monetary Fund.

Orttung, R. (2014) 'Corruption in Russia', *Russian Analytical Digest*, vol. 144, 2–4.

Oxenstierna, S. (2010) *Russia's nuclear energy expansion*, Stockholm: Swedish Defence Research Agency (FOI).

Patel, S. (2013) ',South Korea walks an energy tightrope', *PowerMag*, 1 November, available online at www.powermag.com/south-korea-walks-an-energy-tightrope/ (accessed 21 April 2016).

Pavlov, A. and Rybachenkov, V. (2013) *HEU-LEU project: A success story of Russian-US nuclear disarmament cooperation*, Moscow: Center for Energy and Security Studies.

Pipes, R. (1999) 'Is Russia still an enemy?' *Foreign Affairs*, vol. 76, no. 5.

Ragner, C.L. (2008) 'The northern sea route', in Hallberg, T. (ed.), *The Norden Association's yearbook for 2008*, Stockholm: Arena Norden.

Robinson, N. (2011) 'Russian patrimonial capitalism and the international financial crisis', *Journal of Communist Studies and Transition Politics*, vol. 27, no. 3–4, 434–455.

Rochlitz, M. (2014) 'Corporate raiding and the role of the state in Russia', *Post-Soviet Affairs*, vol. 30, no. 2–3, 89–114.

Rosatom (2012) *Jukka Laaksonen gets a post in Rusatom Overseas*, Rosatom press release, 2 February 2012, available at www.rosatom.ru/en/presscentre/news/f7a675004a040754ab04ef03099b7a0a (accessed 14 April 2016).

Rosatom (2014) *Rosatom annual review: International Business 2013*, Moscow: Rosatom.

Rosefielde, S. (2013) 'Russian economic reform 2012: 'Deja vu all over again'', in Blank, S.J. (ed.), *Politics and economics in Putin's Russia*, Carlisle, Pennsylvania: Strategic Studies Institute and US Army War College Press.

Rutland, P. (2008) 'Putin's economic record: Is the oil boom sustainable?' *Europe-Asia Studies*, vol. 60, no. 6, 1051–1072.

Sakwa, R. (2009) *The quality of freedom: Khodorkovsky, Putin, and the Yukos affair*, Oxford: Oxford University Press.

Schulze, G.G., Sjahrir, B.S. and Zakharov, N. (2013) *Corruption in Russia*, Freiburg: University of Freiburg.

Sim, I., Thomsen, S. and Yeong, G. (2014) *The state as shareholder: The case of Singapore*, Singapore: Center for Governance, Institutions and Organisations/Chartered Institute of Management Accountants.

Sim, L.-C. (2008) *The rise and fall of privatization in the Russian oil industry*, Houndmills, Basingstoke: Palgrave Macmillan.

Sim, L.-C. (2012) 'Re-branding Abu Dhabi: From oil giant to energy titan', *Place Branding and Public Diplomacy*, vol. 8, no. 1, 83–98.

Simola, H., Solanko, L. and Korhonen, V. (2013) *Perspectives on Russia's energy sector*, Helsinki: Bank of Finland Institute for Economies in Transition BOFIT.

Simola, H. (2015) 'Russia's international reserves and oil funds', *BOFIT Policy Brief no. 4*, Helsinki: Bank of Finland Institute for Economies in Transition BOFIT.

Terentieva, A. (2010) 'Russia goes uranium mining around the world', *Global Geopolitics and Political Economy*, 31 March, available online at http://globalgeopolitics.net/wordpress/2010/03/31/russia-goes-uranium-mining-around-the-world/ (accessed 21 April 2016).

Tompson, W. (2006) 'A frozen Venezuela? The 'resource curse' and Russian politics', in Ellman, M. (Ed.), *Russia's oil and natural gas: Bonanza or curse?* London: Anthem.

Transparency International (2016) *Corruptions Perception Index 2015*. Berlin: Transparency International.

Traynor, I. (2014) 'European leaders fear growth of Russian influence abroad', *The Guardian*, 17 November.

Trenin, D. (2013) 'From Damascus to Kabul: Any common ground between Turkey and Russia?' *Insight Turkey*, vol. 15, no. 1, 37–49.

van der Molen, M. (2014) *Country report: Russia*, Rabobank.

Vavilov, A. (2015) 'Introduction', in Vavilov, A. (ed.), *Gazprom: An energy giant and its challenges in Europe*, Houndmills, Basingstoke: Palgrave Macmillan.

Vercueil, J. (2014) 'Could Russia become more innovative? Coordinating key actors of the innocation system', *Post-Communist Economies*, vol. 26, no. 4, 498–521.

Voss, S.S. (2008) 'Russia's future: The precarious balance between Russia's energy and military security', paper presented at PONI Conference, Offutt AF Base, Omaha, US.

Warhola, J.W. and Bezci, E.B. (2013) 'The return of President Putin and Russian-Turkish relations: Where are they headed?' *SAGE Open*, 1–15.

Weir, F. (2014) 'Why Ukraine's freeze on arms sales to Russia will hurt Kiev too', *Christian Science Monitor*, 17 June.

Wellen, R. (2014) 'Is US nuclear energy or isn't it dependent on Russian enriched uranium?' *Foreign Policy in Focus*, available online at http://fpif.org/u-s-nuclear-energy-isnt-dependent-russian-enriched-uranium/ (accessed 21 April 2016).

Wesolowsky, T. (2013) 'Deal at Czech nuclear plant fuels US-Russian economic rivalry', *Christian Science Monitor*, March, available at www.csmonitor.com/World/Europe/2013/0304/Deal-at-Czech-nuclear-power-plant-fuels-US-Russia-economic-rivalry (accessed 18 April 2016).

Westerlund, F. (2011) *Russian nanotechnology in R&D*, Stockholm: Swedish Defence Research Agency (FOI).

Wezeman, P.D. and Wezeman, S.T. (2015) *SIPRI fact sheet: Trends in international arms transfers, 2014*, Stockholm: Stockholm International Peace Research Institute.

WNA (2014) *Supply of uranium*, London: World Nuclear Association, available online at www.world-nuclear.org/info/Nuclear-Fuel-Cycle/Uranium-Resources/Supply-of-Uranium/ (accessed 21 April 2016).

WNA (2015) *Nuclear power in Russia*, London: World Nuclear Association, available online at www.world-nuclear.org/info/Country-Profiles/Countries-O-S/Russia--Nuclear-Power/ (accessed 21 April 2016).

Wright, G. and Czelusta. J. (2007) 'Resource-Based Economic Growth, Past and Present', in Lederman, D. and Maloney, W.F. (eds.), *Natural resources: Neither curse nor destiny*, Redwood City, California: World Bank/Stanford University Press.

Yudanov, A. (2008) '"Gazelle firms", growth, and qualitative changes in the Russian economy', in *Moscow 'Services Management' Symposium on Wealth and Prosperity in the Period of Global Transformation: Experience of Russia and Asia*, The Financial Academy (Government of Russia).

9 Kazakhstan's diversification strategy

Are policies building linkages and promoting competition?

Peter Howie

9.1 Introduction

Kazakhstan is a small open middle-income economy with a per capita income in 2013 of about US$13.2 thousand, or US$23.2 thousand when adjusted by purchasing power. The country spans a vast territory (about 2.7 million km^2; it is the ninth largest country in the world) which is inhabited by a relatively small population (17.3 million inhabitants) and is, hence, characterised by a low population density. Furthermore, Kazakhstan has a high proportion of rural residents as its rural population contributes about 45% of the country's total population. Almaty (the country's financial centre and old capital), Astana (the country's new capital), and oil-rich regions next to the Caspian Sea have been developing fast; on the other hand, depressed regions exist in the north and south. Annual per capita GDP growth has averaged almost 8% between 2000 and 2013. Kazakhstan's fundamental characteristics include: i) significant natural resource endowments; ii) limited scope in its markets due to substantial geographical barriers to the neighbouring markets of China, the very long distance to the major European markets and a small domestic population; iii) the fact that it is landlocked; and iv) very poor transportation infrastructure.

Currently, Kazakhstan risks getting caught in the middle-income trap – being neither a low cost imitator nor a high value-added innovator. Past strategies have been successful in driving industrial transformation from low GDP levels reliant on agriculture, ferrous and non-ferrous metals and, to a minor extent, oil at independence in 1991. Today the oil and gas industry is the 'engine' of Kazakhstan's economy, and since 2000 it has accounted for the greatest share of foreign investment and technology inflow. The three giant oil and gas fields – Karachaganak, Tengiz and Kashagan – have accounted for the majority of foreign direct investment in the country since 2000. The Kashagan field, found in 1999, is the largest discovery worldwide since the 1970s and is considered to be the second largest oil field in the world after Prudhoe Bay Oil Field in Alaska (Interfax, 2015). The total expected cost of developing the field is estimated at US$53 billion (Williams et al., 2015; Interfax, 2014).[1] In 2013, hydrocarbon resources accounted for over 64% of Kazakhstan's exports, more than 12% of its GDP (Figure 9.1), and 47% of government revenues. Oil and gas production has expanded by 135% between 2000 and 2010, from 0.72 to 1.67 million barrels per day, and has stayed fairly constant thereafter (United States EIA, 2014). The non-energy GDP has grown by 7.5% on average during the period from 2002 to 2013, comprising mainly real estate activities (14.7% of GDP in 2013), manufacturing output (12.4% of GDP in 2013), trade (12.2% of GDP in 2013), transport and communication (11.5% of GDP in 2013), government activities (8.9% of GDP in 2013), construction (7.7% of GDP in 2013) and agriculture (6.2% of GDP in 2013). Nevertheless, the recent low oil-GDP growth rates (0.6% during 2011–2013) could be considered a signal for the government to focus more of its attention away from the oil and gas production sector to ensure that the country grows sustainably.

The aim of this chapter is to critically evaluate the following question: 'Is Kazakhstan is on the 'proper' path of sustainable development?' In spite of the potential difficulty of answering this question, the chapter will attempt to critically review Kazakhstan's development strategies and plans with specific attention to industry competitiveness and individual firm efficiency and interconnectedness with economic diversification, using Morris, Kaplinsky and Kaplan's (2012) 'building linkages' conceptual framework. This analysis is performed in order to identify areas that require immediate attention as well as identify policies that have been effective. That is, the major objective of this chapter is to identify the strengths and weaknesses of Kazakhstan's development plans with respect to their usefulness in promoting economic diversification.

The government of Kazakhstan has a well-developed vision for the development of the country. However, what is seriously needed is a quantitative analysis of the country's diversification strategy at the macro, meso and micro levels. To date, most of Kazakhstan's policy documents lack 'explicit acknowledgement of

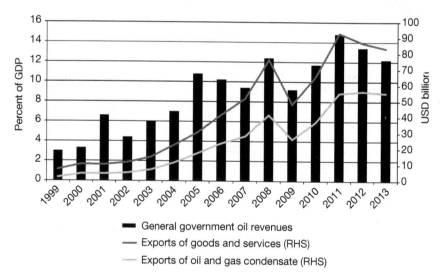

Figure 9.1 Kazakhstan's dependence on oil revenues.
(Kazakhstan National Statistics Agency).

relevant past initiatives and an analysis of the problem they were supposed to address. When analysis was included, it was crude, ad hoc and lacked any reference or indication of modern tools of policy analysis' (Khakimzhanov and Seitenova, 2013: 23). Furthermore, any assessment of Kazakhstan's diversification initiatives faces two additional problems: i) the initiatives are in their very early stages and may take years or decades for the full effects to come to fruition; and ii) there are relatively few studies that specifically assess diversification (some of the exceptions are Asian Development Bank, 2013; Islamic Development Bank, 2011; World Bank, 2013b). Therefore, most of the ensuing analysis is based on evidence from academic papers that have examined specific development issues as well as secondary statistical data (e.g. the Business Environment and Enterprise Performance Survey (BEEPS), the World Economic Forum (WEF) Global Competitiveness Index (CGI), Kazakhstan National Statistics Agency (KNSA) and the National Bank of Kazakhstan).

The chapter is organised as follows. Section 9.2 provides a synopsis of Kazakhstan's economic history. Section 9.3 summarises Kazakhstan's economic development policies since independence that promote diversification. Section 9.4 discusses the concept of linkages in resource-dependent countries. Section 9.5 discusses the promotion of linkages in Kazakhstan in some detail, using Malaysia, a successful upper middle-income country that has used state-sponsored economic planning to diversify its economy away from natural resources, as a comparator. The last section (Section 9.6) concludes.

9.2 Kazakhstan's economic history

The Kazakh people have been heavily influenced by Russian politics, economics and culture since the eighteenth century. By the end of the eighteenth century Russian trade became more important for the Kazakhs than their exchange within the Central Asian khanates (Malikov, 2006). However, one must remember that prior to the 1920s the economic development of the region was quite limited. The area's predominant external access was via the Trans-Siberian and Orenburg-Tashkent railways as well as by river transport on the Irtysh River to Omsk and the Ural River to the Caspian Sea in the west (Peck, 2004). Kazakhstan entered the Soviet Union in 1920 as a member of the Kyrgyz Autonomous Soviet Socialist Republic. In 1936 the whole territory was elevated to a Soviet Republic, called the Kazakh SSR. By that time ethnic Kazakhs were a minority and many of them emigrated to Turkey, China and Mongolia. During the 1930s the Soviet State allotted large budgets for the investigation of mineral and metal industry development. Large development projects included the Karaganda coal basin, the Balkhash copper works and the Emba oil field. Researchers have estimated that Kazakhstan's industrial output grew at an average annual rate of 28% over the period between 1929 and 1940 (Alampiev, 1959 in Peck, 2004). This resulted in industry's share of Kazakhstan's economy in 1937 being 57% compared to just 6.3% in 1920 (Tolibekov, 1963). Following World War Two the development of mineral reserves and grain production was a state priority. The investment in mining and processing facilities as well as infrastructure continued at a high rate until the mid-1970s. Afterwards there was substantially less expansion in both new operations and the renovation of existing operations (Peck, 2004). By independence most of the mines were technologically outdated and were connected to markets through antiquated transportation infrastructure (Engineering and Mining Journal, 2010). In the 1950s the Virgin Lands programme brought about twenty-five million hectares into cultivation (i.e. over 60% of the current arable land). Northern Kazakhstan became a major producer of wheat and barley (Pomfret, 2007a). Agricultural production was carried out on large state or collective farms whose size averaged 35–40,000 hectares, and on over three million small private plots which produced over a third of total output (Green and Vokes, 1997). It is important to realise that within the Soviet system, Kazakhstan was basically used as a primary product supplier of grain, coal, minerals and metals for Soviet industrialisation, remaining closed for external exports (Pomfret, 2007b). As a result, Kazakhstan's regions had stronger links with the rest of the Soviet Union than with each other. 'In 1960, for example, 61% of all rail shipments (by weight) from cities in the northern two-thirds of the country were destined for locations outside of Kazakhstan. Of the remaining 39% of rail shipments, 26% were to other locations in the northern region and only 13% were to locations in the southern third of the country' (Peck, 2004: 53).

At independence in 1991 the Soviet legacy had left Kazakhstan an economy of massive and technologically outdated capital, severe sectoral misallocation of resources due to administratively imposed prices, very large and specialised enterprises that were heavily dependent for both input supply and output demand on very distant enterprises in other parts of the Soviet Union, and enterprises led by managers who were content with inferior product quality and a serious lack of business initiative (Puffer, 1996). These and other conditions led to a severe contraction of Kazakhstan's industrial output by 64.1% from 1991 to 1995 (EBRD, 1999/2002).

The decade of the 1990s was one of severe hardship as Kazakhstan's economy was hit by multiple shocks – the end of central planning, the dissolution of the Soviet Union, hyperinflation, and the Russian Crisis in 1997–98 (Figure 9.2). From 1991 to 1995 policy focussed on nation-building, market-oriented reforms, privatisation of state-owned enterprises, price liberalisation and securing foreign participation in developing the country's energy reserves (Cohen, 2008; Jeffries, 2013). In the absence of markets, the prices of power, oil and gas, and nonferrous metals were significantly below world market prices while the prices of timber and paper, light manufactured goods and food were inflated (IMF, 1998). The changes in relative prices between sectors induced the reallocation of factors. Labour and capital moved towards the fuel and metallurgical sectors and away from machine building, construction materials, light industry and the construction sector (Figure 9.3). In addition to economic turmoil, Kazakhstan's population decreased by 7.2% due to international migration between 1990 and 1999, and this migration was more prominent in urban areas where population declined by 9.4% (An and Becker, 2005). Most of the émigrés were well-educated and skilled young ethnic Europeans adults (An and Becker, 2005; Pomfret, 2005) and, as a result, the mass migration resulted in substantial brain drain (Pomfret, 2005).

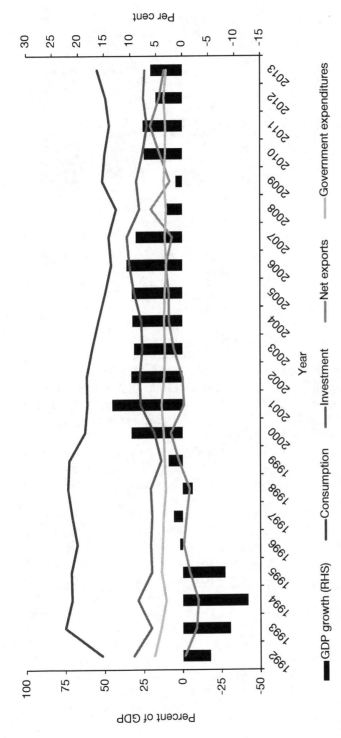

Figure 9.2 Kazakhstan's GDP growth and component shares 1992–2013.
(Source: KNSA).

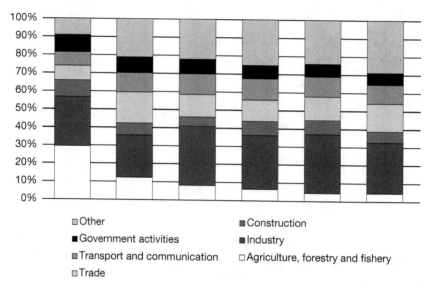

□ Other   ■ Construction
■ Government activities   ■ Industry
▩ Transport and communication   □ Agriculture, forestry and fishery
□ Trade

Figure 9.3 Kazakhstan's GDP by sector 1991–2013.
(Source: KNSA).

Since 2000 Kazakhstan has experienced high economic growth with the exception of the impact of the 2008–2009 Global Financial Crisis. Per capita GDP in Kazakhstan more than doubled in real terms from 2000 to 2013. This corresponded to an increase from US$1,230 in 2000 to US$13,171 in 2013. This improvement in per capita GDP was reflected in an eight-fold growth in average monthly earnings, from US$45 in 2000 to US$370 in 2013, or a real increase in wages greater than 300%. Several factors contributed to this impressive performance: i) the sharp expansion of oil and gas production; ii) commodity exporters generally, and oil and gas exporters particularly, enjoying favourable prices in world markets; iii) a favourable external financial environment until 2007 which facilitated Kazakh banks' access to external credit at modest cost; iv) structural and institutional reform measures; and v) the success of the macroeconomic management in maintaining the right balance among the fiscal, monetary and exchange rate policies (Islamic Development Bank, 2011). Furthermore, the country's labour force increased by 25% from 2000 to 2013, compared with only 12% population growth. People who had stayed out of the labour market because of disenchantment with lack of job opportunities and low wages in the 1990s started returning to the market from 2000, encouraged by new opportunities and rising incomes. The unemployment rate declined from 12.7% in 2000 to 5.2% in 2013, and the labour force participation rate increased from 66% in 2000 to 72% in 2013.

Sectoral GDP growth rates in the economy, with the exception of the construction sector in 2009 and the agricultural sector, have been positive since 2000 (Figure 9.4). However, some sectors' increases have not been keeping pace with those of others; therefore, their shares of total GDP have been diminishing. For example, agricultural value added has recorded a 130% increase since 2000, but its share of GDP has gradually declined from 8.1% to 4.6% over the same period (Figures 9.5 and 9.6). Similarly, the manufacturing output index has more than doubled from 2000 to 2013, but its share in total value added has declined from 16.5% to 12.0% over the same period. Behind these changes were huge expansions in oil, gas and metal-related production in the mining sector and its growing share in GDP, which has been the driving force in the development of the economy. The rapidly growing mining sector output and the resulting injection of purchasing power into the economy promoted demand for services and construction. This has resulted in the share of services in GDP gradually increasing from 47.5% in 2000 to 57% by 2013, and the share of construction in GDP increasing from 5.9% in 2000 to 10.6% in 2006, falling back to 8.2% in 2013.

Since January 2010 Kazakhstan has been one of the three members, along with Russia and Belarus, of a Customs Union (CU). The CU enforced a common external tariff resulting in an average tariff rate of 11.5% compared to Kazakhstan's previous rate of 6.7% (Islamic Development Bank, 2011). Since the launch of the Customs Union, Kazakhstan's trade (exports plus imports) with Russia and Belarus has almost doubled from US$12.9 billion in 2009 to US$24.6 billion in 2013. Imports from CU countries increased from US$9.3 billion to US$18.7 billion, while exports to CU countries grew from US$3.6 billion to US$5.9 billion. It is important to realise that in 2013, CU-destined exports contributed only 7% of Kazakhstan's total exports while CU-originated imports contributed almost 39% of Kazakhstan's total imports. These values suggest that the CU has impacted the places from which Kazakhstan receives its imports significantly more than where it sends its exports. Kazakhstan's capital account has also been affected by the CU. Foreign direct investment to the non-mining and oil and gas sectors has increased by more than 30% per year. As a result, its share in the total foreign direct investment grew from 29% to 41% from 2010 to 2013.

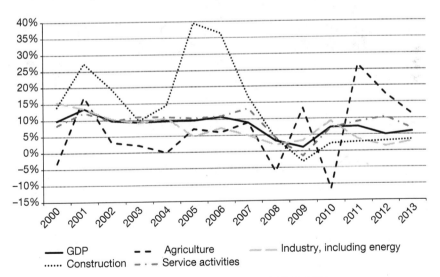

Figure 9.4 Kazakhstan's growth rates for sectoral GDP 2000–2013.
(Source: KNSA).

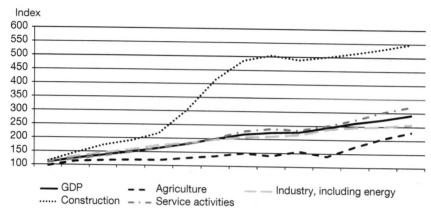

Figure 9.5 Kazakhstan's sectoral GDP indexes 2000–2013 (1999 = 100).
(Source: KNSA).

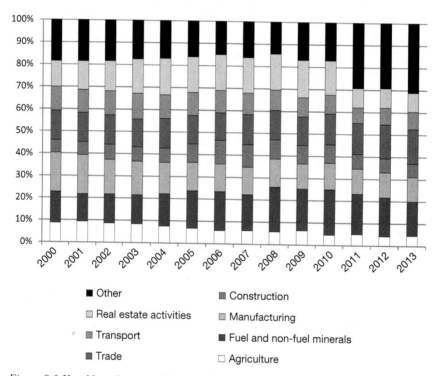

Figure 9.6 Kazakhstan's sectoral shares of GDP 2000–2013.
(KNSA).

9.3 Kazakhstan's economic development policies since independence

A key objective in Kazakhstan's sustainable development programme and the corresponding economic and industrialisation policies is 'to promote the diversification of the economy, particularly given its extensive natural endowments' (World Bank, 2003: 7). Tables 9.5 and 9.6 in the Appendix provide a summary of the country's most important development strategies and plans.

Kazakhstan has been making economic strategies and plans since 1992 and has issued more than twenty trade and industrial policy statements, each with a policy horizon of at least three years (Khakimzhanov and Seitenova, 2013). Few plans lasted long enough to reach their termination date as the majority were discarded ahead of schedule and replaced with revised versions. Only six were in effect as of the end of 2013. Some of most important institutions to come out of these plans are the Development Bank of Kazakhstan (now Samruk-Kazyna) in 2001, the Investment Fund of Kazakhstan (KIF), the National Innovation Fund (NIF), the Export Insurance Corporation (now KazExportGranat) and the National Fund of Kazakhstan. The latter, Kazakhstan's oil fund, was implemented in 2000 and is managed by the National Bank of Kazakhstan. Its objectives are two-fold: the accumulation of funds for future generations, and reducing the adverse effects of both internal and external shocks.

When the country's economic plans are assessed as a group, it becomes evident that the overarching goals of the plans can be separated into three themes: attracting foreign investment, avoiding the 'resource curse', and building linkages. Attracting foreign investment has been a central pillar of Kazakhstan's economic development policy since independence as Kazakhstan has used its comparative advantage in oil, first to kick-start its ailing economy and second to ensure that the revenues from its oil reserves are sustainable for the long term. During the 1990s it was essential that the country offered attractive legal and fiscal terms to the multi-national oil companies to attract the necessary capital. In the late 1990s the government changed the focus of its economic plans towards 'avoiding the resource curse' (Khakimzhanov and Seitenova, 2013). The National Fund was set up to deal with the serious macroeconomic and fiscal challenges that mineral-dependent countries commonly face. The Kazakhstan 2030 Strategy and accompanying multi-year plans aimed to vaccinate Kazakhstan from the perils of Dutch disease by addressing the low competitiveness of the non-resources traded sectors, the poor conditions of social and fiscal infrastructure, and the 'low' quality of institutions. Since 2010, 'building linkages' has received more attention. The development of both 'upstream' and 'downstream' linkages in Kazakhstan's traditional sectors (oil and gas, ferrous and nonferrous metals, and agriculture) have been identified as priorities. Furthermore, consumption linkages have been targeted by developing industries with the principal interest of supplying the home market. A good example of this is the importance given to the national pharmaceutical and automobile industries.

9.4 The concept of linkages in a resource-dependent country

It is widely accepted that long-term and sustainable economic growth in Kazakhstan requires industrial development and an expansion of knowledge-intensive and innovative industries (ADB, 2012). The success of the Asian Tiger economics has led many resource rich low and middle income countries, including Kazakhstan, to attempt to emulate their success by developing industries and services which are unrelated to their resource sector or sectors. However, emulating the success of the Asian Tigers' industrial development is now increasingly difficult or impossible because the global conditions that allowed the Tigers to succeed are no longer available (Morris, Kaplinksy and Kaplan, 2012). As a result, economists have recently been promoting the 'building linkages' approach to developing a resource-dependent economy (e.g. Morris, Kaplinksy and Kaplan, 2012; Dietsche, 2014; Farooki and Kaplinsky, 2014). Hirschman (1977) developed the first formal theory that notes the causal effects of linkages on a resource-dependent country's development. He distinguished three types of linkages: production, fiscal, and consumption. Production linkages are further separated into backward (or upstream) and forward (or downstream). Backward linkages involve the production of inputs, both goods and services, used in the production of the natural resource product. Forward linkages entail that the natural resource product is used as an input.

Recently, Morris, Kaplinksy and Kaplan (2012) have extended Hirschman's forward linkages by distinguishing between 'processing' and 'beneficiation': 'Processing involves a deepening of value added, as a commodity is refined or processed prior to being passed on to user industries. ... By contrast, beneficiation describes a process of transformation in which the processed commodity is converted into an entirely different product, generally in an unrelated manufacturing activity' (p. 24). Fiscal linkages are created when resource rents are used to fund public investments either related or unrelated to the natural resource commodities, for example investments to upgrade or construct new highways, railways and telecommunication infrastructure. Consumption linkages arise from the economic activities created by the local spending of income earned by those directly employed in the production of the natural resource commodity. Purchasing of automobiles, apartments and other durable goods by households directly employed by the resource sector during a resource boom is an example of consumption linkages in action. In Morris, Kaplinksy and Kaplan's (2012) report on economic diversification in sub-Saharan Africa, the authors added the concept of horizontal linkages to Hirschman's model. Horizontal linkages are a 'set of linkages made up of suppliers and users in the chain, who develop capabilities to feed into other industrial and service chains' (p. 24).

Two of the principal findings of Morris, Kaplinksy and Kaplan's (2012) report are that coordination and collaborative action across three levels of industrial policy is necessary for effective linkages to develop and remain sustainable. These three levels are the macro-level, the meso-level and the micro-level. Macro-level policies are those that define and promote efficient property rights, fiscal stability, stable exchange rates that reflect the country's capabilities and skill endowments, efficient financial intermediation between savings and investment, national institutions that support and enhance technological development, and corridor infrastructure development (UNIDO, 2012; Farooki and Kaplinsky, 2014; Morris, Kaplinksy and Kaplan, 2012). Historical development has shown that properly implementing these policies was an important contributor to industrial development in both Africa and Latin America. However, the authors maintain that well-designed and implemented macro-level policies are not sufficient to ensure sustainable growth.

Meso-level policies 'address both the promotion of key sectors and particular regions and industrial clusters ... to achieve dynamic comparative advantage' (UNIDO, 2012: 61). These policies support inter-firm externalities and learning but should not 'pick winners'. Instead, they should support emerging sectors of significance. Such policies include supporting cluster development and partially financing technical institutions, such as Academies of Science, and technical associations.[2] Micro-level policies are aimed at addressing firm-level and value-chain efficiency. Policies effective in increasing efficiency levels include reducing the level of corruption, allowing higher levels of foreign ownership of firms, the promotion of SME capabilities, improving access to financing, improving judicial effectiveness in resolving business disputes, and improving labour quality.

Economists (for example, Wright and Czelusta, 2007; David and Wright, 1997) provide evidence that government policies can inhibit the exploitation of a country's natural resources even if the country is blessed with abundant surface and subsurface resources. That is, there is both an exogenous component related to any natural-resource dependent industry – a gift of nature – and an endogenous component related to the country's economic conditions. The authors argue that investment in world-class science and engineering education during the nineteenth century, combined with a favourable regulatory environment for exploring and developing its mineral resources, accounted for the expansion of mineral production between 1890 and 1920 in the United States (Wright and Czelusta, 2007). In contrast, the authors argue that Australia's mineral boom was delayed until the 1960s due to specific policies and regulations that inhibited earlier discovery and exploitation (David and Wright, 1997). These policies included embargoes on mineral exports at particular times as well as underinvestment in education in areas relevant to mineral discovery and development. Furthermore, McLean (2012) suggests that the United States' sustained industrial development during the late nineteenth and early twentieth centuries is a direct result of the country's low-cost water transport infrastructure, well-defined and effective property rights, the rise of competitive industry, and favourable conditions for risk-taking by entrepreneurs.

For the purpose of examining the likelihood of success of Kazakhstan's diversification policies, it is necessary to examine the institutional characteristics that were in place at the time of the surge in oil and gas foreign direct investment during the 1990s and how these characteristics have changed during the first two decades of the twenty-first century. It is also essential to compare Kazakhstan to similar or historical resource-dependent countries. For this study, Malaysia is used as the comparison country as it is widely accepted as a well-functioning upper-middle income country that has used state-sponsored economic development since the 1970s to, in part, diversify its economy away from a heavy reliance on natural resources (Reinhardt, 2000). Moreover, the Malaysian government's commitment to and support for small and medium enterprises started in the early 1970s, and they are now considered the pillar of industrial development in the country (Saleh and Ndubisi, 2006). Finally, the President of Kazakhstan, Nursultan Nazarbayev, has often referred to the economic success of Malaysia and has appealed for efforts to adopt its practices since 1997 when the Kazakhstan government implemented its 'Kazakhstan 2030 Strategy'.

9.5 Kazakhstan's promotion of linkages

This section focusses on a series of contextual drivers that affect the development of linkages into and out of Kazakhstan's main commodities sectors: oil and gas, non-fuel minerals, and agriculture. Specifically, the following contextual drivers will be examined:

1   The nature and quality of infrastructure
2   The nature of capabilities, skills and the system of innovation
3   The effectiveness of property rights
4   Access to financial services
5   Local content policies
6   The effectiveness of national oil fund and exchange rate policy for the non-oil and gas sectors

For each case there will be a discussion of the factors that are anticipated to determine the impact of each of these drivers on linkage development. This is followed by a review of the literature and an analysis of the available data to explore the impact of these drivers on linkages.

Infrastructure

Infrastructure is commonly separated into two categories, 'hard' and 'soft'. Hard infrastructure is 'embodied in road and rail transport, utilities (energy and water) and telecommunication networks. In each of these cases the effectiveness of infrastructure development is a function of reliability, quality of provision and the cost to the user'. Soft infrastructure 'reflects the efficiency and cost of the administrative and regulatory regime which supports the productive sector' (Kaplinsky, Morris and Kaplan, 2011: 72). Four sets of factors are important in determining the role played by infrastructure in the development of linkages into and out of the commodities sector: i) the nature of the commodities that a country exports; ii) the nature of the infrastructure itself; iii) the infrastructural needs of the lead commodity firms and those of the firms involved in backward and forward linkages to the commodities sector; and iv) the extent to which infrastructure is a public good.

Economists commonly categorise commodities as 'soft', 'hard' and 'energy'. Soft commodities include comestible goods, industrial agrarian goods and animal products. Hard commodities comprise precious, industrial and ferrous metals. Energy commodities can be further subdivided into fossil, nuclear and alternative sources. 'Soft commodities have low technological content, lend themselves to small scale production, are labour intensive, require heterogeneous and diffused infrastructure, and often have short shelf lives, necessitating processing soon after production. Hard commodities generally embody complex technologies and involve large-scale and capital-intensive production ... tend to make intensive use of infrastructure (but this can be used by other sectors – for example road and rail links) and produce output with long shelf life. The energy commodities are generally very technology, scale and capital intensive and require infrastructure which has few externalities to other sectors' (Morris, Kaplinsky and Kaplan, 2012: 22). The primary soft commodities in Kazakhstan are grains, cotton, livestock, dairy and fisheries. Hard commodities comprise both ferrous and non-ferrous metals as well as precious metals. Energy commodities consist of oil, gas, coal and radioactive chemicals.

Second, the nature of the infrastructure inherently affects the development of linkages. Some infrastructure, such as oil pipelines, is highly specific to a particular commodity and has very low potential for positive spill-overs that could promote growth of backward, forward or horizontal linkages. This is the situation of the oil industry in Kazakhstan (Figure 9.7) with approximately 78% of the exports in 2013 using pipelines. Railways carry most of Kazakhstan's refined petroleum, iron ore, refined metals and grain exports. When all international cargo transportation is examined together, in 2009 railways accounted for over 50% of the total freight by weight followed by pipelines (42%), sea (6%), and roads (2%) (Ziyadov, 2011). The railway, port and road infrastructure has the capacity to meet the needs of multiple users, feeding into and out of the mining and agriculture sectors as well as into and out of other sectors of the economy.

Third, it is important to distinguish between the infrastructural needs of the dominant commodity exporter and those of the firms involved in backward and forward linkages to that sector. Kazakhstan's trunk pipelines are mainly controlled by subsidiaries of Kazmunaigaz, the state oil and gas firm, with the notable exception of the Caspian Pipeline Consortium's Tengiz-Novorossiisk oil pipeline, which is controlled by an international consortium in which Kazakhstan has a minority equity stake (20.75%) (Oil News, 2009; Ketenci, 2008). The oil and gas sector is a significant destination of both public and private sector infrastructure development. On average infrastructure investment comprised 2.1% of GDP from 2009–2012 (Kravets, 2013) of which 0.6% was primarily spent on the Kazakhstan-China Oil Pipeline project (i.e. the Atasu-Alashankou pipeline). This can be considered likely to result in enclave infrastructural development, which will hamper the ability of local suppliers or processors to link in and participate effectively in the country's oil and gas value chains.

Fourth, by its nature, infrastructure can be either a public or private good. However, as most of Kazakhstan's oil and gas is exported using pipelines, there is very little positive spill-over to the manufacturing and services suppliers. Therefore, backward and forward linkages are unlikely to be developed with this investment.

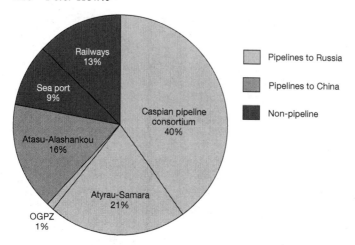

Figure 9.7 Kazakhstan's breakdown of oil exports by route-to-market, 2013.
(Ministry of Oil and Gas of Kazakhstan).
Note: OGPZ refers to the Orenburg gas-processing factory pipeline. During 2013, 72.1 million tons of oil was exported.

In its 2014 Logistics Performance Index (LPI) the World Bank ranked Kazakhstan 88th out of 160 countries with respect to both 'hard' and 'soft' infrastructure. Customs, Infrastructure and International Shipments were the three worst performing indicators. Transportation accounts for 8–11% of the final cost of goods in Kazakhstan, compared to 4% in typical industrialised countries (Yang and McCarthy, 2013). The WEF's Global Competitiveness report 2013/2014 ranks Kazakhstan's roads among the worst in the world (Quality of Roads score = 2.0), and this contributes to the country's low infrastructure score, in comparison to Malaysia (Quality of Roads score = 5.6) which is considered to have the best LPI scores of the group of upper middle income countries. Furthermore, the World Bank in its 2013 Doing Business Survey ranked Kazakhstan as the 186th worst country out of 189 in terms of 'trading across borders'. This is consistent with data which show that Kazakhstan requires almost the highest number of documents for importing goods in the world (twelve, in comparison to two for France) (Yang and McCarthy, 2013). From 2007 to 2014 Kazakhstan's infrastructure has improved with the exception of international shipments, which became significantly worse after 2010 (WEF, 2014). This improvement has been the direct result of a focus on investing in better overall infrastructure (Figure 9.8). However, Kazakhstan (LPI Score of 2.7 in 2014) has a long way to go to improve all aspects of its infrastructure to be at a similar level with Malaysia (LPI Score of 3.6 in 2014).

Since 2008 the government has begun to address the issue of poor infrastructure. However, BEEPS data from 2002 to 2012 show that perceived quality of electricity, telecommunications and transportation services improved between 2002 and 2009, but deteriorated afterwards. Furthermore, the perceived quality of customs and trade regulations has continually deteriorated over the study period. Hence, the BEEPS data suggest that the government is not investing in infrastructure that directly impacts a significant proportion of the business enterprises in Kazakhstan.

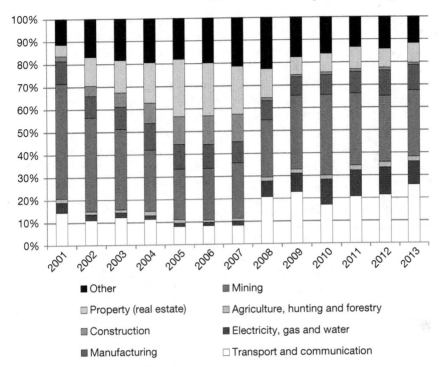

Figure 9.8 Kazakhstan's breakdown of investment by sector.
(KNSA).

Skills development and innovation systems

Given the desire to promote low cost, low inventory production, and the need to ensure the continual availability of capital intensive equipment, oil and gas firms in Kazakhstan not only wish to outsource noncore competences, but also to near-source them. A key component to near-sourcing is the capabilities of local suppliers. Capabilities play a central role in the diversification process as firms need the necessary capabilities to effectively engage with economic opportunities. Moreover, local firms' capabilities need to be continually upgraded to reflect technological development and competition outside the country.

In the discussion of capabilities and their influence on the development of linkages, both the extent to which skills represent a bottleneck and the extent to which capabilities are supported by national, regional and sectoral systems of innovation will examined.

Skills shortages are considered to be one of the weakest links in the diversification process in Kazakhstan. 'The acute shortage of highly skilled professionals, particularly professional managers, is one of Kazakhstan's biggest challenges are pervasive across all of the sectors' (ADB, 2013:43). Firms producing oil and gas as well as the upstream industries identify an acute shortage of qualified personnel as one of the key constraints holding up the industries' development (KAZENERGY, 2013; Islamic Development Bank, 2012). The BEEPS data for 2012 provides further confirmation of the importance of a skill shortage as firms cited inadequately trained labour forces as the second most important constraint after corruption.

This skills shortage will not disappear soon in Kazakhstan as the quality of science, engineering and management programmes have not improved substantially since 2006. In fact, the perception of the quality of scientific research institutions has decreased (WEF, 2014). Furthermore, when Kazakhstan's results are compared to Malaysia it is apparent that Kazakhstan has considerable room for improvement in all aspects. Coupled with low quality standards is low enrolments of students in science and engineering. Data from UNESCO shows that in 2012, only 3% and 20% of university students in Kazakhstan were studying in the science and engineering disciplines, respectively. The 2012 data are consistent with data collected by the US National Academy in 2006 and the composition of Bolashak scholars[3] in 2005. The US National Academy (2007) found that general interest among young people in scientific careers has diminished since independence because well-paying jobs in research and in scientific services have been scarce and the prestige of being a scientist that developed during Soviet times has steadily declined. In 2005, only 18% of students in the Bolashak program were enrolled in science and engineering programs (OECD, 2007). The levels of students enrolled in science and engineering programmes is considerably below the rate in Malaysia for 2010, where 20% and 40% of students were studying in the science and engineering disciplines respectively (UNESCO, 2013).[4]

Data from the WEF indicate that the quality mathematical and science education and the availability of scientists and engineers are considerably lower in Kazakhstan than in Malaysia. In Kazakhstan, during 2014 the average value of these three indicators was 3.5, whereas; the average value for Malaysia was 5.2 (WEF, 2014).

Not only are the quality of tertiary science and math education problematic; but the Programme for International Student Assessment (PISA) scores of the country's fifteen-year-olds indicate that there are serious problems with the teaching of science and mathematics in primary and secondary schools. Table 9.1 presents the percentage share of top performers' PISA scores (i.e. levels 5 and 6) for reading, mathematics and science for Kazakhstan and Malaysia. OECD average scores are included as a comparison with developed-country scores. 'This indicator may be particularly relevant when considering the ability of an economy to innovate and/or adopt new technology' (Commander et al., 2012:60).

The data show that the percentage of Kazakhstani students achieving top grades – defined as level 5 or above – ranged between 0.2% and 1.2% for reading, mathematics and science. By contrast, the OECD average values were approximately 13% for mathematics and slightly above 8% for both science and reading. It is interesting to observe that Kazakhstan's scores are not significantly different to Malaysia's. These low scores have motivated Malaysia to launch its Education Blueprint programme which aims to move Malaysia into the top third of countries in PISA within fifteen years (Asadulla, 2014).

Table 9.1 PISA results in mathematics, science and analytical reading (OECD PISA data)

	Year	Share of top performers			Average scores		
		Math	Science	Reading	Math	Science	Reading
Kazakhstan*	2009	1.2	0.3	0.4	405	400	390
	2012	0.9	0.2	†	423	425	393
Malaysia	2010	0.4	0.2	0.1	404	422	414
	2012	1.3	0.3	†	421	420	398
OECD average	2009	12.7	8.6	7.6	496	501	494
	2012	12.6	8.4	8.4	494	501	497

*: In Kazakhstan, PISA has been administered only in 2009 and 2012.
†: Reporting standards not met.

In conclusion, the percentage of Kazakhstani students achieving top grades is extremely low, with no marked improvement between 2009 and 2012. The evidence suggests that the country needs to radically change its primary and secondary pedagogy to ensure that the skills shortage does not promulgate for several decades. Furthermore, the country needs to focus on increasing the quantity of the science, technology, engineering and medicine programmes provided while ensuring developed-world quality. This is similar to Malaysia's education policy which started with the Third Economic Plan (1975 and 1980), in which the government provided considerable incentives to students to increase the number of engineers and medical specialists to meet the increased requirements of rapid industrialisation (Sirat, 2002).

Fortuitously, the government has started this 'change' with the recent implementation of both the National Intellectual School (NIS) system and Nazarbayev University (NU). The NIS system focusses on the study of maths and physics, chemistry and biology as well as trilingual education (Kazakh, Russian and English) because all of these disciplines are seen as critical to national competitiveness and economic growth (Yakavets, 2014). NU is Kazakhstan's first research-focussed university and has degree programmes in engineering, natural sciences and medicine that conform to 'international standards'. Its mission is 'prepare the best technical and engineering specialists for the industries already developed in Kazakhstan' (Koch, 2014).

A second set of factors that are important for technological development and competition are the extent to which the firms are participating in Kazakhstan's system of innovation, and specifically how this affects both the breadth and depth of linkages into and out of the oil and gas sector. Data from the World Bank, WEF and UNESCO indicate that the development and sustainability of linkages in Kazakhstan are being hampered by low rates of R&D, low numbers of R&D personnel, and low rates and quality of on-the-job training. For example, Kazakhstan's research and development expenditure as a percentage of GDP was only 0.16% during 2011, whereas, Malaysia's was 1.07% (World Bank, 2015). Malaysian businesses employ almost four times the number of R&D personnel per thousand total employees (UNESCO, 2014).

Property rights

Johnson et al.'s (2002) study of Poland, Romania, Slovakia, Ukraine and Russia indicates that secure property rights are both necessary and sufficient to induce investment by entrepreneurs, whether they are active in science and technology or agriculture. Therefore, if Kazakhstan wishes to promote economic diversification through small and medium sized enterprises it needs to ensure that its property rights are both secure and well-functioning. Today, this is not the case. Radosevic and Myrzakhmet (2009) state that the system of intellectual property rights is one of the most important constraints on Kazakhstan's ability to exploit its science and technology potential. Furthermore, the OECD (2013a) and Petrick et al. (2014) both indicate that poorly designed land rights is one of the principal reasons for the very low productivity levels of Kazakhstani agriculture (Figure 9.9). Data published by the Ministry of Agriculture show that in 2011 only 1% of all agricultural land was in full private ownership, while the ownership of the remaining 99% was based on forty-nine-year leases which prohibit subleasing (OECD, 2013a, b). The reason for this high lease rate is that the annual rental fee is set at a guaranteed rate of 0.1% to 0.5% of the cadastral value in 2002, which does not in any way reflect the true market value of the land (OECD, 2013a, b). This system of land rights promotes low mobility of agricultural land, which in turn leads to limited capital investment, low labour productivity and a weakly competitive farming sector (Figure 9.10).

Kazakhstan's weak intellectual property rights may contribute to the country's weak demand for R&D and the low involvement of SMEs (3% of all SMEs) in the manufacturing sector (Korean Development Institute, 2011). The World Economic Forum's GCI data also indicate that property rights is a key policy area that still needs to be addressed, even though they appear to be improving since 2006. There

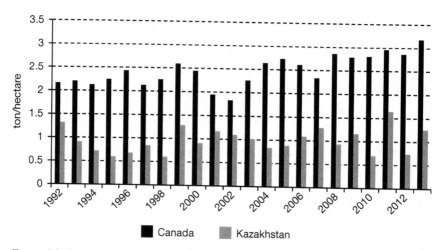

Figure 9.9 Comparison of wheat yields between Kazakhstan and Canada. (OECD-FAO Agricultural Outlook 2014–2023).

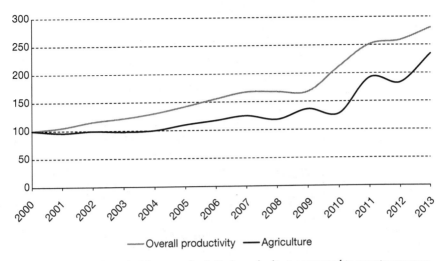

Figure 9.10 Kazakhstan's labour productivity in agriculture compared to country average. (KNSA).

still remains a wide gap between the quality of property rights in Kazakhstan (2014 value of 4.1) compared with Malaysia (2014 value of 5.3).

Access to finance

Businesses in Kazakhstan repeatedly state that access to finance, especially debt financing at sustainable rates, is a key barrier to growth (Radosevic and Myrzakhmet, 2009; OECD, 2011, 2013b). This is reflected in the BEEPS surveys (Table 9.2) which show that in 2012 only 16% of small firms, 25% of medium firms and 31% of large firms had loans or lines of credit. More importantly, the data show that between 2009 and 2012 the use of bank credit has decreased substantially, which is problematic.

The problems of bank financing as well as other types of financing in Kazakhstan are also evident in the WEF's GCI values. Specifically, access to finance is significantly more problematic in Kazakhstan (CGI value of 3.0 in 2014) than in Malaysia (value of 5.6 in 2014). However, this difference is most likely due to the lack support for SMEs from the country's banking sector. That is, the difference is most likely not due to government's lack of support of SMEs because since the early 2000s the government has used SME development policy to undermine support for political opposition (Ostrowski, 2009).

Table 9.2 Per cent of Kazakhstan's firms by size that had loans or lines of credit (BEEPS)

	Small	Medium	Large
2009	22.4	41.0	59.2
2012	16.2	24.7	31.0

Table 9.3 Percentage of Kazakhstan's firms that state access to finance as a major problem to their operations (BEEPS)

	Small	Medium	Large
2009	25.5	30.3	33.8
2012	7.5	9.9	11.3

There are few policies related to loans for SMEs in Kazakhstan. Some policies have become operative recently but are very limited in fund type, support target, size etc. Seed money support policies, which are very effective for start-ups, only began in 2012 (Korean Development Institute, 2013). The BEEPS data provide evidence that access to finance has become less problematic since 2009 as less firms rate accessing finance as a major or severe problem (Table 9.3). In addition, the average nominal interest rate for SMEs has dropped from 18% in 2010 to 13.6% in 2012 (Korean Development Institute, 2011; BEEPS, 2012–2013)

Local content policy

According to the constitution of Kazakhstan all hydrocarbon deposits are state property, and since 2009 mineral rights are only granted under concession agreements.[5] Furthermore, only the Government determines when and what reserves will be put up for tender, what will be the duration of exploration, and when production should start. As a result, the state has significant bargaining power across the oil and gas value chain as current subsurface contracts, which are based on service contracts, commonly contain obligations on the subsurface user to benefit the state. These include: i) using a predetermined amount of local products and services; ii) hiring and training local personnel; and iii) investing in local communities.

Local content was first introduced to the subsoil legislation in 2004 together with the terms 'local manufacturer' and 'local origin' (goods, workers and services of Kazakhstani origin). However, until the adoption of the Law on Amendments to Some Legislative Acts on Kazakh Content in December 2009 (unofficially called 'Kazakh Content Law'), local content did not attract much attention as the majority of multinational companies did not adhere to the rules. The Kazakh Content Law states that if a subsoil user wanted to buy certain equipment or hire a subcontractor for drilling, processing or other subsoil-related activities, it was obliged to obey the following specific local content rules after December 2012: i) a minimum of 15% local content in goods; ii) a minimum of 90% local content in technical workers and 70% for executives; and iii) a minimum of 70% local content in services (Tordo et al., 2013; Ngoasong, 2014).[6] In June 2010 Kazakhstan adopted a new Law on Subsoil and Subsoil Use (the 'Subsoil Law'), which sets a target of 50% certified local procurement as well as mandatory joint ventures with KazMunaiGas, the national oil and gas company, in all new exploration and production contracts (Ngoasong, 2014). In addition to employment and expenditure restrictions, 1% of any project budget must be set aside for training programmes and workforce development (OECD, 2014). The result of the recent modifications to Kazakhstan's local content legislation has localised not only value added, but also ownership.

The second factor driving Kazakhstan's local content programme is the preferential treatment of Kazakhstani firms in the supply of goods and services. A local firm can apply for annual certification of 'local content' if: i) its owner is a citizen of Kazakhstan or the company is legally registered in Kazakhstan and its staff includes no less than 95% Kazakh citizens; and ii) the firm produces goods within the borders of Kazakhstan (Tordo et al., 2013). Firms with local content certification are given a 20% margin of preference in tenders – that is, bid prices received by certified local firms are reduced by 20%. In addition, certified firms are provided interest-free loans, advance payments for equipment and personnel mobilisation, support in certification and technology transfer activities (Tordo et al., 2013).

Oil and gas operators that are noncompliant with procurement rules are subject to a monetary fine equal to 30% of the value of the violation for violations below 50% of the annual investment commitment, and contract termination for violation with a value that equates to 50% or more of the company's annual investment commitment (Tordo et al., 2013). In early April 2010, with new requirements in place, thirty-four contract termination notices were sent out to firms based on noncompliance with local content requirements. Fines attributed to lack of adherence to the local content laws totalled US$1.3 million and US$2.3 million in 2011 and 2012 respectively (OUSTR, 2014). In general, the level of local content in employment, goods and services has improved after the introduction of the Kazakh Content Law with the certification and fines processes (Table 9.4). However, the amount of 'local' goods remains quite low, and for the most part these goods are restricted to fuel and electricity. Furthermore, firms are willing to pay fines to ensure they receive products of consistent quality (KAZENERGY, 2013).

One of the main factors limiting Kazakhstan's further development of local content in the goods sector is the lack of qualified personnel. There is a shortage of skilled graduates in the basic sciences, engineering and mathematics in Kazakhstan. Of specific concern for the oil and gas sector are new graduates in applied disciplines such as geophysics, reservoir engineering, production technology and production chemistry. There is a similar requirement for more well-trained technicians (KAZENERGY, 2013).

Table 9.4 Local content compliance – per cent of Kazakhstan's total[7] (Tordo et al., 2013 and Interfax: Kazakhstan Oil&Gas Weekly, 2014)

	2011	*2012*	*2013*
Goods	12	12.2	16.2
Services	69	66.8	74.4
Works	58	49	

The State Program on Industrial-Innovative Development of Kazakhstan for 2015–2019 has set local content targets of 60% in goods and 90% in works and services (Islamic Development Bank, 2011). Industry groups are unsupportive of these mandatory, general approach goals as they tend to hinder the uptake of newer technology and ultimately limit local company development. Instead, evidence in both Sweden (Blomström and Kokko, 2008), Norway (Noreng, 2004) and Malaysia (Tordo et al., 2013) suggest that to develop internationally competitive expertise in upstream sectors governments should encourage partnerships between foreign and domestic companies.

Compared to Kazakhstan, Malaysia first introduced its local content policies (LPC) in 1974, and Petronas, the state-owned oil company, has been the main vehicle for these policies. Malaysia has pursued a more market-oriented approach in contrast to Kazakhstan's 'command and control' intervention (Tordo et al., 2013). Malaysia's LPCs translate into contractual obligations under production sharing agreements (PSAs) that Petronas negotiates. The terms of these PSAs: i) encourage contractors to maximise the employment of nationals; however, there are no minimum targets; ii) require companies to source all materials and supplies from Malaysian-registered firms or to purchase directly from the manufacturer where no local supplier exists; and iii) support the setting up of local manufacturing activities (Tordo et al., 2013). As the goal of Malaysia's LCPs was to transform the country into a regional hub for oil field services and equipment (OFSE), the country's LCPs would fall short of the government's objectives. However, Malaysia has developed a considerable supply industry that currently competes for projects around the world (Klueh et al., 2009). In 2010 Malaysia modified its key performance indicators to: i) the amount of investment made by OFSE multinationals; ii) the number of mergers of fabricators; and iii) the number of joint ventures between multinationals and local OFSE suppliers (Tordo et al., 2013). These modifications have required the government to focus on 'creating an enabling environment through legal and regulatory reforms, fiscal and nonfiscal incentives, and trade-related measures' (Tordo et al., 2013: 122). Therefore, there has been a movement away from imposing minimum targets and sector restrictions to incentivising foreign investment and joint ventures. This approach has been adapted by other oil producing nations such as Brazil and Trinidad and Tobago. As a result, Kazakhstan should consider modifying its LCPs to improve its local suppliers' penetration into the oil and gas industry supply chain.

Exchange rate and macroeconomic stability policies

Rodrik (2008) argued that a stable and competitive real exchange rate can facilitate growth by enhancing the competitiveness of the tradable sector, which is Kazakhstan's goal to diversify its economy (Kazakhstan, 2010). Furthermore, McLean (2011) in his book 'Why Australia prospered: The shifting sources of economic growth' states that the transitory nature of Australia's sources of finance was a principal reason for the country's severe decline in labour productivity after 1890. Therefore, for a resource-dependent country to sustain economic development through diversifying its economy it needs to deal with Dutch disease effects as well as stabilise or 'smooth out' government expenditures over the long term. Since 2000, Kazakhstan has performed an admirable job of keeping government expenditures at about 22% of GDP and the non-oil deficit averaging 3% (Kyle, 2014) by accumulating significant savings in the national oil fund. To insulate the economy from severe depression during the 2008–2009 global financial crisis, the government accessed in excess of US$21 billion of its National Oil Fund reserves to offset a non-oil fiscal deficit of 10.5% of GDP in 2008 and 13.8% in 2009 (World Bank, 2013a). Kyle (2014) finds that the government's policy decisions during 2008 and 2009 with respect to fiscal stimulus and bank assistance[8] were 'quite close to those which theoretically would gain the majority of the welfare improvements that could be hoped for even under the most optimal 'perfect knowledge' policy that could be devised' (Kyle, 2014: 52). The Kazakhstani economy quickly recovered from the crisis with 6.0% GDP growth in 2010.

In contrast to good fiscal policy, the government's exchange rate policy from 2003 to 2008 deepened the comparative disadvantage in manufacturing (Figure 9.11) as the real effective exchange rate (REER) increased by 30%. After 2008 the REER stabilised. However, there have been two devaluations of the local currency since 2008: by 20% against the US dollar in February 2009 and by 18% against the US dollar in February 2014. In general, it is commonly believed that devaluation constitutes a protectionist measure and insulates domestic industry from foreign competition. However, this ignores the occurrence of foreign-denominated bank loans, which are quite widely used by businesses in Kazakhstan. In December 2013 the National Bank of Kazakhstan estimated that 37% of all corporate loans by value were denominated in either US dollars or euros for a value of over US$18 billion. This is a substantial decrease from over 60% of corporate loans by value being denominated in foreign currency in 2008. Data from BEEPS 2012–2013 suggests that the foreign denominated loans are demanded by a small number of firms (approximately 10%). Nevertheless, the 18% devaluation resulted in an increase in maintenance costs of an equivalent of approximately US$3.25 billion in local currency, which is a substantial cost to local firms.

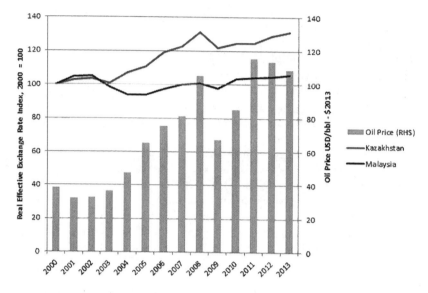

Figure 9.11 Kazakhstan's real effective exchange rates indexes 2000–2013 (2000 = 100).
World Bank, BP Statistical Review of World Energy 2014.

9.6 Conclusion and discussion

Kazakhstan has used industrial policy since 1997 to 'cure Dutch disease' by directing capital to sectors which private capital tended to keep away from (Khakimzhanov and Seitenova, 2013). There was and there still remains a belief that government can produce allocations that are superior to the market's. Furthermore, since the onset of accelerated industrial policies in 2003 there has been a desire to boost competition in the economy via diversification (Kalyuzhnova and Nygaard, 2011). However, history shows that to diversify a resource-dependent country such as Kazakhstan, besides successfully managing its oil revenues government needs to promote high levels of productivity, which in turn will lead to sustained diversification. Norway is an excellent example of promoting diversification and economic growth using 'flexible and competitive product markets, a high degree of exposure to foreign trade, flexible labour markets, adequate education and training ... and significant public spending on research and development' (Ekeli and Sy, 2011: 108). The USA, Sweden and Australia also pursued similar strategies during their diversification processes (David and Wright, 1997; Blomström and Kokko, 2008).

Both the EBRD and the Asian Development Bank acknowledge that poor competition policy limits Kazakhstan's domestic competitiveness (EBRD, 2013; ADB, 2013). Poor competition policy is a legacy of the country's Soviet past and 'Kazakhstisation' or patrimonial policies during the 1990s. The latter policies resulted, for example, in the staffing of the oil industry and its sub-contractors with ethnic Kazakhs who were predominantly not professional oil men, barring non-Kazakh specialists from entering the industry (Ostrowski, 2010). This policy was reversed in the early 2000s as the government adopted strong state-business relationships to suppress political dissent. A consequence of this new strategy has been an improvement of competition; however, the effects of seventy years of Soviet rule and the 1990s will take many years to dissipate.

With the exception of oil and gas pipelines, which have extremely limited positive externalities for both upstream as well as non-oil and gas sector industries, infrastructure remains a key obstacle for Kazakhstani firms to be both domestically and internationally competitive. A recent ADB (2012) report estimated that improving Kazakhstan's transport infrastructure could reduce road travel time between provincial capitals by 35%, rail line-haul time by 71%, and intermodal rail and road container shipment cost by 24%. Furthermore, the EBRD (2013) states that telecommunications infrastructure as well as the water and wastewater infrastructure are obstructed by government involvement. The three-fold increase in the share of investment to the transportation and communication as well as the electricity, gas and water sectors post-2007 has started to address Kazakhstan's infrastructure issues; nevertheless, infrastructure not related to the oil and gas sector needs considerable attention through increased private sector participation and the introduction of public-private partnership structures. BEEPS data show that this hard infrastructure as well as soft infrastructure, which is reflected by both government administration and the regulatory regime, desperately needs improvement to ensure the competitive abilities of the country's SMEs.

The oil and gas sector has recently developed a 'Road map for the scientific and technological development of the oil and gas mining sector in Kazakhstan'. It identifies the country's main challenges in oil and gas development being the 'lack of qualified personnel, a lack of testing facilities and an inflexible system of research funding' (KAZENERGY, 2013: 200). The EBRD (2013) identified similar problems as key challenges in the agriculture as well as the insurance and other financial services sectors. The quality in primary, secondary and post-secondary educational institutions needs to be urgently addressed. There needs to be less concentration on rote learning and more concentration on critical and creative thinking. Singapore's 'Teach Less, Learn More' initiative may be a viable alternative as it focusses on the learning outcomes of knowledge application, effective communication, collaboration and independent learning while ensuring a rigorous mathematics and science curriculum (Ng, 2010).

Furthermore, immediate attention needs to be directed towards reversing the low interest in natural sciences and engineering fields at the university level. The road map proposes to develop a state-level advisory board that includes both industry and academic representatives. However, the road map fails to deal with the low interest levels of school-aged students in science, technology, engineering and mathematics (STEM). What is needed is industry and government support of organisations and national competitions that are set up to inspire young people to take an interest in STEM.

A recent analysis by the World Bank (2013) suggests that the endowments that matter the least for the diversification of Kazakhstan are natural resources and land. The endowments that matter the most are human capital, institutions and financial depth. Property rights are identified as a key component of institutions that needs addressing in energy and mining, real estate, agriculture and SME sectors (EBRD, 2013; Korean Development Institute, 2011). For the promotion of market competitiveness, the government needs to not only address the high rate of poorly performing bank loans, but also promote financial and tax incentives that encourage both technology and manpower development. Specifically, efforts should be made to encourage joint ventures with foreign firms in the upstream oil and gas as well as mining sectors. This approach will advance technology imports and foster a competitive 'local content' sector much like the one that Malaysia has endeavoured to develop.

To sum up, research shows that 'industrial policies have a high failure rate, that is, the results achieved are either much lower than those which could have been achieved, or, in some cases, policies have actually had a negative impact. Instead of promoting industrial growth and diversification, policy structures have held the industrial sector back' (UNIDO, 2012: 75). To ensure success in Kazakhstan, the government needs first to address and promote competition in all sectors with special emphasis on potential export sectors. The government must realise that promoting competitiveness has a higher probability of success than 'selecting' priority sectors. 'Cluster-development schemes rarely work. Success stories are the exception, not the rule' (Wallsten, 2004: 121). As the Asian Development Bank (2013) asserts, Kazakhstan's industrialisation policy, and in turn its diversification policy, needs to be simplified. Promoting competition has been shown to be effective in numerous countries. However, it will be very difficult to sustain diversification in the non-oil and gas sector if Kazakhstan does not change its regulatory regime to promote technology-sharing joint ventures, address the shortage of well-trained scientists and engineers, adjust its property rights policies, and continue to smooth out the high macroeconomic volatility that large oil price swings can transmit. Furthermore, it is essential that the government controls large swings in its real exchange rate.

Notes

1   Kashagan's development cost is approximately 23% of Kazakhstan's 2013 GDP.
2   The Swedish Iron-master's Association, which was partly financed by the state, was very important in the transfer of foreign technology and the wide implementation of best foreign practices across Sweden (Blomström and Kokko, 2008).
3   The Bolashak Scholarship Programme was established in 1994 by the government of Kazakhstan in order to train specialists abroad at both the undergraduate and graduate levels.
4   In 2005, 32% and 31% of students in Malaysia were studying in the science and engineering disciplines respectively (UNESCO, 2013).
5   Prior to 2009, hydrocarbon contracts were based on production sharing agreements (Mills and Howard, 2014).
6   The major operators that operate under production sharing agreements (Tengizchevroil – Tengiz field, Karachaganak Petroleum Operating – Karachaganak field, and the North Caspian Oil Company – Kashagan field) are exempt from local content requirements until 2015 (OUSTR, 2014). Estimates of the share of the local content in

terms of the amount of goods purchased by these three operators does not exceed 3% (KAZENERGY, 2013).

7   The term 'works' represents activities related to construction and the arrangement of primary deposits, with real results. The term 'goods' represents items (things), including semi-finished products or raw materials in solid, liquid or gas state, electric and thermal energy, objectified results of intellectual creative activity, as well as rights in them, under which it can be possible to make the purchase and sales transaction. The term 'services' represents activities aimed at meeting the needs of the customer, with no real results (Samruk-Kazyna, 2012).

8   About US$11 billion of the funds were devoted to direct assistance to struggling commercial banks, while the remainder financed anti-crisis stimulus measures in various sectors of the economy (World Bank, 2013a).

References

Asadulla, M. (2014) *Managing Malaysia's education crisis*, East Asia Forum, available online at www.eastasiaforum.org/2014/12/05/managing-malaysias-education-crisis/ (accessed 25 April 2015).

Asian Development Bank (2012) *Technical assistance report: Preparation of sector road maps for Central and West Asia*, Project Data Sheet (PDS): Details. TA No. 7708. Manila.

Asian Development Bank (2013) *Report to the government of Kazakhstan: Policies for industrial and service diversification in Asia in the 21st century*, Manila: Asian Development Bank.

An, G. and Becker, C.M. (2013) 'Uncertainty, insecurity, and emigration from Kazakhstan to Russia', *World Development*, vol. 42, 44–66.

Blomström, M.E and Kokko, A. (2008) 'From natural resources to high-tech production: The evolution of industrial competitiveness in Sweden and Finland', in Lederman, D. and Francis, W. (eds.), *Natural resources: Neither curse nor destiny*, Stanford University Press and the World Bank.

Cohen, A. (2008) *Kazakhstan: The road to independence*, Central Asia-Caucasus Institute, The Johns Hopkins University, Washington DC, and Silk Road Studies Program, Institute for Security and Development Policy, Stockholm.

Commander, S., Zettelmeyer, J., Nikoloski, Z., Volchkova, N., Plekhanov, A., Isakova, A. and Schweiger, H. (2012) *Diversifying Russia: Harnessing regional diversity*, London: European Bank of Reconstruction and Development.

David, A.P. and Wright, G. (1997) 'Increasing returns and the genesis of American resource abundance', *Industrial and Corporate Change*, vol. 6, no. 2, 203–245.

Dietsche, E. (2014) 'Diversifying mineral economies: Conceptualizing the debate on building linkages', *Mineral Economics*, vol. 27, no. 2–3, 89–102.

Ekeli, T. and Sy, A. (2011) 'The economics of sovereign wealth funds: Lessons from Norway', in Arezki, R., Gylfason, T. and Sy, A. (eds.), *Beyond the Curse: Policies to Harness the Power of Natural Resources*, Washington DC: International Monetary Fund.

Engineering and Mining Journal (2010) 'Kazakhstan – not just another 'Stan'', vol. 211, no. 10, 56.

European Bank of Reconstruction and Development (2013) Strategy for Kazakhstan, London: EBRD.

European Bank of Reconstruction and Development (1999/2002) *Transition report*. London: EBRD.

Farooki, M. and Kaplinsky, R. (2014) 'Promoting diversification in resource-rich economies', *Mineral Economics*, vol. 27, no. 2-3, 103–113.

Fund, K.C.G. (2013) Active support on SME development and preparation for innovative industrial development plan of Kazakhstan. Seoul: Knowledge Sharing Program, Korea Development Institute

Green, D. and Vokes, R. (1997) 'Agriculture and the transition to the market in Asia', *Journal of Comparative Economics*, vol. 25, no. 4, 250–80.

Hirschman, A. (1977) 'A generalized linkage approach to development, with special reference to staples', in Nash, M. (ed.), *Essays on economic development in honor of Bert F. Hoselitz*, Chicago University Press, Chicago.

International Monetary Fund (1998) *Output decline in transition: The case of Kazakhstan*, WP/98/45.

Interfax (2014) 'NCOC to submit pipeline replacement cost for Kashagan by end2014 – energy ministry', *Kazakhstan General Newswire*, 1.

Interfax (Kazakhstan Oil and Gas Weekly) (2015) *COMPANY NEWS: pipe replacement at Kashagan to be completed on schedule during 2nd half of 2016*, available online at http://search.proquest.com/docview/1661339458?accountid=1343 (accessed 25 April 2015).

Islamic Development Bank (2012) Member country partnership strategy for the Republic of Kazakhstan (2012–2014): Strengthening competitiveness for growth and diversification. Jeddah, KSA: IDB.

Islamic Development Bank (2011) 'Enhancing competitiveness and diversification of the Kazakhstan economy', *Muharram*, vol. 1432, December.

Jeffries, I. (2013) Guide to the economies in transition, London: Routledge.

Johnson, S., McMillan, J. and Woodruff, C (2002) 'Property rights and finance', *American Economic Review*, vol. 92, no. 5, 1335–1356.

Kalyuzhnova, Y. and Nygaard, C.A. (2011) 'Special vehicles of state intervention in Russia and Kazakhstan', *Comparative Economic Studies*, vol. 53, no. 1, 57–77.

Kaplinsky, R., Farooki, M., Alcorta, L. and Rodousakis, N. (2012) Promoting industrial diversification in resource intensive economies: The experiences of sub-Saharan Africa and central Asia regions. Vienna: United Nations Industrial Development Organisation.

Kaplinsky, R., Morris, A. and Kaplan, D. (2011) *Commodities and linkages: Industrialisation in sub-Saharan Africa*. Milton Keynes: The Open University Press.

KAZENERGY (2013) *The Oil and Gas Year Kazakhstan 2013*, Astana.

Ketenci, N.S. (2008) Kazakhstani enterprises in transition: The role of historical regional development in Kazakhstan's post-Soviet economic transformation. Stuttgart: Ibidem-Verlag.

Kazakhstan (2010) *2010–2014 State Program of accelerated industrial and innovative development of the Republic of Kazakhstan and cancellation of certain decrees of the President of the Republic of Kazakhstan*. Astana: Republic of Kazakhstan.

Khakimzhanov, S. and Seitenova, A.-G., (2013) *In search of coherence: Kazakhstan's trade and industrial policy*, University of Central Asia Institute of Public Policy and Administration Working Paper No.10.

Klueh, U.H., Pastor, G. and Segura, A. (2009) 'Policies to improve the local impact from hydrocarbon extraction: Observations on West Africa and possible lessons for Central Asia', *Energy Policy*, vol. 37, no. 3, 1128–1144.

Koch, N. (2014) 'The shifting geopolitics of higher education: Inter/nationalizing elite universities in Kazakhstan, Saudi Arabia, and beyond', *Geoforum*, vol. 56, 46–54.

Kravets, O. (2013) *Infrastructure investments in Eastern Neighbours and Central Asia (ENCA)*, EIB Working Papers, No. 2013/01.

Kyle, S. (2014) Mineral revenues and countercyclical macroeconomic policy in Kazakhstan. Working paper, Charles H. Dyson School of Applied Economics and Management, Cornell University (WP 2014-02).

Malikov, Y.A. (2006) Formation of a borderland culture: Myths and realities of Cossack-Kazakh relations in northern Kazakhstan in the eighteenth and nineteenth centuries. Ann Arbor: ProQuest.

McLean, I.W. (2012) *Why Australia prospered: The shifting sources of economic growth*, Princeton: Princeton University Press.

Mills, D. and Howard, B. (2014) 'Oil and gas regulations in Kazakhstan', *Global Practical Law*. Available online at http://uk.practicallaw.co- m/cs/Satellite?blobcol=urldata&blo bheader=application%2Fpdf&blobkey=id&blobtable=MungoBlobs&blobwhere=1247 943878651&ssbinary=true (accessed 22 December 2014).

Morris, M., Kaplinsky, R. and Kaplan, D. (2012) *One thing leads to another: Promoting industrialisation by making the most of the commodity boom in sub-Saharan Africa*. Lulu.com.

Ng, P.T. (2008) 'Educational reform in Singapore: From quantity to quality', Educational Research for Policy and Practice, vol. 7, no. 1, 5–15.

Ngoasong, M.Z. (2014) 'How international oil and gas companies respond to local content policies in petroleum-producing developing countries: A narrative enquiry', *Energy Policy*, vol. 73, 471–479.

Noreng, Ø. (2004) 'Norway: Economic diversification and the petroleum industry', *Middle East Economic Survey*, vol. 47, 45.

OECD (2007) *Reviews for National Policies for Education: Higher Education in Kazakhstan*, Paris: OECD.

OECD (2011) *Competitiveness and Private Sector Development: Central Asia 2011*, Paris: OECD.

OECD (2012) *OECD investment policy reviews: Kazakhstan 2012*, Paris: OECD.

OECD (2013a) *Review of agricultural policies, Kazakhstan 2013*. Paris: OECD.

OECD (2013b) *Improving Access to Finance in Kazakhstan's Agribusiness Sector*, Paris: OECD.

OECD (2014) *Responsible Business Conduct in Kazakhstan*, Paris: OECD.

Office of the United States Trade Representative (OUSTR) (2014) *Kazakhstan Trade Summary*, available online at www.ustr.gov/sites/default/files/2014%20NTE%20 Report%20on%20FTB%20Kazakhstan.pdf (accessed 21 April 2016).

Oil News (2009) *The Caspian Pipeline Consortium: Black Sea Gate for Kazakh oil*, 29 August, available online at http://oilnews.kz/en/home/portraits/46508.html (accessed 21 April 2016).

Ostrowski, W. (2010) *Politics and oil in Kazakhstan*, Routledge: London.

Ostrowski, W. (2009) 'The legacy of the 'coloured revolutions': the case of Kazakhstan', *Journal of Communist Studies and Transition Politics*, vol. 25., no. 2–3, 347–368.

Peck, A.E. (2004) *Economic development in Kazakhstan: the role of large enterprises and foreign investment*. London: Routledge.

Petrick, M., Oshakbaev, D. and Wandel, J. (2014) *Kazakhstan's wheat, beef and dairy sectors: An assessment of their development constraints and recent policy responses* (No. 145). Discussion Paper, Leibniz Institute of Agricultural Development in Central and Eastern Europe.

Pomfret, R. (2005) 'Kazakhstan's economy since independence: Does the oil boom offer a second chance for sustainable development?' *Europe-Asia Studies*, vol. 57, no. 6, 859–76.

Pomfret, R. (2007a) 'Rebuilding Kazakhstan's agriculture', *Central Asia Caucasus Analyst*, 7.

Pomfret, R. (2007b) 'Using energy resources to diversify the economy: Agricultural price distortions in Kazakhstan', *CASE Network Studies and Analyses*, no. 355.

Pomfret, R. (2013) 'Kazakhstan's 2030 strategy: Goals, instruments and performance', in *American Economic Association Annual Conference in Philadelphia*, vol. 4, 2-3.

Puffer, S. (1996) 'Leadership in a Russian context', *Business and Management in Russia*, 38–56.

Radosevic, S. and Myrzakhmet, M. (2009) 'Between vision and reality: Promoting innovation through technoparks in an emerging economy', *Technovation*, vol. 29, no. 10, 645–656.

Reinhardt, N. (2000) 'Back to basics in Malaysia and Thailand. The role of resource-based exports in their export-led growth', *World Development*, vol. 28, no. 1, 57–77.

Rodrik, D. (2008) *The real exchange rate and economic growth*, unpublished manuscript, Boston: Harvard University.

Saleh, A.S. and Ndubisi, N.O. (2006) 'An evaluation of SME development in Malaysia', *International Review of Business Research Papers*, vol. 2, no. 1, 1–14.

Samruk-Kazyna (2012) *Procurement rules for goods, works and services by Joint Stock Company "Sovereign Wealth Fund 'Samruk-Kazyna'" and organisations, fifty or more shares (interest) of which are directly or indirectly owned by 'Samruk-Kazyna' JSC on the right of property or trust management*, available online at sk.kz/page/download/4433?lang=en (accessed 20 December 2014).

Shin, S.H., Chung, Y.S., Chun, S.H. and Lee, E.K. (2011) SME-centered enterprise development strategy for sustained economic development of Kazakhstan. Seoul: Knowledge Sharing Program, Korea Development Institute.

Sirat, M. (2002) 'Managing the interface with the region: The case of the Universiti Sains Malaysia, Pulau Pinang Malaysia', in Pyle, J.L. and Forrant, R. (eds.), *Globalization, universities and issues of sustainable human development*, Cheltenham: Edward Elgar Publishing.

Tolibekov, S.E. (1963) *Economic development of Kazakhstan under socialism*, UNESDOC SS/SP/17; WS/0263.55.

Tordo, S., Warner, M., Manzano, O.E. and Anouti, Y. (2013) *Local content policies in the oil and gas sector*, Washington DC: World Bank Study.

UNESCO (2014) *Education: Distribution of enrolment by field of study: Tertiary education*, Paris: UNESCO, available at http://data.uis.unesco.org/ (accessed 23 November 2014).

UNESCO (2014) *Total R&D personnel per thousand total employment (FTE)*, Paris: UNESCO, available at http://data.uis.unesco.org/ (accessed 23 November 2014).

United States Energy Information Agency (2014) Total Petroleum and Other Liquids Production, available at www.eia.gov/beta/international/ (accessed 19 December 2014).

United States National Academy (2007) *Science and technology in Kazakhstan: Current status and future prospects*, Washington DC: National Research Council.

Wallsten, S. (2004) 'High-tech cluster bombs', *Nature*, vol. 428, 121–122.

Williams, S., Amiel, G. and Scheck, J. (2014) 'How a giant Kazakh oil project went awry', *Wall Street Journal*, March 31, available online at www.wsj.com/articles/SB10001424052702303730804579437492040999738 (accessed 21 April 2016).

World Bank (2003) *The role of a public investment fund in promoting diversification in Kazakhstan*, Background Paper No.1.

World Bank (2012) *Kazakhstan Assessment of Costs and Benefits of the Customs Union for Kazakhstan*, Report No. 65977-KZ.

World Bank (2013a) *Kazakhstan oil rules: Kazakhstan's policy options in a downturn*, Joint Economic Research Program, Report No. 81686-KZ.

World Bank (2013b) Beyond oil: Kazakhstan's path to greater prosperity through diversifying, Volume II: Main Report 82320 – v2.

World Bank (2015) *Development Indicators Database*, Research and Development expenditure (% of GDP), available at http://data.worldbank.org/indicator/GB.XPD.RSDV.GD.ZS (accessed 23 April 2015).

World Economic Forum (2014) *The Global Competitiveness Index Dataset 2005–2014*, available at www3.weforum.org/docs/GCR2014-15/GCI_Dataset_2006-07-2014-15.xlsx (accessed 21 December 2014).

Wright, G. and Czelusta, J. (2007) 'Resource-based growth past and present', in Lederman, D. and Francis, W. (eds.), *Natural resources: Neither curse nor destiny*, World Bank.

Yang, J. and McCarthy, P. (2013) 'Multi-modal transportation investment in Kazakhstan: Planning for trade and economic development in a post-Soviet country', *Procedia-Social and Behavioral Sciences*, vol. 96, 2105–2114.

Yakavets, N. (2014) 'Reforming society through education for gifted children: The case of Kazakhstan', *Research Papers in Education*, vol. 29, no. 5, 513–533.

Ziyadov, T. (2011) 'Azerbaijan as a regional hub in Central Eurasia', Strategic Assessment of Euro–Asian Trade & Transportation, Azerbaijan Diplomatic, 31.

Appendix

Table 9.5 Kazakhstan's development strategies since independence

Year	Name	Objectives
1992	Strategy for Formulation and Development of Kazakhstan as a Sovereign Nation	Promotion of foreign direct investment as a principal vehicle of sustained economic development, development of new markets for exports, prioritised development of manufacturing and science-intensive industries, promotion of import substitution to employ modern domestic and international technology and equipment, and optimal control of the national currency exchange rate
1997	Kazakhstan 2030: Prosperity, Security, and Improvement of Welfare of Citizens of Kazakhstan (or simply 'Kazakhstan 2030 Strategy')	Promotion of national security, domestic stability, economic growth based on an open economy with high levels of foreign direct investment and high domestic savings rates, and high quality health care and education to improve the well-being of Kazakhstani citizens, improvement of transport and communication infrastructure, and professionalisation of the public administration
2004	Diversification of Kazakhstan's Economy through Cluster Development in Non-Extraction Sectors (or simply the 'Cluster Development Plan')	'Create' seven pilot cluster projects: tourism, metallurgy, textiles, construction, agriculture and food processing; oil and gas machinery building, and logistics and transportation – which are intended to become the core of Kazakhstan's competitive economic strength. Later additions were cotton, wine and fish clusters.
2012	Kazakhstan-2050 Strategy	Transitioning to new principles of economic management, comprehensive support for entrepreneurship so it will be a leading force for the national economy, creating a modern and efficient education and health care systems, and increasing accountability, efficiency and functionality of the state apparatus

Table 9.6 Kazakhstan's principal economic development plans since independence

Year	Name	Objectives
1997	Strategic Development Plan for 1998–2000	1 Macroeconomic stability 2 Price liberalisation 3 Strengthening of private property rights 4 Development of energy and other natural resources 5 Diversification of the economy
2001	Strategic Plan 2010	1 Improvement of social services, specifically improvement and increased access to healthcare services, education, and social security system 2 Improvement of agricultural productivity 3 Improvement and construction of new transportation infrastructure 4 Development of policies for environmental protection and controlled use of natural resources 5 Administration of monetary, tax-fiscal policies that is conducive to prolonged economic growth 6 Administration of investment policy that supports sustained growth while reducing the adverse effects of both internal and external shocks 7 Centralised administration of state-owned assets that operate efficiently and profitably by international standards 8 Political and administrative reforms to improve Kazakhstan's international standing to build a business and investment environment most conducive to external and domestic private investors
2003	Innovative Industrial Development Strategy 2003–2015 (IIDS 2003–2015)	1 Increasing GDP in 2015 by 3.5 times compared to 2000 by increasing the share of industry in GDP from 46.5% to 52% by 2015 and curtailing the decline in the share of services in GDP to 40.6% 2 Averaging 8.4% growth for manufacturing industries so as to reduce the decline in the share of manufacturing in GDP to 12% 3 Tripling the labour productivity by 2015 compared to 2000 4 Reducing the countries energy intensity of GDP by 50% 5 Establishing science-intensive and high-tech exports by increasing the share of research and innovations in GDP from 0.9% in 2000 to at least 1.5% in 2015 6 Diversifying exports by targeting goods and services with high value added 7 Transitioning to international quality standards

Year	Name	Objectives
2010	Strategic Plan 2020	1 Ensure sustained growth of Kazakhstan's economy by way of accelerated diversification and industrialisation and infrastructure development so that by 2020 Kazakhstan non-resource exports will contribute more than 45% to all exports 2 Increase the competitiveness of its labour force such that access to skilled labour is no longer a constraint but an asset for domestic and international firms 3 Join the World Bank's 'Doing Business' list of the fifty most competitive countries in the world 4 Join the first one-third of the countries in Transparency International's corruption perception index 5 Decrease the proportion of the population with incomes below the subsistence minimum to 8%
2010	State Programme on the Accelerated Industrial-Innovation Development 2010–14 (AIIDS 2010–2014)	1 'Forced' vertical diversification, both upstream and downstream, of traditional export-oriented industries (oil and gas, ferrous and non-ferrous metals, uranium, and grains) 2 Financial support initiatives in non-oil and gas sectors (e.g. pharmaceuticals, ceramics, aerospace) 3 Accelerating development of light industry products to take advantage of the larger Customs Union market of 170 million people
2014	State Programme on Industrial-Innovative Development 2015-2019 (AIIDS 2015 – 2019)	1 Accelerated development of the manufacturing industry 2 Improving the business climate 3 Promoting entrepreneurship and the development of small and medium sized businesses in manufacturing

10 The role of institutions in economic diversification

The case of the UAE

Hamed Al-Hashemi

10.1 Introduction

The UAE has accomplished remarkable economic growth and made considerable progress in diversifying its economy over the past four decades as a result of many policies that support economic diversification. These have included the development of infrastructure, improving education and health, enhancing the business environment and improving access to trade. The country continues to expand its role as a hub for logistics, a centre for financial services, a destination for tourism and an environment for real estate investment.

The main attributes of the UAE economy are threefold. First, the UAE economy has been the most dynamic in the region, growing at an average rate of approximately 4.2% over the past four decades. Its GDP grew from AED 58.31 million in 1975 to AED 1,448 million in 2013 in current terms. At AED 158,205 GDP per capita (current equivalent) in 2013, the UAE is among the richest countries in the region, despite a very rapid growth in population over the past two decades that was significantly fuelled by the immigration of low-skilled workers.

Second, the economic structure has been transformed from an economy that was dominated by a single natural based commodity – crude oil – to an economy that is well positioned on the path to diversification. Although the oil and gas sector remains the backbone of the economy, the non-oil and gas sector has been growing steadily over the past four decades. The current productive structure of the economy includes plastics, steel, aluminium, copper and machinery, a broad range which demonstrates the diversification that has emerged over the past decade.

Third, the role of government-owned institutions and enterprises has been instrumental in orchestrating economic growth and driving economic diversification. It has manifested in three forms of institutionalised development. The first of these is the entrepreneurial development that has anchored capital intensive firms as the nucleus for the creation of new industries such as logistics, finance, base metals and polymers. The second is competitive development, which has created a robust business environment and special economic zones to support economic growth and diversification. The UAE is ranked first in ease of doing business within the MENA, sixteenth in competitiveness globally, and its special economic zones are among the most dynamic globally. The third form of institutionalised development is the innovative development that is driving innovation initiatives across government-owned institutions and enterprises, bringing about innovation in services and a productive economic structure – e.g. innovation in civil departments and the UAE Space Agency.

On the other hand, based on interviews and focus group discussions with policy makers, private sectors and state-owned enterprises there are still challenges and constraints that hinder the formation of available opportunities for creating and expanding paths for economic diversification. First, the dominance of state-owned enterprises and the limited contribution of the private sector may impact long-term sustainable growth. Second, access to finance due to limited funding channels to support start-ups and working capital for small and medium-sized enterprises (SMEs) is a binding constraint on the growth of related industries downstream of the oil, gas and base metal industries. Third, there is still dependence on subsidised energy for emerging capital-intensive industries such as polymers, aluminium and steel. Fourth, growing sectors are dependent on low-skilled labour, which does not enable the accumulation of knowledge or a capability to drive the economy towards technological frontiers or sophisticated exports.

The policy implications for decision makers are threefold. First, it is necessary to enable the growth of the private sector by easing access to finance, streamlining regulations, financial systems, credit ratings and so on. Second, strategies need to support the creation of integrated industrial platforms that link government-owned enterprises and SMEs, to enable the emergence of complex services and products that are related to existing anchored industries. Third, the role of special economic zones needs revitalising, moving beyond land leasing towards the formation of knowledge and innovation hubs driven by seamless interaction and interplay among various local and global economic actors.

10.2 What determines economic diversification?

The nature of specialisation and diversification matters for economic development, suggesting that industrialisation creates externalities that lead to accelerated growth (Hirschman, 1958; Rosenstein-Rodan, 1943). There are three approaches to explaining countries' patterns of specialisation and diversification.

The first approach focusses on the relative proportions in which countries possess productive factors (physical capital, labour, land, skills or human capital, infrastructure and institutions) and the proportions in which these factors are needed to produce different goods (see Flam and Flanders, 1991). Hence, poor countries specialise in goods that are relatively intensive in labour and land, while richer countries specialise in goods that use more human and physical capital and demand better infrastructure and institutions. According to these models, the speed at which each factor (e.g. physical capital or skills) is accumulated ultimately determines the change in the type of product the country chooses to produce and export. However, the particular products a country produces carry no consequence for future economic performance.

2.2

The second approach emphasises technological differences (Romer, 1990) and therefore needs to be complemented with a theory of what may lie behind these differences and how they may evolve over time. The two dominant theories – the varieties model of Romer and the quality ladders of Aghion and Howitt (1992) and Grossman and Helpman (1991) – assume a continuum of products in some technological space. According to this line of thinking, there is always a slightly more advanced product that countries can move to as they upgrade their technology. The world of products is abstracted away and ignored when thinking about structural transformation and growth.

An alternative measure for patterns of economic diversification is economic complexity, coined by Hausmann and Hidalgo (2011). It views economic development as a diffusion process over a network (Hidalgo et al., 2007). The structure of the network is modelled around export products that require different capabilities, and countries differ in the completeness of the set of capabilities they have. Countries tend to diversify by developing products that are close in the product space to those they already export. As a result, countries face very different opportunities for diversification because they are at very different distances from other products. In a sense, capabilities embedded in export products determine diversification opportunities (Hausmann and Hidalgo, 2014); hence, they condition future capabilities and consequently shape changes in the economic structure and branching into related or nearby products that are in close proximity to pre-existing capabilities (Hidlago et al., 2007).

Economies are complex systems, composed of mechanisms, factors and actors that are in continuous interplay at country, regional, and sector levels and which determine the different pathways for changing the economic structure, particularly the extent of economic concentration and diversification achieved over time. The main factors include the path dependence of existing concentration and the diversification of the existing economic structure, institutional arrangements and environment, and actions taken by various economic agents such as institutions and firms.

Path dependence matters a lot to changing the structure of national and regional economies, particularly for natural resource-based economies such as the UAE, although policy makers would like to assume that new economic growth paths could be created regardless of existing conditions. Sources of path dependence include: wide ranges of existing resources such as oil and gas; capabilities including infrastructure and knowledge such as skills and innovation capacity; and the variety of existing products, services and industries. Countries can diversify into related and unrelated products and services, but products that are distanced from existing accumulated capabilities and knowledge will be difficult to produce, and it will also be difficult to attract and establish new industries that are technologically unrelated to pre-existing industries, as has been the case for the UAE in establishing semiconductor and aerospace industries. Hence, the role of economic agents matters, particularly government institutions and enterprise, to jump-start new unrelated paths for growth and thereby change the structure of the economy. The UAE has pursued a strategy whereby the government assumed the strategy risk to unlock path dependence and diversify into related and unrelated products and services, an essential undertaking without which economic growth as experienced over the past four decades would not have been realised. Moreover, while governments can establish the anchor of an industry such as Strata Manufacturing PJSC for Aerospace, the institutional arrangements and environment will play a crucial factor in promoting the growth of firms and entrepreneurs around the industry.

10.3 Research methodology and data

The most appropriate means to study the role of institutions in the economic diversification of countries and regions is through a mix of quantitative and qualitative research. The scope of this study is a rich case-based dataset focussed on Abu Dhabi in the UAE, including interviews, focus groups and descriptive analysis. The literature review above provides the theoretical foundation but also the theoretical propositions that generated the qualitative research questions for interviews and focus groups. Synthesis of the data from the interviews and focus groups further refined these propositions and introduced new ones.

The questions for the semi-structured interviews and focus groups discussions were as follows:

- What are the key factors that are responsible for the emergence and evolution of new industries?
- How are new industries created?
- What are the mechanisms for creating new industries?
- How do government organisations, e.g. state-owned institutions and 'institutions for collaboration', influence the creation of new paths for diversification?
- What are the strategic and policy implications for the creation of new paths for economic diversification?

Individual interviews and focus groups were conducted with selected government executives and policy makers, representing economic actors in Abu Dhabi from various key government institutions, and selected executives representing state-owned enterprises, special economic zones and private sector firms. The case analysis of Abu Dhabi offers a specific focus on how institutions have influenced the economic development of a regional economy that is characterised by high path dependence on natural resources. However, the main purpose is to generate a broader framework that explains how institutions influence economic diversification, which could be tested at a later stage and extended to cover other countries.

There is an element of prior selective process; as a result, these factors are anticipated to be the main themes for discussion based on literature reviews, previous piloted unstructured studies, and discussions held with a number of government agencies. The main data are focussed around the different factors and challenges facing the creation of new paths for economic diversification in Abu Dhabi, ranging from policy making, the engagement of the private sector in policy directions, easing access to finance, mobilising private firms to branch into new related products, and planting the seeds for new products and industries. In a sense, a preliminary conceptual framework is cognitively shaped, and hence the interviews and focus group discussions act as a confirmation of the key factors. At the same time, however, the process is an exploration of deeper institutional (environmental and arrangement) factors with the purpose of arriving at a deeper understanding of how institutions influence the creation of new paths for growth and diversification.

10.4 Evolution of the UAE's economy

States in development that are aspiring to transition into advanced economies face a dilemma: their economies are not only dependent on natural resources and concentrated on limited variety of services and products, they are also not complex or technologically advanced. In a sense their accumulated capabilities and knowledge are distanced from producing sophisticated products, and as a result they continue to face challenges in diversifying their economies. The evolution of the UAE economy over the past four decades represents a remarkable success story; it achieved continuous economic growth and transformed its services, products and industries, but its future economic growth and sustainability depends on the country's ability to move into advanced technological areas. The UAE has realised that the transformation of its economy and producing novelty in services and products is a complex process that requires leadership, coordinated policies and strategies, and execution to unlock the country's dependency on hydrocarbon and energy and build capabilities and knowledge. The government had to take a leadership role across three facets – entrepreneurship, competition and innovation – for a systematic drive towards advanced economic territory.

Economic performance

The track record of the UAE's macroeconomic performance has been remarkable; it has been growing at an average rate of approximately 8.6% over the past four decades, its GDP grew from AED 58.313[1] in 1975 to 1,447.6 million in 2013 (Figure 10.1). At AED 158,205 GDP per capita (current equivalent) in 2013, the UAE is one of the richest countries and second only to Qatar in the region, despite a very rapid growth in population over past two decades which was largely fuelled by the immigration of low-skilled workers.

The UAE has evolved from an economy that relied on fishery and pearl trading to an economy that produces oil and gas, polymers, aluminium and steel, thereby positioning its economic structure on track towards the manufacture of sophisticated products such as composite materials for aerospace industries. The years up to the 1970s were mainly characterised by fishery and pearl trading, but then towards the end of 1970s Abu Dhabi witnessed the era of crude oil, followed

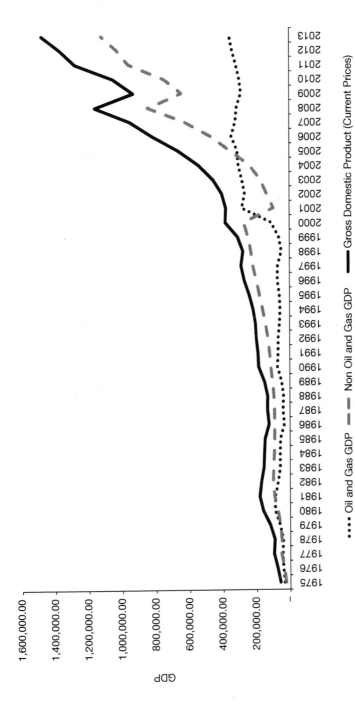

Figure 10.1 The UAE's GDP – current prices in AED millions. (UAE NBS).

by the natural gas industry. The year 1958 marked the first discovery of oil in the emirate, but Abu Dhabi rapidly started exporting oil in 1962 and this sector has been growing to dominate its economy since then. During the 1980s oil and gas income was the sole economic driver, but due to the volatility of oil prices the economy was subjected to large swings and growth was not stable. Nevertheless, local governments used oil and gas revenue to embark on modernisation and social development programmes aimed towards building infrastructure, education and health sectors, which have resulted in raising the standard of living. One noticeable achievement was the Jabal Ali Free Zone (Jafza) that has 'evolved into a dynamic trade catalyst ecosystem that enables business and creates new opportunities for growth. From a modest start in 1985 with just nineteen companies, Jafza today flourishes as a business community with over 7,100 companies including 100 of the Fortune 500s' (Jafza, 2015).

The 1990s witnessed steady economic growth fuelled by the energy sector, which formed a major part of GDP from the 1970s to the 1990s. However, it was evident that the emirate was lacking a vibrant, diverse and sustainable economy with the lack of a strong economic sector beside oil.

In the 2000s the UAE experienced rapid economic growth, witnessing the emergence of new products and industries, and for the first time other sectors of the economy were growing at rate higher than the oil and gas sector, producing a shift in the economic structure and positioning the UAE at a junction of of economic diversification paths.

Over the past decade, every other economic sector (except for a decline in agriculture) out-performed the oil and gas sector. Construction and real estate activities combined grew by 10%, contributed 21.5% to total GDP in 2013 and close to 25% of overall employment (Figure 10.2). Further, the winning bid to host Expo2020 will further boost these activities over the coming five years. Moreover, wholesale trade grew by 4.5% and contributed 11.6% to total GDP and close to 10% to overall employment.

In contrast, manufacturing activities grew by 3.3% and contributed 8.9% to total GDP and around 5% to overall employment. The other main economic activities that contributed to GDP growth as well as employment are banking, transport and communication, government services and utilities. The key conclusion is that emerging economic activities and employment are concentrated in less productive sectors, which not only poses a challenge for future sustainable development but also makes the economy vulnerable as these inherently dependent on the oil and gas sector and are not accumulating advanced and sophisticated knowledge to drive future growth.

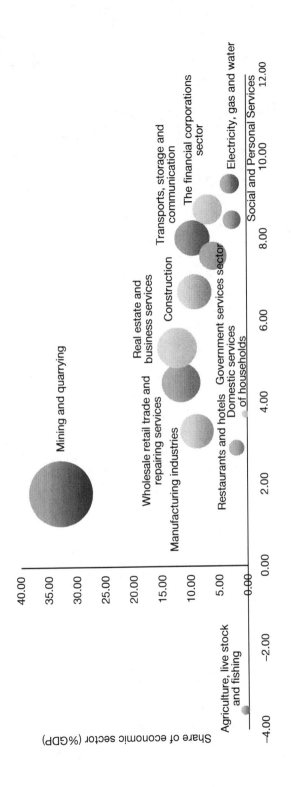

Figure 10.2 The UAE's growth in economic sectors 2011–2013. (UAE NBS).

Table 10.1 Economic indicators (2013) in selected countries

Country	GDP (Constant 2005 US$ in billion)	GDP average growth % 2001–2013	GDP per capita (Constant 2005 US$)	Agriculture	Industry	Manufacturing	Services	Trade	Imports	Exports	FDI
				Value added (% of GDP)					(% of GDP)		
Australia	867.15	3.07	37,489	2.45	26.82	7.13	70.73	41.0	21.1	19.88	3.33
Bahrain	23.32	4.98	17,502	0.00	0.00	0.00	0.00	0.0	0.0	0.00	3.01
Botswana	14.20	4.29	7,027	2.54	36.92	5.68	60.54	115.0	59.9	55.12	1.28
Brazil	1,166.72	3.28	5,823	5.71	24.98	13.13	69.32	27.6	15.0	12.55	3.60
Canada	1,319.29	1.90	37,524	0.00	0.00	0.00	0.00	61.9	31.8	30.08	3.70
Chile	171.41	4.37	9,728	3.44	35.29	11.48	61.28	65.5	32.9	32.56	7.31
Denmark	265.14	0.58	47,230	1.36	22.85	13.73	75.78	102.8	48.5	54.27	0.48
Finland	212.61	1.35	39,086	2.68	26.87	16.62	70.45	77.3	39.1	38.18	-1.98
Iceland	19.21	2.69	59,200	0.00	0.00	0.00	0.00	103.1	47.4	55.73	3.06
Indonesia	452.33	5.45	1,810	14.43	45.69	23.70	39.87	49.5	25.7	23.74	2.68
Korea, Rep.	1,199.88	4.80	23,893	2.34	38.55	31.10	59.11	102.8	48.9	53.92	0.94
Kuwait	102.189	4.76	31,436	0.35	73.31	6.77	35.47	98.1	26.5	71.56	1.05
Malaysia	207.95	1.01	6,998	9.31	40.51	23.92	50.18	154.1	72.4	81.68	3.70
Netherlands	720.79	2.57	42,893	1.97	22.16	12.11	75.88	155.6	72.6	82.94	3.76
New Zealand	130.31	7.77	29,146	0.00	0.00	0.00	0.00	57.5	27.8	29.65	-0.27
Nigeria	183.31	1.55	1,056	21.00	21.99	9.03	57.01	31.0	13.0	18.04	1.07
Norway	331.43	3.54	65,189	1.55	40.79	7.29	57.66	67.0	28.2	38.88	0.51
Oman	43.192	12.13	13,252	1.27	67.34	10.67	31.39	0.0	0.0	0.00	2.04
Qatar	129.89	4.10	59,894	0.09	69.62	9.94	30.28	0.0	0.0	0.00	-0.41
Russian Fed	993.52	4.49	6,923	3.95	36.27	14.82	59.78	50.9	22.5	28.37	3.37
Saudi Arabia	520.66	5.57	18,060	1.84	60.57	10.09	37.59	82.4	30.6	51.79	1.24
Singapore	199.22	5.41	36,898	0.03	25.11	18.76	74.86	358.0	167.5	190.52	21.40
South Africa	313.47	3.27	5,916	2.39	27.58	11.56	70.03	65.1	34.0	31.14	2.32
Sweden	437.39	1.95	45,588	1.44	25.85	16.47	72.71	82.7	38.9	43.79	-0.88
UAE	234.97	4.18	25,141	0.66	59.02	8.53	40.33	176.1	77.7	98.40	2.61
Venezuela, RB	194.65	3.52	6,402	0.00	0.00	0.00	0.00	0.0	0.0	0.00	1.61

Export performance

Export matters for economic diversification. First, it measures the degree of economic diversification; second, it informs us about embedded knowledge and capabilities; and third, it mitigates vulnerability to oil and gas prices.

The economic structure of the UAE, as demonstrated earlier in the distribution of GDP activities, has shifted noticeably over the past decade, with non-oil and gas economic activities reaching 67% of total GDP in 2013. Comparably, the export basket was dominated by oil and gas products which represented a share of around 80% two decades back, but it contributed 70% to total exports in 2013 with other products emerging to take a larger share (Federal Competitiveness and Statistics Authority, 2015). Three major non-oil/gas products have topped the list of growing exports; these are precious metals and gems such as gold and diamonds, aluminium, and polymers, which together contributed approximately 18% of total exports and 55% to non-oil/gas total exports in 2013. The access to low energy feedstock provides a comparative advantage for hydrocarbon and energy-dependent industries such as aluminium, steel, polymers and fertilisers to emerge, while many other products have also developed over time with some now constituting a sizeable share of total exports, such as machinery-manufactured and electrical equipment products. However, these are often re-exports or are not experiencing growth.

A key conclusion that can be drawn from the evolution and emergence of GDP activities and export products is that the UAE continues to face the challenge of breaking out of its hydrocarbon and energy path dependency. Further, downstream industries anchored around capital intensive industries created through entrepreneurial actions of the government are weak because the accumulated capabilities and knowledge embedded in the economy are not yet at the technological frontiers, and there are constraints that limit the growth of private firms in industries. Therefore, the policies of the future for sustainable development should be focussed on establishing a strong export-oriented productive structure that will help the country insulate itself from the vulnerabilities of its domestic economy and the volatility of oil and gas prices.

Patterns of economic diversification

There is no unified measure for evaluating the level of economic diversification. However, the traditional method of measuring diversification in association with economic development is based on income distribution, involving the aggregated variables of GDP. In a sense, the accumulated capital or wealth of a nation is a measure of its economic diversification. Instead, while wealth is one measure, the diversification structure of the economy should also measure variety of economic activities, industries and products. For this chapter, we are applying the concentration ratio and diversification quotient evaluation metrics. The concentration ratio measures how concentrated the particular economy is in any given sector by taking the sum of squares of per cent contribution to GDP.

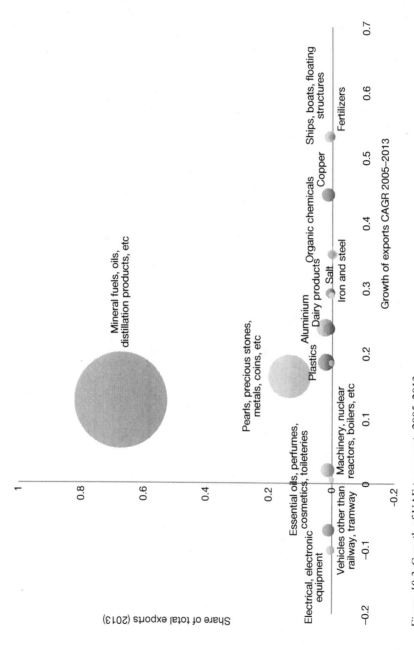

Figure 10.3 Growth of UAE top exports 2005–2013.
(UAE NBS).

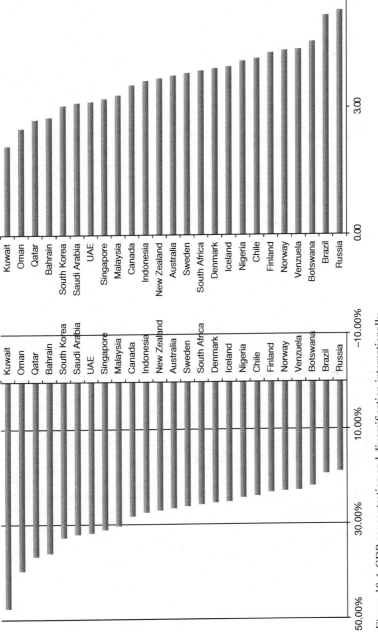

Figure 10.4 GDP concentration and diversification internationally. (Author's calculation).

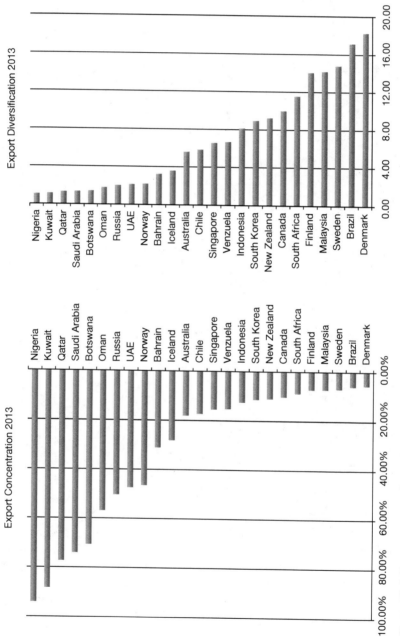

Figure 10.5 Export concentration and diversification internationally. (Author's calculation).

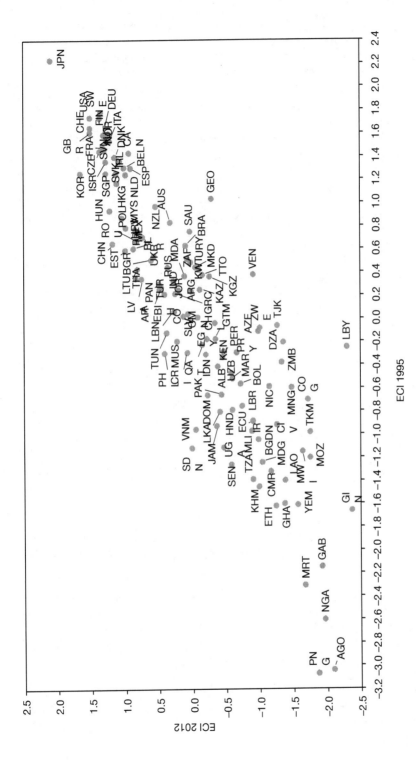

Figure 10.6 Growth of economic complexity: international comparison.
(Centre for International Development at Harvard Kennedy School).

The diversification quotient is the inverse of the concentration ratio. The lower the concentration ratio and the higher the diversification quotient, the more diversified the economy (Shediac et al., 2008). In this report the diversification level of the UAE is compared against GCC countries (Bahrain, Kuwait, Oman, Qatar and Saudi Arabia), other natural resource-based economies (Australia, Brazil, Botswana, Canada, Chile, Indonesia, Malaysia, New Zealand, Nigeria, Russia, South Africa and Venezuela) and selected advanced economies (Denmark, Finland, Singapore, South Korea and Sweden). The concentration ratio and the diversification quotient were measured by calculating GDP distribution across various economic sectors (Shediac et al., 2008) and extended to calculate distribution of export products.

The UAE outperforms other GCC countries, its GDP is less concentrated and more diversified and its export is less concentrated and more diversified, second only to Bahrain. However, the UAE and other natural resource-based economies are more concentrated in their economic activities and exports; hence, their level of diversification is lower than other countries that are less dependent on natural resources, such as Denmark.

On the economic complexity measure, the UAE achieved a complexity level of 322 in 2014 and was ranked 66th globally and 8th among natural resource-based economies, behind Norway, Canada, New Zealand, Malaysia, Russia, Brazil and Indonesia, which were ranked 33rd, 39th, 49th, 50th, 54th and 56th respectively.

10.5 The diversification mechanisms in the UAE

Countries and regions pursue different mechanisms for diversification, conditioned by their economic actors and underlying factors. Some of these factors include path dependence on natural resources, institutional arrangements through the direct involvement of government-owned institutions in creating new paths for growth and diversification, and institutional environments that enhance ease of doing business and competitiveness.

Abu Dhabi is an energy-based economy where access to cheap energy feedstock provides a comparative advantage for energy-dependent industries. Thus, this has determined the nature of the energy-dependent industrial export products that have emerged and evolved over time, including oil, gas, plastics and base metals such as aluminium and steel.

> There are direct and indirect impacts of oil and gas sector on the economy … the existing non and oil gas industries are still somewhat relatively dependent on our strength on the spinal core energy sector … we need to draw the links between our comparative advantage which is the oil and gas sector and spill over impact that is created to the overall economy.

Oil and gas products contributed 78.2% to total exports, while non-oil export products and re-exported products each contributed only 2.2%. Plastic and base metal export products characterise the non-oil productive structure of the Abu

Dhabi economy. The diversification and complexity of the industrial productive structure of Abu Dhabi's economy remains low and dominated by oil and gas products. The energy sector will remain the fundamental backbone of the economy for years to come, fuelling economic growth; further, it will determine the nature of new products and industries that could emerge over time, due to the embedded capabilities and comparative advantages within Abu Dhabi economy.

> We have fundamentals that differ from other areas in the world ... we need to find a model that best suits our needs and requirements ... and identify industries that we like to develop ... existing or new ... and have certain advantages.

While natural resources are main source of path dependency, other indigenous resources such as culture and geographical location have also influenced path dependency. Culture influenced the strategic choice by government to position Abu Dhabi as a cultural tourism destination, whereby the Abu Dhabi Tourism Development Agency started to develop Sadiyat Island as a cultural city featuring international and local museums, art and music premises and events. Geographical location, particularly proximity to Dubai which is a global logistical and trade hub, triggered a similar economic structure – a spillover effect. In a sense, sources of path dependency influence patterns of economic diversification.

The first proposition is that 'path dependence impacts economic diversification', influencing how regions and countries break out of path dependence and create new paths for growth and diversification. The path creation mechanisms as experienced in Abu Dhabi are discussed next.

All in all, the Abu Dhabi Government adopted prudent diversification strategies and undertook a vigorous intervention programme which manifested in four diversification mechanisms: anchoring, branching, clustering, and indigenous creation.

Anchoring

First, the main feature of any diversification mechanism is anchoring capital-intensive industrial firms that are owned by the government as a nucleus for new industries that did not exist previously. The Abu Dhabi Government established and coordinated various SOEs to create new anchor industries that are both related and unrelated to existing economic structures, such as the energy industry, oil and gas, base metals, renewable energy, military, aerospace, semiconductor, and tourism. In the 1970s, 1980s and 1990s the SOEs were directly related to natural resource endowments in oil and gas – e.g. Boroug is a pioneer in anchoring the polymer industry, Emal for aluminium, and Emirates Steel for the steel industry. More recently, in the last decade new SOEs have ventured into unrelated complex products such as ATIC of Mubadala for semiconductors, Masdar for renewable energy, Tawazun for military applications and Strata for the aerospace sector.

It was an essential step for the government to invest and anchor industries, and the rationale is based on self-discovery phenomena since private investors will not invest in a grassroots landscape due to various risks associated with starting up capital intensive industrial ventures and limited domestic demand for generated products. As one policy and strategy executive highlights: 'the private sector will not come because maybe the risk is very high … so the government has got to step in' in order to 'increase confidence of investors, build projects, commitment, remove risk away from investors' – in a sense, to mitigate or remove risks associated with self-discovery.

It is also assumed that the ecosystem and downstream industries will emerge over time, as one industrial executive stated: 'the government invested 10 billion dirhams to build Emirates Steel for certain reasons; a couple of those reasons are to really participate in the development of the infrastructure in UAE, and also to be part of the 2030 vision to diversify the economy of Abu Dhabi, and also to facilitate the development of the downstream sectors'. This could be achieved either by growing domestic SMEs or attracting foreign investment, as emphasised by a policy and strategy executive: 'government becomes an anchor, in which it attracts the private sector to contribute,'. While the diversification approach through anchoring has resulted in the creation of the nucleus of some industries, it should be noted that government may not be able to predict the industry that will flourish over time.

> The government also should be very careful when it comes to taking the decision to enter into a certain sector or industry and ensure that it's not a top-down approach. It should also be based on a thorough analysis and detailing the opportunities, and I think this is what Abu Dhabi is doing. Because at the end of the day, yes you will be attracting the private sector to contribute, but also the private sector will do their own analysis and due diligence to ensure that there is an opportunity and value added. Even if you are also taking the risk and you are leading, it's not necessarily that the private sector will follow you because they have their own… So you have also to be sure that you can convince and you can assure that there is a value added.

Branching

Second, branching is another diversification mechanism where new firms or new products branch off the existing economic structure. Branching is founded on a vibrant SME landscape. SMEs drive economic growth, create jobs and contribute to the development of a dynamic private sector across many economies. There are SMEs that have become established over time around SOEs such as oil and gas manufacturing services; however, in other industries they are are either low in concentration – 'there are only a few real downstream industries that have been created in Abu Dhabi' – or low in the complexity of their products – 'from the steel point of view we do not really have a downstream industry to really support

Emirates Steel ... the wire rod where we have a lot of downstream applications is an example; we only sell 20% in the UAE, the rest goes elsewhere, mostly to Saudi Arabia', as noted by government and industrial executives respectively. The diversification approach through SOEs has not led to the branching of vibrant SMEs or driven downstream industries for polymers, aluminium, steel, aerospace and renewable energy. The economy has not evolved to provide a high level of specialisation around products generated by SOEs. Consequently, the level of diversification and economic complexity remains low, with the UAE ranked sixty-sixth worldwide (Hausmann et al., 2011) as measured by the degree of export sophistication.

Realising the importance of SMEs, Abu Dhabi created the Khalifa Fund to support and finance entrepreneurs, but SMEs still face challenges. The investment climate has been identified as a factor that inhibited the propagation of SMEs, particularly industrial-based SMEs. Regulations, legislation, access to finance, investment promotions and collaboration institutions are key components of cultivating a vibrant business environment. In summary, our interviewees reported that Abu Dhabi has not yet exploited its full existing capabilities and relative comparative advantages that are available in the downstream industries of existing industries, e.g. energy, petrochemicals and base metals. Policy makers should therefore pursue industrial policies and intervention programmes that extend existing capabilities into industries of higher added value and higher complexity. There are many products and industries that could be exploited that are already produced by other countries; hence, the proximity and relatedness of new products and industries to existing anchor-based industries and the opportunity value to be generated should function as the underlying determining factors to set the economy on new paths for growth.

> We will continue to have industries related to energy e.g. aluminium and steel ... and we cannot eliminate energy driven industries ... these industries bring technology and talent to the economy.
>
> The new sectors in an oil and gas economy are and always will be interconnected and we will never be able to disconnect them.
>
> We want to understand the comparative advantage of these industries and the technology that they bring to us.

Government's role should be limited to enabling the investment climate for entrepreneurs and private sector firms to exploit available investment opportunities in emerging industries. Taking into consideration the dominant role of SOEs in the economy, their contribution for the creation of downstream industries becomes crucial, as discussed in the following section.

> Masdar is a new economic development programme to help diversify the economy away from and oil and gas by building on our own strengths and by creating new knowledge based industries that can be sustainable if our oil and gas industry is healthy and fuelling the growth of the economy ... however,

our strengths cannot be centred around one source and we should instead centre it around human capital and technology.

Clustering

Clustering through Special Economic Zones (SEZs) is the third form of economic diversification mechanism in Abu Dhabi. It aims to provide infrastructure and logistics as well as an attractive business environment and legislation to facilitate the growth of local and foreign firms, consequently contributing to economic diversification. There are seven SEZs in Abu Dhabi: ZonesCorp, Masdar and twofour54, which are active with a high level of concentration of firms, and KIZAD, Strata, Tawazun and the Airport Logistics Zone, which currently have low concentrations of firms. ZonesCorp and KIZAD are not directly associated with an SOE, although Emirates Steel and Emal are operating within these zones respectively. Of the others, Masdar, Tawazun and Strata are directly associated with SOEs. These SEZs have enabled the growth of the firm and product mix in Abu Dhabi, but the integration of SEZs with the overall economic diversification strategy and their impact on diversification is not very clear. The value propositions of SEZs, barriers, expectations of policy makers, operators of zones and firms are discussed below.

SEZs are major strategic forms of investment in infrastructure pursued by Abu Dhabi, aiming to facilitate the clustering and growth of firms through enabling sets of laws and regulations, access to land and cheap energy (and therefore price competiveness of products), access to international trade and logistics and linkages with firms located inside and outside the zones. Consequently they contribute to the diversification of the economic structure, or as one policy maker summarises: 'economies cannot develop and grow and be competitive unless they have incentives, policies and regulations that can support industrial companies to be established in their countries, for them to access them to sell their goods overseas, locally or internationally. On that basis the new industrial economic specialised zones were built'. The main value proposition for SEZs is a one-stop-shop service for starting up a firm. Generally firms operating within SEZs are satisfied with the business start-up registration processes; as one investor highlights: 'the main reason we invested in the zone was the fast process to bring in labour', although in some cases firms may still need support and clarity on legal issues, and may be required to approach authorities outside the zones to finalise registration procedures. As another investor states: 'some parts of the license and land allocation process is extremely slow and old fashioned, labour accommodation costs are too high and networking is non-existent, not even a suggestions box is provided'. However, the main concern highlighted by some firms is that business licenses issued by SEZs are sometimes not recognised by some government enterprises, hence restricting these firms form participation in government projects.

Access to land enables foreign firms to lease industrial land for long periods of time, up to fifty years. However, the constraints highlighted by both operators of zones and firms indicate that awareness and clarity of laws and regulations for leasing land are major barrier. A SEZ notes: 'land is available ... the problem is you have to understand exactly what you want to do, what kind of investment you want to create on this land'.

Most firms operating within SEZs have cited cheap energy as one of key attractions to start up their business. This is the result of a deliberate policy direction to economic growth and diversification with SEZs; as a policy executive notes: 'the economic zones provide an area with infrastructure and with a source of energy, which is gas in most cases, better than outside those zones. So light industries can get better, let's say, when it comes to the profit margin for their products it will be higher than outside the economic zones'. An investor taking advantage f this opportunity highlighted that 'I have been to many zones in the UAE and some people do not realise this but this SEZ offers the cheapest electricity rate across the UAE'. However, cheap is not sustainable over a long period of time, taking into consideration changes in energy markets and the burden of energy subsidies on government balance sheets.

Access to logistics and trade is a prerequisite for SEZs to be a success, and thus industrial zones are typically located in close proximity to port facilities to access international markets: 'infrastructure that facilitated building up logistics which led to easing access to trade, hence opening up markets accompanied with flexible trade legislations and minimum tariffs'.

However, beyond access to land, logistics, trade and energy, the essence of SEZs is a vibrant competitive business environment for firms operating within the SEZs, enabling their growth over time. Moreover, there are other viewpoints on the existing anchoring and clustering diversification strategy. The clustering process in Abu Dhabi is embryonic, as one government policy advisor argues: 'we have not yet kicked off the clustering process'. The establishment of SEZs and SOEs is a trigger for clustering because the process of clustering is organic: 'I would say the clustering process is an organic process ... it is kicked off and you've provided the vision, the leadership, the guidance, the direction, the directives and all that, and you've sold yourself fully to the market as being like fully behind this process, then the market will engage in it'.

A policy maker notes that 'you build anchors and then leave the rest to be built organically', and an SOE executive states that 'the government starts with the anchor industry as EMAL and DUBAL ... now the next step is to build a cluster around this main industry ... this is now where the policy should be focussed to build the cluster around this anchor company, or the big company like EMAL and Emirate Steel Company. This will be the next step maybe, and this is maybe the focus in the next industrial strategy for Abu Dhabi, this focus is directly to the medium industry, or the light industry, which can benefit from or bring benefit to what we already have, this is what we feel'. In a sense, once the government-led anchor firms are established stimulating the foundation of new industries, clusters should grow organically around these anchored firms and government intervention should be focussed on other value propositions, such as enhancing the business and competitiveness environment, building innovation capacity and facilitating links between SOEs, SMEs, SEZs that are essential for the branching of new firms and new products. These are discussed below.

> It is not a matter of providing the land and building your project on your plot, it is at the end of the day a chain, meaning how can you get your raw material in the country, how can you bring the best labour to work in your company or manufacturing industry, how can you get the best machines, equipment, knowhow to work on your project? And then surely how to get the right network to send your goods?

Thus, the value propositions stop short of offering to enable the growth of firms by clustering and enabling networking, linkages and collaboration between firms within the zones and across industries.

> When I saw the industrial zones come up, I saw a dream that by default clusters will be built around anchor projects. This has not happened yet. Fair enough, such industries or economies, you do not see the outcomes in a year or two or ten even. We are a very small country, plans, industrial zones have just started, even ten years is a very short time, we literally import over 90% of our goods, so it was a smart move just to leave them, establish their basic manufacturing, needed goods internally, domestic goods I mean.

The impact of SEZs on the overall economy is rather difficult to assess. SEZs are being recognised as an enabler for economic growth and FDI, but these assumptions are not validated on the ground, as the contribution to GDP of firms operating within SEZs is not provided. Moreover, the linkages between SEZs and local firms outside the zones is generally weak, which means that SEZs are islands within the economic structure.

> Some people see that the free zone is not sufficient to the economy, but for me actually it is a very big important role to create FDI, and the free zones bring a lot of the companies inside and this has benefited the economy indirectly. It starts with the export, and extends to offer business opportunities to local firms such as in transportation.

The anchoring diversification strategy via SOEs, which extended to SOEs in special economic zones such as Tawazun for military manufacturing and Strata for the aerospace sector, are yet to create busy clusters around SOEs and within associated zones.

> Manufacturing companies have been established, they started manufacturing, successfully running their businesses, but I think with their number now almost, as I said, between 300 and 400, only in Kizad and ZonesCorp today, we should think seriously about how to build clustering projects around them.

I think the best example would be Strata building parts of aeroplanes with Boeing. This manufacturing company is a state owned company that is today considered one of the main players in building tails of aeroplanes, parts of the tails of the aeroplanes, and is considered a very successful company, meaning a big percentage of their employees are local citizens. It has been built literally in the desert in an area that was inhabited by animals, now today you see literally a small city, a town. After sitting with them, and surely more or less they import their raw material 99.9% from overseas, they said okay, let's take advantage and build a cluster around Strata, which made common sense, and they agreed, and this is one of the main objectives of Strata in such a project.

Indigenous creation

Fourth, Abu Dhabi also ventured into the indigenous creation of industries that are solely based on natural endowments through SOEs, e.g. exploiting the country's geographical location to make it into a global logistical hub for trade and a global tourist attraction. Dubai's Jafza and Abu Dhabi's KIZAD and ZonesCorp developed special economic zones to enable industrial development through logistics and trade. The Tourism Development and Investment Company (TDIC) in Abu Dhabi led the development of the tourism sector including hotels, an island city, residential accommodation and museums.

In summary, the diversification mechanisms employed in Abu Dhabi include indigenous creation, anchoring, branching and clustering, and these are enabled and constrained by various factors. These factors include laws and regulations, access to land, access to logistics and trade, and the availability of cheap energy sources, as well as other factors such as business linkages, access to finance, investment climate, investment and awareness of investment and business opportunities, and innovation capacity. Moreover, diversification mechanisms and factors are influenced by the actions of economic agents such as such the government, special economic zones and state-owned enterprises. The following sections discuss the diversification factors and actors.

In conclusion, the second proposition resulting from the above discussions is that new paths for diversification are created through different mechanisms such as indigenous resources, anchoring, branching, and clustering, which are conditioned by various economic diversification factors and influenced by economic actors.

10.6 The role of the UAE government institutions

The federal government of the UAE and the local governments of Abu Dhabi, Dubai and the other Emirates have played an instrumental leadership role in the social and economic development of the UAE, particularly in terms of the utilisation of indigenous resources, anchoring, clustering and branching of new economic activities and industries. Government has not assumed this role by suppressing market forces or restricting the expansion of private sector activities. Instead its role manifested in visionary, entrepreneurial, competitive and innovative state intervention.

Visionary state

Government leadership and visionary development is demonstrated in its various strategies and policies embraced by the federal government of the UAE and local governments particularly of Abu Dhabi and Dubai.

The UAE Vision 2021 was launched by H.H. Sheikh Mohammed bin Rashid Al Maktoum, Vice-President and Prime Minister of the UAE and Ruler of Dubai, at the closing of a Cabinet meeting in 2010. The Vision aims to make the UAE one of the best countries in the world by the Golden Jubilee of the Union. In order to translate the Vision into reality its pillars have been mapped into six national priorities, which represent the key focus sectors of government action in the coming years. The national strategic priorities are cohesive society and preserved identity, a first-rate education system, world-class healthcare, a competitive knowledge economy, safe public and a fair judiciary, sustainable environment and infrastructure, and strong global standing.

The Abu Dhabi Economic Vision 2030 is a long-term developmental vision that was launched in 2009, setting the strategic direction for diversifying the economy. It outlines key goals, objectives and measures that underpin future policies to branch and create new industries. The main overarching goal is to build a strong, sustainable and diversified economy. The objectives are to first reduce GDP volatility through diversification away from oil into other sectors and ensure more stable and predictable economic growth, whereby Abu Dhabi will focus on capital intensive and export-orientated sectors that represent a comparative advantage. The second goal is to enlarge the enterprise base through the continued growth and expansion of large 'National Champions' (mainly state owned enterprises), the attraction of FDI in leading edge technology sectors, and the stimulation of a more vibrant SME sector. Third, the Vision aims to enhance competitiveness and productivity by bolstering the entrepreneurial SME sector, generating significant economic growth and focussing on capital intensive industries and internationally traded services, aiming to enable companies to make capital and labour work more efficiently and greatly increase the overall competitiveness of the economy. The policy levers include building an open, efficient, effective and globally-integrated business environment, adopting disciplined fiscal policies that are responsive to economic cycles, establishing a resilient monetary and financial market environment with manageable levels of inflation, driving significant improvement in the efficiency of the labour market, developing a sufficient and resilient infrastructure capable of supporting anticipated economic growth, developing a highly skilled, highly productive workforce, and enabling financial markets to become the key financiers of economic sectors and projects.

Dubai has undergone unprecedented growth over the last two decades, transforming this once small pearl-diving town into one of the world's leading cities. The emirate's growth has been anchored by an unwavering vision of establishing a centre to serve an ever-growing region, and a bridge that connects east and west. The Dubai Strategic Plan 2015 (DSP 2015) was launched in 2007 by H.H. Sheikh Mohammad bin Rashid Al Maktoum, UAE Vice-President and Prime Minister and Ruler of Dubai. Through DSP 2015 Dubai established a documented long-term strategy, making it one of the first countries in the region to do so. DSP 2015 set ambitious targets for Dubai's growth in the long-term, highlighting key sectors of focus and priority areas that would shape the emirate as it continued its march forward. DSP 2015 was the driver for change in many sectors, and was the basis for the development of the Government of Dubai's sector strategies as well as several other reform initiatives. Above all, however, DSP 2015 offered guidance to government entities and other players crucial to the Dubai story that helped to ensure coordination among the various stakeholders in pursuit of the vision of the leadership. Dubai has made considerable achievements over the last few years, putting the emirate on the fast track of development. In terms of economic development, it focusses on GDP growth, productivity improvement, economic stability and competitiveness. Moreover, the DSP also covers other focus areas like social development, where priorities include national identity and social cohesion, Emiratis' role in the society and economy, the availability of quality education, healthcare and quality social services, good working environments, and a vibrant cultural life.

Entrepreneurial state

The local governments of Abu Dhabi and Dubai pursued anchoring economic diversification programmes at an accelerated pace through leadership, policies and strategies that were effectively executed by state owned institutions and enterprises. In a sense these actors functioned as entrepreneurs or change agents, introducing novelty in services and products and stimulating economic growth, although with some variations. Dubai focused on logistics, tourism and financial services, while Abu Dhabi pursued capital-intensive industrial diversifications that are associated or branched from energy sectors such as the polymer, aluminium and steel industries.

The last decade witnessed the creation of various state owned enterprises that anchored new industries in Abu Dhabi. In 2002 Mubadala was established to 'help diversify the economy and deliver both financial returns and socio-economic benefits to the emirate'. Consequently, several firms were created covering a variety of industries: Dolphin Energy (2003) for gas transport; Imperial College London Diabetes Centre (2005); Masdar for renewable energy (2006) and Masdar Institute of Science and Technology (2007), both located within Masdar City (2008) which is intended to become a sustainable eco-city economic zone; Al Yah Satellite Communications Company (Yahsat) (2007); Globalfoundries (2009), which is a 100% acquisition in semiconductor manufacturing; Strata for advanced composite aero-structures manufacturing, located within its associated Nibras Al Ain Aerospace Park (2010); and other companies. Emirates Global Aluminium (EGA) is the fifth largest aluminium producer in the world, jointly owned by Mubadala of Abu Dhabi and the Investment Corporation of Dubai, whose core operating assets are Emirates Aluminium (EMAL), which started up in 2013 with an investment valued at approximately AED 38 billion (US$10.2 billion), and Dubai Aluminium (DUBAL), which was commissioned in 1979 and has a combined annual production of 2.4 million tonnes. Emirates Steel was established in 1998, growing in a relatively short period of time from a simple re-roller of imported steel billets to a complex integrated manufacturing plant. In 2012 the Company began producing at a capacity of 3.5 million MTPA, following two expansions and the investment of AED 11 billion – i.e. around US$3 billion (Emirates Steel, 2016). Borouge is a leading provider of innovative, value-creating plastics solutions that started up in 2010, and its production capacity is reaching 4.5 million tonnes of polyethylene and polypropylene (Borouge, 2015).

While services and industries making up the largest share of economic activities and export portfolios are anchored around state owned enterprises, competitiveness and innovation will underpin future growth and sustainable development to bring about variety in new related and unrelated services around and beyond these anchor investments.

Competitive state

The entrepreneurial strategic initiatives undertaken by the government drove the economic growth witnessed from the 1970s through to the 2000s, and over the past decade the UAE government has undertaken steady institutional, environment and competitiveness reforms which have resulted into a remarkable improvement in positioning across various global competitiveness measures. The UAE is ranked third in the region and fortieth worldwide for human development, competitiveness and doing business. It is ranked first regionally and twelfth and twenty-second globally on the Global Competitiveness Index and Doing Business scale respectively. The UAE, and Abu Dhabi and Dubai in particular, have actively pursued a clustering economic diversification strategy through the formation of Special Economic Zones that provide a competitive institutional arrangement and environment for the growth of firms, products and industries. Its competitiveness strategy has already enabled the UAE to become a thriving business hub for firms and entrepreneurs to grow, prosper and contribute to the future sustainable development of the country.

Innovative state

The UAE recognises that its sustainable economic development rests on factors beyond competitiveness, including innovation as the key driving force for a successful progression to become an advanced economy and push the technological frontiers. While the UAE is ranked thirty-sixth on the Global Innovation Index, it is ranked forty-fourth for Economic Complexity because the productive structure of the economy is characterised by low to medium complexity in exported products such as polymers, aluminium and steel. However, this suggests that accumulated innovation capacity should be utilised in the development of technologically advanced products and services to sustain economic growth. The UAE's Prime Minister announced the year 2015 as the year of innovation, coinciding with the release of the UAE Innovation Strategy. In the medium and long term this will facilitate the upgrade of existing knowledge and capabilities, influencing the emergence of sophisticated services and products.

The UAE government in its entrepreneurial, competitiveness and innovation roles has planted seeds for the indigenous creation of new industries, and cultivated the landscape for the growth of firms and entrepreneurs across different services and industries to realise sustainable economic development. On the other hand, there are challenges that still need to be addressed, including the nature of economic diversification, labour and human capital, access to finance, and some institutional issues.

10.7 Challenges for economic diversification

There are six key challenges facing Abu Dhabi and the UAE in its drive towards greater economic diversification. First, emerging economic activities are energy dependent and their complexity level is low to medium, which poses a challenge for generating advanced knowledge and economic growth in the future. The solution is to enable the branching out of new and advanced products around existing capital-intensive industries, e.g. automobile and medical plastic products emerging out of the locally produced polymer industry.

Second, firms and entrepreneurs would produce more such value added products if access to finance was eased. Finance for industrial SMEs has been mainly sourced through the Khalifa Fund for Enterprise Development, a government organisation with a total capital investment of AED 2 billion that was established in 2007 to help develop local enterprises in Abu Dhabi. As one policy maker notes, 'in any strong economy, SMEs play a major role in development. Therefore, it is not only the Khalifa Fund that should be doing the funding – banks should also step in and look at it in a different way and provide support in order to initiate funding, especially local banking, and so there has to be a proper mechanism to do so'. However, banks with ample financial resources have contributed little to SMEs; in 2012, financing SMEs constituted only 4% of banks loans in the UAE. This is because 'financial institutions are not structuring proper funding, nor are they trying to look at the importance of the industrial sector in the economy. Local banks should take the initiative and understand the importance of the industrial sector funding, especially towards SMEs'. The average business lending interest rate in the UAE moved from being in line with regional interest rates up to 2007 to become higher than the rate in any other country by 2011. Supply of loans through and towards the end of the financial crisis dropped as banks became more risk averse, particularly because banks bore the risk of financing in the absence of credit insurance companies. There was a lack of credit information on individuals –the establishment of the Al Etihad Credit Bureau may help this situation, but difficulty in accessing alternative forms of finance by local businesses will remain an obstacle. Nevertheless, lending to the private sector began to rebound in 2013 and 2014. The government has been looking at ways to ease access to finance: 'new access to finance regulations is being looked at which will ensure that there is a proper environment for the private sector to grow and succeed. We have to accept that there will be some probable failures, but generally, these regulations will enable private businesses to become more successful'. One way to avoid failure is for the government to direct local banks to channel some of their loans to industries, since most local banks have local governments as a majority equity shareholder.

Third, awareness of investment opportunities has emerged as an important factor since there are no agencies that collaborate with anchor industries, either to promote demand-side investment or to direct investors towards investments that could be exploited based on regional comparative advantages. The Abu Dhabi Investment Forum, which is held regularly in London, Tokyo and Singapore, is a flagship investment promotion organised by the Abu Dhabi Department for Economic Development in collaboration with bilateral collaboration business councils. It is attended by around three hundred delegates including senior government officials, public and private sector representatives, investors, and industrial, financial and banking organisations. However, investors are demanding more channels to address investment promotions.

Fourth, investors demand the rule of law. The UAE would need to make major reforms to develop comprehensive rules that protect the rights of investors, the enforcing of contracts, and the resolution of insolvency. These are areas that are lacking compared to other nations, as noted in the Doing Business report from the World Bank.

Fifth, the process of issuing an industrial license has been identified as one of the concerns of investors, which influences the business environment. Based on the IMD Competitiveness report,[2] the ease of doing business in Abu Dhabi declined from a ranking of twenty-fifth in 2007 to thirtieth in 2011. However, the number of start-up days in 2007 was 63, improving to 15 days in 2010 – or as an executive from an SEZ said: 'it used to take 365 days and now it takes 50 days ... so there is an improvement'. However, 'the system has to be integrated together to help the investor and be transparent'.

Sixth, human capital as a main factor for economic development has been a key priority for the UAE since its inception; under the leadership of late Sheik Zayed Bin Sultan Al Nahyan, the continuous pursuit of educating both men and women has been reflected in the country's human development indicator, ranked fortieth globally and standing third in the region after Qatar and Saudi Arabia. These achievements reflect the wise utilisation of high income levels to build high quality health and educational institutional capacity. On the other hand, from a broader economic perspective the UAE has a knowledge based economy in its sights, and faces challenges since employment is mainly concentrated in low productive sectors, which explains the high levels of low skilled foreign labour.

10.8 Conclusions

New paths for diversification are created through different mechanisms such as indigenous resources, anchoring, branching and clustering. These are conditioned by sources of path dependence, institutional arrangements and institutional environments, and are influenced by economic actors. The main factors that have contributed to the achievements of the UAE over the past four decades have been the investment of sizeable portions of oil and gas revenues in social, economic and infrastructure development, and the establishment of state-owned enterprises that would not have been realisable without the leadership drive towards social and economic development. This has positioned the UAE on the pathway towards the technological frontiers of advanced economies.

Policies have shaped and orchestrated the role of government institutions through various phases of development, from an entrepreneurial state to a competitiveness state, and towards an innovative state whereby policies and programmes for creating new paths for growth and diversification are harmonised into an integrated and cohesive platform. This enables the emergence and evolution of technologically advanced services and products, and is seen as the most critical activity to be undertaken by the state over coming years in partnership with the private sector.

Notes

1   Source of data for economic performance is UAE National Statistical Bureau – http://www.uaestatistics.gov.ae/
2   The Emirate of Abu Dhabi in World Competitiveness 2011 (a government internal document).

References

Aghion, P. and Howitt, P. (1992) 'A model of growth through creative destruction', *Econometrica*, vol. 60, 323–352.

Asheim, B.T. (2007) 'Differentiated knowledge bases and varieties of regional innovation systems', *Innovation: The European Journal of Social Science Research*, vol. 20, no. 3, 223.

Asheim, B.T. and Coenen, L. (2005) 'Knowledge bases and regional innovation systems: Comparing Nordic clusters', *Research Policy*, vol. 34, no. 8, 1173–1190.

Asheim, B.T., Moodysson, J. and Tödtling, F. (2011) 'Constructing regional advantage: Towards state-of-the-art regional innovation system policies in Europe?' *European Planning Studies*, vol. 19, no. 7, 1133–1139.

Asheim, B.T. Smith, H.L. and Oughton, C. (2011) 'Regional innovation systems: Theory, empirics and policy', *Regional Studies*, vol. 45, no. 7, 875–891.

Audretsch, D., Falck, O., Feldman, M. and Heblich, M. (2008) *The lifecycle of regions*, CEPR discussion paper DP6757, Centre for Economic Policy Research, London.

Audretsch, D.B. and Feldman, M.P. (1996) 'Innovative clusters and the industry life cycle', *Review of Industrial Organisation*, vol 11, 253–273.

Boschma, R. and Capone, G. (2014) 'Relatedness and diversification in the EU-27 and ENP countries', *Papers in Evolutionary Economic Geography*, vol. 14, no. 07, 1–43.

Boschma, R. and Frenken, K. (2011) 'The emerging empirics of evolutionary economic geography', *Journal of Economic Geography*, vol. 11, no. 2, 295–307.

Boschma, R., Heimeriks, G. and Balland, P.A. (2014) 'Scientific knowledge dynamics and relatedness in biotech cities', *Research Policy*, vol. 43, no. 1, 107–114.

Boschma, R. and Lambooy, J.G. (1999) 'Evolutionary economics and economic geography', *Journal of Evolutionary Economics*, vol. 9, no. 4, 411–429.

Boschma, R., Eriksson, R.H. and Lindgren, U. (2014), 'Labour market externalities and regional growth in Sweden: The importance of labour mobility between skill-related industries', *Regional Studies*, vol. 48, no. 10, 1669–1690.

Borouge (2015) *About us*, available online at www.borouge.com/aboutus/default.aspx (accessed 21 April 2016).

Cooke, P. (2002) *Knowledge economies: Clusters, learning and cooperative advantage*, London and New York: Routledge.

Cooke, P. (2007) 'To construct regional advantage from innovation systems first build policy platforms', *European Planning Studies*, vol. 15, 124–46.

Cooke, P. (2012) 'Regional development from clusters to platform policies in regional development', *European Planning Studies*, vol. 20, no. 8, 1415–1424.

Cooke, P. (2012) 'Transversality and transition: Green innovation and new regional path creation', *European Planning Studies*, vol. 20, no. 5, 817–834.

Covin, J.G. and Slevin, D.P. (1990) 'New venture strategic posture, structure and performance: An industry life cycle analysis', *Journal of Business Venturing*, vol. 5, no. 2, 123–135.

Emirates Steel (2016) *About the company*, available online at http://www.emiratessteel. com/index.php/en/

Essletzbichler, J. (2015) 'Relatedness, industrial branching and technological cohesion in US metropolitan areas', *Regional Studies*, vol. 49, no. 5, 752–766.

Federal Competitiveness and Statistics Authority (2015) *Foreign trade statistics analytical report*, available online at: http://www.fcsa.gov.ae/EnglishHome/LatestReportsDetail English/tabid/106/Default.aspx?ItemId=2482 (accessed 21 April 2016).

Flam, H. and Flanders, M.J. (1991). *Heckscher-Ohlin trade theory*, Boston: MIT Press.

Fredin, S. (2014) 'The dynamics and evolution of local industries: The case of Linköping, Sweden', European Planning Studies, vol. 22, 929–948.

Frenken, K. and Boschma, R (2007) 'A theoretical framework for evolutionary economic geography: Industrial dynamics and urban growth as a branching process', *Journal of Economic Geography*, vol. 7, no. 5, 635–649.

Frenken, K., Van Oort, F. and Verburg, T. (2007) 'Related variety, unrelated variety and regional economic growth', *Regional Studies*, vol. 41, no. 5, 685–697.

Grossman, G.M. and E. Helpman, E. (1991) *Innovation and growth in the global economy*, Cambridge, MA: MIT Press.

Hausmann, R. and Hidalgo, C.A. (2010) *Country diversification, product ubiquity, and economic divergence*, Working Paper No-201, Centre for International Development, Harvard University. Cambridge, USA

Hausmann, R., Hidalgo, C.A., Bustos, S., Coscia, M., Chung, S., Jimenes, J., Simoes, A. and Yildirim, M. (2011) *The atlas of economic complexity: Mapping paths to prosperity.* Cambridge, MA: Centre for International Development, Harvard University.

Hidalgo, C.A. (2009) *The dynamics of economic complexity and the product space over a 42-year period*, Working Paper No-201, Centre for International Development, Cambridge, MA: Harvard University.

Hidalgo, C.A. Klinger, B., Barabási, A.-L. and Hausmann, R. (2007) 'The product space conditions the development of nations', *Science*, vol. 317, no. 5837, 482–487.

Hirschman, A.O. (1958) *The strategy of economic development* (No. 04; HD82, H5.), Yale University Press.

JAFZA (2015) *About us*, available online at http://jafza.ae/about-us/ (accessed 21 April 2016).

Klepper, S. (1996) 'Entry, exit, growth, and innovation over the product life cycle', *The American Economic Review*, vol. 86, no. 3, 562–583.

Klepper, S. (2002) 'The capabilities of new firms and the evolution of the US automobile industry', *Industrial and Corporate Change*, vol. 11, no. 4, 645–666.

Klepper, S. and K.L. Simons (2000) 'Dominance by birthright: Entry of prior radio producers and competitive ramifications in the US television receiver industry', *Strategic Management Journal*, vol. 21, 997–1016.

Markusen, A. (1996) 'Sticky places in slippery space: A typology of industrial districts', *Economic Geography*, vol. 72, no. 3, 293–313.

Martin, R. and Simmie, J. (2008) 'Path dependence and local innovation systems in city-regions', *Innovation*, vol. 10, no. 2, pp.183–196.

Martin, R. and Sunley, P. (2003) 'Deconstructing clusters: Chaotic concept or policy panacea?' *Journal of Economic Geography*, vol. 3, no. 1, 5–35.

Martin R. and Sunley, J. (2006) 'Path dependence and regional economic evolution', *Journal of Economic Geography*, vol. 6, 395–437.

Martin, R. (2010) 'Roepke Lecture in Economic Geography: Rethinking regional Path dependence: Beyond lock-in to evolution', Economic Geography, vol. 86, no. 1, 1–27.

Menzel, M.-P. and Fornahl, D. (2009) 'Cluster life cycles – dimensions and rationales of cluster evolution', *Industrial and Corporate Change*, vol. 19, no. 1, 205–238.

Menzel, M.-P., Henn, S. and Fornahl, D. (2010) 'Emerging clusters: A conceptual overview', in Fornahl, D., Henn, S. and Menzel, M.-P. (eds.), *Emerging Clusters*, Cheltenham: Edward Elgar.

Murmann, J.P. and Frenken, K. (2006) 'Towards a systematic framework for research on dominant designs, technological innovations, and industrial change', *Research Policy*, vol. 35, no. 7, 925–952.

Neffke, F. and Henning, M. (2009) 'Revealed relatedness: Mapping industry space', *European Summer School on Industrial Dynamics*, 1–33.

Neffke, F. and Henning, M. (2014) 'Skill relatedness and firm diversification, *Strategic Management Journal*, vol. 316, 297–316.

Neffke, F., Henning, M. and Boschma, R. (2011) 'How do regions diversify over time? Industry relatedness and the development of new growth paths in regions', *Economic Geography*, vol. 87, 237-65.

Notteboom, T., De Langen, P. and Jacobs, W. (2013) 'Institutional plasticity and path dependence in seaports: Interactions between institutions, port governance reforms and port authority routines', *Journal of Transport Geography*, vol. 27, no. SI, 26–35.

Romer, P.M. (1990) 'Endogenous technical change', *Journal of Political Economy*, vol. 98, S71–Sl02.

Rosenstein-Rodan, P.N. (1943) 'Problems of industrialisation of eastern and south-eastern Europe', *The Economic Journal*, vol. 53, no. 210/211, 202–211.

Schumpeter, J.A. (1939) *Business cycles*, London: McGraw Hill.

Shediac, R., Abouchakra, R., Moujaes, C.N. and Najjar, M.R. (2008) *Economic diversification: The road to sustainable development*. Booz & Co., available online at www.ideationcenter.com/media/file/Economic_diversification2.pdf (accessed 21 April 2016).

Utterback, J.M. (1994) *Mastering the dynamics of innovation*, Boston: Harvard Business School Press.

Van Klink, A. and De Langen, P. (2001) 'Cycles in industrial clusters: The case of the shipbuilding industry in the Northern Netherlands', *Tijdschrift Voor Economische En Sociale Geografie*, vol. 92, no. 4, 449–463.

Wolfe, D.A. and Gertler, M.S. (2004) 'Clusters from the inside and out: local dynamics and global linkages', *Urban Studies*, vol. 41, 1071–1093.

11 Double diversification with an application to Iceland

Thorvaldur Gylfason and
Per Magnus Wijkman

11.1 Introduction

Specialisation in production for export, as David Ricardo pointed out, generates gains from trade. However, there can be too much of a good thing. First, specialisation can excessively concentrate economic activity, thereby increasing macroeconomic risk and volatility and undermining economic growth (Aghion and Banerjee, 2005). If the specialised sector is too dominant, its problems may inflict extensive damage on the rest of the national economy. Economic diversification reduces this risk. Second, the specialised sector can have significant adverse spillover effects on other industries. This risk is greater for industries based on natural resources generating rents than for those based on human capital or social capital. The negative externalities, manifest in many countries, include rampant rent seeking, repeated bouts of the Dutch disease and distortions of the political system. In the words of Michael Spence *et al.* (2008: 8–9):

> Economies blessed with abundant oil, minerals, or other natural resources should be able to invest the 'rents' or proceeds at home, raising their growth potential. But the historical experience has most often been the reverse. The pitfalls are well known. Sometimes the state sells extraction rights too cheaply or taxes resource revenues too lightly. Sometimes the money it raises is stolen or squandered by rent-seeking elites and vested interests. When the money is invested, it is not always invested wisely or transparently. And by providing a ready source of foreign exchange, natural resources can also reduce incentives for diversifying exports, a predicament known as 'Dutch disease'. States will improve on this sorry historical record only if they capture an appropriate share of the resource rents; save a judicious amount overseas; and set clear, growth-oriented priorities for absorbing the remainder at home.

Abundant natural resources, if not judiciously managed, may be seized by rent seekers whose forte is the usurpation of wealth, rather than its creation. Abundant natural resource wealth may also breed a false sense of security among politicians as well as the general public, making them feel that it is unnecessary to build up human resources and social capital and to lay a strong foundation for inclusive economic growth.

This chapter views broadly based diversification as an essential aspect of a national risk management policy aimed at promoting social efficiency as well as economic growth. It argues that economic diversification away from dependence on a too narrow economic base, and, similarly, political diversification away from dependence on a too narrow political base, are complementary policies – two sides of the same coin. We first discuss economic and political diversification side by side and demonstrate their relation to long-run economic performance in an empirical cross-country framework. We then apply this analysis to Iceland where the economy used to be dominated by the fishing industry and where economic and political aspects of diversification are intertwined. Today, for the first time, tourism in Iceland generates more foreign-exchange earnings gross than the fishing industry.

11.2 Economic diversification

Most large open economies export a diverse range of merchandise products to other countries, mostly manufactured goods. Other countries, especially those specialising heavily in the production of primary commodities for export, often fail to develop other lines of production. Small countries tend to have less diversified and more open economies than large ones.

An international overview of economic diversification

Figure 11.1 describes different degrees of export diversification by comparing the United States, the United Kingdom, France, Germany, and Canada at one extreme with Chile, Iran, Saudi Arabia, Nigeria, and Iraq at the other. The first group of countries on the left in Figure 11.1 has an export structure that is rather mainstream, that is, similar to the world average, while the second group on the right in Figure 11.1 has an export structure that is quite different from the world average – that is, much less diversified. Notice that New Zealand's specialisation in agricultural exports makes its export structure less diversified than that of Norway, still among the world's chief exporters of oil. Notice also that Iceland's exports of fish and aluminium render its export structure as concentrated as that of Saudi Arabia and Nigeria.

Economic diversification, including in particular diversification away from agriculture and other primary production toward manufactured goods and services, is on the rise around the world. Figure 11.2 describes the rise of manufacturing exports since 1962, highlighting the spectacular expansion of manufacturing exports in Latin America. This is good for growth because increased diversification of the product composition of merchandise trade reduces risk and enhances efficiency – that is, the amount of output that can be squeezed out of given inputs (Gylfason, 1998) – and also because manufacturing has proved to be a reliable source of innovation and spillovers benefitting service industries that claim a steadily higher proportion of world GDP. To stress the point, Figure 11.3 describes the rise of the share of services in GDP, showing how the relative size of the

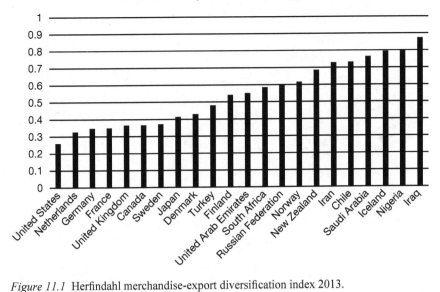

Figure 11.1 Herfindahl merchandise-export diversification index 2013.
(UNCTAD).
Note: The diversification index shows whether the structure of exports by product of a given country differs from the world average. The index ranges from 0 to 1, with values closer to 1 indicating a bigger difference from the world average and hence a relatively more concentrated economy. The index covers only merchandise exports, i.e. exports of goods, not services.

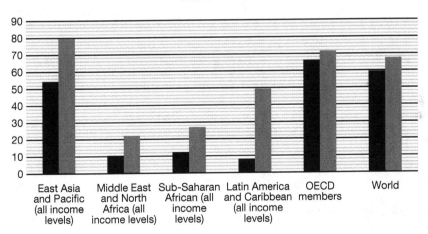

Figure 11.2 Per cent share of manufactured exports in total merchandise exports, selected years between 1962 and 2013.
(World Bank, World Development Indicators).
Note: The data for East Asia and the Pacific refer to 1964 and 2013, the data for the Middle East and North Africa refer to 1974 and 2010, and the data for sub-Saharan Africa refer to 1974 and 2013. The membership of the OECD expanded significantly from 1962 to 2013.

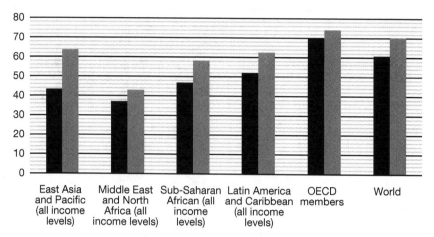

Figure 11.3 Per cent share of services, value added, in GDP, selected years between 1965 and 2013.

(World Bank, World Development Indicators).

Note: The data for East Asia and the Pacific refer to 1970 and 2012 and the data for the Middle East and North Africa refer to 1980 and 2013. The data for the OECD region and the world refer to 1997 and 2012 and 1995 and 2012, respectively. Presumably some of the increase in recorded services is due to improved service statistics due to outsourcing.

service sectors of the emerging economies approaches that of the industrial countries. In countries that have jumped directly from agriculture to services (India is a case in point; see Gylfason (2006) and Panagariya (2008), bypassing the development of a strong manufacturing sector, this may or may not be good for growth because of the beneficial spillover effects of manufacturing on technological development and services (Rodrik, 2013).

Diversification of exports

The experience of several East Asian countries since the 1960s suggests that some exports – certain manufactured goods (e.g. automobiles) and high-tech items (e.g. electronics) – are more conducive to long-run economic growth than others. Therefore, the composition of exports with regard to manufactured goods and other products matters for long-run growth. We shall test this hypothesis informally by considering the relationship between Gross National Income (GNI) per capita and two different measures of export diversification.

Figure 11.4, replicated from Gylfason and Nguessa Nganou (2014), illustrates the cross-country relationship between the share of manufactured goods in merchandise exports and per capita GNI in 139 countries from 1962 to 2012. Each country is represented by a balloon whose size reflects the country's population; hence, India and China are easy to spot in the chart. Here export diversification shown along the horizontal axis, is measured by the average share of manufactures,

Log GNI per person 2012 (USD, ppp)

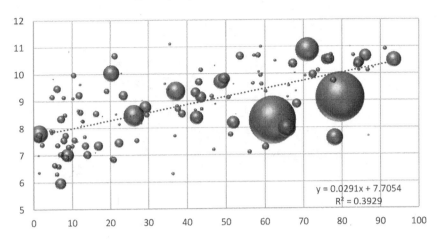

Figure 11.4 Exports of manufactures and per capita GNI.
(Authors' computations based on data from World Bank, World Development Indicators).
Note: The scatterplot shown covers 139 countries, with one observation, or balloon, for each country.
Here, and in other scatterplots to follow, all available observations are included. No outliers are left
out.

in total merchandise exports 1962–2012. Growth is represented by the natural
logarithm of the purchasing power of per capita GNI in 2012 because the level of
current income reflects its rate of growth in the past. The use of only the end-of-
period value of per capita GNI for each country rules out reverse causation (i.e.
from economic growth to export diversification). The relationship shown is
significant in a statistical sense (Spearman rank correlation = 0.62) as well as in an
economic sense. The slope of the regression line (0.029) suggests that, for a
typical country in the sample, a twenty-point increase in the manufacturing share
of exports (e.g. from 40% to 60%) goes along with an increase in real per capita
GNI by well over a half (i.e. by 58%), other things being equal. This suggests that
export diversification toward manufactured goods is good for growth.

Figure 11.5, also replicated from Gylfason and Nguessa Nganou (2014),
illustrates the cross-country relationship between export diversification and
growth in 128 countries from 1962 to 2012. It tells a similar story as Figure 11.4.
Export diversification, shown along the horizontal axis in the chart, is here
measured by one minus the average Herfindahl index for 1996–2012. The
Herfindahl index shows the extent to which the structure of exports by product in
a given country diverges from the world average. The index ranges from zero to
one, with values closer to one indicating a larger divergence from the world
average (recall Figure 11.1). Therefore, the diversification index shown in Figure
11.5 – i.e. one minus the Herfindahl index – rises with diversification. As before,
growth is represented by the natural logarithm of the purchasing power of per
capita GNI in 2012. The relationship shown is significant in a statistical sense

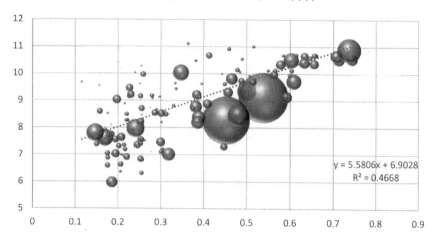

Log GNI per person 2013 (USD, ppp)

$$y = 5.5806x + 6.9028$$
$$R^2 = 0.4668$$

Figure 11.5 Export diversification and per capita GNI.
(Authors' computations based on data from UNCTAD and World Bank, World Development Indicators).
Note: Export diversification is measured along the horizontal axis by one minus the divergence of the structure of a country's merchandise exports from the world average. The higher the index, the greater the diversification of exports.

(Spearman rank correlation = 0.67) as well as in an economic sense. The slope of the regression line (5.58) suggests that, for a typical country in the sample, a twenty-point increase in the export diversification index (e.g. from 40% to 60%), corresponding roughly to the difference between Russia's 0.40 and Japan's 0.59 (again, recall Figure 11.1), goes along with an increase in real per capita GNI by more than a factor of two (i.e. by 112%), other things being equal. Also, this measure of diversification suggests that export diversification is good for growth.

The two measures of diversification compared

Our two measures of export diversification are closely correlated, as shown in Figure 11.6 covering 140 countries (Spearman rank correlation = 0.71). This suggests that either one can be used as a measure of export diversification in empirical work.

The argument for economic diversification rests on the well-understood need to avoid unnecessary exposure to macroeconomic risk (Gelb, 2011). It is supported by the need to avoid excessive concentration which can reduce competition and lead to oligopolistic inefficiency as well as expose an economy to shocks. This is why dependence on a few natural resources, for example, has proved problematic for many countries, resulting in macroeconomic volatility and sluggish growth. We conclude that diversification of exports is essential for economic prosperity.

Export diversification index 1996–2012

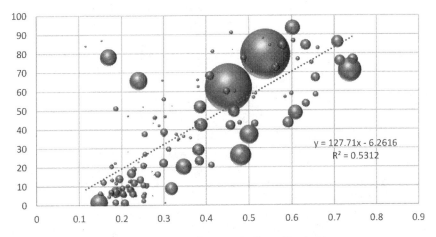

Figure 11.6 Side by side: two aspects of economic diversification.
(Authors' computations based on data from UNCTAD and World Bank, World Development Indicators).

11.3 Political diversification

We next suggest that a similar argument supports the need for political diversification. If the prime responsibility for political decision-making is vested in self-sustaining ruling elites that are shielded from effective competition in the political arena, this concentration of political power can have damaging effects on political life as well as on the economy. Institutions such as free elections, free press, independent courts, a non-corrupt and professional civil service and transparent governance are necessary to expand civil liberties and political rights and ensure healthy electoral competition. Thus, political diversity in the form of competitive political advocates is essential for effective governance just as economic diversification in the form of competitive industries is essential to reduce the risks associated with economic concentration. We shall first consider the expansion of political and democratic rights in recent decades around the world, and thereafter note the relationship between these rights and economic standards of living.

The advance of freedom in the world

Like economic diversification, political diversification has been on the rise around the world. Europe had only five democratic states in 1943: Iceland, Ireland, Sweden, Switzerland and the United Kingdom.[1] Figure 11.7 demonstrates the advance of freedom as measured by indices of civil liberties and political rights in 205 countries, compiled by Freedom House since 1972. Each country score is based on two numerical ratings – each from 1 to 7 – for political rights and civil liberties, with 1 representing the most free and 7 the least free. Countries scoring from 1 to 2.5 are classified as Free, those scoring from 3 to 5 are classified as Partly Free, and those scoring from 5.5 to 7 are classified as Not Free. About fifty countries remain Not Free.

Figure 11.8 uses the same data as Figure 11.7 but shows the trend over time in the average scores of two hundred countries toward more civil liberties and political rights. The average improvement from 4.2 to 3.3 for civil liberties and from 4.5 to 3.3 for political rights is quantitatively significant on a scale from 7 to 1. The consistent improvement ceases after the turn of the century. While the number of countries classified by Freedom House as Free has doubled from forty-four in 1972 to eighty-nine in 2014 (Figure 11.7), that number too has been stagnant since 2002. Several countries have become more democratic, true, but others have slid in the other direction, including Bangladesh, Kenya, Russia, Thailand, and Turkey (Diamond, 2015).

Another measure of democracy is the Polity IV Project's Polity2 variable which reflects the characteristics of democratic and autocratic authority in governing institutions, rather than discrete and mutually exclusive forms of governance. The Polity2 variable spans a spectrum from fully institutionalised autocracies through mixed authority regimes to fully institutionalised democracies, on a twenty-one-point scale ranging from minus 10 (hereditary monarchy) to plus 10 (consolidated democracy). Countries are classified as democratic if their Polity2 score is larger than or equal to plus 6, as neither democratic nor autocratic ('anocracies') if the score lies from plus 5 to minus 5, and as autocratic if their score is smaller than or equal to minus 6.

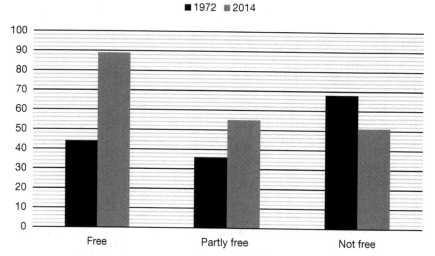

Figure 11.7 Civil liberties and political rights 1972–2014.
(Authors' computations based on data from Freedom House).

Figure 11.9 shows that since 1990 the advance of democracy around the world has gone along with a decrease in the number of autocracies, while the number of anocracies has remained about the same. The number of autocratic regimes began its descent some time before the collapse of communism in Eastern and Central Europe in 1989–1991. The number of democracies stagnated after 2003.

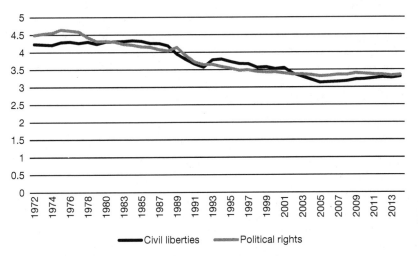

Figure 11.8 Civil liberties and political rights again 1972–2014.
(Authors' computations based on data from Freedom House).
Note: Low scores indicate good performance.

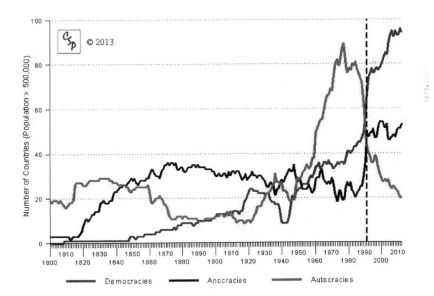

Figure 11.9 Global trends in governance 1800–2012.
(Center for Systemic Peace, Polity IV Project).

The economic effect of democracy

Just as economic diversification spurs growth by transferring labour from low-paying jobs in low-skill-intensive farming and mining to more lucrative jobs in more high-skill-intensive occupations, political diversification can boost growth by redistributing political power from narrowly based ruling elites to broader segments of the people. Replacing a group's monopoly on political power by democracy and pluralism means promoting electoral competitiveness, openness and popular participation. This can be viewed as an investment in social capital, strengthening as it does civil society and promoting good governance and societal institutions that people can trust (Paldam, 2000). This section attempts to assess the economic effects of democracy. As in Section 11.2, we use two standard measures of democracy, one from Polity IV Project and the other from Freedom House.

Figure 11.10, reproduced from Gylfason and Nguessa Nganou (2014), illustrates the cross-country relationship between economic growth and political diversification through democracy in 139 countries from 1960 to 2012. Democracy is measured by the average of the Polity2 variable in each country over the sample period, 1960–2012. Reflecting the possibility that an undemocratic past can have lingering effects, we use the period average of the democracy index rather than its value at 2012. As in Figures 11.4 and 11.5, growth is represented by the logarithm of the purchasing power of per capita GNI in 2012 to rule out reverse causation from growth to democracy. The relationship is significant in a statistical sense (Spearman rank correlation = 0.62) as well as in an economic sense. The slope of the regression line (0.14) suggests that a four-point increase in Polity2 (e.g. from 4 to 8) goes along with an increase in real per capita GNI by a bit more than a half (i.e. by 56%). This is a significant impact.

Log GNI per person 2012 (USD, ppp)

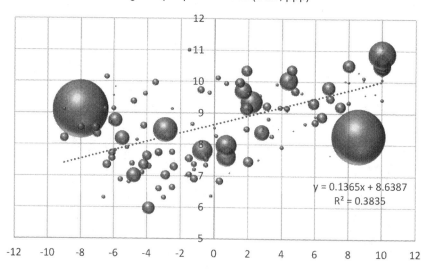

Figure 11.10 Polity2 index of democracy and per capita GNI.
(Authors' computations based on data from Polity IV Project and World Bank, World Development Indicators).

Figure 11.11 tells a similar story as Figure 11.10. It illustrates the cross-country relationship between the average value of Freedom House's indices of civil liberties and political rights during 1972–2014 (displayed in Figure 11.8) and per capita income in 2012 in 111 countries. The Spearman rank correlation is 0.73. The slope of the regression line (0.55) suggests that a one-point increase in the Freedom House index goes along with an increase in real per capita GNI by a bit more than a half (i.e. by 55%). As in Figure 11.10 where an increase in the democracy index spanning about one-fifth of the scale from minus 10 to plus 10 goes along with an increase in per capita GNI by bit more than a half, in Figure 11.11 an increase in the democracy index spanning one-sixth of the scale from 7 to 1 goes along with an increase in per capita GNI by a similar amount. This is an indication that 'democracy matters', also for economic outcomes.

Side by side

Figures 11.10 and 10.11 feature two different democracy indices but illustrate strikingly similar results. The two indices are fairly closely correlated as shown in Figure 11.12, which covers 109 countries. The Spearman rank correlation equals 0.41, and is statistically significant given the sample size of 109.

Log GNI per person 2012 (USD, ppp)

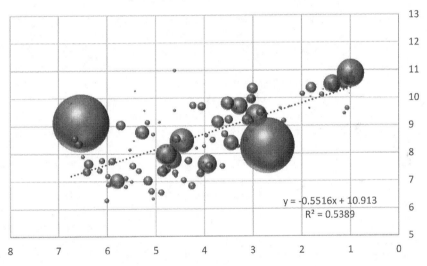

$y = -0.5516x + 10.913$
$R^2 = 0.5389$

Figure 11.11 Freedom House index of democracy and per capita GNI.
(Authors' computations based on data from Freedom House and World Bank, World Development Indicators).
Note: Civil liberties and political rights increase from left to right along the horizontal axis.

Democracy (Polity2) 1960–2012

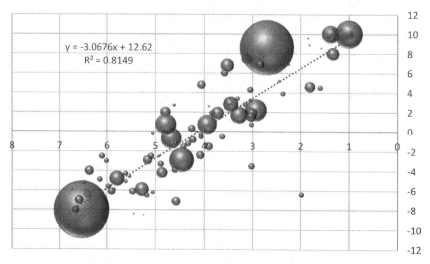

Figure 11.12 Side by side: two aspects of political diversification.
(Authors' computations based on data from Freedom House and Polity IV Project).
Note: Civil liberties and political rights increase from left to right along the horizontal axis.

Notice also the broad similarities between the patterns shown in Figures 11.4 and 11.5 and in Figures 11.10 and 11.11, where in each pair of charts we see a clear tendency for our two different measures of diversification to go hand in hand with per capita GNI in 2012, our indicator of economic growth in the preceding decades. The cross-country patterns are similar for economic diversification in Figures 11.4 and 11.5 and for political diversification in Figures 11.10 and 11.11. Each of the two economic diversification indices in Figures 11.4 and 11.5 is fairly closely correlated with each of the two political diversification indices in Figures 11.10 and 11.11. We should consequently not be surprised that the index of civil liberties and political rights shows a high correlation with measures of export diversification.

Figure 11.13 shows the cross-country correlation between the Freedom House index of democracy and manufacturing exports in 109 countries for which data are available (the Spearman rank correlation is 0.53). Likewise, Figure 11.14 shows the cross-country correlation between the Freedom House index of democracy and the Herfindahl export diversification index in 110 countries (Spearman = 0.56).[2] The bottom line is invariably the same: economic diversification and political diversification go together.

Manufactures exports 1962–2012 (% of total)

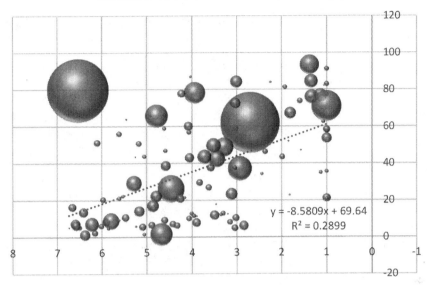

Figure 11.13 Freedom House index of democracy and manufacturing exports.
(Authors' computations based on data from Freedom House and World Bank, World Development Indicators).
Note: Civil liberties and political rights increase from left to right along the horizontal axis.

Democracy (Freedom House) 1972–2014

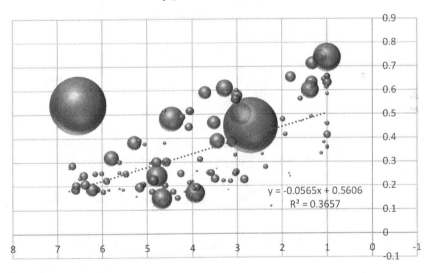

Figure 11.14 Freedom House index of democracy and export diversification.
(Authors' computations based on data from Freedom House and UNCTAD).
Note: Civil liberties and political rights increase from left to right along the horizontal axis.

11.4 Recap: double ascent

To recapitulate, we have argued that economic diversification and political diversification are both good for growth. Furthermore, they go hand in hand across countries: The more diverse the economy, the more diverse the political structure and vice versa. If the absence of democracy enables rent seekers to hold back economic as well as political diversification, the advance of democracy – that is, political diversification – creates conditions for economic diversification. As in finance, effective diversification of economic activity requires production to be dispersed with a reasonable weight distribution across several different sectors whose ups and downs are inversely correlated and thus even each other out. Similarly, risk is reduced if different political parties compete for electoral support. Diversity is not enough, however. Even well-diversified nations and regions – e.g. the United States during 2007–2013 and the Nordic countries during 1989–1994 – experience crises. Arguably, though, the recent US crisis can be attributed in part to intensified power concentration (i.e. decreased political diversity) manifest in the increasing role of money in politics, or perhaps even deeper flaws (Levinson, 2006). In contrast, having learned their lesson from 1989 to 1994, the Nordic countries other than Iceland escaped relatively unscathed from the recent crisis.

Economic diversification and democracy are on the rise around the world. We have already mentioned the transformation of Europe from five democracies in 1943 to a full house today. Among the ten Spanish or Portuguese-speaking countries of Latin America, the number of democracies (countries with Polity2 scores between 6 and 10) grew from three in 1961 to eight in 2012 (source: Polity IV Project), while the share of manufactured goods in total merchandise exports rose from 8% to 46% (recall Figure 11.2). A similar pattern is observed in other regions, but not in Europe and Central Asia where manufactured goods now comprise about 70% of total exports as they already did fifty years ago.

On the whole, the double ascent of economic diversification and democracy bodes well for general prosperity and growth. Even so, there are signs in several countries of insufficient diversification on both fronts and even reversals in some cases. Russia is an unsurprising case in point where a 50% drop in oil prices in world markets caused the ruble to lose half its value in 2014, mainly due to the Russian economy's excessive dependence on oil exports. Meanwhile, in Norway next door the krone only lost a sixth of its value thanks to Norway's judicious management of its oil wealth. Next, however, we shall present a surprising case of insufficient economic diversification in Europe: Iceland.

11.5 Not by fish alone: the case of Iceland

Since acquiring Home Rule in 1904 as a nation of peasants where economic life had stood still for centuries, Iceland has developed into a modern market economy evidencing some of the problems described in the preceding section associated with 'double concentration'. This section describes Iceland's dependence on natural resource exports, the overrepresentation of these natural resources in the political process, the industry capture of economic policy and institutions and the consequent problems of inflation and inefficiency.

Insufficient economic diversification

Through the ages, Icelandic waters have been full of fish. With the mechanisation of fishing vessels, the education and training of the labour force, and the gradual extension of Iceland's economic jurisdiction to two hundred nautical miles in the twentieth century, fish became a significant export commodity. Export earnings matter a great deal for small countries, enabling them to import many goods and services from abroad. Iceland's population is only 330,000.

Figure 11.15 describes the evolution of Icelandic exports since the late 1950s. In 1957, fish products constituted more than 90% of merchandise exports and accounted for 65% of total exports of goods and services. The share of fish in total merchandise exports hovered around 40% to 50% in the 1970s and 1980s and thereafter dropped little by little to 17% in the mid-2000s. This computation takes merchandise exports to equal exports of goods. On this assumption, the share of fish exports in total exports of goods and services shown in Figure 11.15 is defined as the share of fish exports in merchandise exports times the share of the exports of goods in total exports of goods and services. Statistics Iceland has made a poor job of documenting foreign trade in services despite the rapid rise of such trade. Figure 11.16 reports a higher share of fish in total exports, 26% in 2013 (the discrepancy may be related to the conversion described above).

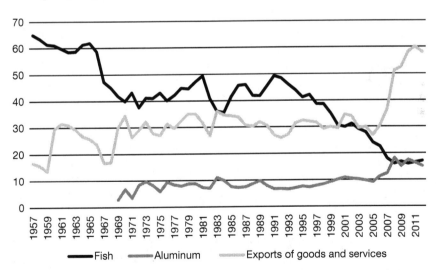

Figure 11.15 Iceland – level and composition of exports 1957–2012 in percentage. (Authors' computations based on data from Statistics Iceland).
Note: Fish exports and aluminium exports, including ferrosilicon, are expressed as a percentage of total exports of goods and services, which in turn are expressed as a percentage of GDP.

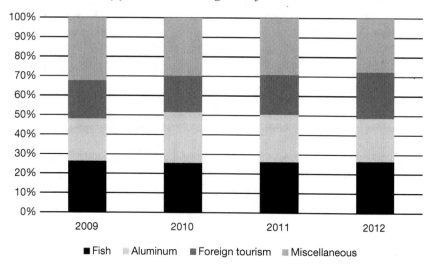

Figure 11.16 Iceland – composition of export earnings 2009–2013 in percentage.
(Authors' computations based on data from Statistics Iceland).
Note: Fish exports, aluminium exports, including ferrosilicon, and foreign-exchange earnings from tourism are expressed as a percentage of total exports of goods and services.

The decline in the share of fish in exports and GDP was a natural consequence of conservation measures taken in the mid-1980s, when fish stocks appeared close to collapsing due partly to overfishing. In response the government began issuing catch quotas based on the concept of maximum sustainable yield. With a fixed, quota-bound tonnage of fish in the numerator of the ratio and gradually expanding total exports in the denominator, it was natural for the share of fish products in total exports to dwindle over time.

Fish and aluminium together account for a third of export earnings from 1957 to 2012 (Figure 11.15), rising to a half for 2009 to 2013 (Figure 11.16). Exports of goods and services doubled as a proportion of GDP following the depreciation of the Icelandic króna by a third in real terms before and after the financial crash of 2008. This was a textbook example of a currency depreciation that boosted export earnings and slashed imports, thereby closing the huge deficit in the balance of payments that had developed as a counterpart to the financial capital inflows preceding the crash of 2008 (Gylfason and Zoega, 2014). Thus, natural-resource-based exports (fish, aluminium and ferrosilicon) fell from 65% of total exports in 1957 to 34% (or 48% in Figure 11.16) in 2012.

Iceland has diversified away from fisheries, primarily as a result of the growth of services, in particular foreign tourism, to account for nearly 70% of GDP, close to the OECD average (Figure 11.17). No longer a fish-based economy or even a natural-resource-based economy, Iceland has developed into a diversified service-oriented economy with a tiny manufacturing sector apart from aluminium and ferrosilicon. Except for artificial limbs, computer games, fish processing equipment and generic drugs, Iceland's exports are on the whole remarkably

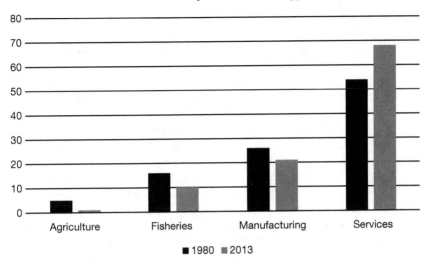

Figure 11.17 Iceland – composition of GDP 1980 and 2013 (% of GDP).
(Statistics Iceland).

low-tech. The diversification away from fisheries was not the result of deliberate government policy. Rather, it was market-induced. Deliberate economic diversification would probably have been more conducive to lasting success than the accidental, incomplete economic diversification that took place, and would, moreover, have been more likely to be accompanied by commensurate political diversification, to which we now turn.

Insufficient political diversification

Iceland was an overwhelmingly agricultural society until 1900, more so than much of the rest of Europe. This meant that the Icelandic Parliament, even following Home Rule in 1904, was under the control of farmers. To protect their turf, farmers wrote electoral laws granting voters in rural areas disproportionate influence in parliamentary elections. This was done through a blatant form of gerrymandering – that is, by dividing the country into electoral constituencies such that in the emerging towns, including the capital Reykjavík, it took up to four times as many votes to elect a member to Parliament as it took in rural constituencies. In one election, for example, the Progressive Party, the party of the farmers, obtained a majority in Parliament with only 33% of the popular vote. As a result of this electoral bias, the minority of voters left behind in rural areas as people flocked to the emerging fishing towns around the coast, as well as to Reykjavík, retained a majority or at least a disproportionate influence in Parliament. This imparted a provincial, inward-looking bias to policy making.

This bias persists, even if it has diminished with time through piecemeal and marginal constitutional reform. Today it takes about twice as many votes to elect a member to Parliament in the Reykjavík area where two thirds of the country's electorate resides, as it takes in rural areas.

The disproportionate political influence of rural residents has manifested itself in a protectionist farm policy regime, restricting since the 1920s imports of farm commodities that could compete with local produce, mainly dairy products and meat. These import restrictions, still largely intact, reduced the demand for foreign exchange as import restrictions are wont to do, thus imparting an upward bias to the exchange value of the króna.[3] More importantly, however, as the twentieth century progressed and the fishing industry bypassed agriculture as Iceland's main economic activity, the fisheries began to share in the political clout that had earlier been the prerogative of the farm lobby. Hence, the privileges accorded agriculture through import protection, generous farm subsidies, subsidised credits from state banks and so on were extended to the fishing industry. A telling sign of this arrangement is the names given to two of the country's three large state banks from the 1930s onward: the Agricultural Bank and the Fisheries Bank. In 1960 subsidies to the fishing industry absorbed 43% of government outlays, prompting a new reform-minded government to slash the subsidies to 3% of government outlays and to compensate the fishing industry by a big devaluation of the króna. This switch, necessary though it was, set a precedent for repeated devaluations to shore up the profitability of the fishing industry, thereby reducing its financial self-responsibility and cost consciousness.[4] If costs became too high or profits too low, the government could be counted on to devalue the króna.

The devaluation cycles were in part a symptom of the scourge of overvaluation resulting even more strongly from the government's generous support of the fisheries sector than from the farm policy regime. Just as farm protection increases the exchange value of the domestic currency by reducing the demand for imports, government subsidies to fish exports, overt or not, increase the exchange value of the currency by encouraging export supply.

Inflation bias and overvaluation

Insufficient economic and political diversification helps to explain the systemic overvaluation of the Icelandic króna. The long-standing excessive political clout of farmers – that is, of agriculture and later also of fisheries[5] – impacted economic policy.

Iceland is unique among high-income countries in that the exports-to-GDP ratio was stagnant from 1870 (this is not a misprint) until the crash of 2008. The main reason for the failure of exports to grow more quickly than domestic output, which is the general rule around the world, is a systemically overvalued currency which, whether under a fixed exchange-rate regime or under flexible rates, restrained exports and, by design, kept imports artificially inexpensive. Such an overvaluation strategy is, or at least used to be, commonly observed in developing countries, and helps to explain persistent current account deficits and the attendant accumulation of external debts.

Iceland has had the second highest inflation rate in the OECD region since 1960, second only to Turkey. High inflation is an independent source of systemic overvaluation. Since 1939 the Icelandic króna has lost 99.95% of its value vis-à-vis the Danish krone. When inflation reached 83% in 1983 and the government decided to clamp down on it by, among other things, introducing price indexation of financial obligations to bring real interest rates above zero, the fishing industry was compensated by the introduction of a system of catch quotas, allocated free of charge to vessel owners and based on arbitrary rules considered by many to be discriminatory. On grounds of efficiency and fairness a number of economists and others had advocated a market-friendly regulation of the fisheries, either through fishing fees or quota auctions with revenues accruing to the citizen-owners of the common resources (for early warnings in English, see Wijkman 1976, 1982), but their advice was not heeded. Instead, one form of subsidy was thus replaced by another. The original quota legislation is known to have been drafted in the offices of the Vessel Owners Association. By a stroke of the pen, parliament produced a class of local oligarchs – billionaires – by granting them free access to a hugely valuable common property resource, a controversial decision from the outset that has had important political ramifications, to which we now turn.

Capture of the constitution by vested interests

The system of gratis quota allocations turned a dispersed natural resource – i.e. fish – into a concentrated one like oil, with all the potential for political capture and cartelisation that implies. Iceland's situation contrasts starkly with that of Norway which – unlike Russia, for example – has managed its oil wealth in a way that has not created a class of oligarchs in Norway. The word 'oligarch' is never heard in Norwegian political debate. In Iceland, on the other hand, the words 'quota king' and 'quota queen' are commonly used in political discourse, for a good reason. Iceland has not managed to avoid the pitfalls that Norway has so effectively stayed clear of. While Norway's democratic credentials have not in any way been adversely affected by its discovery and export of oil since 1970, Iceland's discriminatory management of its fishing industry has thrown its standing among fully democratic European nations into question.

In 2007, the United Nations Committee on Human Rights issued a binding opinion instructing Iceland to remove the discriminatory element from its system of fisheries management and to pay damages to the two fishermen who brought their complaint before the committee. The Icelandic government responded by promising a new constitution with a provision on natural-resource management, declaring that Iceland's natural resources belong to the people without any discrimination.

After the crash of 2008, parliament resolved to initiate a revision of the 1944 constitution of Iceland, a seventy-year old promise that parliament had so far failed to keep (Gylfason, 2013). A constituent assembly elected by the nation drafted a constitution bill containing, among other reforms, provisions on equal voting rights (one person, one vote, no gerrymandering) as well as on national ownership of natural resources, stipulating that 'government authorities may grant permits for the use or utilisation of resources or other limited public goods against full consideration'. In a national referendum called by parliament in 2012, 67% of the voters accepted the constitution bill as a whole as well as the provision on equal voting rights, and 83% of the voters accepted the provision on national ownership of natural resources. Even so, parliament has thus far declined to respect the will of the people as expressed in the results of the constitutional referendum, the clearest sign to date of the danger of according disproportionate political power to a special interest group. It has never before happened in a democracy that the national legislature has failed to adopt the overwhelming result of a constitutional referendum.

The Icelandic parliament's refusal to ratify the new post-crash constitution shows clearly how differently Norway and Iceland have met the challenge laid out at the end of the quote from Spence et al. (2008) in Section 11.1. Norway used its oil wealth to build up an Oil Fund, later renamed the Pension Fund, to reflect its intended use. At present the fund exceeds $800 billion. It is invested overseas and is the world's largest sovereign wealth fund, equivalent to $170,000 per person in Norway. On the other hand, following its financial meltdown in 2008, Iceland carries a crushing debt burden despite abundant fish and energy resources. Export concentration sometimes translates into concentration of political power, a problem that Norway judiciously avoided but Iceland did not (Gylfason, 2015).

Whether Iceland's ongoing economic diversification away from the fisheries through the advance of tourism will be followed by political diversification away from parliamentary subservience to the fishing lobby remains to be seen. A comparison between Iceland and Mauritius may be relevant here. Until the 1980s Mauritius was a natural-resource-based economy. Its sugar cane industry was the country's main foreign exchange earner (Frankel, 2012). As tourism gained momentum, however, the importance of the sugar industry in economic activity waned and the political clout of the plantation owners declined accordingly. This could also happen in Iceland.

Failed attempts to pick the winners

We have already described the decline of the share of fish products in total exports as a natural and inevitable consequence of fixed catch quotas in a growing economy. At about 200,000 tons per year the cod catch in Icelandic waters is about the same today as it was in 1945, even if Iceland's economic jurisdiction was far smaller in 1945 than it is now (cod is Iceland's most valuable fish species). Total fish catches are larger today than in 1945, true, but they are smaller than they were a generation ago, in 1980 (Figure 11.18).

While the main reason, and a legitimate one, for tight-fisted fish quotas is conservation of endangered fish stocks, quota holders clearly also have a financial incentive to keep the quota allocations under control so as to increase their value, a strategy well known to many oil producers. So, the declining weight of fisheries in the Icelandic economy did not result from government strategy but was rather an inevitable outcome dictated mostly by nature.

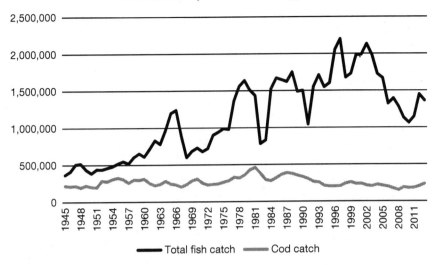

Figure 11.18 Iceland – fish catches 1945–2013 in tonnes.
(Statistics Iceland).

The government's first strategic response to the decline of the fisheries was to start harnessing waterfalls as well as geothermal energy for use in the production of aluminium and ferrosilicon, energy-intensive products of low weight that are relatively easy to transport as a way of indirectly exporting energy. Plans to harness waterfalls for industrial use in the early years of the twentieth century had come to naught partly for environmental reasons, but the decline of the fishing sector in the 1960s induced the government to change its mind. Hence, a new natural-resource-based industry was intended to pick up the slack left by the natural decline of the old one. This was long before problems associated with excessive reliance on natural resources began to attract the attention of economists and policy makers (Sachs and Warner, 1995).

In response to the declining contribution of fish to export earnings, hydropower projects in conjunction with mostly foreign-owned and highly energy-intensive aluminium and ferrosilicon plants were launched in the late 1960s. The share of aluminium and ferrosilicon hovered around 10% of total exports until the mid-2000s, when their share of foreign-exchange earnings rose to match that of fish products.

From the outset, Iceland's energy sector was mired in controversy for environmental reasons as well as due to opposition to foreign involvement in Iceland's economy and, importantly from an economic perspective, because the price at which the energy was sold to foreign aluminium and ferrosilicon producers was not made public, triggering suspicions that the price was lower than it could have been. One reason why the price may have been low is the habit of Icelandic politicians to prematurely promise aluminium plants and iron smelters to the voters ahead of time, thus undermining the ex post negotiating position of the government vis-à-vis the foreign firms. Without publicly available information on the price of energy, it is impossible to assess the contribution of the energy sector to Iceland's economy apart from registering its share in export earnings (Figure 11.16), employment etc. Only recently did the National Power Company of Iceland begin publishing the average price of energy to big industry.

On the other hand, there no conscious government strategy to support the build-up of manufacturing or services which is why the high-exchange-rate policy remained in place until the crash of 2008. All the emphasis by the government was on energy as a substitute for fish. As a result, manufacturing for the domestic market or for export markets did not have a chance to develop in earnest (Figure 11.19). While manufactures in neighbouring countries typically account for two thirds of merchandise exports, their share in Iceland is far less. At 14% in 2012, the share of high-tech manufactures in total manufactures was lower than in the 1990s when it was 20% (not shown). In manufacturing, the cheaper króna after the crash of 2008 was not enough to offset or outweigh the adverse consequences of the crash that made GDP contract by 10% during 2008–2009 and resulted in negative net investment – that is, a declining real capital stock – four years in a row, from 2009 to 2012.

Growth of tourism – a market response to the cheaper króna

The number of foreign tourists visiting Iceland has risen sharply since 2002, reaching a multiple of the country's population, a rare feat in an international comparison (Figure 11.20). The rapid rise of tourism was propelled first, in part, by the foreign-credit-driven banking boom before the financial crash of 2008 and thereafter by the collapse of the króna. Tourism in Iceland is not kept in check on

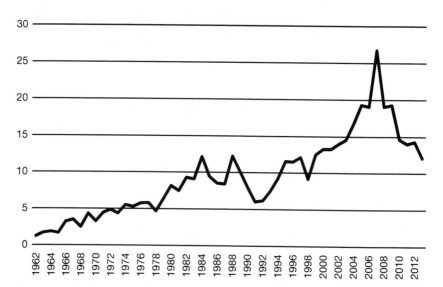

Figure 11.19 Iceland – manufacturing exports 1962–2013 as a % of merchandise exports. (World Bank, World Development Indicators).

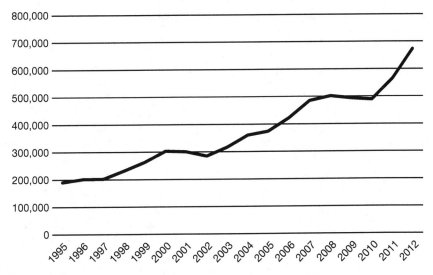

Figure 11.20 Iceland – foreign tourist arrivals 1995–2012 (number of persons).
(World Bank, World Development Indicators).

environmental or other grounds. There is as yet no limit on the number of tourist arrivals comparable to the catch quotas placing a limit on the number of fish caught each year in Icelandic waters. Tourism, which already generates more foreign exchange each year than the once-dominant fishing industry (recall Figure 11.16), may in the years ahead permanently surpass the fishing industry as Iceland's main foreign exchange earner. This would provide a strong boost to the domestic economy. Unlike fish exports which are paid for abroad, a significant part of tourism services is paid for on location, at home. Further, tourism seems likely to generate positive externalities, learning by doing and the like, resulting in significant political diversification away from government acquiescence to the densely concentrated fishing industry dominated by a few firms holding much of the catch quotas granted to them by the government virtually free of charge, and toward diversified tourist-related services which, as experience from other countries shows, usually create few political problems related to rent seeking and power concentration (Gylfason and Zoega, 2014).

These contrasts notwithstanding, there are some striking parallels. Both tourism and fishing exploit natural resources with attendant risks of overexploitation of common-property resources at public expense. By common consent, access to fishing grounds, a common-property resource by local law as well as by international human-rights covenants, needs to be restricted by market-friendly, non-discriminatory methods in the interest of efficiency and fairness. Likewise, access by tourists to public infrastructure as well as to natural wonders needs to be regulated to forestall environmental degradation. Specifically, just as catch quotas need to be sold or auctioned off on a level playing field to vessel operators wishing to exploit the common property resource at sea, with anything less than full price amounting to an implicit government subsidy, admission tickets need to be sold to tourists in one way or another.

Key policy implications of insufficient diversification in Iceland

Iceland's economic diversification away from heavy dependence on export earnings from fisheries was not the result of deliberate government policy. Rather, it was market-induced, and ultimately initiated by a financial meltdown in 2008 that reduced the real value of the Icelandic króna by a third. This created for the first time reasonably favourable economic conditions for new types of exports, especially tourism services. Further, Iceland's economic diversification has not yet been accompanied by commensurate political diversification. Agricultural and especially fishery interests retain disproportionate political influence. This influence has permeated four important national issues with profound consequences: electoral laws, fisheries policy, EU accession, and the Icelandic constitution.

Electoral laws: Iceland saw its first written proposal of equal voting rights – i.e. one person, one vote – in 1849, but to no avail. The laws governing elections to parliament were originally written by farmers for farmers, and have to this day remained biased in favour of residents of rural areas at the expense of the inhabitants of the Reykjavík metropolitan area where the bulk of the electorate resides. In recent years foreign monitors of parliamentary elections in Iceland have repeatedly condemned the continued discrimination among voters inherent in the electoral laws.

Fisheries: Successive governments have long undercharged vessel owners for use of Icelandic fishing grounds. The government granted access to the resources to vessel owners free of charge from 1984 to 2002 when nominal fishing fees were levied on vessel owners. These fees amounted to only a small fraction of the market value of the fishing rights as established by competitive auction. While the fishing grounds are by law a common-property resource belonging to the country's citizens, the resource thus benefits primarily the fishermen. Even after the crash of 2008 when the government faced an acute shortage of revenues, it shied away from significantly raising fishing fees.

EU accession: Despite fairly consistent though not strong majority support for EU membership reflected in public opinion polls from the early 1990s until the crash of 2008, Parliament showed no interest in applying for membership or holding a national referendum on the issue except briefly after the crash. Instead, Parliament sided with the farm lobby and the fishing lobby, which feared losing its privileged access to Icelandic fishing waters. At present the Icelandic Parliament shows no interest in joining the European Union.[6] Parliament did not file a membership application until after the crash of 2008 when public opinion had swung against EU membership, partly because some voters blame foreigners, including the EU, for Iceland's home-made financial meltdown and partly because of the EU's current debt problems. The application has been put on hold by the government in office since 2013. The new government has even attempted, unsuccessfully so far, to circumvent Parliament by withdrawing Iceland's application as opposed to just putting it on hold.[7]

Constitution: Parliament invited the electorate to a national referendum on a new post-crash constitution in 2012. A specially elected constituent assembly had drafted the bill in full accordance with the conclusions of a national forum in 2011, and passed it unanimously. The national forum comprised 950 Icelanders selected at random from the national register, meaning that every Icelander had an equal chance of being invited to participate in the forum. The bill was accepted by two thirds of the voters in the 2012 referendum, as were its most important individual provisions on equal voting rights (67%), national ownership of natural resources (83%), and direct democracy through increased use of national referenda (73%). A majority in parliament (32 members out of 63) declared in public that they wanted to ratify the new constitution in keeping with the result of the referendum. However,, Parliament adjourned in 2013 without ratifying the bill, inviting the new parliament elected in 2013 to put the bill on ice as if no referendum had taken place (Gylfason, 2014). This is an example of how a narrow political base favours special interests at the expense of general welfare.

11.6 Conclusion

Economic diversification and political diversification both confer economic benefits through socially productive diversity and pluralism and both reduce macroeconomic risk. A broad industrial base comprising manufacturing, trade, and services confers economic gains that can be compared to the political benefits of checks and balances, accountability, and transparency, the hallmarks of good governance. Economic and political diversification both reduce the risk of macroeconomic damage caused by excessive industrial concentration and insufficient competition – hence the need to diversify away from agriculture that tends to perpetuate poverty as well as from excessive dependence on natural resources which, if not well managed, may stifle or delay the development of modern manufacturing and services. Further, modern economies need democratic pluralism with broad political participation to provide the people with an efficient and fair way of exercising their political will through free elections and to safeguard their human rights. Without democracy, bad governments tend to last too long. The need for political diversification is particularly urgent in some resource-rich countries that often face a double jeopardy – that is, natural wealth that is concentrated in the hands of relatively small number of elites who seek to preserve their privileges by blocking both economic and political diversification that would disperse their power and wealth (Ross, 2001). Rent-seekers typically resist reforms – economic diversification as well as democracy – that would redistribute the natural resource rents to their rightful owners: the people. A people's right to their natural resources is a fundamental human right proclaimed in international law and enshrined in many national constitutions (Wenar, 2008).

Specialisation in production for export is an essential source of economic efficiency and long-run growth. However, excessive concentration of economic activity can, by increasing national risk and volatility, pose a threat to efficiency, growth and welfare. Shockwaves in the specialised sector may spread to other parts of the national economy. This risk calls for economic diversification. Likewise, political concentration can amplify national risk by facilitating the adoption of economic policies that favour special interests, disregard common interests and lack economic rationality. Economic and political diversification is thus an essential feature of national risk management aimed at promoting efficiency and growth. Both types of diversification are vital to protecting and promoting national welfare. A narrow economic base as well as a narrow political base increases the risk of economic losses. Also, they tend to be mutually reinforcing. A modern, service-oriented economy with a well-educated workforce is easier to diversify than an agrarian or natural-resource-based economy.

We have provided evidence over time and across countries showing that worldwide, long-term income growth goes along with diversification of exports and of political institutions. Double diversification pays off! We have presented indications that natural-resource based economies are more prone to retain a narrow base than economies based on manufactured goods or services. More work needs to be done to clarify the pattern of spillover effects across different types of production. More work is also needed to establish the important interactions between economic and political diversification to identify how to establish positive feedbacks with cumulative effects.

Policy prescriptions will differ from country to country depending on each country's history and specific circumstances. We have offered a case study of Iceland, stressing the capture of policy by special interest groups made possible by their overrepresentation in the political system. The example of Iceland demonstrates how the failure to diversify exports and other economic activity can in time weaken or even undermine political diversity and ultimately pose a threat to liberal democracy, unless the people find a way to prevail in the political arena.

Acknowledgements

The authors thank Gylfi Magnússon and Hans Sjögren for their comments on a version of the text that was presented at the 17th Annual Conference on European Integration organised by the Swedish Network for European Studies in Economics and Business (SNEE) in Mölle, Sweden, 19–22 May 2015.

Notes

1 The Polity IV Project classifies Finland as fully democratic from 1944 onward. Switzerland granted women the right to vote in 1971.
2 Corresponding charts showing the cross-country correlations between the Polity2 index of democracy, manufacturing exports and the Herfindahl index are presented in Gylfason and Nguessa Nganou (2014, Figure 7).
3 True, agriculture uses imported inputs. The magnitude of the net effect of farm import restrictions on the exchange rate has never been investigated, and remains unknown.
4 Not so long ago, when asked how his fishing firm was doing, a CEO responded: 'Very well, thank you, except financially.'

5 Agriculture and fisheries have always been viewed as separate occupations in Iceland, even though fishing began as the extracurricular activity of farmers sending their farm workers out to sea in small boats, and did not emerge as a separate activity until the twentieth century when bigger, mechanised boats had entered the scene.

6 The parliaments of oil-rich Norway and super-neutral Switzerland are the only other national legislatures in Europe opposed to EU membership, both in accordance with public opinion as expressed in national referenda.

7 A withdrawal without parliamentary consent would, if the EU were to go along with such a violation of democratic practice, make it necessary for a new parliament to restart the application process from scratch, securing renewed individual approval by each member country – a tall order.

References

Aghion, P. and Banerjee, A. (2005) *Volatility and growth*, Oxford: Oxford University Press.

Diamond, L. (2015) 'Facing up to the democratic recession', *Journal of Democracy*, vol. 26, no. 7, 141–155.

Frankel, J. (2012) 'Mauritius: African success story', CID Working Paper No. 234, April, in Edwards, S., Johnson, S. and Weil, D. (Eds.), *African Economic Successes*, Chicago: University of Chicago Press.

Gelb, A. (2011) 'Economic diversification in resource-rich countries', in Arezki, R., Gylfason, T. and Sy, A. (eds.), *Beyond the curse: Policies to harness the power of natural resources*, Washington DC: International Monetary Fund.

Gylfason, T. (1998) *Principles of economic growth*, Oxford: Oxford University Press.

Gylfason, T. (2006) 'How do India and China grow?' *Challenge*, vol. 49, no. 1, 74–89.

Gylfason, T. (2013) 'From collapse to constitution: The case of Iceland', in Paganetto, L. (ed.), *Public debt, global governance and economic dynamism*, Amsterdam: Springer.

Gylfason, T. (2014) *Constitution on ice*, CESifo Working Paper No. 5056, November.

Gylfason, T. (2015) 'Iceland: How could this happen?' in Andersen, T.M., Bergman, M. and Hougaard Jensen, S.E. (eds.), *Reform capacity and macroeconomic performance in the Nordic countries*, Oxford: Oxford University Press.

Gylfason, T. and Nguessa Nganou, J.-P. (2014) *Diversification, Dutch disease, and economic growth: Options for Uganda*, CESifo Working Paper No. 5095, November.

Gylfason, T. and Zoega, G. (2014) 'The Dutch disease in reverse: Iceland's natural experiment', Oxford: Oxford University, OxCarre Research Paper 138, available online at http://www.oxcarre.ox.ac.uk/files/OxCarreRP2014138.pdf (accessed 9 April 2016).

Levinson, S. (2006) *Our undemocratic constitution: Where the constitution goes wrong (and how we the people can correct it)*, Oxford: Oxford University Press.

Paldam, M. (2000) 'Social capital: One or many? Definition and measurement', *Journal of Economic Surveys*, vol. 14, no. 5, 629–653.

Panagariya, A. (2008), *India: The emerging giant*, Oxford: Oxford University Press.

Rodrik, D. (2013) 'Unconditional convergence in manufacturing', *Quarterly Journal of Economics*, vol. 128, no. 1, 165–204.

Ross, M. (2001) 'Does oil hinder democracy?' *World Politics*, vol. 53, 325–361.

Sachs, J.D. and Warner, A.M. (1995, revised 1997, 1999), 'Natural resource abundance and economic growth', NBER Working Paper 5398, Cambridge, Massachusetts.

Spence, M. et al. (2008) *The growth report: Strategies for sustained growth and inclusive development*, Washington DC: Commission on Growth and Development, The World Bank.

United Nations Human Rights Committee (2007) *International covenant on civil and political rights*, CCPR/C/91/D/1306/2004, 14 December, available online at www. ccprcentre.org/wp-content/uploads/2012/12/1306_2004-Iceland.pdf (accessed 21 April 2016).

Wenar, L. (2008) 'Property rights and the resource curse', *Philosophy and Public Affairs*, vol. 36, no. 1, 1–32.

Wijkman, P.M. (1976) 'Comments on the exploitation of common property natural resources', *Fjármálatíðindi*, vol. 22, no. 2, Central Bank of Iceland.

Wijkman, P.M. (1982) 'Managing the global commons', *International Organization*, vol. 36, no. 3, 511–536.

Wijkman, P.M. (1982) 'UNCLOS and the redistribution of ocean wealth', *Journal of World Trade*, vol. 1, 27–48.

12 Industrial diversification processes and strategies in an oil economy

Norway

Olav Wicken

12.1 Introduction

Background

Norway is a natural resource based economy with high productivity and rapid long-term growth. Since the 1970s it has emerged as one of the world's major exporters of oil and gas. In addition it specialises in industries like fish and marine resources, and primary metals and chemicals. It has low specialisation in high-tech industries and financial services. In this way it belongs to a group of industrialised countries which can be defined at natural resource based economies which have achieved long term economic growth and social welfare. A characteristic of these economies is the ability to develop new industries and specialisations in their natural resource based sector, or to develop goods and services linked to these industries. In this chapter we discuss the extent to which Norway has managed to remain a diversified economy during the period where oil and gas have become a dominant export sector.

A natural resource based industrial economy

In this section we present some generalised facts about Norway's economy and economic development. We first present the long-term growth of the economy and some indicators of its contemporary position, and go on to present some data to characterise Norway as a natural resource based or industrial economy. There is no consensus about the definition of what constitutes a natural resource based economy (NRBE), but the main indicators are normally the share of natural resource based industries (NRBI) in the country's gross national product or its exports (Sachs and Warner, 1995, 2000; Gylfason, 2001, 2004). There is also no general consensus about how to measure NRBI. Our studies use international industrial statistics (NACE) and select specific sectors as NRBI (Sachs and Warner, 1995, 2001). For a well-developed industrial economy like Norway we chose to use economic specialisation (export) as main indicator. The indicator used in this chapter is a combination of share of NRBI in export statistics.

Norway was an industrial latecomer compared to other countries in the northwest of Europe. GDP per capita remained lower than the average among

European countries throughout the nineteenth century, and from the middle of the twentieth century Norway's productivity reached the average European level. It was as an oil economy from 1970 that its GDP per capita became higher than other industrial economies. Today Norway is a wealthy industrialised nation with a high level of welfare.[1] It is a relatively small society and a medium-sized economy. Today the population is approximately 5.2 million people (ranked as number 118 globally). However, Norway has a GDP which in 2012–13 was ranked as number 23 or 25 in the world (IMF, 2012; UN, 2013; World Bank, 2013). This position is reflected in a very high GDP per capita during the early 2000s, ranked as second highest in the world by IMF. Also, Norway was at the top of UN's Human Development Index in 2013 and 2014.

Norway has developed into a high-income economy as a NRBE. The percentage of NRBI in exported goods has for most of the period since the mid-nineteenth century been between 80% and 95% (see Table 12.1). During the long growth period (1950–1973) there was a trend towards lower importance of NRBI in the total export statistics, but Norway moved back to its long-term trajectory as a NRBE with the introduction of an expanding offshore oil and gas sector from the 1970s. What is evident from Table 12.1 is the dominant role of oil and gas for export statistics during the twenty-first century, with the sector representing 65% of total exports. The second largest export sector is fish and marine resources, competing with primary metals for this position.

The importance of NRBI in the economy and its export may be illustrated by international comparisons on comparative advantages in manufacturing. This is illustrated by Table 12.2 which compares Norway with some other mid-size economies with similar industrial structure. The table reveals five sectors which constitute a relatively large share of the economy; food, chemicals, basic metals, wood and paper, and machinery. The first four industries are linked to natural resources (fish and agriculture to the food industry, wood and paper to forestry and hydropower, chemicals and metals to hydropower) and the last industry (machinery) is closely linked to NRBI (capital goods industry for the NRBI).

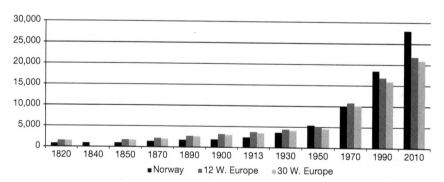

Figure 12.1 GDP/capita in Norway, Western Europe 12 and Western Europe 30 countries, 1820–2010.
(Bolt and vab Zanden, 2013).

Table 12.1 Historical share of export of goods from Norway by 'sector' (for 1880 to 1975, Historical Statistics 1978; for 1995 and 2014 Statistics Norway, Statistikkbanken, Foreign trade)

	1880	1913	1955	1975	1995	2014
Foods	44	40	27	11	8	8
Primary products	44	32	19	4	3	2
Minerals	23	4	3	2	1	1
Fuels	0	0	0	13	48	64
Capital goods	0	3	9	32	15	11
Basic metals	2	4	19	17	12	7
Consumer goods	5	2	1	4	1	1
Other manufacturing	3	15	23	17	13	7
	100	100	101	100	100	101

Table 12.2 Revealed comparative advantages in selected OECD countries (OECD, 2010)

	Food	Chemicals	Basic metals	Wood and paper	Machinery	Manufacturing
Norway	1,7145	1,4174	1,6329	1,1208	1,6186	
NZ	6,2126			3.3541		
Australia	3.1389		3.1978			
Canada	1.1329	1.1114	1.1717	2.6875		1.1159
Denmark	2.7582	1.3336			1.5071	1.1204
Finland				4.1774		1.8701
Sweden			1.2056	3.3895	1.615	

The specialisation within NRBI is reflected in the strong position of Norwegian producers in international trade in selected industries and sectors. By the outset of the financial crisis (2009–2010) Norway was/had the world's:

- second largest exporter of fish and seafood
- second largest fleet of supply vessels for offshore oil and gas
- third largest exporter of natural gas
- fourth largest shipping fleet (20% of global gas and chemicals fleet, 10% of global crude oil tankers)
- sixth largest exporter of primary aluminium
- sixth largest exporter of oil
- leading exporter of oil related products and services (50% of world market in sub-sea production technologies)
- major exporter of silicon for solar cells production

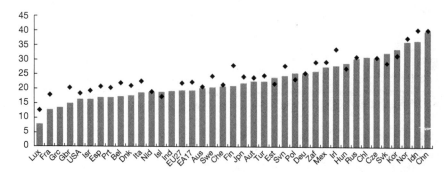

Figure 12.2 Value added in industry, including energy as a percentage of total value added. (OECD).

Norway is an open economy and exports constitute approximately half of GDP. Large and strong NRBI and related industries in the export statistics therefore reflect that Norway is an industrial economy. Only in China is the share of value added in industry – including energy – as part of total economy higher than in Norway (see Figure 12.2).

The rapid long-term economic growth as an oil economy from 1970, and the ability to remain an industrial economy with a large, competitive and export-oriented economy makes Norway an outlier among oil economies during this period. In international literature the concepts 'paradox of plenty' (Karl, 1997) and 'resource curse' (Auty, 1994) have been used to describe how specifically oil economies, but also NRBE in general, experience slow long-term growth. In many studies the slow growth is explained by the idea that booms in NRBI lead to a decreasing role of manufacturing in the economy, called Dutch disease. In the following we briefly discuss this literature in the light of the Norwegian experience.

12.2 Oil economies and the paradox of plenty or resource curse

The idea that an abundance of natural resources is a curse for economic development and growth is closely linked to the experience of oil and gas economies since the early 1970s. The rapid increase in oil prices through OPEC I (1973) and OPEC II (1979) created expectations for future growth and economic development for old and new oil producing economies. When oil prices dropped dramatically during the mid-1980s, it became obvious that high financial income from export of oil had not led to the wider economic development of oil producing countries. This development was contrasted by the emerging 'Asian Tiger' economies which had to import oil for domestic use.

Terry Lynn Karl (1997) made a seminal contribution to the analysis of oil economies in a detailed analysis of political and economic problems in oil exporting countries like Venezuela, Iran, Nigeria, Algeria and Indonesia. She described how financial flows from oil export influenced the behaviour of the elites of the oil economies, which in the longer run destabilised political regimes. The oil economies in her analysis entered a common development path in spite of an initially high degree of diversity between the economies. The common chosen path led to disappointing – and surprising – results. The paradox of plenty represents economies and societies where high financial income from the oil sector resulted in a dysfunctional society, economy and political system. The experience of the oil economies during this period may be seen as extreme cases of the resource curse. Sachs and Warner (1995, 2001) extended the analysis of the resource curse to include a wider range of natural resources in the analysis. However, the resource curse discourse is closely linked to importance of the experience of oil economies for their findings.

A often used model for economic analysis of the resource curse is based on the experience of the Netherlands' expanding gas sector in the North Sea during the 1960s, called Dutch disease by some economists. The idea of this model is that financial flows during boom periods will push prices and costs (salaries) and in this way reduce competitiveness in sectors which compete on international markets. Reduced competitiveness will have an impact on industrial structure. Manufacturing (specifically the traded sector) is expected to lose out and labour and capital will move to sectors not competing internationally (the untraded sector). A long period of financial flows into Norway has certainly increased labour costs, particularly from the early 1990s. In 1995 labour costs were around 17% above those of Norway's trading partners (NOU, 2010: 4); the difference increased to 45% in 2009–2010, and to 55% in 2013 (NOU, 2014: 3).

This implies that traded industries have entered a challenging cost position. Still, there is no clear evidence that this has had a strong negative influence on the growth pattern in manufacturing. In fact, Norway's de-industrialisation during the oil period has been slower compared to its main trading partners. Norway's employment in the manufacturing sector dropped by 23% between 1970 and 2002, compared to 25% among its trading partners (NOU, 2003). In its main trading partner and neighbour, Sweden, manufacturing employment dropped by 30%.

Figure 12.3 shows that the manufacturing sector in Norway experienced a significantly higher rate of growth compared to other industrial economies in the North of Europe between 1990 and 2014.

In this way Norway became a 'black swan' among oil economies. The economic development was not characterised by the resource curse; rather, it became a success story where the oil and gas seemed to be a blessing with few symptoms of Dutch disease (Gylfason, 2001, 2004). Wright and Czelusta (2004a) used 'the case of Norway' as an example of how a recent oil economy had succeeded in combining oil production and high financial income with long-term economic growth and dynamics. Norwegian economic development no doubt inspired local economists Mehlum, Torvik and Moene (2006) to oppose Sachs and Warner's empirical findings about the statistical correlation between natural abundance and growth rates.

Norway's experience during the oil era (1970–2015) therefore contrasts with the idea that oil economies are struck by the paradox of plenty and the resource

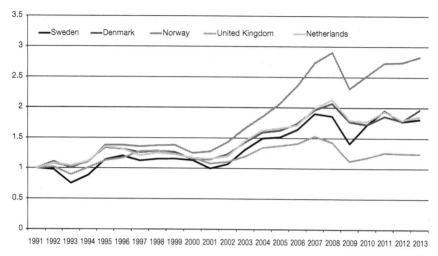

Figure 12.3 Growth in value added in manufacturing sector in selected industrial countries, 1990–2014.
(World Bank – data compiled by Erlend O. Simensen, TIK centre, University of Oslo).

curse. Increased production costs due to high financial income flows from the oil sector did not have a negative impact on long-term growth or the performance of the manufacturing sector relative to Norway's trading partners. This implies that Norway was able to keep a more diversified industrial sector compared to other oil economies. In the following we move from emphasising cost efficiency as a main explanatory factor for long-term industrial development and diversification, focussing on the role of knowledge and learning processes in industrial dynamics.

12.3 The role of knowledge as a competitive advantage

In the early 2000s there was a turning point in the discussion of the resource curse, strongly influenced by historical work on the USA's long-term economic development. Gavin Wright (in collaboration with various researchers) produced a series of papers which documented how natural resource based industries (NRBI) could be analysed and perceived as modern knowledge based production. In his early work Wright (1990) created a link between resource expansion and America's international economic success. His analysis of the factor content of trade in manufacturing exports showed that it was characterised by intensity in non-reproducible natural resources, and that the resource intensity had increased during the period from around 1880 to 1930. With the arrival of Sachs and Warner's thesis of the resource curse, Wright used his historical knowledge of American history to challenge the arguments underlying the resource curse theory. In a paper written in collaboration with Paul David (David and Wright, 1997), they argued that a country's resource abundance was not given by the natural environment. When the USA became the main producer of many minerals during the late nineteenth and early twentieth centuries, this was not a result of an environment rich in these specific minerals, but rather of the ability of American society to discover and extract resources compared to other countries. The resource abundance was not destined by geology, but rather was endogenous to the economy and was therefore a socially constructed phenomenon. The lesson from American history is that a society may increase its natural resource base by investing in knowledge and technology to search for minerals, extract them and then process or market them:

> [T]he abundance of American mineral resources should not be seen as merely a fortunate natural endowment, but is more appropriately understood as a form of collective learning, a return on large-scale investments in exploration, transportation, geological knowledge, and the technologies of mineral extraction, refining, and utilization.
>
> (Wright and Czelusta, 2004a: 10)

The USA's share of world mineral production in 1913 was much higher than its share of world reserves, and Paul David and Gavin Wright identified three elements which caused this: i) an accommodating legal environment, ii) investment in the infrastructure of public knowledge, and iii) education in mining, minerals and metallurgy. The resource abundance of the USA was socially constructed. The stocks of natural resources are not fixed, but rather the dynamic output of investments in various types of knowledge in the economy and society, including science, education, technologies and organisations. This is the basis for the argument that the USA's development in mining in the early twentieth century 'embodied many of the features that typify modern knowledge based economies'. David and Wright (1997) found in their empirical analysis that there was:

> positive feedback to investments in knowledge, spillover benefits from one mining speciality to another, complementarities between public- and private-sector discoveries, an increasing return to scale – both to firms and to the country as a whole.
>
> (David and Wright 1997: 204–205)

The theoretical approach developed through historical analysis has become a competitive perspective to the ideas from the resource curse thesis in policy making institutions. In the World Bank a group of economists has used this approach to discuss the role of natural resources in the contemporary development of Latin American, and in defining policies for development of the region (De Ferranti et al., 2002). The idea presented by Ferranti et al. is that '[i]t is not what you do, but how you do it' that matters for the development process. Countries may succeed with or without an abundance of natural resources. For countries which specialise in natural resources it is how their natural resources are created through socio-economic processes involving various types of knowledge, and how these resources enter into various types of production sectors, as well as how this creates the long-term dynamics of the wider economy, that define the outcome. Wright and Czelusta (2004b: 184–185) describe the same point of view:

> What matters most for resource-based development is not the inherent character of the resources, but the nature of the learning process through which the economic potential of the resources is achieved.

We may argue that this is no different from analysis of the development, growth and dynamics of any other economic process or sector, and that the same type of analytical tools apply. The positive role of natural resources for long-term industrial and economic development, as observed in the USA, have also been noted in other economies. The general argument is that NRBI may be dynamic and may form the basis for long-term economic development.

The move towards analysing long-term economic development with knowledge as the main explanatory factor has become widely accepted in both neo-classical approaches (New Growth Theory) and evolutionary economics (including innovation systems approaches). In this chapter we use a version of the innovation systems approach adapted to the specificity of the industrial dynamics of natural resource industries. The underlying idea is that innovation processes normally involve more than one company or firm, and therefore depend on interactive relationship between firms and other organisations/actors. Innovation processes therefore take place in networks of organisations and the relationships between the actors are structured by the existing institutional framework, which gives the network a systemic aspect (Fagerberg, 2004). This is also the case for NRBEs like Norway (Fagerberg, Mowery and Verspagen, 2009).

Innovation processes in NRBIs are complex, involving a large number of heterogeneous actors with different types of resources and knowledge bases. In many sectors there has been a systematic process to outsource technological development, involving both process and product development, to external companies. This is evident in the oil sector where oil producing companies define performance criteria for the technology they want, and invite firms and organisations with specific skills in the relevant technology to come up with solutions (Ryggvik, 2013). This defines the specific structure of a given innovation system; where NRBI defines the (technological) direction of the production system, and other companies – outside the NRBI – design and develop the new (technological) solutions. This is the basis for analysing dynamics in NRBIs as an inter-sectoral relationship between two types of companies in two sectors of the economy. The two sectors are the NRBI and the 'enabling sector' (Ville and Wicken, 2013, Pol et al., 2002).

This relationship structures learning/knowledge creation processes and shapes knowledge bases and organisations involved in the interaction learning activity. These processes are endogenous to the economy, and they are central in the build-up of institutional and industrial capabilities natural resource industries and economies (Ville and Wicken, 2013). The NRBI and the enabling sectors interact with public knowledge infrastructure (public knowledge organisations), and

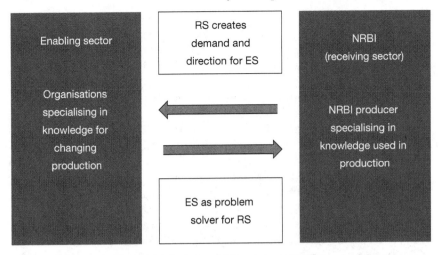

Figure 12.4 A two-sector model for industrial dynamics in NRBEs.

together they constitute the main elements in a country's knowledge bases. As they are distributed over various sectors of the economy and society, we label them distributed knowledge bases (Robertson and Smith, 2008), and they are central resources for the dynamics of a natural resource based knowledge economy (NRB-KE).

Returning to our Norway case and using this model as an analytical tool, we will explore qualitatively – using secondary literature – how these relationships have resulted in knowledge/technology development and how they have contributed to the diversification of the economy. Before we turn to this analysis, however, we will discuss the selection of the industrial sectors for analysis.

12.4 Industry analysis of natural resource based dynamics

In this section, we describe and analyse the dynamics creating diversity in the Norwegian economy. Diversification is a result of the survival and growth of old industries combined with the entry and expansion of new production sectors. We use export industries as an indicator of the existence of competitive sectors, and study four of the main export industries. Table 12.1 shows that export from Norway has historically been dominated by NRBI, normally representing 80–95% of the total value of exports of goods. Only at the end of the long growth period (1950–73) was the export sector characterised by a higher degree of diversity. From that time the offshore oil and gas industry gradually became a dominant export sector, contributing 65% of total exports in 2014. Norway's economy has once more become highly specialised in natural resources, representing approximately 80% of total exports, mainly from oil and gas, fish and marine products, and base metals and chemicals. The strong position of Norway's fishery is the result of the build-up of a globally new industry, fish farming of salmon. Base metals and chemical products are old industries in Norway, based on the availability of abundant cheap hydropower since the early twentieth century. The last of the main export sectors from Norway is 'capital goods'. In this section, we discuss the extent to which the internationalisation of this type of industry is closely related to the development NRBI – i.e. the extent to which this industry today is part of the enabling sector of NRBI.

The analysis of these processes in Norway's four main export sectors is based on the model presented at the end of Section 12.1. We study the entry, expansion and transformation of each NRBI sector, with a focus on the build-up of capabilities for industrial change and international competitiveness. A central part in this process is the co-evolution of an enabling sector (capital goods, R&D, knowledge intensive inputs), and of an institutional framework regulating the interaction between NRBI and firms or organisations in the enabling sector.

We start the empirical discussion by analysing two new industries emerging since 1970 – the offshore oil and gas sector and salmon fish farming. This is followed by a study of the transformation of an old NRBI, the production of base metals. Finally, we look at the expansion of capital goods and services during the early part of the twenty-first century.

Transferring old industry to new country: offshore oil and gas

The initial phase of the oil industry in Norway can be seen in the transfer of the international oil sector to a new location. During the 1960s a small number of MNCs got permission to start exploration for oil in the North Sea. As in other emerging oil regions they brought a system of supply and service industries with which they collaborated globally (Engen, 2009). Until 1971 the government followed a liberal policy with very limited regulation of potential future production. During this liberal phase international oil companies involved some local industrial actors, and shipping became the most significant industrial partner. Parts of the shipping industry got contracts for supply services from the international oil companies operating in the North Sea before 1970, but with some exceptions there was no strong interest from local industry to become involved in the emerging oil sector.

This changed rapidly after the first oil discovery in December 1969. From 1971 the Labour government introduced a policy for national control of the petroleum resources, reducing the role of MNCs. A central aspect of this strategy was the build-up of national, state-owned oil companies. The main economical and policy instrument, the state-owned Statoil, was established in 1972. Historically the largest industrial company in Norway, Norsk Hydro started preparing for a future as an oil company. From the 1980s Hydro became the operator of a large oil and gas field (Ryggvik, 2000; Lie, 2006). National policies supported the build-up of national oil companies. Statoil was given majority control of potentially valuable fields for exploration, and received privileges regarding finance and taxes. As part of the permission to start exploration in the North Sea, international companies had to accept that they would train Norwegian expertise.

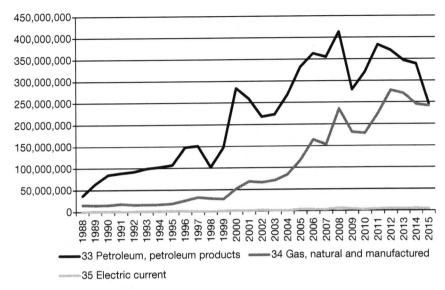

Figure 12.5 Export value of oil and gas from Norway 1988–2014.
(Stat Norway: statistikkbanken).

Statoil and Norsk Hydro gradually acquired competencies and skills relevant for modern oil companies, and become independent operators. Key personnel participated in the planning, engineering and construction of new fields in foreign companies. A key knowledge area was competence in interpreting data from geological surveys. Each company needs highly qualified internal competence in this area to make investment decisions for exploration. Strong local academic communities in geology became central for recruitment and expertise in the area.

The introduction of a local content policy was the result of problems in the existing industry during the recession starting in 1973. Shipping, particularly oil transport, was severely hit by the international economic crises. Ship owners and shipbuilding firms were forced to look for more profitable and expanding markets. The large and growing investments and operations in the emerging oil industry were seen as an alternative market. The build-up of a local supply and service industry was a politically supported response to internal challenges in the economy.

A central policy instrument was the introduction of high standards for safety and environment. The harsh natural environment in the North Sea soon made it evident that existing technology for offshore drilling used in the Mexican Gulf could not be transferred to the new oil region without high risk. This created an opportunity for local industry to develop new technologies with sufficiently low risk in the harsh environment. The main technological breakthrough was Condeep (concrete deep water) – vast concrete platforms positioned on the bottom of the sea. The platforms were placed on top of huge concrete tanks used for the storage of oil. This became the core technology for a 'Norwegian technological style' in offshore oil production. The use of concrete in sub-water constructions was based on long experience and competence from construction of dams for hydro power and competence and research in the development of specific qualities of concrete.

The old international supply industry gradually lost its dominance, and a new group of suppliers emerged linked to the Norwegian technological style. Local engineering companies were responsible for designing and constructing the platforms; other local industries became sub-suppliers. Shipyards were transformed to enable the construction of platforms. Also, other industries turned away from old markets and focussed on supplying the oil sector with knowledge and technology. Norway's emerging high-tech and ICT research community and industry gradually became integrated into the oil sector, building on industrial control technology, computing, nuclear reactor management, space and defence technologies (Njølstad, 1998; Njølstad and Wicken, 1997; Collett, 1995; Sogner, 2015). Owners of fishing vessels moved into supply services in the offshore sector, exploiting their skills to operate vessels in the extremely harsh marine environment with strong winds and cold weather.

From 1978 to 1979 the government introduced policies to link international oil companies more directly to local capability building, establishing incentives for international oil companies to fund R&D projects in local industry and local research organisations (goodwill agreements). The context was a fear of the rapid breakdown of old manufacturing sectors due to high cost levels and lack of competitiveness. The outcome was four large national oil R&D organisations; concentrating on drilling technology, applied geology and improved oil recovery (Nerdrum and Gulbrandsen, 2009). Oil related R&D continued to expand, and during the late 1990s oil and gas companies funded 12% of total R&D in Norway. This instrument linked international oil companies to local oil industry and research (Engen, 2009: 199).

The drop in oil prices from 1986 challenged the high-cost trajectory in North Sea oil production (Olsen and Sejersted, 1997; Engen, 2002). The oil and supply industry, unions and the government established a process (NORSOK) to search for new technological concepts and new forms of organising technological processes. The underlying basis was an acceptance that Norwegian actors in the oil sector 'did not yet possess sufficient competitive capabilities to place [them] among the international elite of the energy producers' (Engen, 2009: 197). The NORSOK development created the basis for an dynamic innovation system where the industrial actors – oil companies and main suppliers – enjoyed greater freedom in choosing technological solutions, partners and geographical locations for production. A core element of what emerged from the process was simplified organisational models and a new technological trajectory characterised by greater use of unmanned installations and computer based technological solutions linked to subsea technologies and new drilling techniques. In the new fields developed, costs were reduced by around 30% compared to the 'Norwegian style' (Engen, 2009: 201).

The technological transformation coincided with organisational concentration. The national oil companies, Statoil and Hydro, achieved total control of the

Norwegian shelf, and in 2007 the two companies merged. A similar development took place in the supply sector where the amalgamation of Aker and Kvaerner in 2001 resulted in only one local firm able to handle large petroleum contracts. The oil sector and its innovation system today are therefore dominated by a relatively small number of powerful local actors. The system became internationalised, and Statoil and Norwegian technology suppliers are involved in development and investments in oil fields in a number of countries. The ambition has been to become global actors, and Norwegian governments have supported this strategy. Today Norwegian companies have diversified into new markets for investment in Asia, Africa, Latin America and North America.

Creating a globally new industry: salmon fish farming

Norway is (as of 2014) the world second largest exporter of marine products, trailing only China. This sector consists of two main parts: traditional sea fisheries and fish farming. The growth in this sector from 1970 reflects the development of the salmon fish farming industry. This industry differed from the oil sector in various ways. First, fish farming of salmon was a globally new industry and could not build on technologies and expertise from other countries. Second, producers were small-scale local entrepreneurs, often with a background in fisheries and agriculture. Third, the regulatory system and public policies differed in many ways from the oil industry.

Fish farming expanded from a production of 100,000 tons during the late 1980s to 400,000 tons around 2000, 900,000 tons by 2010, and 1.3 million tons in 2014. The value increased from NOK 12 billion in 2005 to NOK 42 billion in 2014, reflecting the increase in export value from the marine sector during the same period (Figure 12.6). Improved production technology and efficiency resulted in lower production costs, down from NOK 32 per kg in 1986 to NOK 12 per kg twenty years later. Labour costs represent less than 10% of production total value. This development is the outcome of the long-term interplay between fish farming producers, a complex enabling sector, and public institutions to support the industry and its knowledge bases.

The emergence of the new industry was based on resources and expertise from old industrial sectors, mainly marine industries/fisheries and agriculture. During the early period (before 1990) a large number of local fishermen and farmers entered the industry as producers. Many fishermen had long experience in planning and finance of large capital investments, employing people and running a business, as well as dealing with markets and sales. Some also had sufficient capital to experiment in fish farming independent of subsidies or bank loans, and some had established fish farming production during the early 1970s. The emerging industry became more regulated; from 1973 licenses (as in the oil sector) were needed to start fish farming. The intention of the policy was to promote small-scale and decentralised industry with local owners located along the long coast of western and northern Norway. Most fishermen and farmers did not have sufficient resources to be able to enter fish farming, and public subsidy schemes became

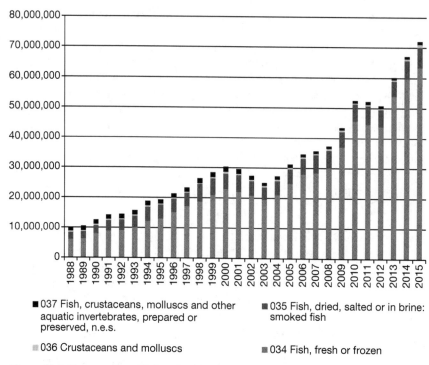

Figure 12.6 Export value of fish and seafood from Norway 1997–2013.

central to the diffusion of small-scale production in various parts of the coast line. Before 1990 more than eight hundred licenses were handed out.

The enabling sector emerged in parallel to the build-up of fish farmer/producer organisations, building three different types of knowledge bases located in different types of organisations: 1) practical knowledge from traditional fisheries; 2) technological knowledge in supply industries; and 3) science-based knowledge from various disciplines in research laboratories.

Fishermen could draw on practical or experience-based knowledge from traditional ocean and coastal fisheries. The first fish farmers using net cages in the sea had experience in keeping saithe alive in large closed nets close to land. They had detailed knowledge of the local natural environment – sea currents, waves, wind, sea bed – which were crucial factors in decisions on the location of net cages and how to moor the net securely in the sea, and also for fish health. They also transferred technological solutions, like using vessels to pump fish out of the net cage, from fisheries. The focus on local environmental conditions made each farmer demand specific solutions for net cages and related products. Fish farmers demanded tailor-made technologies, and in this way influenced the direction of the emerging production system (Berge, 2006). New ideas, practices and technologies diffused rapidly due to open relationships between fish farmers and between fish farmers' consultancy companies, fodder providers and technology suppliers.

Local capital goods industries became providers of technology for the fish farming industry. Gradually more technologically advanced production systems emerged, involving many new knowledge bases. Control technologies and automation were introduced for regulating fodder, weighing, measuring, health control and other operations. An important specialisation was the production of smolt and fodder. During the first phase fishermen used fish caught at sea to feed the salmon, but gradually specialised fodder adapted for salmon became available.

Research institutes started to experiment with aquaculture from the 1960s when researchers at the Norwegian University College for Agriculture started a genetic programme for creating salmon for fish farming. This was based on genetic selection for breeding livestock. The initiative was well received, and in 1971 a research centre, Akvaforsk, was founded. The following year the world's first experimental research lab for fish farming was established in Sunndalsøra funded by the Research Council for Agriculture (W-Aslesen, 2009: 209–10). The main objectives of the R&D projects were to select fish which could grow fast in captivity, the use of fodder, and later resistance to various diseases. Norway became an international research arena for fodder. Systematic research during the 1980s resulted in the introduction of dry-feed. The Institute for Marine Research in Bergen contributed with a breakthrough for the industry when it solved the problem of feeding fish in their larval stage (Schwach, 2000: 23).

Salmon production experienced problems with diseases from its early days. In 1968 fish farmers approached the Institute for Marine Research seeking support to solve health problems among hatchery-produced fish. The rapid expansion during the 1980s and 1990s made health a key problem for fish farming. Scientists worked on remedies against parasites, bacterial and viral infections, etc. (Aslesen, 2004). From 1983 public research programmes on Healthy Fish were launched, and became a long-lasting public support area. The programme also developed an efficient vaccination procedure which drastically reduced the amount of antibiotics used. The research sector linked to fish farming is considerable, consisting of twenty public or semi-public research institutes with 1,600 researchers, scientists and other experts (Aslesen, 2009).

Role of public policy in transforming the industry

The emerging fish farming industry was shaped by public policies. As mentioned, the government supported the build-up of public research institutions which created fast-growing species of salmon. The strong research centres became core elements of the 'public knowledge infrastructure' for fish farming; in addition, courses for training in fish farming were introduced at various levels (university as well as pre-university level). Regulations introduced before 1981 supported small-scale vertical and horizontal integration, mandating a producer cartel similar to those in fisheries (Aslesen, 2009: 211). Laws also *de facto* excluded external investors, securing local ownership.

The small-scale decentralised industry entered economic crisis which culminated in 1991. Public authorities rapidly changed the regulatory framework of the industry. The government removed laws that protected sales cartels and allowed horizontal integration since one owner could control more than one concession or licence. In the following period there was a strong concentration of ownership, and large nationals and MNCs entered the industry. As discussed above, the transformed industry experienced rapid growth from the late 1990s, and Norwegian producers invested in fish farming in other countries (notably Scotland, Chile and Canada). Parts of the supply industry such as fish fodder producers and R&D organisations followed producers to new markets. Norwegian fodder producers established a presence in all major salmon producing markets (Aslesen, 2009: 212–213). In many ways, the fish farming industry followed in the footpath of the oil industry in becoming a global enterprise.

Diversification from old industry: electro-intensive production

The discussions on the emergence of new industries – offshore oil production and salmon fish farming – illustrate the importance of existing technological capabilities in the economy for this type of diversification. The offshore oil sector drew on resources, competences and knowledge from a wide range of industries like shipping, shipbuilding, engineering industry, ICT, construction and fisheries. In a similar way fish farming could build on experience, resources and capabilities from ocean fisheries, equipment producers and suppliers for fisheries and shipbuilding, farming, and biological research. This implies that the existence of strong and dynamic industries and their enabling sectors have been a prerequisite for the creation of new industrial export sectors. We now change the perspective away from analysing emerging industries, and we focus on how old industries may become a basis for diversification processes. We emphasise their role in creating new production sectors which are linked to or related to the old industries and their existing knowledge bases or industrial activities. The new industrial production is related to the old in the sense that they draw on the same knowledge bases, and we call this related variety or diversification (Boschma and Lammarino, 2009). As a special case, we discuss how specialisation within a commodity may become a basis for higher value creation and growth processes within a NRBI.

As illustrated in Table 12.1, Norway is specialised in the production of primary products based on abundant and cheap hydropower. It is the largest producer of primary aluminium in Western Europe, globally ranked as number seven; 80–90% is exported. It is also a major producer of ferro-silicon. Timber-based products – pulp and paper – have historically been a major export sector, but the production has gradually been reduced and most production units are closed down. The problems of the paper industry illustrate challenges for firms located in a high cost economy and competing globally. For the largest company in the industry, Norske Skog, its ambition from 1990 was to become a world-leading producer of paper for newspapers. This industry is characterised by the large-scale production of a standardised product where competition in price is central. The stagnation in demand for newspaper and over-capacity in production created economic problems. The relatively high cost of production in Norway resulted in the closure of all except two of the firm's domestic production units.

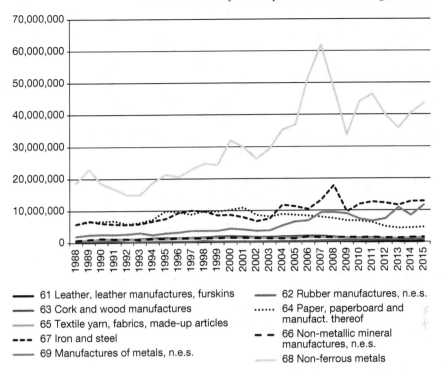

61 Leather, leather manufactures, furskins
62 Rubber manufactures, n.e.s.
63 Cork and wood manufactures
64 Paper, paperboard and manufact. thereof
65 Textile yarn, fabrics, made-up articles
66 Non-metallic mineral manufactures, n.e.s.
67 Iron and steel
68 Non-ferrous metals
69 Manufactures of metals, n.e.s.

Figure 12.7 Exports of Norway.
(1000 NOK).

Other natural resource and energy intensive industries are faced with similar cost challenges, but have chosen diversification strategies which have made them less dependent on Norway's cost level. Borregaard was historically Norway's largest wood processing company, and chose a more transformative and innovative strategy. As one of few similar companies globally it has succeeded in becoming what is often called a bio-refinery. The strategy is to develop methods and processes which can turn bio-mass into high value-added products, like new materials or bio-energy. The success of Borregaard has been dependent on long-term capability building as a combined pulp and paper and chemistry company from WW2 onwards (Bergh and Lange, 1989). The company can draw on a dual competence base, and this was used to transform the company into a bio-refinery. The main development and production unit is still located in Norway.

In the base metal industry we observe strategies of related variety and diversification in many forms. Norsk Hydro used its competences and resources in metallurgical processes to develop a new method for the production of magnesium. This was a completely new product area for the company when the first production unit started in the mid-1980s (Andersen and Yttri, 1996). Many firms have moved into the production of specialised products directed towards users who require specific quality specifications for the material. The old industries of aluminium and ferro-silicon production illustrate the point. Ferro-silicon is traditionally an input for the aluminium industry (used in alloys). In addition the material has a market in the semi-conductor industry and the solar energy industry. The two latter industries demand a very high purity of silicon for their products, and Norwegian firms were among the early actors in developing processes for this quality of silicon. Elkem, REC and others succeeded in achieving a stronghold in the expanding markets for solar energy during the 1990s, and became global providers for the emerging solar energy market (Sogner, 2004). Before the financial crisis in 2008 Norwegian firms were among the world's leading exporters of silicon for solar energy. The entry of Chinese firms into this market illustrates the importance of costs for survival in a specific location. Market prices were rapidly reduced, and Norwegian firms responded by moving production abroad (Hanson, 2013).

Also in fertilisers, special qualities and varieties adapted to specific user environments were introduced. Originally Norwegian production of fertiliser was nitrogen-based, of high quality and with high costs. In the 1990s this type of fertiliser lost market share in Western Europe, which was the only market for Norwegian fertiliser. In order to expand exports to other parts of the world, Norsk Hydro (today Yara) developed a global strategy by adapting fertilisers to variations in natural environments and individual markets, and also by moving into special products like fodder for livestock (Lie, 2006: 329, 335).

Public policy interventions

The cases of pulp and paper and the silicon industries indicate that labour costs are important for producers in international markets. In the electro-intensive industry high wages have been a driving force for the introduction of automated production technology. Labour costs have become less important, with electricity prices the more important cost factor. Policy instruments and firm strategies are directed towards reducing the costs of energy in production. An important instrument is public policy measures to increase production of renewable energy (Tradable Electricity Certificates). Higher supply in the power market has rapidly reduced electricity prices, and prices are expected to stay low for a long period. Companies develop production technologies using less energy, as illustrated by Hydro's investment decision in a new a pilot plant for aluminium production in Western Norway (Karmøy) in 2015. This technology is regarded as environmentally friendly, and EU legislation therefore provides for public subsidy (NOK 1.5 billion) of the pilot plant, which the Norwegian government has provided.

The electricity intensive industry is an important part of climate and energy policy, as the processes demand large amounts of electricity and energy and also contribute significantly to climate emissions (one quarter of Norway's total emissions). As all electricity in Norway is renewable, there are no climate emissions from the use of electricity. Norwegian producers of aluminium have introduced new technologies to reduce the emissions created by the chemical processes gradually since 1990. The production therefore has relatively small emissions and is energy efficient. The combination of low emissions, low energy intensity, and abundant and cheap renewable electricity capability may create an opportunity for the future location of electro-intensive industry in Norway.

Enabling sectors as new specialisations

In 2013 a consultancy report concluded that a new industry had become Norway's second largest export sector (Melbye et al., 2012). Export from the supply industry of the oil and gas sector had surpassed fish and metals in this ranking. The report was ordered and financed by the oil supply industry, but nevertheless there is evidence that exports from the enabling sector for offshore oil and gas have become a major export oriented industrial sector (Ryggvik, 2013). Table 12.1 shows that capital goods today (2014) are the second largest export sector (trailing only oil and gas), and Figure 12.8 illustrates the growth and levels of production in the SITC sectors most relevant for capital goods exports.

The report on the internationalisation of the supply industry for oil and gas (Melbye et al., 2012) showed that the industry is diverse, covering major parts of the value chain in oil and gas production. The largest export sub-sector was drilling and well services (NOK 58 billion), but geological and seismic services were also significant (NOK 18 billion). The other major export sub-sector was field development (NOK 60 billion) which was divided into two sub-sectors: development topside (above sea level, NOK 39 billion), and subsea fields (NOK 21 billion). The third major export industry is operation support (NOK 28 billion). The diversity of capital goods and services directed towards international markets for oil and gas investments and services may be compared to the similar diversity of export product sectors within the SITC 7 (Machinery) sector (illustrated in Figure 12.8).

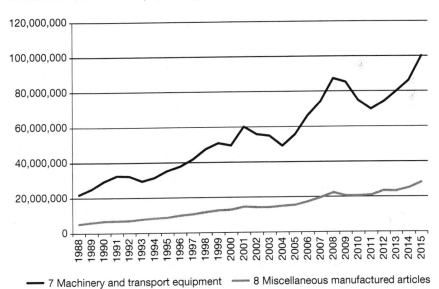

Figure 12.8 Norway's exports of machinery and transport and equipment (SITC 7), and miscellaneous manufactured articles (SITC 8).

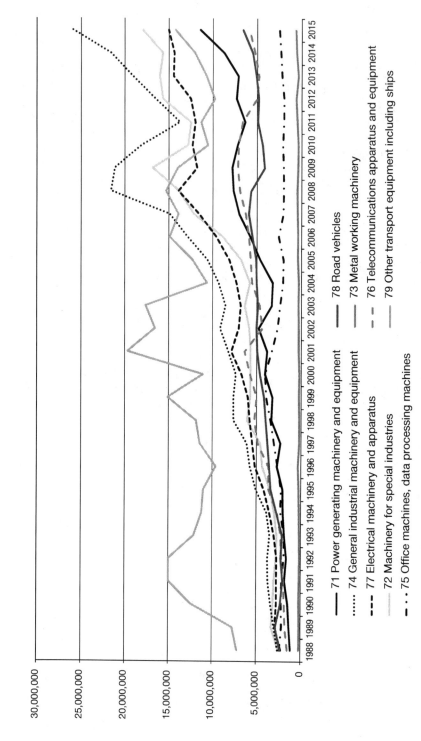

Figure 12.9 Export value from Norway 1988–2014, Machinery and Transport Equipment, SITC 7. (NOK 1000).

As discussed earlier in this chapter, the enabling sectors emerged in co-evolution with domestic NRBIs, in oil and gas, fish farming, metals and chemicals. They started primarily as providers of technology and input to domestic industry. How did they become export oriented and global industries? Based on the evidence from this study, the main factor seems to be the close co-evolution with national NRBI: when Norwegian NRBI firms became global operators, the enabling sector followed. When fish farming companies entered into markets in Europe (UK, Scotland, Ireland), North America (USA, Canada) and South America (Chile), the supply industry followed into the same markets. The export orientation of the oil and gas supply industry took place in parallel to Statoil's internationalisation strategy, and mainly within the same markets as Statoil entered. Export statistics also reflect changes in the oil and gas value chain. From the 1990s many Korean firms became main contractors for large projects in the Norwegian petroleum sector. The Korean contractors sub-contracted specific modules of the production to Norwegian suppliers. In this way exports in the statistics reflect the entry of global contractors in an industry where Norwegian firms used to play this role (Ryggvik, 2013). The internationalisation of the enabling sector also involved foreign direct investment, and many Norwegian firms established new companies or acquired established subsidiaries in the new markets.

Globalisation of the industry changed the role of the national government to shape the inter-relation between NRBI and the enabling sector. The government's formal policy instruments to create links between oil companies and the national enabling sector were removed when Statoil became a player in the global oil industry. However, it may be argued that the government still plays an important role in supporting national industrial interests in the internationalisation process. The Foreign Office and its embassies are active in building links between Norwegian companies and local political and industrial actors in large oil and gas markets. The government also markets the Norwegian model in its development programme called 'Oil for Development', with a number of emerging oil economies participating in the programme. The effects of these policy instruments are unknown, but they support an argument that the triangle of oil industry, enabling sector and governmental agencies still constitutes a central part of the Norwegian model for natural resource based industrialisation.

12.5 Strategies and policies for diversification in an oil economy

In this section we discuss the policy implications of the empirical studies presented in previous sections. We have used the model illustrated in Figure 12.4, and we use the findings to discuss the role of public policy in industrial diversification. In the following we first describe two main types of interventions for diversification of the economy: instruments supporting *knowledge capability* building; and instruments supporting the creation of *platforms* for inter-sectoral learning processes. These two elements represent policy instruments to establish an innovation system for innovation and industrial dynamics, which are preconditions for diversification processes. Diversification and the establishment of new production sectors demand more than the existence of knowledge capabilities. We draw on ideas from the technological innovation systems (TIS) literature to discuss how policy instruments are used in the development of new industries to secure experimenting, investment and other resources, and the creation of initial markets in the early phase of the industry. We will also see how new policy instruments have been used to transform new industries as they grow and become more mature.

Policies for capability building and inter-sectoral learning

When oil production started in 1970, the Norwegian public sector had for a very long period of time established organisations for education, research and innovation relevant to the economy's natural resource based industries. Particularly since 1950 governments had introduced a number of instruments to promote knowledge creation, particularly by expanding investments in higher education and in a public technological research institute sector (Wicken, 2009b, Nerdrum and Gulbrandsen, 2009). This strategy continued during the oil era. The 'local content' policy in the oil sector from the late 1970s (with the introduction of the goodwill agreements) increased financial support from multinational companies to local research institutes and universities (Wiig, 1993). During the economic crises from the end of the 1980s the government rapidly increased public funding for higher education as well as industrial R&D. The combination of increased public support for research and education in universities and increased R&D procurement from large oil producers resulted in higher capabilities for innovation and industrial diversification in the university and research sectors. The increasing capacity of higher education and the R&D system reflect the growing importance of the petroleum sector in society. Also, other NRBIs experienced increased public support for R&D and innovation, and a number of research labs for the emerging fish farming industry were established.

As discussed earlier, the introduction of standards and regulations in safety and environment became central industrial instruments. The demands linked to the Norwegian technological style made existing capabilities and competences in the Norwegian economy relevant for the emerging oil sector. Over time the oil sector attracted a significant part of the established industry to move into offshore oil, shipping, shipbuilding, mechanical engineering, ICT and machinery. This made Norway's economy less heterogeneous, and the oil sector became gradually more dominated by the development of the petroleum sector. However, it also resulted in a very large and internationally highly competitive supply industry.

The enabling sector constitutes a part of the economy's distributed knowledge system, and is an important resource for the creation of new industries and diversification. However, the capability of the enabling sector is not sufficient. NRBI firms need to link up with relevant research labs and knowledge intensive industries in order to be able to use their competences and resources in innovation processes. Public policies contribute to the establishment of platforms for inter-sectoral learning (Nelson, 2003; Ville and Wicken, 2013). The introduction of

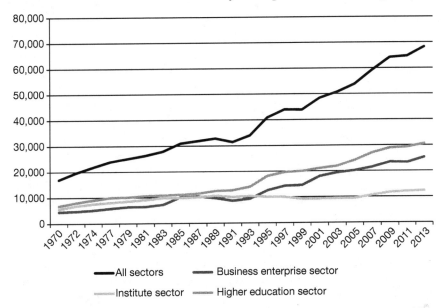

Figure 12.10 Man-years in Norwegian R&D organisations, R&D Institutes, universities, industry and in total.
(Man-year: SSB, Statistikkbanken, Innovasjon og teknologi).

'user oriented development projects' in Norway may illustrate this type of policy instrument. Public institutions financially support R&D projects where (NRBI) companies invite R&D institutions or knowledge intensive companies to participate in a common project to develop a new product or improve product quality or production technology. The project becomes an arena or platform for communication between various types of organisations participating in learning processes. In Norway this type of policy was introduced during the 1960s, and it became a dominating type of industrial R&D policy from 1990 (Wicken, 2009b). Universities have gradually engaged in this type of R&D project in collaboration with industry.

State ownership of NRBI firms has been a tool to secure interaction with local enabling sector. Statoil became a dominant operator on the Norwegian shelf, and also worked closely with local suppliers. It may be argued that state ownership in Hydro has been a driving force in continuing the production of aluminium in Norway, which is important for long-term collaboration with national research communities. In the early period of fish farming, local ownership resulted in the use of local providers of equipment and other input.

Policies for platforms seem to be particularly important during an early phase of new industries. In many cases the initial meeting between various actors results in the institutionalisation of relationships. As both NRBI firms and enabling sector organisations become stronger and more competitive, the dependence on public support may be significantly reduced. The inter-sectoral learning processes become institutionalised and part of business-as-usual.

Policies to initiate new industries

We have discussed the emergence of two new NRBIs – the offshore petroleum industry and salmon fish farming – as examples of two different types of new industries. In addition, we have mentioned the entry of new industrial/production sectors like new metals (magnesium, silicon for solar energy), bio-materials, and renewable energy sectors (solar and wind power, bio fuels). In all these attempts to establish new industries, public sector policies and interventions have been important. In order to structure the discussion on the role of public policies in the emergence on new industries, we draw on literature studying how new technologies are developed, produced, and become diffused in the economy (Bergek et al., 2008, Hekkert et al., 2007). A core element is that all creation processes involve the implementation of a number of core processes which fulfil specific functions, like entrepreneurial experimentation, knowledge development, the formation of markets or the mobilisation of resources.

The new industries emerging in Norway started with local entrepreneurs getting involved in the new industry before there was any intervention from public authorities. This was the case for fish farming, where fishermen, farmers and other local actors started experimentation locally before fish farming was on the political agenda. In offshore petroleum Norwegian firms entered into contracts with multi-national oil companies during a period characterised by a liberal policy regime. In electro-intensive industries there are large local firms with sufficient resources to develop new processes and processes without public support. They are often able to shape policy institutions to develop policy instruments which are well adapted to the needs of the industry. Supporting processes which are initiated by economic actors may make policy interventions more efficient.

However, most new products or production technologies demand experimentation – pilot plants or demonstration projects – which often are capital intensive and involve high risk for investors. Some form of public subsidy or support system may be necessary to prompt firms and investors to engage in this type of experimentation. The subsidy (NOK 1.5 billion) to build a pilot plant for a more energy efficient method to produce aluminium developed by Hydro illustrates the role of public interventions. Hydro Aluminium would most likely not invest in this technology (at least not in Norway) without such financial support. In fish farming there are ongoing experiments to start production of other species than salmonids, which also are subsidised through various mechanisms. Even in the oil and gas sector costly experimentations are heavily subsidised. Since oil companies pay almost 80% tax on profits, most of the costs of experimentation (which is tax deductible) will be covered by the state. In addition, experimentation on exploration in marginal fields and to extract more oil and gas from old fields may be fully covered by the tax authorities even when costs are higher than the total taxes paid by company. Policy instruments to support the development of new technologies and industries in renewable energy involve large-scale public funding for experiments in carbon capture and storage (CCS) at Mongstad test centre, as well as support for experimentation with floating offshore wind turbines and other renewable technologies.

New industries normally struggle to compete with established producers. New production technologies are normally less efficient compared to old forms of production. Today this is illustrated by the high cost of producing renewable energy using new technologies and energy sources. Wind, power, bio and other sources cannot compete with old technologies like hydropower or fossil fuel based technologies. Still, new technologies may have the potential to become competitive. Public authorities therefore introduce various types of support systems to create markets for infant industries – in Norway one example is tradable electricity certificates. Public procurement is also used as an initial market for new industries and technologies; in Norway publicly owned transport firms have been early users of bio fuels. However, not all new industries need public support to get access to the market. In cases where the new industry involves transferring existing industry and production systems to a new territory – like oil and gas in Norway – it may not be necessary to create subsidised initial markets. In salmon fish farming this was also not necessary. Salmon was a luxury consumer product with a high price on the market, and even relatively inefficient production technology was profitable from the start.

Creating profitable markets for new industries and technologies is an instrument to encourage firms and investors to invest in emerging industries. Many modern NRBIs are highly capital intensive with complex and advanced production systems (offshore oil and gas, mining petrochemicals, base metals). From a public policy perspective, the question is how to make (private) companies invest sufficiently to allow new industries to expand rapidly. We observe different types of instruments directed towards mobilising financial resources for diversification or developing new industries. Fish farming was from its outset regarded as a small scale industry where fishermen, farmers and other local actors were the main agents. Many lacked sufficient capital for investment or could not raise capital on the commercial market, and state banks became core institutions for funding. In oil and gas the situation is very different. Large multinational oil firms controlled vast financial resources, and a high tax level combined with tax deduction for investments promoted a very high level of investments. In the energy intensive industry there are subsidised investments in pilot projects but (probably) not for full scale production. The policy is rather to make Norway an attractive investment region by reducing costs on input factors like electricity, and to support R&D and knowledge capabilities. In renewable energy we find a combination of direct investment subsidies and indirect support through feed-in tariffs or TES.

12.6 Concluding remarks

The description of policy interventions which are used to support the creation of new industries and keep old industries competitive in Norway indicates the demand for a complex set of policy instruments. The basis is the long-term build-up of knowledge capabilities and institutions which enables industry and other actors to engage in diversification and innovation processes. In addition, we observe that there is a diverse variety of policy instruments directed towards the specific challenges of each industry. We find that successful policies often support the demands of emerging industries for the implementation of specific types of processes – experimentation, the formation of initial markets, and the mobilisation of financial or human resources. Policy instruments seem to be contextual, designed for specific challenges in specific industries located in an environment with specific characteristics. Diversification in an oil economy demands policies tailor-made for each case.

Note

1   Norway is also ranked eleventh on the World Bank's competitive index 2013 and 2014, in line with the other Scandinavian countries (2014: Finland 4, Sweden 10 and Denmark 13). The Gini coefficient ranks Norway third lowest (after Slovenia and Denmark). In the UN's list of 'most happy societies' Norway ranked second (following Denmark).

References

Andersen, K.G. and Yttri, G. (1997) *Et forsøk verdt. Forsøk og utvikling i Norsk Hydro gjennom 50 år*, Oslo: Pax Forlag.
Andersen, K.G (2006) *Flaggskip i fremmed eie. Hydro 1905–1945*, Oslo: Pax Forlag.
Asheim, B., Coenen, L., Moodysson, J. and Vang, J. (2005) *Regional innovation system policy: A knowledge-based approach*, CIRCLE paper 2005/13, Lund.
Aslesen, H.W. (1999) *Governance and the innovation system in the fish-processing industry in Northern Norway*, STEP Research Report 12, 1999.
Aslesen, H.W. (2004) *Knowledge intensive service activities and innovation in the Norwegian aquaculture industry*, part project report for the OECD KISA study, STEP Research Project.
Aslesen, H.W. (2009) 'The innovation system of Norwegian aquacultured salmonids', in Fagerberg, J.E., Mowery, D.C. and Verspagen, B. (eds.), *Innovation, path dependency and policy: The Norwegian case*, Oxford: Oxford University Press.
Auty, R. (1994) 'Industrial policy reform in six large newly industrializing countries: The resource curse thesis', *World Development*, vol. 22, no. 1, 11–26.
Berge, D.M. (2006) 'Havfiske inn i nye næringer', in Bjarnar, O., Berge D.M. and Melle, O. (eds.), *Havfiskeflåten i Møre og Romsdal og Trøndelag, Vol 2: Fra fri fisker til regulert spesialist*, Trondheim: Tapir Akademisk Forlag.
Bergek, A., Jacobsson, S., Carlsson, B., Lindmark, S. and Rickne, A. (2008) 'Analyzing the functional dynamics of technological innovation systems', *Research Policy*, vol. 37, no. 3, 407–429.
Bergh, T. and Lange, E. (1989) *Foredlet virke: Historien om Borregaard 2889–1989*, Oslo: Ad Notam Forlag.
Bolt, J. and vab Zanden, J.L. (2013) *First update of the Maddison Project: Re-estimating growth before 1820*, Maddison Working Paper 4.
Boschma, R. and Lammarino, S. (2009) 'Related variety, trade linkages, and regional growth in Italy', *Economic Geography*, vol. 85, no. 3, 289–311.
Collett, J.P. (1995) *Making sense of space. The history of Norwegian space activities*, Oslo: Scandinavian University Press.
David, P. and Wright, G. (1997) 'Increasing returns and the genesis of American resource abundance', *Industrial and Corporate Change*, vol. 6, no. 2, 203–245.

De Ferranti, D., Guillermo, E.P., Lederman, D. and Maloney, W.F. (2002) *From natural resources to the knowledge economy*, Washington DC: World Bank Latin American and Caribbean Studies, World Bank.

Engen, O.A. (2002) *Rhetoric and realities: The NORSOK programme and technical and organisational change in the Norwegian petroleum industrial complex*, Dr. Polit thesis, University of Bergen.

Engen, O.A. (2009) 'The development of the Norwegian petroleum innovation system: A historical overview', in Fagerberg, J.E., Mowery, D.C. and Verspagen, B. (eds.), *Innovation, path dependency and policy: The Norwegian case*, Oxford: Oxford University Press, 179–207.

Fagerberg, J.E. (2004) 'Introduction', in Fagerberg, J.E., Mowery, D.C. and Nelson, R.R. (eds.), *The Oxford handbook of innovation*, Oxford: Oxford University Press.

Fagerberg, J., Mowery, D.C. and Verspagen, B. (2009) 'The evolution of Norway's national innovation system', *Science and Public Policy*, vol. 36, no. 6, 431–444.

Gulbrandsen, M. (2009) 'University-industry relations in Norway', in Fagerberg, J., Mowery, D.C. and Verspagen, B. (eds), *Innovation, path dependency and policy: The Norwegian case*, Oxford: Oxford University Press.

Gylfason, T. (2001) 'Natural resources, education and economic development', *European Economic Review*, vol. 45, no. 4, 847–59.

Gylfason, T. (2004) *Natural resources and economic growth: From dependence to diversification*, available online at www.cer.ethz.ch/resec/sgvs/029.pdf (accessed 21 April 2016).

Hanson, J. (2013) *Dynamics of innovation systems for renewable energy technology: The role of post-introduction improvements*, PhD dissertation, University of Oslo.

Hekkert, M., Suurs, R.A.-A., Negro, S.O., Kuhlmann, S. and Smits R.E.H.M. (2007) 'Functions of innovation systems: A new approach for analyzing technological change', *Technological Forecasting and Social Change*, vol. 74, no. 4, 413–432.

International Monetary Fund (2012) *World economic outlook 2013*, Washington DC: IMF.

Karl, T.L. (1997) *The paradox of plenty: Oil booms and petro states*, Berkeley, CA: University of California Press.

Lie, E. (2006) *Oljerikdommer og internasjonal ekspansjon. Hydro 1977–2005*, volume 3 in *History of Hydro 1905–2005*, Oslo: Pax Forlag.

Mehlum, H., Moene, K. and Torvik, R. (2006) 'Institutions and the resource curse', *Economic Journal*, vol. 116, 1–20.

Mellbye, C., Fjose, S. and Jakobsen, E.W. (2012) *Internasjonalisering av norsk offshoreleverandørindustri 2011*, Menon Report.

Narula, R. (2000) *Explaining 'inertia' in R&D internationalization: Norwegian firms and the role of home country effects*, Research Memorandum 021, MERIT, Maastricht University.

Nelson, R.R. (2003) *Physical and social technologies and their evolution*, LEM Working Paper 2003/9, Pisa.

Nerdrum, L. and Gulbrandsen, M. (2009) 'The Technical-Industrial Research Institutes', in Fagerberg, J.E., Mowery, D.C. and Verspagen, B. (eds.), *Innovation, path dependency and policy: The Norwegian case*, Oxford: Oxford University Press, 327–348.

Njølstad O. (1998) *Strålende forskning: Institutt for atomenergi 1948–1998*, Oslo: Tano Ashehoug.

Njølstad, O. and Wicken, O. (1997) *Kunnskap som våpen. Forsvarets Foskningsinstitutt 1946–1975*, Oslo: Tano Aschehoug.

NOU (2003) *Konkurranseevne, Lønnsdannelse og kronekurs*, Oslo: Ministry of Finance.

NOU (2010) *Grunnlaget for inntekstoppgjørene 2010*, Oslo: Ministry of Labour.

NOU (2014) *Grunnlaget for inntekstoppgjørene 2014*, Oslo: Ministry of Labour and Social Affairs.

OECD (2010) available online at http://stats.oecd.org/Index.aspx?QueryId=47827 (accessed 5 April 2015).

Olsen, O.E. and Sejersted, F. (eds.) (1997) *Oljevirksomheten som teknologiutviklingsprosjekt*, Oslo: Ad Notam Gyldendal.

Pol, E., Carroll, P. and Robertson, P. (2002) 'A new typology for economic sectors with a view to policy implications', *Economics of Innovation and New Technology*, vol. 11, no. 1, 61–76.

Ryggvik, H. (2000) *Norsk oljevirksomhet mellom det nasjonale og det internasjonale. En studie av selskapsstruktur og internasjonalisering*, PhD dissertation, University of Oslo.

Ryggvik, H. (2013) *Building a skilled national offshore oil industry: The Norwegian experience*, Oslo: NHO Department for internationalization and European Policy.

Ryggvik, H. (2015) 'A short history of the Norwegian oil industry: From protected national champions to internationally competitive multinationals', *Journal of Business History*, vol. 89, no. 1, 3–41.

Sachs, J.D. and Warner, A.M. (1995) *Natural resource abundance and economic growth*, National Bureau of Economic Research Working Paper, no. 5398, December.

Sachs, J.D. and Warner, A.M. (2001) 'The curse of natural resources', *European Economic Review*, vol. 45, no. 4–6, 827–38.

Schwach, V. (2000) *Havet, fisken og vitenskapen. Fra fiskeriundersøkelser til havforskningsinstitutt 18602000*, Bergen: Ocean Research Institute.

Sejersted, F. (2002) *Demokratisk kapitalisme*, Oslo: Pax Forlag.

Smith, K.H. (2002) 'What is the 'knowledge economy'? Knowledge intensity and distributed knowledge bases', INTECH Discussion Paper Series 2002/6, United Nations University.

Robertson, P.L. and Smith, K. (2008) 'Distributed knowledge bases in low- and medium-technology industries', in Hirsch-Kreinsen, H. and Jacobsen, D. (Eds.) *Innovation in Low-Tech Firms and Industries*, Cheltenham: Edward Elgar.

Sogner, K. (2004) *Skaperkraft gjennom 100 år. Elkem 1904–2004*, Oslo: Messel Forlag.

Sogner, K. and Petersen, T. (2015) *Strategisk samspill. Kongsberggruppens historie 1987-2014*, Oslo: pax Forlag.

Statistics Norway (2015) *Statistikkbanken*, Oslo: Statistics Norway.

Statistics Norway (1978) *Historisk statistikk*, Oslo: Statistics Norway.

Sæther, B., Isaksen, A. and Karlsen, A. (2011) 'Innovation by co-evolution in natural resource industries: The Norwegian experience', *Geoforum*, vol. 42, no. 3, 373–381.

United Nations (2013) *National accounts main aggregates database 2013*, Washington DC: United Nations Statistics Division.

Ville, S. and Wicken, O. (2013) 'The dynamics of resource-based economic development: Evidence from Australia and Norway', *Industrial and Corporate Change*, vol. 22, no. 5, 1341–1371.

Wicken, O. (2009a) 'The layers of national innovation systems: The historical evolution of a national innovation system in Norway', in Fagerberg, J., Mowery, D.C. and Verspagen, B. (eds.), *Innovation, path dependency and policy: The Norwegian case*, Oxford: Oxford University Press.

Wicken, O. (2009b) 'Policies for path creation: The rise and fall of Norway's research-driven strategy for industrialization', in Fagerberg, J., Mowery, D.C. and Verspagen, B.

(eds.), *Innovation, path dependency and policy: The Norwegian case*, Oxford: Oxford University Press.

Wiig, H. (1993) *Olje mot forskning. En oppgave om Goodwillavtalen i norsk forskningspolitikk, og om teknologioverføring i FoU-samarbeidene*, Master's thesis in Social Geography, University of Oslo.

World Bank (2013) available online at databank.worldbank.org/data/downloads/GDP.pdf (accessed 5 April 2015).

Wright, G. (1990) 'The origins of American industrial success, 1879–1940', *American Economic Review,* vol. 80, no. 4, 651–68.

Wright, G. and Czelusta, J. (2004a) 'The myth of the resource curse', March-April, 6–38.

Wright, G. and Czelusta, J. (2004b) *Mineral resources and economic development*, working paper no. 209, February, Berkeley: Stanford University.

13 Old and new directions for economic diversification policies

Yasser Al-Saleh

13.1 Learning from policy successes and failures

Economic diversification policies have been a feature of government policy for over half a century, with varying degrees of success. While common sense may stipulate a tendency both to avoid blunders and simply to cultivate what 'already works', it is important to recognise that no 'finite line' can be drawn which will differentiate success from failure. Success may not only be judged differently by different parties and/or criteria, but assessments are also likely to vary over time. Public policy studies are littered with tales of seemingly short-term failures that have turned into long-term successes and vice versa (e.g. see the Routledge Handbook of Public Policy, 2012).

Irrespective of any snapshot assessment of public intervention, there is no doubt that governments can learn from both policy success and failure, as policy-making remains by and large a juggling process of successive experimentation. In the words of Charles Lindblom in his renowned paper 'The science of muddling through': 'Making policy is at best a very rough process ... Policy-making is a process of successive experimentation on some desired objectives in which what is desired itself continues to change under reconsideration' (Lindblom, 1959: 86).

A desire to diversify the economic base should be 'too difficult to dismiss' in terms of mitigating the potential risks associated with excessive specialisation. Yet, the contributors in this book demonstrate how governments have varied in terms of the priority they give to a diversification agenda. Hernandez and Manzano, for example, note that economic diversification has been a desired outcome among Latin American policy-makers since the 1950s. However, economic performance in Latin America has not progressed in line with those set expectations, partly due to political instability. On the other hand, Kazakhstan is an example of an oil-producing country with a relatively nascent history of economic diversification. Efforts in this regard have been hampered by both unfair market competition and under-developed human capital. While diversification policies there have largely been considered an implicit element of a nation-building undertaking, Abdillah Noh argues that redistributive efforts in plural societies like Malaysia have a strong social cohesion dimension to avoid potential social unrest. Russian resource policies are often viewed as a subset of regime sustainability and foreign policies, whereas diversification in Australia is essentially a subset of an economic liberalism agenda to ward off fears of becoming 'a banana republic'. Outsiders' analysis of economic policy in Saudi Arabia reveals a more mixed outcome, even though internal political affairs are usually geared to social welfare and the creation of new industries to address rapidly growing youth unemployment.

Regardless of the underlying political intentions, the contributors to this volume show that the most problematic stage of the policy-making process is implementation as opposed to rationale or design formulation. Considering potential success factors as far as policy implementation is concerned, many of the fortunes documented in the Norwegian and Malaysian – and to a lesser extent Russian – experiences can be explained by the respective governmental understanding that sound economic policies are futile without supportive institutional and political terrains. Phillimore and Leong point out that a key factor behind the relative success of Australia has been a genuine effort to replace protectionist policies with an emphasis on openness, flexibility and competitiveness. Reflecting on the Kazakhstani experience, Peter Howie suggests that promoting broad economic reforms has a higher probability of success than the practice of protecting handpicked priority sectors. On the other hand, Olav Wicken argues that while no all-encompassing national industrial policy exists in Norway, its ongoing search for diversity is underpinned by several sector-level policies and processes. While useful policy lessons can be drawn from such an instructive range of international experiences, this book strongly suggests that when it comes to policy-making, there is no such thing as a one-size-fits-all.

13.2 A policy panacea remains missing

The absence of a 'silver-bullet' policy solution is a message that is repeatedly recounted in the public policy literature. The contributions to this book have emphasised the importance of local context in the understanding of policy-making and economic development realities. Although it has never been the remit of this book to offer universal policy prescriptions, as these would differ from one jurisdiction to another depending on historical factors and local circumstances, it is useful to reflect on what we can take away from the various diversification approaches adopted by different natural resource-based countries.

History is of great importance and path dependency plays a major role in economic development. The Australian experience shows that not only do politicians have to work within a context of inherited institutional arrangements, but also that their ideas are likely to be a product of history and past learnings. Timing and status quo also play a role, as is demonstrated by the Malaysian story. Some countries may have the luxury of investing natural resource-based funds into sovereign wealth accounts, while others can only afford to cover their current expenditures. In Canada, it appears that windfalls from natural resources have not been invested wisely, let alone set aside, but rather used to fuel government spending. A valuable lesson – learned the hard way from the Canadian oil sands experience – is not to depend on booms continuing in order to finance the future.

The chapter on Uganda embraces the adoption of fiscal policies that emulate those in Chile. That country has been successful in avoiding over-spending in boom times while simultaneously only allowing deviations from a target surplus in response to permanent (or at least, long-term) price changes in commodities. Despite all this, government budgets in most oil-producing nations remain highly vulnerable to volatile oil prices.

The chapter by Li-Chen Sim on Russia nicely reminds us that diversification requires not just financial commitment but also institutional reforms in terms of the way the economy is managed. In fact, the quality of institutions, human and physical infrastructures are all critical determinants of the success of the economic diversification process. As vividly argued by Gylfason and Nganou in relation to Uganda, the build-up of human resources and essential infrastructure – such as schools, hospitals and roads – are conducive to sustaining long-term economic growth. Furthermore, this process is just as much political as economic, especially in countries with a fragmented population and/or high youth unemployment. In the example of Iceland, Gylfason and Wijkman illustrate how failure to diversify economic activities in a timely manner can undermine political diversity and ultimately also pose a threat to a liberal democracy. They emphasise that diversification of the political system is an essential part of the successful diversification of the economy, and vice versa.

As noted by Richard Hawkins, beginning in the early 1980s many OECD countries including resource-abundant Canada witnessed a major policy shift, from a vertically-oriented focus on building new industries to a horizontally-oriented emphasis on individual firms, particularly SMEs and start-ups. Further evidence from Norway, and also to some extent from Malaysia and the UAE, points to economic success being underpinned by the existence of related capabilities. Leveraging legacies to venture into new but yet still related industries has emerged as an effective economic diversification policy to adopt. In essence, this presents a promising trend that moves away from the traditional focus on pursuing either vertical or horizontal diversification strategies.

13.3 Epilogue: which way now?

Recurrent financial downturns and volatility in commodity prices serve as telling calls that natural resource-dependent nations are highly vulnerable to various external shocks. Economic diversification – in terms of both products and exports – is therefore destined to remain at the top of government agendas in several resource-rich regions and countries around the world. Given the significance of this topic, it comes as no surprise that it has attracted extensive scholarly discussions and policy debates. However, since so much of that attention has been documented in ad hoc policy reports and/or subscription-based academic journals, progress has been made here through providing an in-depth historical compilation involving a wide range of international experiences.

It has become clear that deepening our understanding of the policy-making factors affecting economic diversification remains a fundamental area for research.

As a whole, the chapters in this book highlight the importance of institutions, relatedness, path dependency, policy timing, economic reforms, governance and regulatory quality – among other factors – each of which represents a key theme onto which researchers might shed more light. Additional future research should examine in detail some of the key variables that remain relatively unexplained, such as exchange rates, fiscal policy and sovereign wealth funds. Another area for pursuing future research involves the development and empirical testing of conceptual and analytical frameworks – such as the ones presented in the first chapter – as they provide useful avenues for learning and research in terms of economic diversification policies. Here it is believed that conducting comparative work and developing public policy indicators will be particularly relevant to advancing our understanding with regard to the art and craft of economic diversification policies.

References

Araral, E., Fritzen, S., Howlett, M., Ramesh, M. and Wu, X. (eds.) (2012) *Routledge Handbook of Public Policy*, London: Routledge.

Lindblom, C.E. (1959) 'The science of "muddling through"', *Public Administration Quarterly*, vol. 19, no. 2, 79–88.

Index

Mexico 61–5, 67, 79–82, 92, 98–9
microeconomics 155–61, 194
middle-income economies: Kazakhstan
203, 205, 212–16; LAC countries
59–60, 75; Russia 177
minerals: Australia 151, 154, 156, 164;
Canada 10, 13, 21; Iceland 267;
Kazakhstan 111, 205–6, 210–14;
Norway 297, 300–1; Russia 181, 186;
Uganda 129–30
mining: Australia 150–2, 160, 163–71;
Iceland 276; Kazakhstan 205–6, 209,
215, 217, 227–8; LAC countries 79;
Malaysia 100, 115; Norway 301, 319;
Russia 189; Saudi Arabia 37, 41–2;
Uganda 130, 133–4
modernisation, Russian economy 181–3

NACE, Norway 295
nanotechnology, Russia 184, 187–8
'National Champions' 258
national political economy, Canada 12–15
National System of Innovation (NSI),
Canada 11, 24–6, 28
New Economic Policy (NEP), Malaysia
103, 107–15
new firms/ventures, survival 6
New Zealand 44–5, 134, 154, 250, 268–9
NGO *see* non governmental organisations
Nigeria 62–3, 65, 67, 98–9
non-existing markets 3–4
non governmental organisations (NGO) 122
non-satisfied markets 3–4
Norway 129, 226, 285–6, 295–323, 325
NSI *see* National System of Innovation
nuclear industry 176, 184–96

oil industries: Australia 150–1, 163, 167,
171; Canada 9–32; Kazakhstan 203–11,
213–19, 222–8, 233, 235; LAC
countries 59–99; Malaysia 100–7,
111–15; Norway 295–320; Russia
175–88, 191–5; Saudi Arabia 37–45,
48–52, 55–6; Uganda 118–31, 141–4;
United Arab Emirates 236–42, 245–6,
250–4, 258, 263; Venezuela 61–3,
65–8, 78, 86–92, 98–9
oil sands 10–17, 23, 26–7, 30, 325
Oman, LAC exports 62–3, 65, 67, 98–9

Ontario, Canada 12, 23
overvaluation aspects 284–5
ownership aspects: Canada 13, 17; Iceland
286, 291; Kazakhstan 213, 220, 223;
LAC countries 84–5; Malaysia 106,
108–11; Norway 309–10, 317; Russia
177, 183, 185, 193

palm oil 5–7, 100, 103, 105, 111
paper industries 296–7, 310, 312
'paradox of plenty' 298–300
Pastrana administration 74
path dependency 102–7, 238–9, 250–1,
257, 263
patronage aspects 183–4, 186–7
PDP *see* productive development policies
Pearson correlation 131–2, 135–42
People's National Movement (PNM)
government 82, 84
petrochemicals *see* gas industries; oil
industries
Petroleum Nasional Berhad (PETRONAS)
106
physical capital 125–8, 237
plastics 41, 55, 236, 246, 250, 260–1
Plaza, Galo 76
PNM *see* People's National Movement
policy options: Australia 149–61, 164–72;
Canada 10, 22–32; Iceland 268–92;
Kazakhstan 204–6, 211–14, 219–22,
225–8, 234; LAC oil industries 59–99;
Malaysia 102–9, 112–14; Norway 301,
304–19; Russia 176–9, 182–3, 186–9,
192–3; Saudi Arabia 38, 41, 48–56;
successes and failures 324–5; Uganda
121–4, 134; United Arab Emirates
237–40, 252, 254–5, 258, 261
politics: Australia 149–50, 153, 158,
165–7, 171; Canada 12–15; Iceland
267–8, 273–92; Kazakhstan 221, 227;
LAC countries 70, 79, 81, 88–9, 91–2;
Malaysia 103–11, 114–15; Norway
298–9, 305, 315, 318; political rights
273–9, 285–6, 291; Russia 176,
180–94; Uganda 118, 121, 123–5,
128–9, 134–40, 144
Polity IV Project's Polity2 variable 274–6
population: Canada 14; Iceland 281, 288;
Kazakhstan 203, 206, 208, 235; Norway